Microsoft®
Excel VBA
Programming
for the
absolute
beginner

Premier
Press DUANE BIRNBAUM

ISBN: 1-931841-04-7

Library of Congress Catalog Card Number: 2001099839

Printed in the United States of America

02 03 04 05 BH 10 9 8 7 6 5 4 3 2

Publisher:
Stacy L. Hiquet

Marketing Manager:
Heather Buzzingham

Managing Editor:
Sandy Doell

Series Editor:
Andy Harris

Project Editor:
Estelle Manticas

Editorial Assistant:
Margaret Bauer

Technical Reviewer:
Greg Perry

Copy Editor:
Linda Seifert

Interior Layout:
Shawn Morningstar

Cover Design:
Mike Tanamachi

Indexer:
Sherry Massey

Proofreader:
Jenny Davidson

Acknowledgments

Special thanks to my family—Jill, Aaron, and Joshua. You were all wonderfully patient with me while I worked on this book. Your love and understanding are greatly appreciated.

Thanks to all the people at Premier Press, especially Stacy, who gave me the opportunity to write this book, and to everyone else behind the scenes who worked to make it look good. Special thanks to Estelle for all the help, and for putting up with my numerous changes during the review process.

I would also like to thank Andy Harris for recommending me to Premier, and for his guidance in the early development of the book. Thanks to Greg Perry for an outstanding technical review. I only wish I'd had time to include more of his suggestions; doing so would have made the book even better.

Finally, thanks to all of the contributors of the software and support files on the CD and to the reader who supports them (and who, of course, also purchases this book).

About the Author

Duane Birnbaum began programming in graduate school, where he wrote custom software for interfacing the various electronic devices required for his experiments and analyzing the data obtained from them. Since completing his Ph.D. in physical chemistry, he has been working as a post-doctoral and research scientist in academia and industry while continuing to teach on a part-time basis. For the last five years he has been working as a research scientist in the biotechnology industry and serving as a part-time lecturer in the Computer Science department of Indiana University/Purdue University. He teaches introductory classes in data analysis, database design, and Visual Basic.

Contents

CHAPTER 3   Procedures and Conditions . . . 51

CHAPTER 4   Loops and Arrays 87

CHAPTER 5 · Basic Excel Objects 133

CHAPTER 6 · Enhancing VBA Programs: Adding Multimedia and Intelligence 187

UserForms and Additional Controls 227

Data Access, File I/O, Error Handling, and Debugging. . . . 269

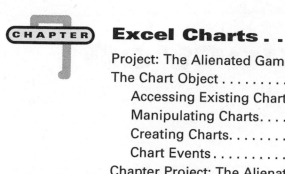

Introduction

Visual Basic for Applications (VBA for short) is a programming environment designed to work with Microsoft's Office applications (Excel, Word, Access, etc.). Components in each application (for example, worksheets or documents) are exposed as objects and made available to the programmer to use and manipulate to a desired end. Anything you can do through normal use of the Office applications can also be automated through programming.

You can also extend the abilities of the application through the use of additional reusable objects provided for the programmer. These reusable objects are referred to as *ActiveX controls*, and I will demonstrate their use throughout this book. ActiveX controls are pre-built, reusable programming components that you can add to your own programming projects. Common examples include text boxes, buttons, labels, and image controls. They are very useful to program developers because they are reusable and serve to handle common programming tasks. Because ActiveX controls are reusable they only have to be developed once, thus saving valuable time. VBA includes several common ActiveX controls for use in Office projects. You can also import ActiveX controls from third party vendors, though licensing and copyrights may restrict their use in your VBA project.

Why VBA?

As a beginning language, VBA will suit your needs well. VBA is not as vast as many popular languages because such extensiveness is simply unnecessary. VBA was built to work with and extend the capabilities of MS Office applications, so it doesn't need the substance of a programming language used to build full-blown applications from scratch. The relative simplicity of VBA makes it easier for people to pick up and learn and also makes it less intimidating to the beginner. However, VBA does share many of the programming constructs common to all languages, so it also serves as a great introduction to programming. For these reasons, and the fact that MS Excel is the most popular spreadsheet application available, I am writing this book.

As a scientist I never really gave the business-orientated Excel a chance. At first, it didn't even have graphical capabilities, and even after they were added, Excel still couldn't match other spreadsheet applications geared toward the scientist.

After ignoring Excel for several years, I started a new job where Excel was the only spreadsheet application available; it was then that I discovered that it used a macro language based on the already very popular Visual Basic. I started writing programs to handle some of the routine data analyses required around the lab, and the time I have saved using these programs has sold me on Excel as a valuable component in any lab or business.

Who Should Read This Book?

The goal of this book is to help you learn VBA programming with Excel. No prior programming experience is required or expected. Although you do not have to be an Excel user, you should have a good understanding of the basic tools involved in using any spreadsheet application. This includes a basic understanding of ranges and cell references, formulas, built-in functions, and charts. If you're not comfortable with spreadsheet applications or it's been a while since you have used a spreadsheet, then I recommend you consider purchasing another introductory book on how to use the Excel application (*Microsoft Excel Fast & Easy*, by Faith Wempen, is a good choice). In addition to spreadsheets, I also expect you to have a basic understanding of the Windows operating system.

What's in This Book?

I developed the programs in this book using Excel 2000 for Windows. It doesn't matter if you're using a slightly older or newer version of Excel (97 or XP); VBA has changed very little between these three versions. I have added folders to the accompanying CD-ROM that include versions of the chapter projects that run without error in these other versions. If you are a Macintosh user, you can still use the programs in this book. There are small differences in the object model for Excel Windows and Excel Macintosh but in most cases you will not notice them. The most notable difference is in how each operating system specifies a file path (Windows uses a backslash and Macintosh a colon).

The chapter projects in this book feature the development of games using VBA with Excel. This is somewhat unusual in the sense that prior to writing this book, I had never seen an Excel application that runs any kind of a game. However, it does serve to make programming more fun. After all, what's the first thing anybody does when they get a new computer? Answer: Find the games that are installed and start playing. With this book, you get to write the program and then play the game. It actually works very well. The games developed in this book illustrate the use of basic programming techniques and structures found in all programming languages as well as all of the common (and some less common) components in Excel.

What's on the CD-ROM?

The CD that accompanies this book includes two "bonus" chapters, Chapters 11 and 12. These chapters are in PDF (Portable Document Format), and must be viewed with the Adobe Acrobat Reader software. If you do not currently have the Acrobat Reader software, you can download it for free from http://www.adobe.com.

Chapter 11 shows you how to import data from external sources (MS Access database, the World Wide Web, and text files) into an Excel worksheet. Chapter 11 also covers some Web-related objects and methods that allow you to view and save your worksheet as a Web page, and add hyperlinks to a worksheet. The programming project uses several of the objects and methods discussed in the chapter to import data from an MS Access database for use in the game of Hangman.

Chapter 12 shows you how to create custom toolbars and menus that appear when your VBA programs are loaded into Excel. In addition, you will learn how to store your VBA programs as add-ins that can be loaded by the user when needed. The programming project uses the Excetris and Hangman programs from Chapters 10 and 11 and connects them to a custom toolbar with two buttons used to start each game. The project is stored as an add-in, so it can be easily loaded and run in any worksheet.

In addition to the bonus chapters, the CD-ROM also includes the following:

- All source code from the book, including all supporting image and sound files.
- Links to several helpful VBA and Excel Web sites.
- The GIMP, a powerful graphics creation and editing tool.
- Sawcutter 1.0, a software synthesizer and wave editor that allows waveforms to be hand drawn. You can also load external sound files and run them through several banks of effects that can be adjusted in real-time
- Audacity. Records audio directly and also imports/exports WAV, AIFF and MP3 files. Supports envelope editing, mixing, simple built-in effects, and plug-in effects, all with unlimited undo.

Sample VBA programs for Excel. A collection of add-ins and worksheets with attached VBA programs for your perusal and enjoyment.

Visual Basic for Applications with Excel

I n this first chapter I will introduce you to the programmer's tools available through Excel. These tools include the VBA IDE (Integrated Development Environment), controls and functions available through the main Excel application, and online help from both the Excel and VBA environments. Finally, I will take you through a very short and simple program that takes textual input from the user, places it in a spreadsheet cell, and then formats the cell with a large font, bright colors, and a border.

Specifically this chapter will cover:

- The VBA IDE and its components

- Programming tools within Excel

- Installing and using the online help

- Chapter project: Colorful Header

Project: Colorful Header

The project in this chapter is short and simple but will serve as your first introduction to the VBA programming environment, ActiveX controls, event-driven programming, and using VBA to interact with your spreadsheet. Figure 1.1 shows a view of the Colorful Header spreadsheet.

HINT

Event-driven programming refers to the creation of a program that is designed to run when the user generates a stimulus. For example, a keystroke or a mouse click may trigger specific pieces of a program to execute. The event-driven programming model has been popular for years and is now commonplace. It is vastly superior to older programs that did not allow for much user interaction because the programmers dictated the flow of the program. In event-driven programming, the user dictates the flow of the program, and it is up to programmers to anticipate the user's needs.

Don't concern yourself with syntax at this time. In later chapters I will show you the tools you need to build VBA projects. For right now I just want you to see how easy it is to make something work, and for you to recognize that many of the keywords we use in VBA programming projects in this book are already familiar to you as an Excel user.

HINT

Keywords are words used by the programming language for a special purpose, and are therefore reserved. This means you cannot use a keyword in your program for anything other than what was designed into the language.

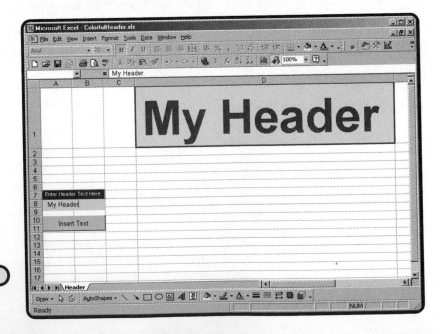

FIGURE 1.1

The Colorful Header project

The VBA Integrated Development Environment (IDE)

Before learning how to program in VBA you have to learn how to use the software required for creating your projects. The VBA development software is included with each component of the Microsoft Office suite of programs, including Excel. Starting the VBA development software places you in the VBA programming environment IDE, which provides you with a number of tools for use in the development of your project.

Getting to the IDE from Excel

Before you begin creating projects with VBA you must know your way around the IDE. You can access the IDE from Excel in a couple of different ways. In Excel, select Tools, Macro, Visual Basic Editor (as shown in Figure 1.2), or use the keystroke Alt+F11.

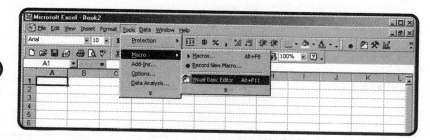

FIGURE 1.2

Accessing the VBA IDE from the Tools menu in Excel

IN THE REAL WORLD

An *IDE* is software used by programmers for rapid application development (RAD). IDEs are available for numerous programming languages and are often quite expensive to purchase (several hundred dollars or more for a single license). The price is worth it because IDEs provide tools that enable programmers to develop applications quickly, saving them considerable time and money. But the most important component of any development software is the compiler, which for many languages can be obtained at no cost. The compiler converts your program into the binary code your computer understands. If you have the compiler, all you really need to create an application, albeit with considerably more effort, is a text editor. Excel comes with its own IDE and VBA compiler, thus making it more of a value than you may realize. Yet there are many companies that purchase large site licenses for Excel only to use the application side, never taking advantage of the enhancements VBA can provide.

Alternatively, select the Visual Basic toolbar from the View/Toolbars menu item in Excel. When the toolbar is displayed, select the Visual Basic Editor icon in the middle of the toolbar (see Figure 1.3).

Components of the IDE

After opening the VBA IDE you may find yourself looking at a window similar to that shown in Figure 1.4. This figure shows the VBA IDE and some of the tools that can be used to create projects.

Like in most applications, there is a menu bar across the top of the window. You may only recognize a few items that exist within this menu, but don't worry. I'll show you the function of most of these items as we proceed through the book.

The Standard toolbar is one of four toolbars available from the IDE. Like any toolbar, its function is to give the user fast access to common tools available within the application. Again, I will explain the use of many of these functions, as well as the use of other toolbars, as we proceed through the book.

Of particular importance is the Project Explorer window, shown in the upper left corner of the IDE window in Figure 1.4. The Project Explorer lists all projects currently open, including those opened by Excel upon startup. The Project Explorer

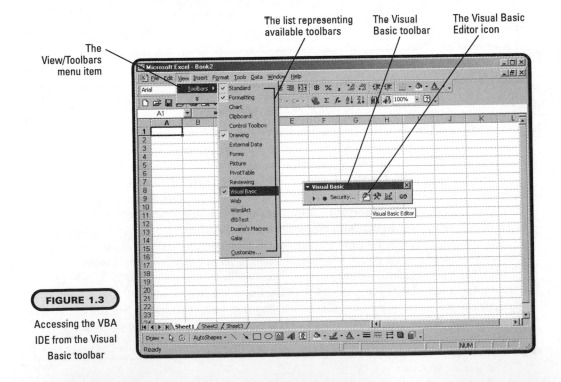

FIGURE 1.3

Accessing the VBA IDE from the Visual Basic toolbar

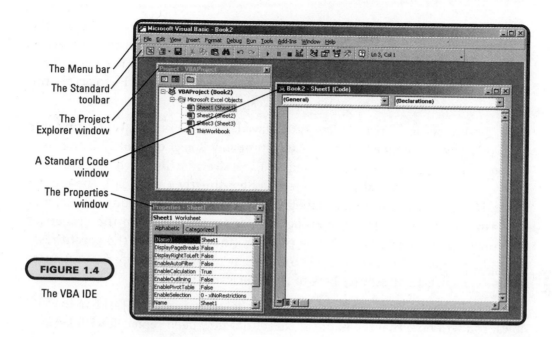

FIGURE 1.4

The VBA IDE

The Menu bar
The Standard toolbar
The Project Explorer window
A Standard Code window
The Properties window

also lists the components of any opened projects. For example, Figure 1.4 shows that there is currently one project, called Book2, open, and that this project contains four Excel objects: Sheet1, Sheet2, Sheet3, and ThisWorkbook. I will discuss Excel objects in detail in Chapter 5. For right now, recognize that these objects represent familiar components from Excel (the workbook and worksheets it contains).

Prior to opening the IDE, I created a new workbook from the file menu in Excel. Excel gave the default name Book2 to the workbook (I had already closed Book1), and the workbook includes three worksheets (default names Sheet1, Sheet2, and Sheet3) because that's what I have set in my options from the Tools menu in Excel. If I open more workbooks, or add more worksheets to a currently open workbook in Excel, then their names will appear on the component list in the Project Explorer window.

Just below the Project Explorer window in Figure 1.4 is the Properties window. The Properties window displays a list of attributes or properties of the currently selected object in the Project Explorer window. These properties are used to manipulate the behavior and appearance of the object to which they belong. The properties of Sheet1 are displayed in Figure 1.4 because it has been selected in the Project Explorer. Choosing a different object will result in a different properties list in the Properties window, as not all objects have the same properties. As a simple exercise in manipulating the properties of a worksheet, open a new workbook in Excel, note the name of your workbook and any worksheets it contains (do not change any names), then open the VBA IDE. Once in the IDE, display the Project Explorer and Properties windows. If the Project Explorer and Properties windows are not already displayed you can access them through the View menu item (see Figure 1.5). You can also use the keystrokes Ctrl+R and F4 to access the Project Explorer and Properties windows, respectively.

Once the Project Explorer window is displayed, find the project that represents the workbook you opened while in Excel (probably Book1 or Book2). If the components of the workbook you opened in Excel are not displayed, click on the + sign next to the Microsoft Excel Objects folder directly underneath the project name. Now find the component labeled Sheet1, select it with your mouse, and then turn your attention to the Properties window. Scroll down the Properties window until you come to the Name property (the one without the parentheses around it). Delete the text entered to the right of the Name property and enter MySheet. Figure 1.6 illustrates how to find the Name property.

Toggle back to Excel by pressing Alt+F11, or select it from the taskbar in Windows. You will note that the name of Sheet1 has now been replaced with MySheet in your Excel workbook, as shown in Figure 1.7.

See how easy it is to alter properties of a worksheet in Excel using VBA? As VBA developers, however, we will seldom, if ever, alter the properties of a workbook or worksheet at design time. The bulk of the work affecting workbooks and worksheets will occur at run time; however, we will alter properties of ActiveX controls at design time.

Design time refers to project development and the manipulation of object properties using the VBA IDE prior to running any code. Conversely, run time will refer to the manipulation of object properties using a program, thus, the properties of the object do not change until the code is executed.

Finally, I will show you one more component of the VBA IDE. If you look back at Figure 1.4 you will also see a Standard Code window. Windows such as these are used as containers for your program(s). This is where you type in the code for your program, so these windows are essentially text editors very similar to Notepad. You must be aware that there are pre-defined code windows for specific Excel objects, namely the workbook (for example, ThisWorkbook) and the worksheets (for example, Sheet1). The code window displayed in Figure 1.4 represents Sheet1 contained within the workbook Book2.

You will also be able to add components to your project and they will have their own code windows. I will explain how to use code windows more thoroughly as we proceed through this book. For now, know that you can open a code window by

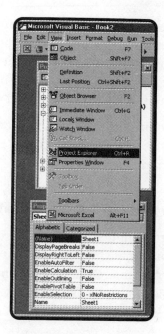

FIGURE 1.5

Accessing the
Project Explorer
and Properties
windows

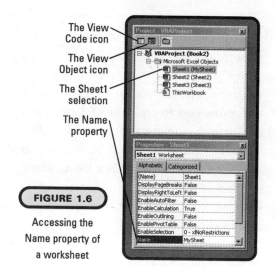

FIGURE 1.6

Accessing the
Name property of
a worksheet

The View
Code icon

The View
Object icon

The Sheet1
selection

The Name
property

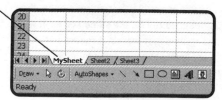

The worksheet
name

FIGURE 1.7

The altered
workbook in Excel

double-clicking on any object listed in the Project Explorer. You can also select the object in the Project Explorer and click on the View Code icon at the top left of the window (refer to Figure 1.6), select Code from the tools menu, or hit F7 (refer to Figure 1.5). Note that you can also view the selected object in Excel by selecting the appropriate item from these same locations (refer to Figures 1.6 and 1.7).

There are, of course, more components to the VBA IDE, but I've shown you enough to get you started for now. As the need arises, I will introduce more tools from the IDE that will aid in the development of various projects.

Programming Components within Excel

Not everything of interest to the VBA programmer can be found in the VBA IDE. There are a few programming-related components that you access from the Excel application. The components I am referring to are the Macro items found under the Tools menu, and three of the available toolbars—Visual Basic, Control Toolbox, and Forms—found in the View menu in Excel.

Macro Selection

Now that you've had an introduction to the VBA IDE, it's time to look at development tools accessed directly from Excel. To begin, take a closer look at the Macro selection from the Tools menu, shown back in Figure 1.2. Notice two other items displayed in Figure 1.2 that I have not yet discussed: Macros and Record New Macro. Essentially the Record Macro tool will allow you to create a VBA program by simply selecting various tasks in Excel through the normal interface. The Record Macro tool is quite helpful, as you'll see in Chapter 4 when I discuss it in detail. The Macros menu item will simply display a dialog box with a list of some or all of the currently loaded VBA programs. Again, I will explain the Macro menu item in more detail later in the book, but for now remember that it is one way to access and run desired VBA programs. Figure 1.8 shows the Macro dialog box.

HINT

Macros typically refer to programs that are recorded as the user executes a series of tasks from the normal application interface. They are useful when a user repeatedly performs the same tasks in Excel. Instead of having to repeat tasks, the user can simply record his/her actions once, then "play back" the macro when he/she needs to repeat the same series of tasks. However, it is possible to access programs that were not recorded through the Macro menu item, thus I will use the term *macro* to refer to both recorded programs and those programs written from scratch.

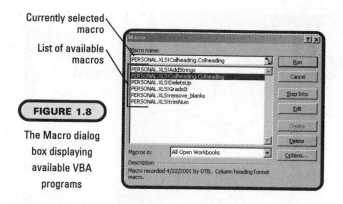

Currently selected macro

List of available macros

FIGURE 1.8

The Macro dialog box displaying available VBA programs

The Visual Basic Toolbar

The Visual Basic toolbar shown in Figure 1.3 provides another set of tools for the VBA developer. We have already seen how selecting the Visual Basic Editor icon from this toolbar gives us access to the VBA IDE. There are several other useful items on the Visual Basic toolbar—including Run Macro, Record Macro, and Design Mode—that we will discuss later. Also included on the Visual Basic toolbar is an icon for the Control toolbox, denoted by the crossed hammer and wrench, as shown in Figure 1.9. The Control toolbox can also be accessed via the Toolbars item on the View menu.

The Control toolbox provides you with the ActiveX controls mentioned earlier (see the Introduction for a discussion of these controls). The Text Box, Command Button, Label, and Image controls are just some of the controls available and are specifically labeled in Figure 1.9. You place controls on a worksheet by first clicking on the desired control and then drawing it onto the worksheet. Start by selecting the Command Button control and drawing it on a worksheet, as shown in Figure 1.10.

After the Command Button is placed on the worksheet, you will notice that it is selected and the application is currently in Design Mode (check that the Design Mode icon in the upper left corner of the Control toolbox appears "pressed in").

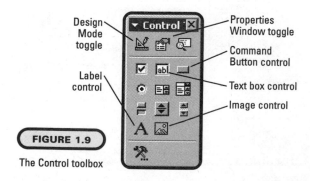

Design Mode toggle

Properties Window toggle

Command Button control

Label control

Text box control

Image control

FIGURE 1.9

The Control toolbox

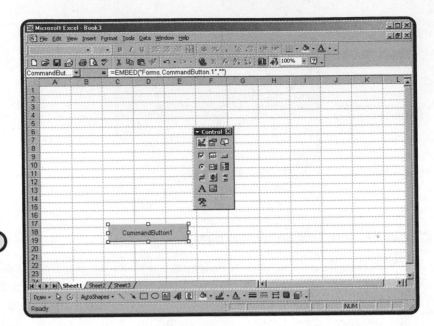

FIGURE 1.10

The Command
Button control
placed on a
worksheet

You can access the properties of the Command Button control while in design
mode. With the Command Button control selected while in design mode, select
the Properties icon from the Control toolbox. A window much like the Properties
window in the VBA IDE will appear. The Properties window lists all of the attributes or properties used to describe the Command Button control. Figure 1.11
shows the Properties window.

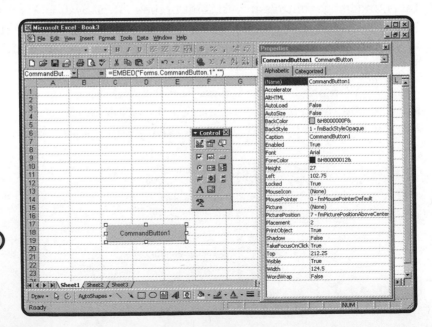

FIGURE 1.11

The Properties
window of the
Command Button
control

In the Properties window of the Command Button control, change the Caption property to Click Me and then notice how the new caption is displayed on the control. Changing the Name property to cmdColorChange allows you to experiment with some of the other properties, such as Font, ForeColor, BackColor, Width, and Height to change the appearance of the control. You can even display a picture within the Command Button control through the Picture property, and then select an image file from your computer.

TRICK

The Name **property is an important property of any ActiveX control. The value of the** Name **property should be changed to something meaningful as soon as the control is added to the worksheet. Typically, an abbreviated word telling us the type of control (the** cmd **at the beginning of the name above denotes a Command Button) and its function in the program, will work well. The** Name **property of an ActiveX control should be changed if you will refer to it in your program. A meaningful name will help you remember it, as well as make the code more readable.**

Once the appearance of your Command Button control is to your liking, select the View Code icon from the Control toolbox, or double-click on the Command Button control to access the code window. You will be taken immediately to the VBA IDE. Now it's time to make the Command Button control functional, and you can only do that by adding code to its code window. Figure 1.12 shows the code window for the Command Button control.

The title bar tells us the object to which this code window belongs. In this case, the code window belongs to the worksheet named Sheet1 in the workbook named Book2. This is because I placed the Command Button control on Sheet1 of Book2 in the Excel application. You may recall that I changed the name of the worksheet in Excel to MySheet, but the name of the worksheet as it will have to be referenced in code is still Sheet1. In the upper left corner of the code window is a dropdown

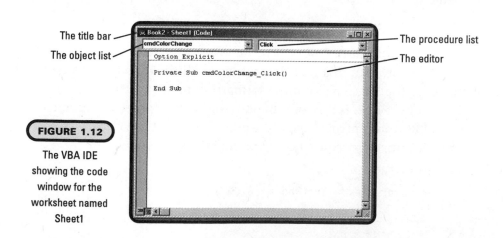

FIGURE 1.12

The VBA IDE showing the code window for the worksheet named Sheet1 list box containing the names of all objects contained within the selected worksheet. The name of the Command Button control is displayed because the cursor in the editor is within an event procedure of this Command Button control.

Event procedures are self-contained blocks of code that require some type of stimulus in order to run. The stimulus often comes directly from the user (for example, a mouse click), but may also result from another piece of code.

Event procedures are pre-defined for ActiveX controls and other Excel objects, such as workbooks and worksheets. All event procedures for the selected object are listed in the upper right corner of the code window in a dropdown list box. I will discuss event procedures in more depth in Chapter 3. For now, just take a look at the Click() event. The Click() event is a very common event procedure that is built into most ActiveX controls. Any code placed within the predefined procedure will trigger when the user clicks once on the object—in this case, the Command Button control named cmdColorChange. The procedure is defined and listed in Figure 1.12 with the following two lines of code:

```
Private Sub cmdColorChange_Click()
End Sub
```

The name of the procedure will always be the name of the object with an underscore followed by the name of the event. You cannot change the name of a predefined event procedure. If you do change the name of the event procedure, the code within the procedure will not run when you want it to. The keyword Sub is required and is used as the defining opening of any procedure—event-type or programmer-defined. Private is an optional keyword; I'll discuss it in Chapter 3. The second line, End Sub, is always used to close a procedure. Now type the following line of code within the Click() event procedure of the Command Button control named cmdColorChange.

```
Cells.Interior.ColorIndex = Int(Rnd * 56) + 1
```

This line will set the fill color of all cells in the worksheet to one of 56 possible colors. This is the equivalent of a user first selecting all the cells in a worksheet and then changing the fill color from the formatting toolbar in the Excel application. The color of the cells is chosen randomly and will change with each click of the Command Button control because the above code will run once with each click event. So the entire procedure now looks like the following:

```
Private Sub cmdColorChange_Click()
   Cells.Interior.ColorIndex = Int(Rnd * 56) + 1
End Sub
```

Return to the Excel application and exit the design mode by toggling the icon on the Control Toolbox (refer to Figure 1.9). Now test the program by clicking on the Command Button control. The color of all cells in the worksheet will change color with each click. Figure 1.13 shows my worksheet after one click on the Command Button control.

You can save the workbook as you would an Excel workbook. The Command Button control and event procedure code will be saved with the workbook.

Getting Help with VBA

I can't emphasize enough how important it is that you become comfortable with the online help in the VBA IDE (not to mention in the Excel application). The online help provides fast access to solutions for any programming problems you have with your project. Books make good resources, and are much better at teaching you how to program, but they don't cover everything. Often all you need to see is a simple example of how to use a particular function or other keyword, and the online help does contain documentation on every keyword, programming construct, and object you might use in your project. The bottom line is: there is always something helpful online, it's just a matter of finding the right document.

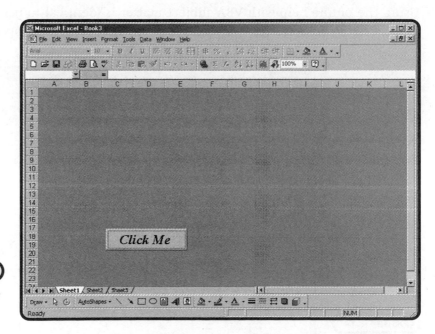

FIGURE 1.13

The Color Changer program

Excel Help

If you are a regular Excel or MS Office user then chances are you've used the online help. Whether or not you use the Office Assistant, you probably know how to get to the Help window shown in Figure 1.14. No matter what your opinion concerning that paper clip, it is absolutely critical that you get comfortable with the online help.

You can select this window from the Help menu in the Excel application. If you have the Office Assistant turned on, then you must access the Help window after first going through its paces. Once the Help window is displayed, keywords can be entered in order to get a list of potential documents that may be helpful. Select the document and view it on the right side of the window. Personally, I find the index option the most useful, and I use it exclusively, though I recommend you at least explore the table of contents and Answer Wizard. Finding the answers you need is usually a matter of typing in the right keywords. I can't teach you how to choose the right keywords, but I know from experience that you will get better as you gain experience with Excel and VBA and develop a better understanding of the subject matter.

VBA Help

Using the online help with VBA subject matter is identical to using the online help in Excel. To access the VBA help, you must have the IDE open and active.

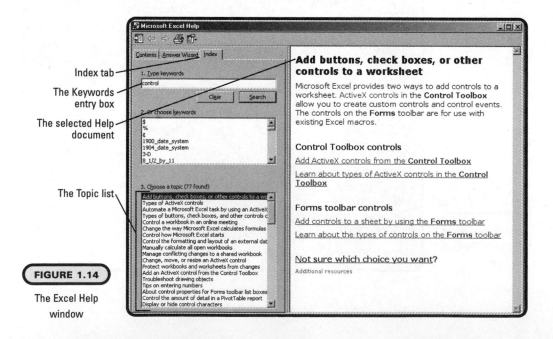

Index tab
The Keywords entry box
The selected Help document
The Topic list

FIGURE 1.14

The Excel Help window

Otherwise everything is exactly the same, from the Help menu to the Help window and even to the Office Assistant, if you choose to use it.

To look up documentation concerning a known keyword in VBA, (for example, the syntax requirements for a particular VBA keyword), first select that keyword in the code, hit F1, and the document that describes that keyword will immediately appear in the Help window.

Installing VBA Help Files

Unfortunately, the VBA help files are not installed with Excel or the Office suite of programs with the typical installation. You must custom-install VBA help files yourself. Don't worry—it's quick and easy to do so. I'll take you through the custom installation of VBA help files for Office XP. The selections that appear with the installation of previous versions of Office will be slightly different, but you should get the general idea as to what needs to be done.

With the Excel or Office CD inserted into the appropriate drive, do the following:

1. Select Settings/Control Panel from the Start menu.
2. From the Control Panel window, select Add/Remove Programs.
3. From the resulting dialog box, select Microsoft Office XP, Microsoft Excel, or similar item, and click on Add/Remove.
4. Select Add or Remove Features, then click Next.
5. From the displayed list of components, open Office Shared Features, then open Visual Basic for Applications.
6. Select Visual Basic Help and click Update.

With the help files installed you will now be able to access the VBA documentation online.

Constructing the Colorful Header Program

Before I begin a programming project, I like to break up the problem I'm trying to solve into specific pieces. I begin with a simple statement of what I am trying to accomplish, followed by a statement of what tools I know are available for me to use in the project. I then write an *algorithm*, or approach, that I will follow when beginning the project. Andy Harris, a computer science instructor at Indiana University Purdue University at Indianapolis, first introduced this method to me. The method is intuitive and I think you'll probably realize that you've used a similar approach when solving problems of your own.

Project Statement

I want to create a program demonstrating the use of ActiveX controls on a worksheet. The program will accept text from the user and then display this text in a spreadsheet cell. The text should be formatted with color, a large font size, and a matching color border.

Project Tools

Now I'll list the tools I know are available for creating the project defined above. It is often hard to think of every tool available, so I try to be aware of this and look for more or different tools as I work on the project.

The project will use three ActiveX controls: the Text Box control, the Label control, and the Command Button control. Each of these controls will be placed on a single worksheet in Excel, and will interact with a single spreadsheet cell. The Click() event procedure of the Command Button control will contain all of the code for the project.

Project Algorithm

The controls will be placed in a logical location near the upper left corner of the worksheet. The Label control will serve to let the user know to enter text for the header in the Text Box control. The Command Button control will hold all the program code in its click event procedure. Table 1.1 shows just some of the values I chose for the properties of the ActiveX controls. I recommend that you change a few more properties in order to get comfortable with these controls.

To view the properties of a particular control, either select the specific control first or select the desired control from the drop-down list at the top of the Properties window (refer to Figure 1.11).

 TRICK Label controls are often used to describe what should be entered in a Text Box or other control. Thus, Label controls are not often referred to in code. For this reason, it is not necessary to change the name property of a Label control unless it will be referred to in code.

When the user clicks on the Command Button control, the text entered in the Text Box control will be copied to a spreadsheet cell, and that cell will be formatted with the following specifications:

- Bold text
- Arial font

TABLE 1.1 SELECTED PROPERTIES OF ACTIVEX CONTROLS USED IN THE COLORFUL HEADER PROJECT

ActiveX Control	Properties	Value
Label	Caption	Enter Header Text Here
	BackStyle	Opaque
	BackColor	Black
	ForeColor	White
Text Box	Name	txtHeading
	BackColor	Light Gray
	ForeColor	Black
	Text	None...left blank
	BackStyle	Opaque
	BorderStyle	None
Command Button	Name	cmdInsertHeading
	Caption	Insert Text
	Visible	Makes Command Button visible or not during runtime
	Font	Arial

- Font size: 72
- Font color: Dark Blue
- Cell Color: Cyan
- Thick border
- Border Color: Dark Blue

Adding the Code

As I stated in the algorithm, all of the code is to be placed in the `Click()` event procedure of the Command Button control. The code window can be accessed via the VBA IDE by double-clicking on the Command Button control while in design mode. You can also select the appropriate object (cmdInsertHeading) from the object drop-down list in the code window for the worksheet on which the ActiveX controls were placed (see Figure 1.15).

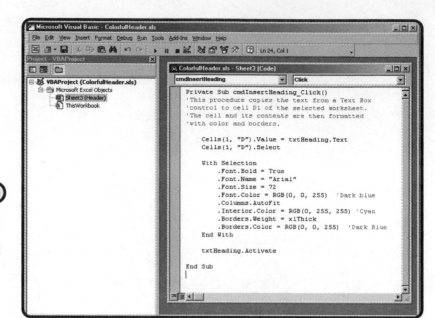

FIGURE 1.15

VBA IDE showing the code window for the worksheet containing the ActiveX controls of the Colorful Header project.

As you can see, the following code was placed in the `Click()` event procedure of the `cmdInsertHeading` Command Button control. Now let's take a closer look at each line of code.

The very first and last lines define the type of procedure as a `Click()` event, as described earlier in this chapter. Immediately following the opening line of code are four lines of comments.

Comments (or remarks) are notes left in the code by the programmer to help describe the function of the program. Comments make it easier to find problems with the code, or add different features to the code at a later time. Enter comments into the code by beginning the line with an apostrophe (or Rem). You must enter another apostrophe for each new line, and the VBA text editor will color each comment line green. Comments are not part of the program, and are ignored when the program runs; thus, comments do not decrease the execution speed of a program.

```
Private Sub cmdInsertHeading_Click()
'This procedure copies the text from a Text Box
'control to cell D1 of the selected worksheet.
'The cell and its contents are then formatted
'with color and borders.
```

```
    Cells(1, "D").Value = txtHeading.Text
    Cells(1, "D").Select

    With Selection
        .Font.Bold = True
        .Font.Name = "Arial"
        .Font.Size = 72
        .Font.Color = RGB(0, 0, 255)   'Dark blue
        .Columns.AutoFit
        .Interior.Color = RGB(0, 255, 255) 'Cyan
        .Borders.Weight = xlThick
        .Borders.Color = RGB(0, 0, 255)   'Dark Blue
    End With

    txtHeading.Activate

End Sub
```

I will discuss code structures, Excel objects, and object syntax in subsequent chapters. If you are even somewhat familiar with Excel, however, you probably have a pretty good idea as to what's happening in the above code. First, the text entered in the Text Box control (txtHeading) is placed in cell D1 of the worksheet, and this cell is selected as if the user clicked on this cell with the mouse. With cell D1 selected, it is formatted in the manner stated in the algorithm. After formatting cell D1, the cursor is placed in the Text Box control by making it the active object.

That's all there is to it! This code will run once each time the Command Button control is clicked (don't forget to exit the design mode first). If you want a different heading, just enter new text in the Text Box control and click on the Command Button.

Chapter Summary

Well, I didn't show you very much program code in this chapter, but you did get a solid introduction to the VBA programming environment. You learned how to access the VBA IDE and how to view, and use, some of its major components. You also learned how to add ActiveX controls to a worksheet, change their properties, and add code to their event procedures. After a brief look at using the online help and installing the VBA help files, you developed a small project that used ActiveX controls on a worksheet to insert a column header into a worksheet and format the cell with color, font properties, and a border.

In Chapter 2 you'll learn about some basic programming concepts and tools, variables and data types; I'll focus particularly on the string data type.

CHALLENGES

1. Open a new workbook in Excel, then access the VBA IDE to find the names of the different Event procedures for a worksheet. In particular note the `SelectionChange` Event procedure of any worksheet.

2. While in the Excel application, add a Label Control to a worksheet. Change the name property of the Label control to `lblCellAddress`. Change the caption and appearance properties as desired.

3. Add the following line of code to the `SelectionChange` Event procedure of the worksheet to which you added the Label control:

```
lblCellAddress.Caption = "You selected cell " & Target.Address
```

4. Return to the worksheet, exit design mode, and click on any cell in the worksheet containing the Label control. What happens?

5. Return to the VBA IDE and the line of code above. Place the cursor within the word `Caption` and hit F1. Repeat with the `Address` keyword.

Beginning Programs with VBA

Now that you know your way around the VBA IDE for Excel, it's time to introduce some basic programming concepts common to all languages. The next three chapters are devoted to these basic programming structures that, although they may not be that exciting, are essential for developing VBA projects.

Specifically, in this chapter you will examine:

- **Variables and data types**

- **Constants**

- **Simple input and output**

- **String functions**

- **Chapter project: Time of Your Life**

Project: Time of Your Life

The Time of Your Life spreadsheet begins by asking for the user's name and birth date. The program then calculates the length of the user's life in years, months, days, hours, and seconds. Following the user input, the user's name, birth date, and age (in several units) are displayed in the worksheet (see Figure 2.1).

This program demonstrates the use of several variable types, including numbers, text, and dates. The program also demonstrates the use of some of VBA's built-in functions—primarily those used to manipulate text and dates.

Variables, Data Types, and Constants

Because this book focuses on a spreadsheet application, it's only natural that I introduce variables by asking you to think about what types of values can be entered into a spreadsheet cell, and how you might use them. You know that you can enter numbers and text into any spreadsheet cell in Excel. You may also know that the format of a spreadsheet cell can be changed to one of several possibilities. For example, a number can be formatted such that the value is displayed with or without digits to the right of the decimal point. Numbers can also be formatted as currency or as percentages (along with a few other options). Text can be displayed as entered or be automatically converted to a date or time. The contents or value of a spreadsheet cell can be changed or deleted at any time.

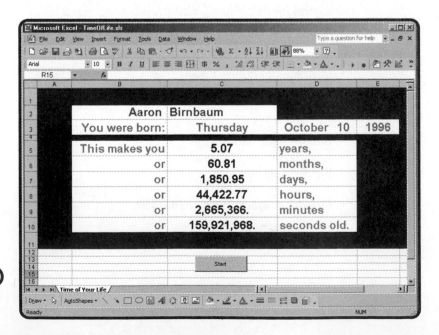

FIGURE 2.1

The Time of Your Life spreadsheet

HINT The contents of a spreadsheet cell (text or numbers) in Excel will be referred to as its *value*. You have already seen in the Chapter 1 project, and will continue to see throughout this book, the use of the Value property to access or change the contents of a spreadsheet cell.

In essence, spreadsheet cells are temporary storage containers for numbers and text that can be displayed and used in a number of different formats. The last sentence also describes a variable in any programming language. You can use variables in programs for temporary storage of data. For example, if you ask the user for input (possibly from a Text Box control), then the value entered by the user could be stored in a variable and used later in the program. In the Colorful Header project from Chapter 1, the following line of code acts a lot like a variable:

```
Cells(1, "D").Value = txtHeading.Text
```

Here the value from the Text Box control is copied to a spreadsheet cell. I could have just as easily copied the value from the Text Box control into a program variable first and then copied the contents of the variable to the spreadsheet cell. I didn't use an additional program variable because I wanted to save a couple of steps and because, as discussed earlier, spreadsheet cells already act a lot like variables. To accomplish the same task using a program variable, use the following:

```
Dim myHeading as String
myHeading = txtHeading.Text
Cells(1,"D").Value = myHeading
```

The variable myHeading is first declared (declaration is discussed in the next section) and then assigned the value from the Text Box control. The value of spreadsheet cell D1 is then assigned the value stored in the variable myHeading.

Declaring Variables

To *declare* a variable is to tell the computer to reserve space in memory for later use. To declare a variable, use a Dim (short for *Dimension*) statement.

```
Dim myVar As Integer
```

The name of the variable is myVar. The name must begin with an alphabetic character, and cannot exceed 255 characters or contain any spaces. You should avoid the use of punctuation marks or other unusual characters in the variable name, as many of them are not allowed. However, the underscore character *is* allowed and works well for separating multiple words contained within a single variable name (for example, First_Name). Avoid using reserved VBA keywords and don't repeat variable names within the same scope (discussed later in this chapter). As a convention, the variable name should be descriptive of the value it will hold. For example, if you use a variable to hold someone's first name, then a good name for that variable might be firstName or FirstName. My preference is to begin a variable name with a lowercase letter and then capitalize the first letter of any subsequent words appearing in the name. I try to keep the length to a minimum (fewer than12 characters) only because I don't like typing long names. Of course, you can adopt your own conventions as long as they don't contradict rules established by VBA.

Use Option Explicit **in the general declarations section of a module window to force explicit variable declarations (see Figures 2.2 and 2.3). Otherwise variables can be dimensioned implicitly (without a** Dim **statement) as they are required in code. In other words, you can begin using a new variable without ever declaring it with a** Dim **statement if you don't use the** Option Explicit **statement. This is not good programming practice, as it makes your code harder to read, and subsequently more difficult to debug. You can automatically have** Option Explicit **typed into each module window by checking the Require Variable Declaration option in the Tools/Options menu item of the VBA IDE.**

Following the variable name, the data type is specified for the variable. In the example above, the variable is declared as an integer data type. This tells VBA what kind of data can be stored in this variable and how much memory must be reserved for the variable. I will discuss data types in detail later in this chapter.

Component and Standard Modules

Modules refer to a related set of declarations and procedures. Each module will have a separate window in the VBA IDE and, depending on the origination of the module, it will have different behavior with regard to variable declarations. I will refer to the module window shown in Figure 2.2 as a *component* module.

VBA makes no distinction between component and standard modules. You may run across the term *standard module* in the online help, but *component module* is a term I have invented to help distinguish between modules created by VBA for various components of the Excel application and modules created by the programmer. As you shall soon see, identical syntax in these two types of modules can result in significantly different program behavior.

This module will automatically contain all event procedures associated with the worksheet Sheet1, and any ActiveX controls added to this worksheet. Component modules may also contain programmer-defined procedures (I cover procedures in Chapter 3, "Procedures and Conditions"). Each worksheet will have a separate code window, as will the workbook.

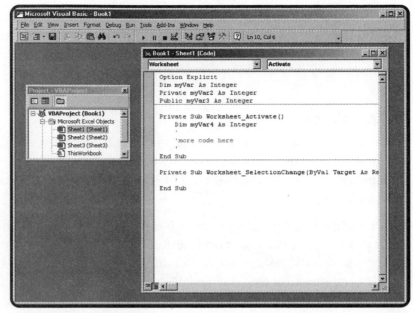

A standard module must be added to the project via the Insert menu of the VBA
IDE, as shown in Figure 2.3.

Standard modules are contained within a separate folder in the Project Explorer
and may be renamed in the Properties window (see Figure 2.3). Standard modules
contain variable declarations and programmer-defined procedures.

Adding a
module from
the Insert menu

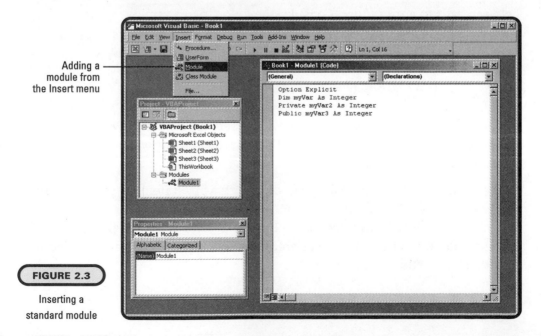

Modularized code aids in the encapsulation of program code. *Encapsulation* **is the process of breaking a large programming problem into several smaller problems and then solving each of these smaller problems separately. Encapsulation is vital in the development of software applications.**

Variable Scope

Scope in the context of variables refers to the time when a variable is visible, or available to the program. When a variable is in its scope, it can be accessed and/or manipulated. When a variable is out of scope, it is unavailable—essentially invisible to the program.

A variable declared within the code block of a procedure (such as the Click() event procedure of the Command Button control) is a *procedural level* variable. Procedural level variables are only available while program execution occurs within the procedure that the variable was declared. In Figure 2.2, the variable myVar4 is only visible to the program while the code in the Worksheet_Activate() event procedure executes. When program execution is triggered by the Worksheet_Activate() event, the variable myVar4 is dimensioned in memory. Program execution proceeds through the event procedure until reaching the End Sub line of code, after which the variable is released from memory and is no longer available. Each time the procedure executes, the variable is created and destroyed. Thus, myVar4 will not retain its value between calls to the procedure. If necessary, the Static keyword can be used to tell VBA to remember the value of the variable between calls to a procedure. Consider the following example:

```
Private Sub Worksheet_Activate()
                Static myVar4 As Integer
     myVar4 = myVar4 + 1
End Sub
```

In this procedure the variable myVar4 will increment its value by one with each call to the procedure. If you replace the Static keyword with Dim, myVar4 will never exceed a value of 1.

Declaring a variable outside of a procedure with a Dim statement makes it a *module level* variable. The scope of a module level variable depends on the type of module in which it is declared, as well as the keyword used in the declaration. For example, in Figure 2.2 the variables myVar, myVar2, and myVar3 are declared outside all procedures.

The area outside of any defined procedure is known as the *general declarations* section of a module (component or standard). This area can only be used for declarations.

These three variables are declared with the Dim, Private, and Public keywords. The Private and Public keywords are only allowed for variable declaration in the general declarations section of a module. Each of the three variables, myVar, myVar2, and myVar3 are visible to any procedure within this module and nowhere else in the project. Thus, the Dim, Private, and Public keywords have identical functions in a component module.

Now consider the standard module shown in Figure 2.3. Again the variables myVar, myVar2, and myVar3 are declared outside of any procedure in the general declarations section of the module. Again, each of the three variables, myVar, myVar2, and myVar3 are visible to any procedure within this module. However, the variable myVar3, declared with the Public keyword, is also visible to every procedure in the project, regardless of the module. In fact, the variable myVar3 is visible to all projects in all Office applications that are currently open. Variables that are visible throughout a programming project are often called *global*, although VBA refers to them as *public* variables.

To summarize: the keywords Dim and Private have the same function in variable declarations when used in the general declarations section of any module; the Public keyword can be used to declare module level variables in a component module and global variables in a standard module.

 Use Dim or Private, not Public, to declare module level variables in a component module. Because Public can be used to declare global variables in a standard module, it can be confusing if it is also used in a component module.

Data Types

Data types define the kind of value that may be stored within the memory allocated for a variable. As with spreadsheet cells, there are numerous data types; the most common are defined in Table 2.1.

TABLE 2.1   COMMON DATA TYPES

Data type	Storage size	Range
Boolean	2 bytes	True or False
Integer	2 bytes	-32,768 to 32,767
Long	4 bytes	-2,147,483,648 to 2,147,483,647
Single (floating-point)	4 bytes	-3.402823E38 to -1.401298E-45 for negative values; 1.401298E-45 to 3.402823E38 for positive values
Double (floating-point)	8 bytes	-1.79769313486231E308 to -4.94065645841247E-324 for negative values; 4.94065645841247E-324 to 1.79769313486232E308 for positive values
Date	8 bytes	January 1, 100 to December 31, 9999
Object	4 bytes	Any Object reference
String (variable-length)	10 bytes+ string length	0 to approximately 2 billion
String (fixed-length)	Length of string	1 to approximately 65,400
Variant (with numbers)	16 bytes	Any numeric value up to the range of a Double
Variant (with characters)	22 bytes + string length	Same range as for variable-length String
User-defined (using Type)	Number required by elements	The range of each element is the same as the range of its data type.

Numbers in Table 2.1 that end with an E followed by a number are written in sci-entific notation. *Scientific notation* is a type of shorthand notation used to express very large or very small numbers. The number to the right of the E refers to the number of times the value to the left of the E should be multiplied by 10 (positive numbers) or divided by 10 (negative numbers). For example, the number 3.45E3 is the equivalent of 3.45 x 10 x 10 x 10 or 3,450. Likewise, the number 3.45E-3 is the equivalent of 3.45/10/10/10 or 0.00345. Thus, the largest value that can be stored in a variable of type Single is 340,282,300,000,000,000,000,000,000,000,000,000,000.

Numerical Data Types

The numerical data types listed in Table 2.1 are Integer, Long, Single, and Double. A variable declared as an integer or long data type can hold whole numbers or non-fractional values within the specified ranges. If you need a variable to hold fractional or "floating point" values, then use a single or double data type. Pay attention to the value of the number that might have to be stored within the variable. If the value gets too large for the data type your program will crash. For example, the following code will generate an overflow error because the value 50000 is outside the allowed range for an integer data type:

```
Dim myNum As Integer
MyNum=50000
```

You must also be careful about mixing numerical data types, because you may not get the result you want. The following code will execute without errors, but the variable answer will hold the value 32 after execution of this block, not 31.8 as you might want.

```
Dim answer As Integer
Dim num1 As Single
Dim num2 As Integer
num1 = 5.3
num2 = 6
answer = num1 * num2
```

Changing the variable answer to a single data type will correct the problem. Using the code as shown above is a good way to ensure that an integer is stored within a variable that receives its value from a computation involving floating point numbers. Notice that the value stored in answer is rounded to the nearest whole integer.

By using variables with numerical data types, you can carry out mathematical operations as you normally would using just the numbers the variables contained. You can add, subtract, multiply, and divide variables. You can square and cube numerical variables or raise them to any desired power. See Table 2.2 for a list of the operators used for common mathematical operations in VBA.

TABLE 2.2 COMMON MATHEMATICAL OPERATORS USED IN VBA

Operation	Operator
Addition	+
Subtraction	-
Multiplication	*
Division	/
Exponential	^

Basically, any mathematical operation that can be performed on a number can be performed on a numerical variable. The following are a few examples:

```
Dim num1 As Integer
Dim num2 As Integer
Dim answer As Integer
num1 = 10
num2 = 5
answer = num1 + num2   ' answer Holds 15
answer = num1 - num2    ' answer Holds 5
answer = num1 * num2    ' answer Holds 50
answer = num1 / num2    ' answer Holds 2
answer = num1 ^ 2         ' answer Holds 100
answer = 2 ^ num2         ' answer Holds 32
```

After declaring the variables num1, num2, and answer, a few mathematical operations are carried out over several lines of code. The result of each line is given as a comment within the same line of code. In the code above, the equals (=) does not designate equality; instead it works as an assignment operator. For example, the variable answer gets the result of adding the two variables num1 and num2.

Next, I will look at a fairly simple spreadsheet that uses integer variables and some simple math.

TRICK Although not required, it is a good idea to place all variable declarations for a procedure at the start of your code. With variable declarations at the beginning of your code, you will be able to find them quickly when you need to debug.

Magic Squares

I think I was first introduced to magic squares in seventh grade math. The idea is to fill a square grid with numbers such that the sum of all rows, columns, and diagonals add up to the same value. The number of columns/rows in the grid is an odd number and you can only use each value once. For example, a 3 × 3 grid must be filled with the numbers 1 through 9 so that everything sums up to 15. A 5 × 5 grid uses 1 through 25 and all rows, columns, and diagonals add up to 65. The 3 × 3 is pretty easy even if you don't know or see the pattern.

Figure 2.4 shows the spreadsheet containing the 3 × 3 grid. The Magic Square spreadsheet is available on the CD-ROM that accompanies this book.

The Magic Square spreadsheet is preformatted for colors, borders, and font size.

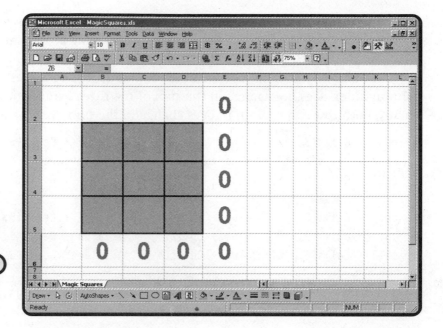

FIGURE 2.4

A 3 × 3 Magic
Square

The program will be contained entirely within the Worksheet_SelectionChange()
event procedure of the worksheet. To get to the Worksheet_SelectionChange() event
procedure, double click the worksheet name in the VBA Project window to open its
component module. Select Worksheet from the object's dropdown list, then select
SelectionChange from the procedure dropdown list. The program will simply
calculate the sum of all rows, columns, and diagonals in the magic square and
display the result in adjacent cells. The program code is listed below. The
Worksheet_SelectionChange() event procedure will trigger every time the user
selects a new cell in the worksheet.

First, variables are declared for holding the summations of the rows, columns, and
diagonals in the magic square. I am using integer data types because I know that I
will not be working with floating point values, and the numbers used will be small.

```
Private Sub Worksheet_SelectionChange(ByVal Target As Range)
    Dim row1 As Integer
    Dim row2 As Integer
    Dim row3 As Integer
    Dim col1 As Integer
    Dim col2 As Integer
    Dim col3 As Integer
    Dim diagonal1 As Integer
    Dim diagonal2 As Integer
```

Next, the values of three cells are added and stored in the previously-dimensioned variables. The values of the individual spreadsheet cells are obtained in what should now be a familiar way. Notice that within a row, the row index in the Cells property does not change in the sum of the three values. Similarly, the column index does not change in the sum of the three values within a column. Finally, both row and column indices change in the sum over the diagonals.

```
row1 = Cells(3, "B").Value + Cells(3, "C").Value + Cells(3, "D").Value
row2 = Cells(4, "B").Value + Cells(4, "C").Value + Cells(4, "D").Value
row3 = Cells(5, "B").Value + Cells(5, "C").Value + Cells(5, "D").Value

col1 = Cells(3, "B").Value + Cells(4, "B").Value + Cells(5, "B").Value
col2 = Cells(3, "C").Value + Cells(4, "C").Value + Cells(5, "C").Value
col3 = Cells(3, "D").Value + Cells(4, "D").Value + Cells(5, "D").Value

diagonal1 = Cells(3, "B").Value + Cells(4, "C").Value + Cells(5, "D").Value
diagonal2 = Cells(5, "B").Value + Cells(4, "C").Value + Cells(3, "D").Value
```

Next, the contents of these summations are copied to the spreadsheet cells in the corresponding row or column.

```
Cells(6, "B").Value = col1
Cells(6, "C").Value = col2
Cells(6, "D").Value = col3

Cells(3, "E").Value = row1
Cells(4, "E").Value = row2
Cells(5, "E").Value = row3

Cells(6, "E").Value = diagonal1
Cells(2, "E").Value = diagonal2
End Sub
```

As the user enters the numbers into the Magic Square, the procedure above is triggered and the values of the summations are updated, as shown in Figure 2.5.

I could have bypassed using variables and simply copied the summation of the three cells directly to the appropriate spreadsheet cell, but using variables with descriptive names makes it a little easier to understand the function of the program.

You have probably realized that the Magic Square isn't anything you couldn't do with formatting and formulas directly in the Excel application. However, if you use a program you can show the spreadsheet to a friend or colleague who knows

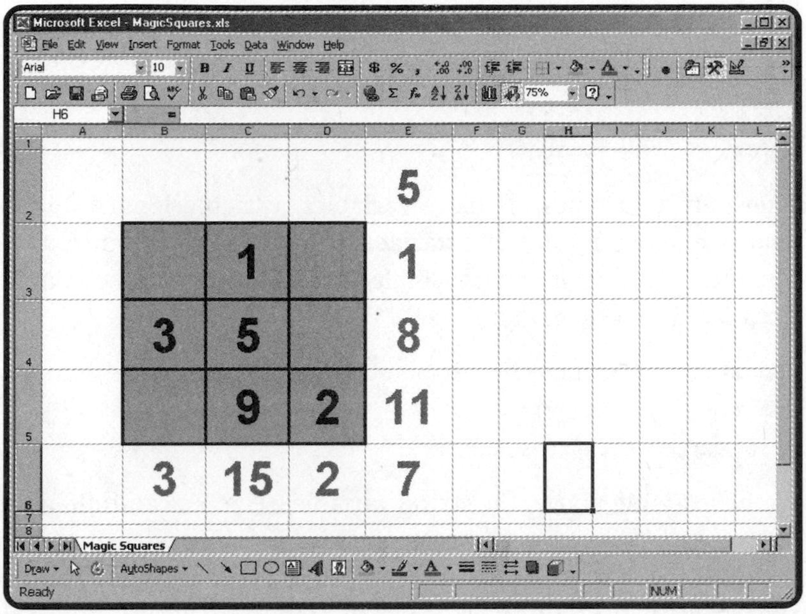

FIGURE 2.5

Magic Squares in action

Excel and he or she will wonder how you did it, as there aren't any formulas in the spreadsheet cells that hold the summations of the rows and columns. Your friend might even be impressed. You can also try a 5 × 5, or any size grid as long as the number of rows and columns is odd and equal. The median value of the number set multiplied by the grid dimension will tell you the sum that the values in all rows, columns, and diagonals should equal.

> **TRICK**
>
> As you may have realized by now, VBA is not case-sensitive. That is, it does not matter if you type your code with uppercase or lowercase letters. However, VBA does preserve capitalization wherever it's used. This is helpful with variable definitions. If you use uppercase letters when declaring a variable, any additional references to that variable within the same scope will automatically follow the same capitalization scheme. So after a variable is defined with a Dim statement, you can type additional references to that variable using all lowercase letters and VBA will automatically convert the capitalization for you. This is a handy feature to ensure that you are spelling your variable names correctly as you type them in your code.

String Data Types

Variables with string data types are used to hold characters as text. The characters can be numbers, letters, or special symbols (for example, punctuation marks). Basically, just about anything you can type on your keyboard can be held within a string variable. To declare a string data type, use the String keyword. To initialize a string variable, place the string value within double quotes.

```
Dim myText As String
myText = "VBA is fun"
```

There are two types of string variables, variable length and fixed length. The example above is that of a variable length string because myText can hold just about any length of text (see Table 2.1). Following is an example of a declaration for a fixed length string:

```
Dim myString As String * 8
Dim myNum As Integer
myString = "ABCDEFGHIJKL"
```

In the example above, the string variable myString can hold a maximum of eight characters. You can try to initialize the variable with more characters (as was done above), but only the first eight characters in this example will be stored in the variable. The value of myString is then "ABCDEFGH." Fixed length strings are more commonly used as a part of a user-defined data type discussed in a later chapter. In most cases, you will not know the length of the string to be stored in a variable, so you should use the variable length type.

I will discuss string manipulation a little later in this chapter. Next I will finish my discussion on data types by looking at variants and a few less common data types.

Variant Data Types

Variant data types are analogous to the General category in the number format of a spreadsheet cell in the Excel application. Variables are declared as variants by leaving off the type designation.

```
Dim myVar
```

IN THE REAL WORLD

A lot of what programmers do with strings revolves around extracting desirable information out of them. For example, a search engine on the Internet will look for certain keywords on a Web page and store them in a database. The search engine may load the entire textual content of a Web page into a string variable and then extract various keywords from that variable. Then when a user searches that database by entering in various keywords, the user's keywords are stored in string variables and compared to database content.

Variant type variables can hold any type of data except a fixed length string. Variant data types relax the restrictions on the value a particular variable can hold and thus give the programmer more flexibility. However, variant data types can also be dangerous if overused—they can slow down program execution, and programs with a large number of variant data types can be very difficult to debug. So while I don't recommend using them, I do recognize that many programmers do use variants, and the online help is filled with examples using variants, so I will offer a brief example here:

```
Dim myVar As Integer
myVar = 10
myVar = "Testing"
```

The example above will generate a type mismatch error because an attempt is made to enter the string "Testing" into an integer variable. However, if you change the variable myVar to a variant, the code will execute and myVar will hold the string value "Testing" when all is complete. The following code will run without error:

```
Dim myVar
myVar = 10
myVar = "Testing"
```

Using variants allows you to use the same variable to hold multiple data types (one at a time). The variable myVar holds the integer value 10 (albeit briefly) before being assigned the string value "Testing."

You are probably starting to see the danger of using variant data types. Imagine a large program with numerous procedures and variables. Within this program are two variables of the type that initially hold numerical values and will need to be used within the same mathematical operation before the program is finished executing. If one variable is mistakenly reinitialized with a string before the mathematical operation, an error will result and may crash the program (or at least taint the result). Debugging this program may present problems that depend on how hard it is to find the string initialization of the variant variable, and additional problems associated with the string variant. So even though it may be tempting to use variants as a way to prevent errors that crash your program (as in the example above), in actuality the use of variants make your code "loose," and may result in logic errors that are difficult to find.

HINT Logic errors are the result of a mistake in a programming algorithm. They may or may not cause your program to crash, depending on the specific nature of the error. Trying to multiply variables of a string and integer data type would crash program execution, making the error relatively easy to find. Adding when you should have multiplied is a type of logic error that will not crash a program, but will certainly give you the wrong result. Logic errors can be very serious because you may never find them or even know they exist.

Other Data Types

There are just a couple more data types that need to be mentioned. You will see them in action in subsequent chapters.

The Boolean data type holds the value true or false. You can also represent true as a 1 and false as a 0. Boolean variables will be very useful when dealing with programming structures that use conditions, as you will see in the next chapter. Declare and initialize a Boolean variable as follows:

```
Dim rollDice As Boolean
rollDice = False
```

You can also specify variables of type date. Variables of type date are actually stored as floating point numbers with the integer portion representing a date between 1 January, 100 and 31 December 9999, and the decimal portion representing a time between 0:00:00 to 23:59:59. The date data type is mostly a convenience when you need to work with dates or times. There are a handful of VBA functions that use variables of type date that add to this convenience. You will see a couple of examples of date functions in the chapter project.

Constants

Constants allow you to assign a meaningful name to a number or string that will make your code easier to read. This is analogous to using named ranges in your spreadsheet formulas. There are numerous mathematical constants for which it makes sense to use constant data types. A constant string might be used when you need frequent use of a particular spreadsheet label. Constants are declared using the Const keyword as shown below.

```
Const PI = 3.14159
Dim circumference As Single
Dim diameter As Single
diameter =10.32
circumference = PI* diameter
```

The declaration and initialization of a constant occur in the same line of code. The value of a constant can never change, so it is a good idea to use constants when you need the same value throughout the life of your program. Constant names are uppercase as a convention only; it is not required by VBA.

Simple Input and Output with VBA

You have already seen how to get input from the user through the use of the Value property of a spreadsheet cell. Conversely, you can generate output for the user through the spreadsheet. Yet there may be times when you want something more dynamic and dramatic than a spreadsheet cell. The easiest method for gathering input from the user and sending output back is using the InputBox() and MsgBox() functions.

HINT

Just as Excel comes with a large number of functions for the user to use in spreadsheet formulas (for example, the SUM() function), VBA contains numerous functions for the programmer. VBA programming functions, just like Excel functions, typically require one or more values (called *parameters*) to be passed to them, and then return one or more values (most commonly one) back to the program.

Collecting User Input with InputBox()

When you need to prompt the user for input and want to force a response before program execution continues, then the InputBox() function is the tool to use. The InputBox() function sends to the screen a dialog box that must be addressed by the user before program execution proceeds. Figure 2.6 shows the dialog box.

The InputBox() function returns the data entered by the user as a string if the OK button is clicked or the Enter key is pressed on the keyboard. If the user clicks the Cancel button, then a zero-length string is returned (""). Here is the syntax required for creating an InputBox() (parameters in brackets are optional):

```
InputBox(prompt [,title] [,default] [,xpos] [,ypos] [,helpfile, context])
```

The prompt is the only required parameter that must be passed to the function.

FIGURE 2.6

The InputBox() dialog box

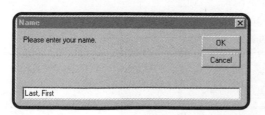

Typically, the prompt, title, and sometimes the default are used. You must assign the return value of the function to a variable of type string.

```
Dim name As String
name = InputBox("Please enter your name.", "Name", "Last, First")
```

The prompt and title must be strings, which is why they are enclosed in double quotes. Alternatively, you can use string variables for these parameters. The title parameter is displayed in the title bar of the dialog box. The default parameter is displayed in the text box of the dialog box. Including a little help in the prompt or default parameter will increase the chances of getting the desired input returned. In the example above, I included a default parameter that serves to tell the user in what format I want the name entered.

Output with MsgBox()

The `MsgBox()` function outputs a message to the user in the form of a message box like the one shown in Figure 2.7.

The `MsgBox()` function is a good way to alert the user about some type of problem, or ask a question that requires a yes/no answer. Here is the syntax for the `MsgBox()` function:

```
MsgBox(prompt[, buttons] [, title] [, helpfile, context])
```

The prompt is the only required parameter, although buttons and title are usually included. The following example was used to generate the message box in Figure 2.7:

```
userResponse = MsgBox("Testing the Message Box", vbInformation + vbOKOnly
+ vbMsgBoxHelpButton, "Message")
```

The prompt must be a string or string variable and is used as the message you want the user to read. The buttons parameter requires a numeric expression (either an integer or constant) and tells VBA what buttons and/or icons are to be placed on the message box. There are several choices for buttons, including OK, OK/Cancel, Abort/Retry/Ignore, and Yes/No. You can also display an icon (warnings or information type), a help button, and add some additional formatting

FIGURE 2.7

The Message box

with your choice of buttons. For a complete list of button choices, look up the MsgBox() function in the on-line help by typing **msgbox** in the keyword field of the help window (see Figure 2.8). The references vbOKOnly, vbInformation, and vbMsgBoxHelpButton in the preceding expression are actually constants associated with this function. For example, the value of vbOKOnly is zero. I used the constant expression because it's easier to read the code and know exactly what I am asking for in the appearance of the message box. Finally, the title can be included as a string or string variable.

The MsgBox() function returns an integer between 1 and 7, depending on the button selected. Obviously this is only useful when there is more than one button. The return value should then be used to select a course of action in your program.

Finally, you should take care not to use too many message boxes in your program. Always ask yourself if you can get the input or display the message in another way when you are thinking of including a message box. Most users (including myself) find it extremely annoying to have to answer a message box when it's not really necessary.

Manipulating Strings with VBA Functions

Now it's time to get back to strings and have a little fun. Strings are more of an unknown to the programmer in the sense that you seldom know how long they are, or how much of the string actually represents useful information. Thankfully, there

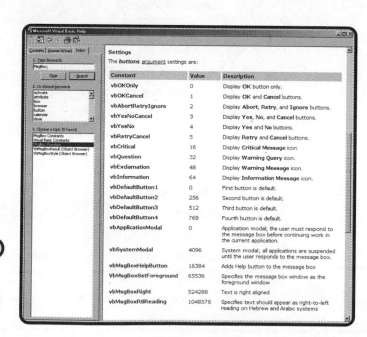

FIGURE 2.8

Settings for the buttons argument with the MsgBox() function is a plethora of functions designed to work on string variables that you can use to extract the information you need. Table 2.3 summarizes many of these functions.

As with most functions, the string functions require one or more parameters be passed. All functions must return a value, so the syntax will look something like this:

```
myVar = FunctionName(parameter list)
```

where myVar is a variable of the proper type for the return value of the function, FunctionName is the name of the VBA function, and parameter list is a list of one or more values to be passed to the function. Parameters can be literals (for example, 5.2 or "Hello"), but are usually in the form of variables.

Fun with Strings

The best way to learn these functions is to use them, so let's create a program that asks for the user's name and then outputs components of the name to a worksheet. I call it "Fun with Strings," and Figure 2.9 shows the spreadsheet, which can also be found on the CD-ROM.

TABLE 2.3 VBA STRING FUNCTIONS

Function Name	Returns
Str()	A string representation of a number
Val()	A numerical representation of a string
Trim()	A string with leading and trailing spaces removed
Left()	A portion of a string beginning from the left side
Right()	A portion of a string beginning from the right side
Mid()	Any portion of a string
InStr()	A number representing the place value of a particular character within a string
Len()	A number of characters in a string
LCase()	A string with all characters lowercase
UCase()	A string will all characters uppercase
StrConv()	A string converted to one of several possible formats
StrComp()	A number indicating the result of a string comparison
Asc()	Number representing the ANSI code of a character
Chr()	One character string representing the ANSI code of a number

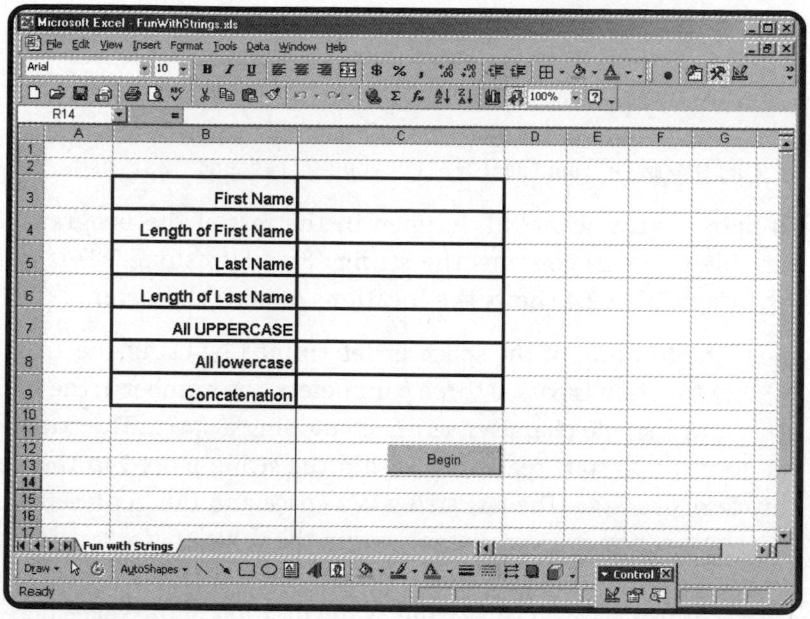

FIGURE 2.9

Fun with Strings

Specifically, the program will output the user's first name and last name along with the number of characters in each name to separate cells in the spreadsheet. The program will also convert the user's name to all uppercase and all lowercase characters as well as reverse the order of the first and last name. The code is placed in the Click() event procedure of a Command Button control placed on the worksheet. The name property of the Command Button control was changed to cmdBegin and the Caption property to "Begin." When the user clicks on the command button, code execution begins. After some variable declarations, the InputBox() function is used to prompt the user for his/her first and last name. You will notice that I am assuming the user enters his/her first name followed by one space and then the last name.

 HINT Input validation is an important component in any program that requires user input. I have not yet covered enough programming constructs to discuss input validation; I will wait until Chapter 4 to discuss it.

Everything entered by the user is stored in the string variable userName.

```
Option Explicit
Private Sub cmdBegin_Click()

    Dim userName As String
    Dim firstName As String
```

```
Dim lastName As String
Dim strLength As Integer
Dim spaceLoc As Integer

userName = InputBox("Enter your first and last name.", "Name")
```

To help picture what will happen in the rest of the program, let's assume the variable userName contains the string "Fred Flintstone." This string is 15 characters long; Table 2.4 shows the locations of each character.

Next, the location of the space is determined by using the InStr() function. The InStr() function is passed three parameters, the number 1, the string variable userName, and a single character string containing a space. The parameter 1 represents the location to start searching within the string passed in the next parameter, in this case, userName. The last string is a space and this represents the character the InStr() function is searching for within the value of userName. The InStr() function then returns an integer value representing the location of the space within the userName string. This integer value is the location of the space between the first and last name of the user, location 5 in this example (see Table 2.4), and is stored in the integer variable spaceLoc. The Left() function is then passed two parameters, the userName string, and the length of the portion of the userName string to return. The variable spaceLoc is holding the location of the space (5 in our example), so using spaceLoc - 1 for the length parameter in the Left() function returns just the first name (Fred). The Len() function is used to return the length of the firstName string as an integer and this value is stored in the variable strLength. The values of the firstName string and strLength variables are then copied to the worksheet.

```
spaceLoc = InStr(1, userName, " ")
firstName = Left(userName, spaceLoc - 1)
Cells(3, "C").Value = firstName
strLength = Len(firstName)
Cells(4, "C").Value = strLength
```

TABLE 2.4 CHARACTER LOCATIONS IN A STRING

Character	F	r	e	d		F	l	i
	n	t	s	t	o	n	e	
Location	1	2	3	4	5	6	7	8
	9	10	11	12	13	14	15	

The `Mid()` function is used to return the last name of the user to the string variable `lastName`. The `Mid()` function takes three parameters: the original string `userName` (Fred Flintstone), the starting location of the new string (`spaceLoc - 1`), and the length of the string to return (`strLength - spaceLoc`). The variable `strLength` was reinitialized to the length of `userName` prior to using the `Mid()` function. Again, the variables holding the last name and the number of characters in the last name are copied to the worksheet.

```
strLength = Len(userName)
lastName = Mid(userName, spaceLoc + 1, strLength - spaceLoc)
Cells(5, "C").Value = lastName
strLength = Len(lastName)
Cells(6, "C").Value = strLength
```

The `UCase()` and `LCase()` functions convert the `userName` string to all uppercase and all lowercase letters, respectively. Finally, the ampersand (&) character is used to concatenate strings and rearrange the user's name such that the last name is first, followed by a comma and the first name.

```
Cells(7, "C").Value = UCase(userName)
Cells(8, "C").Value = LCase(userName)
Cells(9, "C").Value = lastName & ", " & firstName
End Sub
```

HINT

String concatenation is the process of combining one or more strings together to form a new string. The strings are combined from left to right using either the ampersand (&) or addition (+) operators. To avoid ambiguity with the addition operator, I recommend that you always use the ampersand (&) operator for string concatenation.

You did not see all the string functions in action in the Fun with Strings program. You will see more in the next project and throughout this book. I will explain their use in detail as they appear in various code snippets and programming projects. In the meantime, I recommend you play with the string functions I have already discussed in order to get comfortable using them.

Constructing the Time of Your Life Program

This project will utilize several of the VBA programming components discussed in this chapter. The project contains several different examples of data types, including integer, floating point, string and date types. I introduce some new functions designed to work with the date and string data types. The project also demonstrates nesting functions, the use of constants, and some simple mathematical operations.

Project Statement

I want to create a program that will take the user's name and birth date as input, then calculate the time of the user's life in several units. These time units should then be displayed in a worksheet along with the user's name and birth date formatted to display the day of the week and month (see Figure 2.1). As always, the project spreadsheet can be found on the CD-ROM.

Project Tools

Possible tools for this project include the InputBox() function for getting information from the user, numerical, string, and date data types for processing the information, and numerous functions that work with string and date values for manipulating the information. Possible functions include the string functions listed in Table 2.3 and numerous date functions, two of which are Now and DateDiff().

The VBA function Now is a rare example of a function that is not passed any arguments. No information is required by the Now function because all it does is return the current time and date from the computer's clock. VBA functions that do not accept arguments will be written without ending parentheses.

The Click() event procedure of a Command Button control can be used to hold and start the program. The worksheet can be preformatted for font, borders, and color with the Excel application.

Project Algorithm

You will develop the project by doing the following:

1. Formatting the worksheet with a large font (Arial 20 pt) and color.
2. Entering data input from the program in ranges B2:C2 for the user's name, C3:E3 for the user's birth date, and C5:C10 for the various lengths of time converted from the user's birth date.

3. Adding appropriate labels to adjacent cells.

4. Filling in black the columns and rows that border the working area of the worksheet.

5. Adding a Command Button control to the worksheet. Change its name property to `cmdStart` and its `Caption` property to "Start."

6. Placing all code in the `Click()` event procedure of the Command Button control.

7. Writing code that will accept user input (name and birth date) using the `InputBox()` function.

8. Calculating the length of the user's life in seconds using the `Now` and `DateDiff()` functions.

9. Converting the length of the user's life to units of minutes, hours, days, months, and years using simple mathematical operations.

10. Formatting variables holding the user's birthday such that the day and month are displayed as text (for example, Sunday, January, etc.).

11. Separating the user's first and last names into new variables using suitable string functions.

12. Copying all information to the appropriate cells in the worksheet.

See Figure 2.1 as a guide to spreadsheet cell locations for labels and variable output by the program.

Adding the Code

Variable declaration is required by adding `Option Explicit` to the general declarations section of the component module for the Time of Your Life worksheet. All other code is added to the `Click()` event procedure of the Command Button control named `cmdStart`. Variable declarations are placed at the top of the procedure. Several string variables will be used to hold the information obtained from the user. Numerical variables will be used for holding the various lengths of time the user has been alive and the numerical components of the user's birthday.

```
Option Explicit
Private Sub cmdStart_Click()

    Dim userName As String
    Dim firstName As String
    Dim lastName As String
    Dim yearsPassed As Single
```

```
Dim monthsPassed As Single
Dim daysPassed As Single
Dim hoursPassed As Single
Dim minutesPassed As Long
Dim secondsPassed As Single
Dim userBirthday As Date
Dim currentDate As Date
Dim bDay As String
Dim bMonth As String
Dim bDay2 As Integer
Dim bYear As Integer
Const secsPerMin = 60
Const minsPerHour = 60
Const hoursPerDay = 24
Const daysPerYear = 365.25
```

Input is gathered from the user with the InputBox() function. Notice that I placed the InputBox() function inside the parameter list of the LCase() function. This is called *nesting functions*. In nested functions, the innermost function runs first, in this case InputBox(), then whatever the user enters in the input box is passed to the next function, LCase(). The string entered by the user is then stored in the userName variable with all characters lowercase. Another InputBox() function is used to retrieve the user's birthday. Again the InputBox() is nested in another function. The DateValue() function is used to convert the string entered by the user in the form of date to an actual value of type date. The date is then store in the variable userBirthday.

```
userName = LCase(InputBox("What is your first and last name?", "Name"))
    userBirthday = DateValue(InputBox("When was your birthday?
(month/day/year)", "Age"))
```

Now you must process the information obtained from the user. First get the current date and time by using the Now function and store it in the date variable currentDate. The Now function is somewhat unusual in that it does not take any parameters. The currentDate and userBirthday variables are passed to the DateDiff() function along with the single character string "s" The DateDiff() function calculates the difference between two dates in the interval specified, in this case "s" for seconds. Once the user's life in seconds is known, it's a simple matter to convert this number to minutes, hours, days, months, and years using the constants defined earlier.

HINT

The `DateDiff()` function returns a value of type variant (long). This means that the function will return a long integer unless the value exceeds its range (2,147,483,647), in which case it will promote the return value to the next largest data type with integer values. In the Time of Your Life program, the range of the long data type will be exceeded by anyone more than 68 years old. Thus, to avoid a possible data-type error, the variable `secondsPassed` was declared as a single data type. This ensures the value from `DateDiff()` will be within the variable's allowed range of values. I did not want a floating-point number for the value of `secondsPassed`, but I don't need to be concerned because I know the `DateDiff()` function will only return a whole number.

```
currentDate = Now
    secondsPassed = DateDiff("s", userBirthday, currentDate)
    minutesPassed = secondsPassed / secsPerMin
    hoursPassed = minutesPassed / minsPerHour
    daysPassed = hoursPassed / hoursPerDay
    yearsPassed = daysPassed / daysPerYear
    monthsPassed = yearsPassed * 12
```

The `Format()` function can be used with numerical, string, and date data. Here `Format()` is used to return the weekday the user was born, and the month as text rather than the numerical representation. The dates are passed as variables along with format strings (`"dddd"` and `"mmmm"`). These strings tell the function what format to use on the return value. For example, `"dd"` would return the numerical value for the day of the month, and `"ddd"` would return the three-letter abbreviation.

Next, the `Day()` and `Year()` functions are used to return the day of the month and year as integers.

```
bDay = Format(userBirthday, "dddd")
bMonth = Format(userBirthday, "mmmm")
bDay2 = Day(userBirthday)
bYear = Year(userBirthday)
```

Using some of the string functions from Table 2.3, the first and last names are extracted from the `userName` string and formatted to ensure the proper capitalization. Two approaches are used for the first and last names in order to demonstrate a couple of different string functions. The first name is extracted form `userName` with the `Left()` function, then a nested `Instr()` function is used to determine the length parameter that must be passed to the `Left()` function. The next line formats the firstName string for proper case. The first letter of the firstName string is extracted with the Left() function and is converted to uppercase with the UCase() function. The first letter is then concatenated with the rest of the name, which was extracted with the Right() function and a nested Len() function to set the length parameter. You have probably noticed that the firstName string variable being passed to the functions is the same variable to which the result is stored. This is perfectly acceptable when you don't need the current value of the variable, so you pass it to a function for altering and overwrite the old value.

```
firstName = Left(userName, InStr(1, userName, " "))
    firstName = UCase(Left(firstName, 1)) & Right(firstName,
Len(firstName) - 1)
```

Extract the user's last name from the userName string with the Right() function with nested Len() and Instr() functions to set the length parameter. Then use the StrConv() function to convert it to proper case, where vbProperCase represents a numerical constant of the function. This is considerably easier than the method used with the firstName variable, and illustrates the fact that there can be more than one way to work with available functions for solving a problem.

```
lastName = Right(userName, (Len(userName) - InStr(1, userName, " ")))
lastName = StrConv(lastName, vbProperCase)
```

Finally, now that all values have been calculated and formatted as desired, they are output to the appropriate cells in the worksheet. The only new element here is the Str() function which converts a numerical value to a string data type. The Str() function is not really needed for the conversion in this case. Since the & is used as the string concatenation operator, VBA assumes I want the variable bDay2 treated as if it were a string when the Str() function is omitted. If + is used as the string concatenation operator, then the Str() function must be used to avoid a type mismatch error.

 HINT The converse of the Str() function is the Val() function. The Val() function is used to convert string data to numerical data.

```
Cells(2, "B").Value = firstName
Cells(2, "C").Value = lastName
Cells(3, "C").Value = bDay
Cells(3, "D").Value = bMonth & "   " & Str(bDay2)
Cells(3, "E").Value = bYear
Cells(5, "C").Value = yearsPassed
Cells(6, "C").Value = monthsPassed
```

```
    Cells(7, "C").Value = daysPassed
    Cells(8, "C").Value = hoursPassed
    Cells(9, "C").Value = minutesPassed
    Cells(10, "C").Value = secondsPassed
End Sub
```

That concludes this chapter's project. Although it's not exactly a long program, you may be feeling a bit overwhelmed by the number of functions used. Don't worry about learning all the functions available in VBA and how to use them—you can't! There are way too many, so it's a waste of time to try to memorize them all. I am familiar with the string functions because I use them quite often, although I still had to look up syntax and parameter lists a couple of times while writing this project. The date functions are another matter. I didn't know any of the date functions before writing this program. What I did know is the essence of how a function works. I also realized that VBA was very likely to have a number of functions that worked on the date data type. Then it was a simple matter of searching the online help and looking at my choices.

Chapter Summary

This chapter introduced you to some important basics of programming, including variables, data types, and constants. I placed particular emphasis on the most common data types, numbers, and strings. I also took a look at programming modules in VBA and their effect on the scope of a variable. Finally I discussed several functions used to manipulate values of type string and date.

In Chapter 3 I will give you a more in-depth look at VBA modules and procedures. Then I will examine some more basic programming constructs with conditional operators and If/Then/Else type structures.

CHALLENGES

1. Write a program that will add two numbers input by the user and display the result in a spreadsheet. Use an input box and the Val() function to convert the user input to a numerical data type.

2. Place a Command Button control on a worksheet and write a program in the Click() event procedure that increments a variable by 5 with every click of the mouse. Output the value of this variable in a message box.

3. Write a program that extracts the time from the string returned by the Now function and outputs it in a message box.

Procedures and Conditions

A lthough the two topics in this chapter title don't necessarily go hand in hand, they do represent basic constructs essential for any program. In this chapter you'll take a close look at both procedures and conditions in order to establish some basic tools with which to work in VBA.

Specifically, in this chapter I will discuss:

- **Sub procedures**

- **Function procedures**

- **Event procedures**

- **Conditional logic**

- **Conditional statements and the** `If/Then/Else` **and** `Select/Case` **code structures**

- **Chapter project: Poker Dice**

Project: Poker Dice

Poker Dice is a variation of five-card draw using dice instead of cards. This is the first functional program that can't be created in the Excel application alone. The Poker Dice spreadsheet is shown in Figure 3.1.

The program introduces two new controls (Check Box and Image controls) and a conditional programming structure (If/Then/Else).

VBA Procedures

I briefly discussed programming modules in Chapter 2. You may remember that a module is a segment of your project that contains a related set of declarations and procedures. You may also remember that every module has its own window within the VBA IDE and, depending on whether or not it is a component module or a standard module, slightly different behavior regarding variables. Programming procedures can be constructed within each of these module windows if they are not already defined. Let's take a look at the different type of procedures that can be used and/or built using VBA.

Event Procedures

You have already seen a few examples of event procedures, such as the Click() event procedure of a command button and the SelectionChange() event procedure of a worksheet. These procedures are predefined by VBA in the sense that we cannot change the name of the procedure, component, or object within Excel to which the procedure belongs, or the conditions under which the procedure is triggered. For the most part, all we can do with these procedures is add the code to be executed when the event is triggered. Typically, several events are associated with each Excel

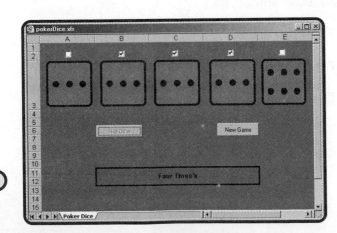

FIGURE 3.1

The Poker Dice program

object, whether it is a worksheet, workbook, chart, or ActiveX control. Figure 3.2 shows the component module for a worksheet and displays all of the events associated with a worksheet in Excel.

Event procedures are defined with the Sub keyword followed by the name of the procedure.

```
Private Sub Worksheet_Activate()
                'Event procedure code is listed here.
End Sub
```

The name of the procedure listed above is Worksheet_Activate(), although it will be more commonly referred to as the Activate() event. No parameters are passed to this procedure because the parentheses are empty. This procedure is triggered when the worksheet to which it is associated is activated. That is, when you switch between two different windows or worksheets, the Activate() event of the currently selected worksheet is triggered. The procedure ends with the line End Sub, unless the statement Exit Sub is used within the procedure code.

Private, Public, and Procedure Scope

The Private and Public keywords used with procedure definitions have a similar function to that used with variable declarations. Private and Public are used to define the procedure's scope. The Public keyword makes the procedure visible to all other procedures in all modules in all projects. The Private keyword ensures

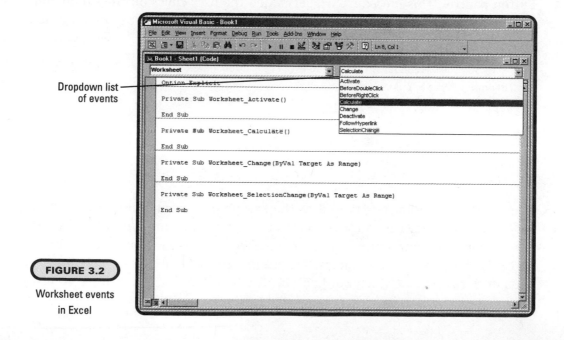

FIGURE 3.2

Worksheet events in Excel

that the procedure is visible to other procedures within the same module but keeps it inaccessible to all other procedures outside the module in which it is defined. The `Private` and `Public` keywords are optional, but VBA includes them in predefined event procedures. If `Private` or `Public` is omitted, then the procedure is public by default.

Use the `Option Private` **statement in the general declarations section of a module to keep public modules visible only within the project. Omit** `Option Private` **if you want to create reusable procedures that will be available for any project.**

Parameters with Event Procedures

Parameters are the list of one or more variables or literals passed to the event procedure when it is triggered. The values of the parameters passed to the event procedure contain information related to the event. A comma separates multiple variables, and the variable data type is also declared. VBA defines everything about the parameters passed to the event procedure, including the number of parameters, the name of each parameter and their data types, and the method in which they are passed. Although it is possible to change the name of the variables in the parameter list under certain circumstances, I do not recommend editing the event procedure definition in any way.

The following example shows the `MouseDown()` event procedure of a Command Button control. This procedure triggers when the user clicks on the Command Button control with the mouse. The first and last lines of the procedure are automatically created by VBA. I added the four lines of code within the procedure.

```
Private Sub CommandButton1_MouseDown(ByVal Button As Integer, ByVal Shift
As Integer, ByVal X As Single, ByVal Y As Single)
    Cells(2, "A").Value = Button
    Cells(2, "B").Value = Shift
    Cells(2, "C").Value = X
    Cells(2, "D").Value = Y
End Sub
```

There are four parameters passed to the `MouseDown()` event procedure: `Button`, `Shift`, `X`, and `Y`; they have all been declared as numerical data types. These parameters contain numerical information describing the event that just occurred, and they can be used as variables within the procedure because they have already been declared. The `ByVal` keyword will be discussed later in this chapter, so just ignore it for now. The previous code was added to the MouseDown() event procedure of a Command Button control placed on a worksheet with a few column headers, as shown in Figure 3.3.

The values of the parameter variables are copied to the appropriate cells in this worksheet when the user clicks on the Command Button control with his or her mouse. The variable Button represents the mouse button that was clicked—a value of 1 for the left mouse button, 2 for the right mouse button, and 3 for the middle mouse button (if it exists). The variable Shift represents the combination of Shift, Ctrl, and Alt keys held down while the mouse button was clicked. Since there are eight possible combinations of these three keys, the variable Shift can hold an integer value between 0 and 7. The variables X and Y represent the location of the mouse cursor within the Command Button control when the mouse button was clicked. The values of X and Y fall within 0 to the value of the Width property of the Command Button control for X, and 0 to the value of the Height property for Y. The upper left corner of the Command Button control is X = 0, Y = 0.

You now see how helpful the information within these parameters can be. For example, a programmer might use the MouseDown() and MouseUp() event procedures of an ActiveX control to catch a right click of the mouse button over that control. The MouseDown() event procedure might be used to display a menu with various options, and the MouseUp() event procedure would then be used to hide the menu. Does this sound familiar?

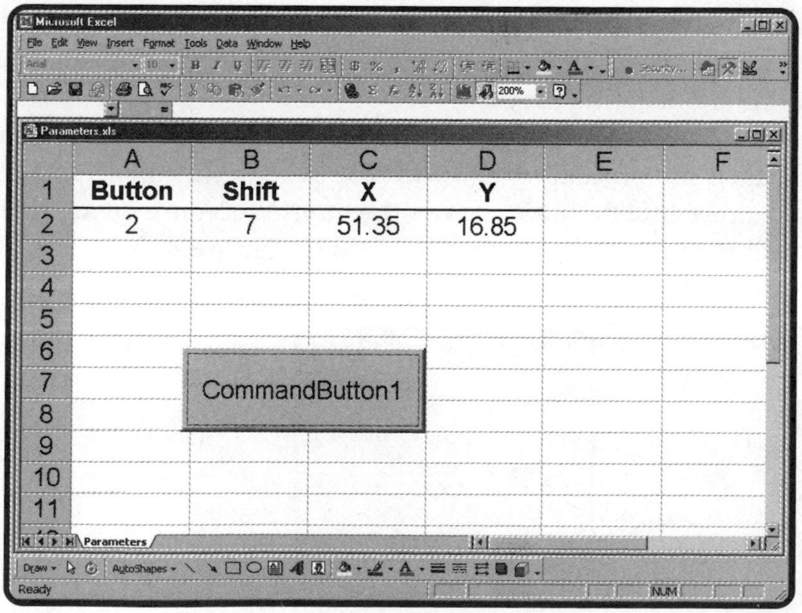

FIGURE 3.3

Parameter values of the MouseDown() event procedure

It is both impractical and unnecessary to discuss all of the event procedures of all Excel objects and ActiveX controls in this book. The examples you have seen so far are a good representation of how to use event procedures in VBA. In order to establish which event procedures (if any) should be used in your program, do the following:

- Ask yourself, "When should something happen?"

- Search for the event procedure(s) that will be triggered by the answer to the question, "When should something happen?" The event procedures have sensible names related to the action that triggers them, however it may be useful to look up the description of the event procedure in the online help.

- If you cannot find an event procedure that triggers when desired, re-design your program with ActiveX controls that do contain a useful event procedure. If you still can't find anything, then there are probably errors in the logic of your algorithm.

- Test possible procedures by writing simple programs such as the one for the MouseDown() event procedure described earlier.

- Insert the code that carries out the tasks you want once you recognize the proper event procedure.

Sub Procedures

Although all procedures are really sub (short for *subroutine*) procedures, I will use the term to refer to those procedures created entirely by the programmer. The basic syntax and operation of a sub procedure is the same as for an event procedure. You define the procedure with the scope using the Public or Private keywords, followed by the keyword Sub, the procedure name, and the parameter list (if any). Sub procedures end with the End Sub statement. You can either type in the procedure definition or use the Insert/Procedure menu item to bring up the "Add Procedure" dialog box, as shown in Figure 3.4.

FIGURE 3.4

The Add Procedure
dialog box

```
Private Sub myProcedure(parameter list)
    'Sub procedure code is listed here.
End Sub
```

Sub procedures differ from event procedures in that

- the programmer defines the procedure name and any variable names in the parameter list.
- the programmer decides how many (if any) variables are in the parameter list.
- they can be placed in both component and standard modules.
- execution begins when they are "called" using code from other parts of the program and cannot be automatically triggered.

The following program collects two numbers from the user, adds them, and outputs the result. This program can reside in any module. For simplicity, I tested this program by running it directly from the VBA IDE. To begin program execution from the VBA IDE, first insert the mouse cursor within the procedure to be executed, and then hit F5 or select the appropriate icon from the Standard toolbar or Run menu, as shown in Figure 3.5.

First, variable declaration is required with Option Explicit and a module level variable (answer) is declared.

```
Option Explicit
Dim answer As Integer
```

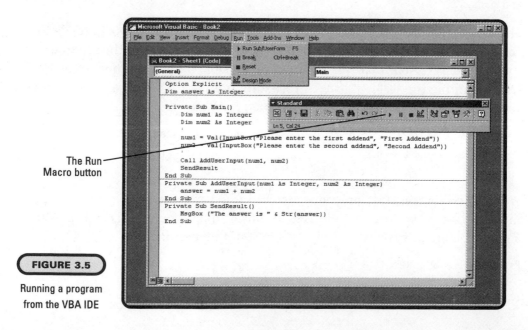

The Run Macro button

FIGURE 3.5

Running a program from the VBA IDE

The sub procedure `Main()` is declared as `Private` and serves as the central procedure for the program. Two procedure-level integer variables (num1 and num2) are declared and assigned to the return value of input boxes. The `Val()` function is used to convert the string type return value from the `InputBox()` function to a numerical value.

```
Private Sub Main()
    Dim num1 As Integer
    Dim num2 As Integer
    num1 = Val(InputBox("Please enter the first addend", "First Addend"))
    num2 = Val(InputBox("Please enter the second addend", "Second
Addend"))
```

The `Call` keyword is used to send program execution to the sub procedure called `AddUserInput()` and the variables num1 and num2 are passed to this procedure. The `Call` keyword is required when passing parameters; otherwise it is unnecessary. After the `AddUserInput()` procedure executes, program execution resumes in the `Main()` procedure where it left off. The line `SendResult` is another procedure call and sends program execution to the `SendResult()` sub procedure. As no parameters are passed, the `Call` keyword is omitted (although you may include it if you like). The `Main()` procedure, and consequently the program, terminates after program execution returns from the `SendResult()` procedure.

```
    Call AddUserInput(num1, num2)
    SendResult
End Sub
```

The `AddUserInput()` procedure's only purpose is to accept the two addends from the `Main()` procedure, add them together, and store the result in the module level variable answer. Note that I used the same variable names for the two addends when defining the `AddUserInput()` procedure. This is perfectly legal, as this is outside the scope of the original num1 and num2 variables.

```
Private Sub AddUserInput(num1 As Integer, num2 As Integer)
    answer = num1 + num2
End Sub
```

Finally, the `SendResult()` procedure is used to output the answer using a basic message box. A `Str()` function is used to convert the numerical variable answer to a string before it is concatenated to the rest of the message.

```
Private Sub SendResult()
    MsgBox ("The answer is " & Str(answer))
End Sub
```

Keep your procedures as short as possible. You will find that as your procedures get longer, they get harder to read and debug. As a general rule I try to keep my procedures to a length such that all of the code is visible on my monitor. If your procedure gets much longer than one screen, break the procedure into two or more procedures.

ByVal and ByRef

You should have noticed the ByVal keyword in the parameter list of the MouseDown() event procedure shown earlier in the chapter. The ByVal keyword tells VBA to make a copy of the value stored in the accompanying variable. Thus, any manipulation of the copied value within the procedure does not affect the original variable.

The alternative to passing a variable by value is to pass a variable to another procedure by reference; the ByRef keyword is used to do so. When you pass by reference you are essentially passing the original variable to the procedure. Any manipulation of the variable in the new procedure is permanent, so the variable does not retain its original value when program execution proceeds back to the calling procedure. This is true even if you use a new variable name in the procedure that accepts the variable passed by reference. Passing by reference is the default behavior, so you can omit the ByRef keyword if you want to.

The following short program will make the behavior of ByVal and ByRef clear. I suggest inserting a new module into a project, adding the code below, and running the program from the procedure Main().

```
Private Sub Main()
    Dim num1 As Integer
    Dim num2 As Integer
    num1 = 10
    num2 = 15
    Call passByRef(num1)
    Call passByVal(num2)
    MsgBox (num1 & "  " & num2)
End Sub
Private Sub passByRef(ByRef num3 As Integer)
    num3 = 20
End Sub
Private Sub passByVal(ByVal num2 As Integer)
    num2 = 20
End Sub
```

Figure 3.6 shows the message box output by this program.

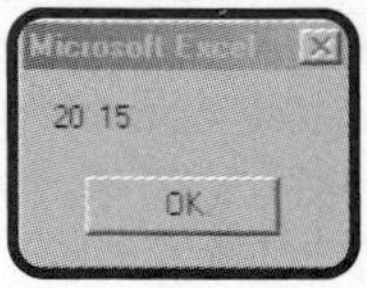

FIGURE 3.6

Message Box output from sub procedure Main()

First, two integer variables are declared and initialized to the values 10 and 15. The first variable, num1, is passed by reference to the procedure passByRef() in a variable called num3. The value 20 is assigned to the num3 variable inside the passByRef() procedure. Next the variable num2 is passed by value to the passByVal() procedure, where it is copied to another variable called num2. The num2 variable in the passByVal() procedure is then assigned the value 20. The program ends with the output of the original num1 and num2 variables in a message box.

Now ask yourself: "What values are output in the message box?" The answer is 20 for the num1 variable, and 15 for the num2 variable. The variable num1 holds the value 20 at the end of the Main() procedure because it was changed in the passByRef() procedure. Even though a different variable name was used in the passByRef() procedure, the num3 variable still refers to the same memory location holding the value assigned to the num1 variable. Essentially, we have one variable with two names, each with its own scope. The num2 variable retains its value of 15 at the end of Main() procedure because it had been passed by value to the passByVal() procedure. Passing by value makes a copy of the variable's value to a new variable, even if the variable in the accepting procedure (passByVal) has the same name. In this case, there are two variables with the same name.

IN THE REAL WORLD

At the most basic level, you can think of a memory location in your computer as a sequence of electrical switches that can be on or off. With these two possible conditions we have the basis for the binary language a computer understands (0 for off and 1 for on). The values stored by a programming variable are then just a patterned sequence of switches that are either on or off.

Some languages, such as C or C++, allow the programmer to directly access memory locations of variables. This extends the power of a programming language dramatically, but is not without dangers. For example, if you change the state of the wrong memory location you can easily cause the computer to crash. VBA handles memory management for you, so it is inherently safer than these other languages. However, with this safety you sacrifice some powerful capabilities.

You pass a variable by reference to a procedure in order to change the value of the original variable, or when the variable is needed in the procedure but its value does not have to be changed. If the variable needs to be altered for another purpose but must retain its original value, then pass the variable by value using the ByVal keyword.

Function Procedures

Function procedures are very much like other procedures, but with one significant difference: they return a value to the calling procedure. Now you might be concerned or confused by the fact that I used the term *functions* back in Chapter 2 in reference to Excel's spreadsheet functions and VBA's string and date functions. So, what's the difference? There is no difference. Everything I have called or will call a function is essentially the same thing. A *function* is a small program built with a specific purpose that, when used, will return a value to the calling procedure or spreadsheet cell(s).

If you are familiar with the built-in functions available in the Excel application, such as SUM(), AVERAGE, and STDEV(), then you already have a basic understanding of how they work. Functions are often (but not always) passed one or more values and they always return at least one value. For example, if I enter the formula **=AVERAGE(A2:A10)** into cell A11 on a worksheet in the Excel application, I know that the average of the nine values given in the range A2:A10 will be calculated and returned to cell A11. Excel recognizes the AVERAGE keyword in the formula as one of its built-in functions. Excel then calls the function procedure AVERAGE() and passes the range of values specified in parentheses—in this case, nine values. The function procedure AVERAGE() then calculates the average of the values passed in as parameters and returns the result to the spreadsheet cell containing the formula. In VBA, you can also call function procedures such as Left(), Mid(), and DateDiff(), as we have seen in previous examples. You can even use the built-in functions of the Excel application. Finally, you can create your own function procedures in VBA.

Creating Your Own VBA Functions

The basic syntax for creating a function procedure in VBA is as follows:

```
Private/Public Function FunctionName(paramter list) as type
                'Function procedure code is listed here
                FunctionName = Return value
End Function
```

This is similar to the syntax for any procedure with the procedure name, parameter list, and an End statement. You can, and should, include a `Private` or `Public` keyword to define the scope of the function. One obvious difference is the `Function` keyword replaces `Sub`. Also, you should define a return type to the function. The return data type is used for the value that the function sends back to the calling procedure. If you do not specify the data type, then the function's return value will be of type variant. The function returns a value by assigning the desired value to the name of the function, although the return value is usually stored in a variable.

 TRICK Use `Exit Sub` or `Exit Function` **if you need to return program execution to the calling procedure before the rest of the code in the procedure executes.**

Functions are called from expressions where you would normally insert a variable or literal. For example, instead of assigning a literal to a variable, a function call can be used to assign the function's return value to the variable.

```
myVar = MyFunction(param1)
```

Here, the variable `myVar` is assigned the return value of the function named `MyFunction` that is passed one parameter in the form of a variable named `param1`.

Now let's consider an example of a function that mimics one of Excel's built-in functions. The following function calculates the result of raising a number to a specified power. I named the function `PowerDB` and set its return value as type double. The `PowerDB` function accepts two numerical values for input, the number to which the exponent will be applied (`number`), and the value of the exponent (`n`). The function has been given public scope.

The code is really very simple. The value of the variable `number` is raised to the power of the value of the variable `n`, and then the result is restored in the variable `number`. The value of the variable `number` is assigned to the function so that it may be returned to the calling procedure.

```
Public Function PowerDB(ByVal number As Double, n As Single) As Double
    number = number ^ n
    PowerDB = number
End Function
```

A procedure that uses the `PowerDB` function can be written as follows:

```
Private Sub testPower()
    Dim number As Double
    Dim n As Single
    Dim result As Double
```

```
    number = Val(InputBox("Enter a number.", "Number"))
    n = Val(InputBox("Enter the value of the exponent.", "Exponent"))
    result = PowerDB(number, n)
    MsgBox (number & "^" & n & " = " & result)
End Sub
```

The only new idea here is the line that calls the PowerDB() function, result = PowerDB(number, n). The variable result is assigned the return value of the function and output in a message box. The variable number was passed to the PowerDB() function by value because if I passed it by reference its value would be changed by the function. Since I want to use the original value of number in the final output, I must pass it by value. The variable n was passed by reference because I did not change its value in the function procedure and VBA is more efficient when passing values by reference.

A public scope for the function PowerDB makes it visible to all other office projects and the Excel application. Thus, this function can now be used like any other function in Excel. Returning to the Excel application and entering the formula **=PowerDB(2,8)** into any worksheet cell will return the value 256 to that cell. The PowerDB function is even listed in Excel's paste function tool, as shown in Figure 3.7 and 3.8.

You now see that I named the function PowerDB in order to avoid a conflict with Excel's POWER() function. You can create your own library of VBA functions to use in your spreadsheet applications. Toward the end of the book, I will show you how to create add-ins with Excel and have your VBA functions, as well as any other programs you create, automatically available every time you run Excel.

FIGURE 3.7

Step 1 of the Paste Function tool in the Excel application

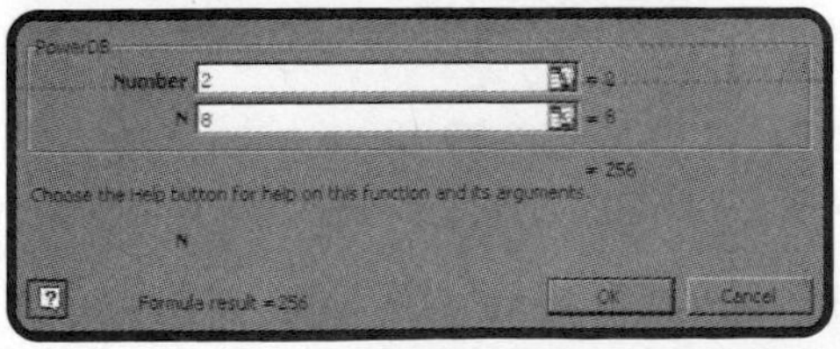

FIGURE 3.8

Step 2 of the Paste Function tool in the Excel application

Using Excel Application Functions in VBA

Now that you know how to write functions in VBA and make them available to your spreadsheets, you are also aware that you can re-create any function already available in the Excel application. Although re-creating Excel's functions would be a good way to improve your VBA programming skills, it's certainly not a practical use of your time. Why re-invent what's already been created for you? It would be nice if you could use Excel's application functions in your VBA code, as they are mostly complimentary, not repetitive, to VBA's set of functions. That way, if you need a specific function performed in your program that is not already included with VBA, you don't have to write it yourself.

Well, there *is* a method to use the Excel application functions, of course, and it is really quite simple.

```
result = Application.WorksheetFunction.Power(number, n)
```

Replacing the call to the PowerDB() function in the testPower() Sub procedure shown earlier with the line of code above will give the exact same result. The difference is that this code uses Excel's POWER() function and not the PowerDB() function. The syntax will be explained in detail in Chapter 5, "Basic Excel Objects," but you can probably guess what's happening from the names used in this line of code. The component Application.WorksheetFunction will return all functions available from the Excel application. From there it is a simple matter of adding on the name of the function and inserting the required parameters into the parentheses. Two more examples illustrate the use of the AVERAGE() and STDEV() functions from the Excel application.

```
myVar = Application.WorksheetFunction.Average(5, 7, 9)
myVar2 = Application.WorksheetFunction.StDev(3, 7, 11)
```

The examples above will return the value 7 to the variable myVar and 4 to the variable myVar2.

Logical Operators in VBA

Logic as applied to a computer program is evaluating an expression as true or false. An expression is typically, but not always, a comparison of two variables such as var1>var2 or var1=var2 (see Table 3.1 for a list of available comparison operators). A programmer reads these expressions as asking the questions

- Is the value of var1 greater than the value of var2?
- Is the value of var1 equal to the value of var2?

then answering the questions with true or false.

Imagine a simple device that takes a single expression as input, evaluates that expression as true or false, spits out the answer, and then moves on to the next expression. The evaluation of the expression is a simple task since there are only two choices and computers are very good at assigning 1's (true) or 0's (false) to things. The difficulty arises from trying to make sense out of the expressions that have been evaluated as true or false. This is where Boolean (after the nineteenth-century mathematician George Boole) algebra comes in to play. Boolean algebra refers to the use of the operators AND, OR, NOT, and a few others to evaluate one or more expressions as true or false. Then, based on the result of the logic, the program selects a direction in which to proceed.

AND, OR, and NOT Operators

VBA uses logical AND to make a decision based on the value of two conditions. The value of each condition can be one of two values, true or false. Consider the following two conditions.

Condition1   Condition2

myVar > 10   myVar < 20

The expression "Condition1 AND Condition2" evaluates as true only if Condition1 and Condition2 are both true. If either or both conditions evaluate to false then the overall result is false. The evaluation of expressions using logical operators is easily displayed in truth tables. Table 3.2 shows the truth table for logical AND.

The logical operator OR returns true from an expression when at least one of the conditions within the expression is true.

TABLE 3.1 COMPARISON OPERATORS IN VBA

Operator	Function
=	Tests for equality
<>	Tests for inequality
<	Less than
>	Greater than
<=	Less than or equal to
>=	Greater than or equal to

TABLE 3.2 TRUTH TABLE FOR THE AND OPERATOR

Condition1	Condition2	Condition1 AND Condition2
True	True	True
True	False	False
False	True	False
False	False	False

The expression "Condition1 OR Condition2" evaluates as true when either Condition1 or Condition2 is true or if both conditions are true. Table 3.3 shows the truth table for logical OR.

The NOT operator simply returns the opposite logic of the condition. So if the condition is false, NOT will return true and vice versa. Table 3.4 shows the truth table.

There are a few other logical operators (Xor, Eqv, and Imp) but they are seldom used or needed, so let's turn our attention to the practical use of Boolean algebra within the code structures If/Then/Else and Select Case.

TABLE 3.3 TRUTH TABLE FOR THE OR OPERATOR

Condition1	Condition2	Condition1 OR Condition2
True	True	True
True	False	True
False	True	True
False	False	False

TABLE 3.4 TRUTH TABLE FOR THE NOT OPERATOR

Condition1	NOT Condition1
True	False
False	True

Conditionals and Branching

It may seem like I've covered a fair amount of VBA programming, but in reality, I've barely even started. Right now you can't really do much with the VBA programs you've created so far, because you haven't yet learned any programming structures. However, that is about to change as I begin to examine a simple yet very useful VBA code structure. The If/Then/Else structure is known as both a conditional and branching structure because it uses conditional statements to change the flow or direction of program execution.

If/Then/Else

There are several ways to implement this code structure. The most basic uses the two required keywords If and Then.

```
If (condition) Then Code statement
```

In the example above, the code statement following Then will execute if condition evaluates as true, otherwise code execution proceeds with the next statement. The entire structure takes just one line of code. It's convenient when you have just one brief code statement that needs to be executed if the condition is true. Multiple statements can be entered on the same line if you separate them with colons (:), but then your code may be hard to read. If you need more than one code statement executed, then for the sake of readability you should use the block form of If/Then/Else .

```
If (condition) Then
    'Block of code statements
End If
```

Again, the condition must be true or the block of code statements will not execute. When using more than one line in the program editor for If/Then you must end the structure with End If.

The following procedure is a simple number-guessing game where the computer comes up with a number between 0 and 10 and asks the user for a guess. Three If/Then structures are used to determine the message output to the user depending on the guess.

```
Private Sub NumberGuess()
    Dim userGuess As Integer
    Dim answer As Integer
```

The variable `answer` is used to store a number generated by the `Rnd` function that returns a random number of type single between 0 and 10. Using an integer data type for the variable `answer` ensures that the calculated value is rounded and stored as an integer.

```
answer = Rnd * 10
userGuess = Val(InputBox("I'm thinking of a number between 0 and 10.
Try and guess.", "Number Guess"))
```

The `If/Then` structures each use one condition that compares the values stored in the `userGuess` and `answer` variables. Only one of these conditions can be true, and the message box in the `If/Then` structure with the true condition executes.

```
If (userGuess > answer) Then
    MsgBox ("Too high!")
    MsgBox ("The answer is " & answer)
End If
If (userGuess < answer) Then
    MsgBox ("Too low!")
    MsgBox ("The answer is " & answer)
End If
If (userGuess = answer) Then MsgBox ("You got it!")
End Sub
```

If you know you want one block of code executed when a condition is true and another block of code executed when the same condition is false, then use the `Else` keyword.

```
If (condition)
    'This block of code executes if the condition is true
Else
    'This block of code executes if the condition is false.
End If
```

The `If/Then` structures in the number guess procedure can also be written as follows, where <> is the "not equal" operator (see Table 3.1):

```
If (userGuess <> answer) Then
    MsgBox ("Wrong! The answer is " & answer)
Else
    MsgBox ("You got it!")
End If
```

This time, instead of using additional `If/Then` statements the keyword `Else` is used to direct the program to another block of code that is executed if the condition (`userGuess <> answer`) evaluates to false.

There is no limit on the number of conditions you can use with an `If/Then` code structure. The condition

```
If (userGuess <> answer) Then
```

can also be written as

```
If (userGuess < answer) Or (userGuess > answer) Then
```

Where the logical operator `Or` is used in the expression for the conditional. Thus, if only one conditional evaluates as true, then the expression returns true and the logic is maintained. You can use more than two conditionals if needed; however, your code will get harder to read as the number of conditionals in one line of code increases. You will see an excessive use of conditionals in the Poker Dice project at the end of this chapter.

There are numerous possibilities for achieving the same logic when using `If/Then/Else` and conditionals. You can also nest the `If/Then/Else` code structure if you want to. The procedure below outputs a short message to the user depending on the current time and day of the week. After some variable declarations, a few familiar date functions are used to determine the current time and day of the week.

```
Private Sub myTime()
    Dim time As Date
    Dim theHour As Integer
    Dim theDayOfTheWeek As Integer
    time = Now
    theHour = Hour(time)
    theDayOfTheWeek = Weekday(time)
```

The first `If/Then/Else` structure is checking whether the time of the day is between 8:00 A.M. and 5:00 P.M., since the variable `theHour` holds an integer value between 0 and 23. If the expression is true then another `If/Then/Else` structure will execute. This `If/Then/Else` structure is "nested" in the first one and is checking the value for the day of the week. If the day of the week is Monday through Friday, then a message box is used to display the string "You should be at work." (Remember that it had to be between 8:00 A.M. and 5:00 P.M to get to this point.) Otherwise, the nested `If/Then/Else` outputs the message "I love weekends." If the time of day is not between 8:00 A.M. and 5:00 P.M, then the message "You should not be at work!" is displayed in a message box.

```
    If (theHour > 8) And (theHour < 17) Then
        If (theDayOfTheWeek > 0) And (theDayOfTheWeek < 6) Then
            MsgBox ("You should be at work!")
        Else
            MsgBox ("I love weekends")
        End If
    Else
        MsgBox ("You should not be at work!")
    End If
End Sub
```

There is no limit to the number of nested If/Then statements you can use; however, after three or four levels, keeping track of the logic can be difficult and your program may be difficult to read and debug.

 It is a good idea to indent your code with each level of logic. You will find your programs much easier to read and debug if indented properly.

Another option regarding If/Then/Else structures is the ElseIf clause. The ElseIf clause is used like the Else clause with a conditional expression. You must also include Then when using ElseIf. The following example uses a series of ElseIf clauses to display the day of the week in a message box.

```
    If (theDayOfTheWeek = 0) Then
        MsgBox ("It's Sunday!")
    ElseIf (theDayOfTheWeek = 1) Then
        MsgBox ("It's Monday!")
    ElseIf (theDayOfTheWeek = 2) Then
        MsgBox ("It's Tuesday!")
    ElseIf (theDayOfTheWeek = 3) Then
        MsgBox ("It's Wednesday!")
    ElseIf (theDayOfTheWeek = 4) Then
        MsgBox ("It's Thursday!")
    ElseIf (theDayOfTheWeek = 5) Then
        MsgBox ("It's Friday!")
    Else
        MsgBox ("It's Saturday!")
    End If
```

There is no limit to the number of ElseIf clauses that can be used. However, ElseIf cannot be used after an Else clause. You can also nest more If/Then/Else structures inside an ElseIf clause.

Select Case

There are innumerable ways to accomplish the same task with If/Then/Else and ElseIf code structures. But keep in mind that using a large number of If/Then/Else and ElseIf statements can make it difficult to follow the logic of your program. You should consider using the Select/Case code structure in situations where you find yourself using a large number of ElseIf statements. The Select/Case code structure is used when you need to test the value of a variable multiple times and, based on the outcome of those tests, execute a single block of code. The Select/Case syntax is fairly simple and easy to understand.

```
Select Case expression
    Case condition1
        'This block of code executes if condition1 is true.
    Case condition2
        'This block of code executes if condition2 is true.
    …'There is no limit on the number of cases you can use
    Case Else
        'This block of code executes if none of the other conditions were true.
End Select
```

A Select/Case structure must begin with Select Case and end with End Select. The expression immediately following Select Case is typically a variable of numerical or string data type. Next, a list of one or more code blocks is entered just beneath the keyword Case and a condition. The condition is a comparison to the expression in the opening line of the structure. VBA proceeds down the list until it finds a condition that evaluates as true, then executes the block of code within that case element. Any additional case elements following one that evaluates as true are ignored, even if their conditions are also true. Thus, order of the case elements is important. The last case element should use Case Else. This ensures that at least one block of code executes if all other conditions are false.

The following example uses a Select/Case structure in a VBA function designed to work with an Excel spreadsheet. The input value should be numerical and expressed as a percentage. This percentage represents a student's score and is passed into the function and stored in the variable studentScore. The variable studentScore is used as the test expression for the Select/Case structure.

```
Public Function AssignGrade(studentScore As Single) As String
    Select Case studentScore
        Case 90 To 100
            AssignGrade = "A"
        Case Is >= 80
            AssignGrade = "B"
        Case 70 To 80
            AssignGrade = "C"
        Case Is >= 60
            AssignGrade = "D"
        Case Else
            AssignGrade = "F"
    End Select
End Function
```

There are two forms for writing the conditionals in the case elements; both are shown in this example. The first case element uses Case 90 To 100. This condition is specified as a range of values with the lower value inserted first followed by the To keyword and then the upper value of the range. This condition evaluates as true if the value stored in the variable studentScore is greater or equal to 90 and less than or equal to 100.

If the value of studentScore is less than 90, VBA proceeds to the next case element, which is Case Is >= 80. This is the other form for a condition using the Is keyword to specify a range with a comparison operator >= (greater than or equal to). If the value of studentScore is greater than or equal to 80 this condition is true and the block of code within this element executes. Again, VBA will proceed down the list until it finds a true condition and then evaluate that case element's code block. If Case Is >= 60 and the AssignGrade() function is placed at the top of the Select/Case structure, then all students with a percentage higher than 60 would be assigned a grade of "D," even they have a score of 100%.

Constructing the Poker Dice Program

Poker Dice is a variation on five-card draw using dice instead of cards. Since there are six possible values per die instead of 13 and no suits, you will get much better hands with this game. This program illustrates the use of conditionals with If/Then/Else and ElseIf code structures. The code for Poker Dice will be contained in two Click() event procedures of Command Button controls and one sub procedure. Poker Dice will also introduce you to a couple of new ActiveX controls, the

Image control and the Check Box control. The project along with the images of the dice can be found on the accompanying CD.

Project Statement

I want to create a program that simulates five-card draw using images of dice instead of cards. The program should use an Excel spreadsheet as the interface and display five dice when started. The user should be given one draw before the final result of the hand is displayed. Thus, the program should be able to evaluate the user's hand.

Project Tools

The images of the dice will be displayed on the spreadsheet in Image controls. Command Button controls will be used to start the game and take a draw, and Check Box controls will be used to hold a die so it is not replaced on a draw. I will use multiple If/Then/Else code structures to determine the value of a hand. A spreadsheet cell or a Label control can be used to display the value of the hand, and the worksheet containing the game can be preformatted for the desired appearance. The code will be placed in `Click()` Event procedures of the Command Button controls as well as any Sub procedures that may be deemed necessary.

The Image Control

The Image control is used to hold images of type bitmap (.bmp extension). This is somewhat of a nuisance if your images are not in the bitmap format, but you can use just about any image-editing software to convert them. The Image control can be added to a worksheet from the control toolbox like any other ActiveX control. Figure 3.9 shows the icon for the Image control.

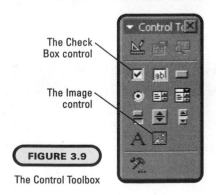

FIGURE 3.9

The Control Toolbox

Image files can be loaded into the Image control at design time or run time via the `Picture` property. Table 3.5 summarizes some of the more important properties of the Image control.

The image control also has several event procedures, most notably the `Click()`, `BeforeDragOver()`, and `BeforeDropOrPaste()` event procedures. Although we will not be using any of the Image control event procedures in the Poker Dice program, you should at least know how to use the `Click()` event procedure by now.

The Check Box Control

The Check Box control is a familiar and relatively easy control to use. Figure 3.9 shows the icon for the Check Box control. Check Box controls are designed to give the user multiple selections from a group.

 TRICK **Use the OptionButton control if you wish to limit the user to only one choice.**

Table 3.6 lists the most important properties of the Check Box control.

Most of the properties of the Check Box control are related to its appearance, and you will have to use more than what is listed in Table 3.6. However, these are the properties most commonly manipulated at run time. The `Name` property is used to reference the Check Box control and the `Value` property is used to test whether or not the user has it selected. The Check Box control has several event procedures associated with it, but you will seldom use anything other than its `Click()` event procedure.

TABLE 3.5 SELECTED PROPERTIES OF THE IMAGE CONTROL

Property	Function
Name	Used for referencing the control in your program
AutoSize	If true, the control will automatically resize itself to fit the image size.
BackStyle	Use the transparent setting if you don't want the user to know it's there until an image is loaded.
Picture	The path to the image file to be displayed
PictureAlignment	Aligns the image to the specified location
PictureSizeMode	Clip, Stretch, or Zoom. Not important if AutoSize is true. May distort the image.

TABLE 3.6 SELECTED PROPERTIES OF THE CHECK BOX CONTROL

Property	Function
Name	Used for referencing the control in your program
Caption	Displays text that describes a choice for the user
Value	True if checked

Project Algorithm

Follow these instructions to create the Poker Dice program:

1. Format the worksheet for the desired appearance.

2. Add five image controls in a neat row. Set their properties as listed in Table 3.7.

3. Add five Check Box controls, placing one each centered above an Image control. Set the properties of the Check Box controls as listed in Table 3.8.

4. Add two Command Button controls to the worksheet and center under the dice. Set their Name properties to cmdRollDice and cmdClear, and their Caption properties to Roll Dice and New Game.

5. Format the range B11:D12 to merge the cells and center the text. Give the merged region a thick black border. This area will be used to hold the result output by the program.

TABLE 3.7 PROPERTY SETTINGS OF IMAGE CONTROLS IN THE POKER DICE PROGRAM

Property	Value
Width, Height	75
Name	imgDice1, imgDice2, etc.
BackStyle	transparent
AutoSize	True
BorderStyle	None
SpecialEffect	Flat

TABLE 3.8 PROPERTY SETTINGS OF CHECK BOX CONTROLS IN THE POKER DICE PROGRAM

Property	Value
Name	ckBox1, ckBox2, etc.
BackStyle	Transparent
Caption	Empty
SpecialEffect	Sunken
Value	False

6. Use the `Click()` event procedure of `cmdRollDice` to load the images into the Image controls where the associated Check Box control is left unchecked. The image to be displayed should be selected randomly.

7. Display the result of the hand in the worksheet with each roll of the dice. Use a sub procedure and `If/Then/Else` code structures to determine the result of the hand. Disable `cmdRollDice` after two selections and enable `cmdClear`.

8. Use the `Click()` event procedure of `cmdClear` to clear the contents of the Image controls, Check Box controls, and worksheet cell containing the result. Enable the Command Button `cmdRollDice` and disable the Command Button `cmdClear`.

Adding the Code

As stated in the algorithm, the program used two click event procedures and one sub procedure. All code will be added to the component module of the Poker Dice worksheet. The general declarations section of this module contains `Option Explicit`, so variable declaration is required.

```
Option Explicit
```

The `Click()` event procedure to the Command Button control named `cmdClear` is fairly straightforward. First the value property of all Check Box controls is set to false to remove any checks selected by the user.

```
Private Sub cmdClear_Click()
    ckBox1.Value = False
    ckBox2.Value = False
```

```
ckBox3.Value = False
ckbox4.Value = False
ckBox5.Value = False
```

The value property of the merged cells on the worksheet is set to an empty string. Note that when referring to cells that have been merged, use the row and column indices of the upper left cell in the merged group.

```
Cells(11, "B").Value = ""
```

Set the enabled property of an ActiveX control to true in order to activate the control for use. Set the enabled property of an ActiveX control to false to make it unavailable to the user (Note: the caption will be grayed out).

```
cmdRollDice.Enabled = True
cmdClear.Enabled = False
```

Remove the images from the Image controls by passing an empty string to VBA's LoadPicture() function.

```
imgDice1.Picture = LoadPicture("")
imgDice2.Picture = LoadPicture("")
imgDice3.Picture = LoadPicture("")
imgDice4.Picture = LoadPicture("")
imgDice5.Picture = LoadPicture("")
End Sub
```

The Click() event procedure of the Command Button control named cmdRollDice is used to load images of dice into Image controls. The image for each control is selected randomly from one of six choices.

```
Private Sub cmdRollDice_Click()
```

A static integer variable is used to keep track of how many times the user has clicked on this control. The user is only allowed two clicks per game. Additional string variables are used to hold the name of the file and path to that file.

```
Static I As Integer
Dim imageFile As String
Dim imagePath As String
```

The file path is stored in a variable so that if it needs to be changed later, there is only one line of code to edit. (The syntax used to get the file path string will make more sense after you have read Chapter 5.) When the workbook containing Poker Dice is loaded, Excel keeps track of the file path to the loaded workbook (pokerDice.xls). The line of code below accesses this information using the Path property of the Workbook object. This will actually prevent a "file not found" error if the workbook is copied to a new location on the same, or another, computer. An additional backslash is concatenated onto the string for later use.

```
imagePath = Workbooks("pokerDice.xls").Path & "\"
```

The variable I is incremented by one and the Command Button name cmdClear is disabled. Next the Randomize statement is used to initialize VBA's random number generator. Without any arguments passed to it, Randomize will use the system clock to set a seed value for random number generation. Without the Randomize statement, the same seed value will be used for random number generation. As a result, the same random number sequence will be reproduced each time the program is run.

```
I = I + 1
cmdClear.Enabled = False
Randomize
```

An If/Then/Else code structure is used to check the Value property of the Check-Box controls. If the value is false, then a randomly-chosen image is loaded into the Image control. The random number is converted to an integer with the Int() function. As written, the value of the random number can only fall between 1 and 6. I am storing the random number in a spreadsheet cell because I will need to access this value in another procedure later in the program in order to check the result of the hand. Alternatively, I could use a set of module-level variables to hold the result from the random number generation. The entire path to the desired image file is stored in the string variable imageFile. I used filenames "1.bmp," "2.bmp," etc., for my image files in order to make the string concatenation easy. Finally, the image is loaded into the Image control by passing the file path to the LoadPicture() function. This If/Then/Else block is repeated for each of the five Image controls.

```
If ckBox1.Value = False Then
    Cells(1, "A").Value = Int(Rnd * 6) + 1
    imageFile = imagePath & Trim(Str(Cells(1, "A").Value)) & ".bmp"
    imgDice1.Picture = LoadPicture(imageFile)
End If
If ckBox2.Value = False Then
    Cells(1, "B").Value = Int(Rnd * 6) + 1
    imageFile = imagePath & Trim(Str(Cells(1, "B").Value)) & ".bmp"
    imgDice2.Picture = LoadPicture(imageFile)
End If
```

```
If ckBox3.Value = False Then
    Cells(1, "C").Value = Int(Rnd * 6) + 1
    imageFile = imagePath & Trim(Str(Cells(1, "C").Value)) & ".bmp"
    imgDice3.Picture = LoadPicture(imageFile)
End If
If ckbox4.Value = False Then
    Cells(1, "D").Value = Int(Rnd * 6) + 1
    imageFile = imagePath & Trim(Str(Cells(1, "D").Value)) & ".bmp"
    imgDice4.Picture = LoadPicture(imageFile)
End If
If ckBox5.Value = False Then
    Cells(1, "E").Value = Int(Rnd * 6) + 1
    imageFile = imagePath & Trim(Str(Cells(1, "E").Value)) & ".bmp"
    imgDice5.Picture = LoadPicture(imageFile)
End If
```

Another If/Then/Else structure is used to test the value of the variable I. The Command Button controls named cmdRollDice and cmdClear are disabled and enabled, respectively, after the user has rolled twice. The variable I is reinitialized to zero for the next game.

```
If I = 2 Then
    cmdRollDice.Enabled = False
    cmdClear.Enabled = True
    I = 0
End If
```

The sub procedure DisplayResult() is called without passing parameters in order to determine the result of the user's hand.

```
    DisplayResult
End Sub
```

The sub procedure DisplayResult() determines the result of the user's hand by using several If/Then/Else code structures, and numerous conditional expressions, to recognize the various combinations the dice can exhibit. The DisplayResult() procedure is somewhat long but the logic is easy to follow, so I did not break it up into more than one sub procedure.

```
Private Sub DisplayResult()
```

Several integer variables will keep track of possible dice combinations and a string variable will hold the result of the hand.

```
Dim numOnes As Integer
Dim numTwos As Integer
Dim numThrees As Integer
Dim numFours As Integer
Dim numFives As Integer
Dim numSixes As Integer
Dim result As String
```

The first set of If/Then code structures checks the value of the dice stored in the first row of the spreadsheet for each possible value. A variable is then incremented if its associated value is found in a spreadsheet cell. These If/Then code structures effectively determine how many dice show the value 1, 2, 3, 4, 5, or 6.

```
If Cells(1, "A").Value = 1 Then numOnes = numOnes + 1
If Cells(1, "B").Value = 1 Then numOnes = numOnes + 1
If Cells(1, "C").Value = 1 Then numOnes = numOnes + 1
If Cells(1, "D").Value = 1 Then numOnes = numOnes + 1
If Cells(1, "E").Value = 1 Then numOnes = numOnes + 1

If Cells(1, "A").Value = 2 Then numTwos = numTwos + 1
If Cells(1, "B").Value = 2 Then numTwos = numTwos + 1
If Cells(1, "C").Value = 2 Then numTwos = numTwos + 1
If Cells(1, "D").Value = 2 Then numTwos = numTwos + 1
If Cells(1, "E").Value = 2 Then numTwos = numTwos + 1

If Cells(1, "A").Value = 3 Then numThrees = numThrees + 1
If Cells(1, "B").Value = 3 Then numThrees = numThrees + 1
If Cells(1, "C").Value = 3 Then numThrees = numThrees + 1
If Cells(1, "D").Value = 3 Then numThrees = numThrees + 1
If Cells(1, "E").Value = 3 Then numThrees = numThrees + 1

If Cells(1, "A").Value = 4 Then numFours = numFours + 1
If Cells(1, "B").Value = 4 Then numFours = numFours + 1
If Cells(1, "C").Value = 4 Then numFours = numFours + 1
If Cells(1, "D").Value = 4 Then numFours = numFours + 1
If Cells(1, "E").Value = 4 Then numFours = numFours + 1

If Cells(1, "A").Value = 5 Then numFives = numFives + 1
If Cells(1, "B").Value = 5 Then numFives = numFives + 1
If Cells(1, "C").Value = 5 Then numFives = numFives + 1
If Cells(1, "D").Value = 5 Then numFives = numFives + 1
If Cells(1, "E").Value = 5 Then numFives = numFives + 1
```

```
If Cells(1, "A").Value = 6 Then numSixes = numSixes + 1
If Cells(1, "B").Value = 6 Then numSixes = numSixes + 1
If Cells(1, "C").Value = 6 Then numSixes = numSixes + 1
If Cells(1, "D").Value = 6 Then numSixes = numSixes + 1
If Cells(1, "E").Value = 6 Then numSixes = numSixes + 1
```

The potential hands we will test for first are when the user has either a 5 or 6 high straight or nothing. The opening If/Then/Else code structure uses six conditional expressions. I said earlier in the chapter there would be an excessive use of conditionals—at this point, it can't be helped much, but I have used a line continuation character (_) in an effort to make the code easier to read.

 TRICK The line continuation character (_) tells VBA that I really want just one line of code but I need to type it on more than one line in the editor. Make sure there is a single space between the last character and the underscore before proceeding to the next line.

In the next chapter, I will introduce more code structures that will help clean up this code. The six conditionals are all linked with logical AND. This means that all conditionals must be true if the block of code within the first If/Then statements is to be executed. If the number of occurrences of each die value is equal to or less than one, a nested If/Then/Else code structure is then used to determine if the hand is a "6 High Straight," a "6 High," or a "5 High Straight."

```
If (numOnes <= 1) And (numTwos <= 1) And (numThrees <= 1) And _
    (numFours <= 1) And (numFives <= 1) And (numSixes <= 1) Then
    If (numSixes = 1) And (numOnes = 0) Then
        result = "6 High Straight"
    ElseIf (numSixes = 1) And (numOnes = 1) Then
        result = "6 High"
    Else
        result = "5 High Straight"
    End If
End If
```

Next we test for one pair of dice with the same value. Another If/Then/Else code structure and six condition expressions for each If/Then or ElseIf/Then statement will determine whether the user has just a single pair of dice with the same value.

```
If (numOnes = 2) And (numTwos <= 1) And (numThrees <= 1) And _
    (numFours <= 1) And (numFives <= 1) And (numSixes <= 1) Then
    result = "Pair of Ones"
```

```
ElseIf (numOnes <= 1) And (numTwos = 2) And (numThrees <= 1) And _
       (numFours <= 1) And (numFives <= 1) And (numSixes <= 1) Then
    result = "Pair of Twos"
ElseIf (numOnes <= 1) And (numTwos <= 1) And (numThrees = 2) And _
       (numFours <= 1) And (numFives <= 1) And (numSixes <= 1) Then
    result = "Pair of Threes"
ElseIf (numOnes <= 1) And (numTwos <= 1) And (numThrees <= 1) And _
       (numFours = 2) And (numFives <= 1) And (numSixes <= 1) Then
    result = "Pair of Fours"
ElseIf (numOnes <= 1) And (numTwos <= 1) And (numThrees <= 1) And _
       (numFours <= 1) And (numFives = 2) And (numSixes <= 1) Then
    result = "Pair of Fives"
ElseIf (numOnes <= 1) And (numTwos <= 1) And (numThrees <= 1) And _
       (numFours <= 1) And (numFives <= 1) And (numSixes = 2) Then
    result = "Pair of Sixs"
End If
```

To test for two pair of dice with the same value, all possible scenarios are tested for with conditional expressions. This time logical OR is used with logical AND to find the combination of dice that make up "two pair." Pay close attention to the use of parentheses in the conditional expression. I am using parentheses to group each possible combination of dice that returns "two pair." For example, (numOnes = 2 And numTwos = 2) is one possible combination. Each of these combinations are linked with logical OR because if only one of them is true, then the result is "two pair."

```
If (numOnes = 2 And numTwos = 2) Or _
   (numOnes = 2 And numThrees = 2) Or _
   (numOnes = 2 And numFours = 2) Or _
   (numOnes = 2 And numFives = 2) Or _
   (numOnes = 2 And numSixes = 2) Or _
   (numTwos = 2 And numThrees = 2) Or _
   (numTwos = 2 And numFours = 2) Or _
   (numTwos = 2 And numFives = 2) Or _
   (numTwos = 2 And numSixes = 2) Or _
   (numThrees = 2 And numFours = 2) Or _
   (numThrees = 2 And numFives = 2) Or _
   (numThrees = 2 And numSixes = 2) Or _
   (numFours = 2 And numFives = 2) Or _
   (numFours = 2 And numSixes = 2) Or _
   (numFives = 2 And numSixes = 2) Then
       result = "Two Pair"
End If
```

The next `If/Then/Else` code structure tests for three of a kind, or three dice with the same value. There is nothing new here, so take a close look and try to follow the logic.

```
    If (numOnes = 3 And numTwos < 2 And numThrees < 2 And numFours < 2
And numFives < 2 And numSixes < 2) Then
        result = "Three Ones"
    ElseIf (numOnes < 2 And numTwos = 3 And numThrees < 2 And numFours <
2 And numFives < 2 And numSixes < 2) Then
        result = "Three Twos"
    ElseIf (numOnes < 2 And numTwos < 2 And numThrees = 3 And numFours <
2 And numFives < 2 And numSixes < 2) Then
        result = "Three Threes"
    ElseIf (numOnes < 2 And numTwos < 2 And numThrees < 2 And numFours =
3 And numFives < 2 And numSixes < 2) Then
        result = "Three Fours"
    ElseIf (numOnes < 2 And numTwos < 2 And numThrees < 2 And numFours <
2 And numFives = 3 And numSixes < 2) Then
        result = "Three Fives"
    ElseIf (numOnes < 2 And numTwos < 2 And numThrees < 2 And numFours <
2 And numFives < 2 And numSixes = 3) Then
        result = "Three Sixs"
    End If
```

Testing for four and five values that are the same is easy because there is only one variable to test with each conditional expression.

```
    If numOnes = 4 Then result = "Four Ones"
    If numTwos = 4 Then result = "Four Twos"
    If numThrees = 4 Then result = "Four Threes"
    If numFours = 4 Then result = "Four Fours"
    If numFives = 4 Then result = "Four Fives"
    If numSixes = 4 Then result = "Four Sixs"
    If numOnes = 5 Then result = "Five Ones"
    If numTwos = 5 Then result = "Five Twos"
    If numThrees = 5 Then result = "Five Threes"
    If numFours = 5 Then result = "Five Fours"
    If numFives = 5 Then result = "Five Fives"
    If numSixes = 5 Then result = "Five Sixs"
```

Finally, we test for a full house, where three dice have the same value and the other two dice have the same value but are different from the other set of three.

This is just like the test for two pair, except we have more combinations to test.

```
If (numOnes = 3 And numTwos = 2) Or (numOnes = 3 And numThrees = 2) Or _
    (numOnes = 3 And numFours = 2) Or (numOnes = 3 And numFives = 2) Or _
    (numOnes = 3 And numSixes = 2) Or (numTwos = 3 And numOnes = 2) Or _
    (numTwos = 3 And numThrees = 2) Or (numTwos = 3 And numFours = 2) Or _
    (numTwos = 3 And numFives = 2) Or (numTwos = 3 And numSixes = 2) Or _
    (numThrees = 3 And numOnes = 2) Or (numThrees = 3 And numTwos = 2) Or _
    (numThrees = 3 And numFours = 2) Or (numThrees = 3 And numFives = 2) Or _
    (numThrees = 3 And numSixes = 2) Or (numFours = 3 And numOnes = 2) Or _
    (numFours = 3 And numTwos = 2) Or (numFours = 3 And numThrees = 2) Or _
    (numFours = 3 And numFives = 2) Or (numFours = 3 And numSixes = 2) Or _
    (numFives = 3 And numOnes = 2) Or (numFives = 3 And numTwos = 2) Or _
    (numFives = 3 And numThrees = 2) Or (numFives = 3 And numFours = 2) Or _
    (numFives = 3 And numSixes = 2) Or (numSixes = 3 And numOnes = 2) Or _
    (numSixes = 3 And numTwos = 2) Or (numSixes = 3 And numThrees = 2) Or _
    (numSixes = 3 And numFours = 2) Or (numSixes = 3 And numFives = 2) Then
    result = "Full House"
End If
```

Finally, the result is displayed in the spreadsheet.

```
    Cells(11, "B").Value = result
End Sub
```

That concludes Poker Dice. It really is a pretty simple program. The difficulty is in following the logic of the large number of conditions contained in the expressions with the If/Then/Else code structures. The DisplayResult() Sub procedure is a longer procedure than I normally write because of the number of conditionals involved. As you may have already guessed, the DisplayResult() Sub procedure can be simplified significantly with the use of different programming structures and techniques. You will look at a couple of these structures in the next chapter.

Chapter Summary

In this chapter you covered a considerable amount of material on some of the tools required to help you build a strong programming foundation. You started by taking an in-depth look at procedures in VBA—specifically, event, sub, and function procedures. You learned how to use and build these procedures while considering the procedures scope, available parameters, and return values (function procedures). You even learned how to build new function procedures to use within formulas created in the Excel application. Finally, you saw two new code structures, If/Then/Else and Select/Case, and you learned how to use Boolean logic within conditional expressions so a program could branch off in different directions in terms of code execution. In essence, you learned how to write a program that can make simple decisions.

CHALLENGES

1. Draw a simple image of a smiley face using MS Paint then load the image into an Image control placed on a worksheet in Excel. Using the MouseDown() Event procedure of the Image control, write a program that displays a message to the user every time the user clicks on the image. The message should tell the user if he/she clicks on the eyes, nose, mouth, or face of the image and which button they used. The message can be displayed with a message box, or in a Label control, or on the spreadsheet.

2. Write a function procedure in VBA that returns the square root of a number. The function should be made available to the Excel application.

3. Write a sub procedure in VBA that either adds, subtracts, multiplies, or divides two numbers. The procedure should be called by another sub procedure that collects the two numbers from the user and asks the user which mathematical operation is desired. The calling procedure should also output the result, displaying the original values and the answer.

4. Add a few Check Box controls or Option Button controls to a worksheet, then use a Select/Case code structure in a sub procedure that outputs a message to the user telling them which check box has been selected.

CHAPTER 4

Loops and Arrays

In Chapter 3, "Procedures and Conditions," you started building your programming foundation with the branching structures If/Then/Else and Select/Case. In this chapter you will significantly expand on that foundation with looping code structures and arrays. Loops and arrays are fundamental to all programming languages; they expand the capabilities of a program significantly and make them easier to write. You'll begin this chapter by looking at the different looping structures available in VBA before moving on to arrays.

Specifically, this chapter will cover:

- Do **loops**
- For **loops**
- **Input validation**
- **Arrays**
- **Multi-dimensional arrays**
- **Dynamic arrays**
- **Recording macros**
- **The Forms toolbar controls**
- **Chapter project: Math Game**

Project: The Math Game

The Math Game is a natural choice for programming with a spreadsheet application like Excel. The Math Game requires only basic math skills, so it may be more fun for kids to play, but it's a lot of fun for adults to write. To play the Math Game, you answer as many questions as you can in the allotted time. After you finish, the questions are reviewed and scored. The Math Game spreadsheet is shown in Figure 4.1.

Looping with VBA

Program looping is the repetition of a specific block of code a specified number of times. The number of times the block of code is repeated may be well defined or based on a conditional statement. All computer languages have looping structures because these structures are excellent at solving problems that would otherwise require repetitive code. Imagine a program that had to search for a specific name in a column of data with one hundred entries. A program with one hundred If/Then statements testing the value property of each cell for the required name will solve the problem. The program would be technically easy to create, but it would be a pain to type in all that repetitive code and it would look awful. Fortunately, we have looping code structures to help us.

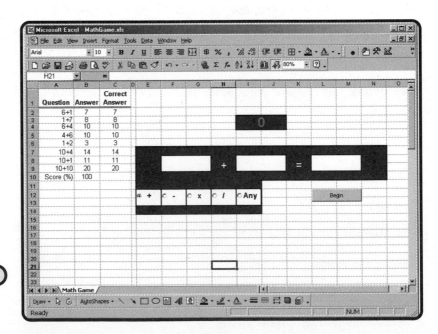

FIGURE 4.1

The Math Game project

HINT Each execution of the block of code inside a looping structure represents one iteration of the loop.

Do Loops

Do loops will execute a given block of code repetitively based on the value of a conditional expression. The three required keywords are Do, Loop, and While or Until. The keywords are used to build four basic representations of the Do-Loop. The first two representations use the keyword Until with a conditional statement that determines if, and how many times the code inside the loop executes. With the conditional statement at the end of the loop, the code inside the loop executes at least one time.

```
Do
   'Block of code executes at least once and continues to loop if condition
is false.
Loop Until (condition)
```

When the conditional statement is at the beginning of the loop, the code inside the loop will not be executed unless the logic of the conditional statement allows it. When using Until, the code inside the loop will execute if the conditional statement is false.

```
Do Until (condition)
   'Block of code executes only if condition is false.
Loop
```

The next two representations of the Do-Loop use the keyword While with a conditional statement that determines if, and how many times, the code inside the loop executes. When While is used, the code inside the loop executes when the conditional statement is true.

```
Do
   'Block of code executes at least once and continues to loop if condition
is true.
Loop While (condition)
```

When deciding on which representation of the Do-Loop to use, ask yourself whether you need the code inside the loop to execute at least once. If you do, then put the conditional at the end. The choice of While or Until depends on the logic of the conditional expression.

```
Do While (condition)
    'Block of code executes only if condition is true.
Loop
```

Beware of creating loops that never stop repeating, otherwise known as *infinite loops*. When constructing your Do-Loop, create it with a conditional expression that will change its logical value (true to false and vice-versa) at some point during execution of the code within the loop. It is easier to create an infinite loop than you might think. The following example is supposed to find the first occurrence of the string Flintstone in the first column of a worksheet, output a message to the screen, and then quit:

```
Dim I As Integer
I = 1
Do
        If (Cells(I, "A").Value = "Flintstone") Then
                MsgBox ("Yabba Dabba Do! I found a Flintstone in row " &
Str(I))
        End If
          I = I + 1
Loop Until (Cells(I, "A").Value = "Flintstone")
```

The loop will always fail for two reasons. First, if the string Flintstone does not appear in the first column of the worksheet, then the loop is infinite because the conditional statement at the end of the loop, (Cells(I, "A").Value = "Flintstone"), will never be true. Second, even if the string Flintstone does appear in the first column of the worksheet, the output from the MsgBox() function will not appear because the conditional statement at the end of the loop will be true before the conditional statement associated with the If/Then structure.

 If you find your program stuck in an infinite loop, use Ctrl+Alt+Break to suspend program execution.

In most cases you can construct a loop with logical expressions that will work with both While or Until, so using one or the other is simply a matter of personal preference. The following Do-Loops have the exact same function, but the first loop uses While and the second uses Until:

```
Dim I As Integer
I = 1
Do
        If (Cells(I, "A").Value = "Flintstone") Then
                MsgBox ("Yabba Dabba Do! I found a Flintstone in row " &
```

```
Str(I))
    End If
    I = I + 1
Loop While (Cells(I, "A").Value <> "")
```

If I change the conditional operator to = (is equal to), then I change the logic of the conditional statement, so I must use the keyword Until to get the same result from the loop.

```
Dim I As Integer
I = 1
Do
    If (Cells(I, "A").Value = "Flintstone") Then
        MsgBox ("Yabba Dabba Do! I found a Flintstone in row " &
Str(I))
    End If
    I = I + 1
Loop Until (Cells(I, "A").Value = "")
```

Both of these loops search the first column in a worksheet for the string Flint-stone. Once the desired string is found, a message box outputs a statement with the index of the worksheet row in which the string was found. In both examples, the Do-Loop continues until an empty cell is found. Both loops will execute at least once, because the conditional expression is at the end of the loop. Neither loop will be infinite because Excel will always add empty rows to the end of a spreadsheet as more rows of data are added.

For Loops

When you know the number of iterations required from a loop, the For/Next loop is the best choice of structures. The syntax is very simple.

```
For variable = start To end Step value
                'Block of code
Next variable
```

The required keywords are For, To, and Next. A counting variable is also required to keep track of the number of iterations through the loop. Starting and ending values for the counting variable are also required. The keyword Step is optional, but if it's used, the value that follows it is used to denote the step size of the counting variable with each iteration through the loop. The value of the step can be any positive or negative integer; the default value is +1 when Step is omitted. Table 4.1 lists a few examples of For/Next loops.

TABLE 4.1 EXAMPLES OF FOR/NEXT LOOPS IN VBA

Loop Example	Output from Message Box
For I = 0 To 10 MsgBox (I) Next I	11 iterations: 0, 1, 2, 3, 4, 5, 6, 7, 8, 9, and 10
For I = 0 To 10 Step 2 MsgBox (I) Next I	6 iterations: 0, 2, 4, 6, 8, and 10
For I = 0 To 10 Step 3 MsgBox (I) Next I	4 iterations: 0, 3, 6, and 9
For I = 10 To 0 Step –5 MsgBox (I) Next I	3 iterations: 10, 5, and 0

The variable I in Table 4.1 should be declared as an integer prior to use, and the ending value for the loop is usually another variable rather than a constant. In most cases, you will want to use the default step size of +1, so the keyword Step is omitted.

TRICK Use the statement Exit Do **or** Exit For **to force code execution to leave a looping structure and proceed with the first line of code after the loop. Normally,** Exit Do **or** Exit For **will be within a branching structure (**If/Then **or** Select/Case**) inside of the loop.**

The following example of a VBA function mimics the FACT function in the Excel application by calculating the factorial of an integer:

```
Public Function Factorial(myValue As Integer) As Long
    Dim I As Integer
    Dim factorialValue As Long
    '
    factorialValue = 1
    For I = 2 To myValue
        factorialValue = factorialValue * I
    Next I
    Factorial = factorialValue
End Function
```

IN THE REAL WORLD

The factorial function can also be written as a recursive procedure. A *recursive* procedure is one that calls itself.

```
Public Function Factorial(N As Integer) As Integer
    If N <= 1 Then
        Factorial = 1
    Else
        Factorial = Factorial(N - 1) * N
    End If
End Function
```

Although the factorial example above is a nice illustration of recursion, it is not a practical example. Recursive procedures can be very demanding on system resources and they must contain logic that will eventually stop the procedure from calling itself.

Recursive procedures are most often and most effectively applied to tree-like data structures such as the file system on a computer.

The For/Next loop is a natural choice, because you need the looping variable to increment by one with each iteration until it reaches the value of the integer passed into the function. Each iteration through the For/Next loop multiplies the next factor by the previous result, effectively producing the factorial of the value stored in the variable myValue. For example, if myValue is 5 then the variable factorialValue will be calculated as 1×2×3×4×5.

Finally, consider the most obvious example of looping in spreadsheet applications, which is looping through a range of cells in a worksheet. For now, I will illustrate looping through a worksheet range using a For/Next loop.

```
For I = 1 To 10
    For J = 4 To 7
        Cells(I, Chr(J + 64)).Value = I * J
    Next J
Next I
```

The looping structures I have discussed so far are not the best choice for looping through a range of cells, even though doing so is a simple enough task. A better looping structure for handling this task is the For/Each **loop discussed in Chapter 5, "Basic Excel Objects."**

The example just given uses two nested For/Next loops to loop through the worksheet range D1:G10. The nested (inside) loop will execute to completion (four iterations) with each iteration of the outer loop. In the example just given, the value of J iterates from 4 through 7 for each value of I. The code loops through the range by rows, as the variable used for the row index (I) is also the counting variable for the outer loop. The Chr() function is used to convert a numerical input representing an ASCII (American Standard Code for Information Interchange) value to its corresponding keyboard character. In this case the values 68 through 71 will be converted to the uppercase letters D through G. The Chr() function in VBA works with values 0–255. Table 4.2 lists a few of the more common characters in the set.

Input Validation

Trusting that a user will input the type of data required by your program is a leap of faith. You can, and should, provide hints to the user indicating the type and format your program requires. However, you should also include code in your program to check what the user enters against a required format. The process of checking user input for correctness is known as *validation*. Validation should be

TABLE 4.2 SELECTED ASCII CONVERSION CHARACTERS

ASCII Value	Keyboard Character
8	backspace
9	tab
10	line feed
13	carriage return
32	space
48-57	0-9
65-90	A-Z
97-122	a-z

included whenever input is required from the user and the format of that input cannot be guaranteed. Examples discussed thus far in this book include the InputBox() function, the Text Box control, and spreadsheet cells. This may seem like a daunting task at first, but asking where the validation code needs to be entered in a program, and when it needs to run, simplifies the task considerably.

Validation with the InputBox() Function

In the Chapter 3 project, the program asks the user to input his/her name and birthday. The program assumed the user would enter the information in the proper format. For the user's name, the desired format was first name-space-last name and for the user's birthday, a date format had to be used (for example, 3/4/86 or 3-4-1986). The DateValue() function handled some of the input validation for us by allowing multiple date formats, but more validation is required.

Consideration of where the validation code should go and when it should run is easy with the InputBox() function. The validation should occur as soon as the user enters the data. The best way to do this is to put the InputBox() function inside a Do-Loop. In the Time of Your Life project in Chapter 2, user validation could be added as follows:

```
Dim userName As String
Dim userBirthday As Date
Dim nameOk As Boolean
```

The InputBox() function is inserted inside a Do-Loop where the return value is tested by the function procedure ValidateName(). The ValidateName() procedure returns true if the name satisfies the desired format, otherwise it returns false. The loop is repeated if the ValidateName() name procedure returns false, or the user hits the Cancel button (InputBox() returns an empty string) on the input box.

```
nameOk = True
Do
        userName = InputBox("What is your first and last name?", "Name")
        If (userName <> "") Then nameOk = ValidateName(userName)
Loop While (nameOk = False) Or (userName <> "")
```

The ValidateName() function procedure accepts the string entered by the user as input and tests for the number of spaces inside the string.

```
Private Function ValidateName(userName As String) As Boolean
    Dim strLength As Integer
    Dim I As Integer
```

```
Dim numSpaces As Integer
Dim tempString As String
Dim msb As Integer
```

Any leading or trailing spaces on the string entered by the user are removed using the Trim() function, so extra spaces before or after the names are forgiven. The length of the resulting string is then stored in the strLength variable for use in the subsequent For/Next loop.

```
userName = Trim(userName)
strLength = Len(userName)
```

The For/Next loop tests the leftmost character for equality to a space before removing this character. If the character is a space, then a variable keeping track of the number of spaces in the string is incremented by one. Essentially, the For/Next loop iterates through each character in the string and counts the number of spaces found within that string.

```
For I = 1 To strLength
    If Left(userName, 1) = " " Then
        numSpaces = numSpaces + 1
    End If
    userName = Right(userName, Len(userName) - 1)
Next I
```

If more than one space (or less than one space) is found in the string entered by the user, then the function returns false; otherwise it returns true.

```
If  (numSpaces <> 1) Then
   ValidateName = False
   msb = MsgBox("Please enter just two names separated by one space",
vbCritical, "Error")
 Else
   ValidateName = True
 End If
End Function
```

For example, if the user enters either of the strings **FredFlintstone** or **Fred J Flintstone** in the input box, then the ValidateName() function returns false to the calling procedure just after outputting the message Please enter just two names separated by one space in a message box.

Obviously, the ValidateName() function procedure does not test for all possible mistakes users might make entering in their names, but it does illustrate how to use input validation with the InputBox() function. To test for other potential errors by the user, simply add more code (specific to the type of error you are looking for) to the ValidateName() function procedure.

Validation with a Spreadsheet Cell

Validating input from a specific spreadsheet cell can be a bit more complicated, although the basic idea of writing a validation procedure to test the input for the desired format is the same. Validating input in one or multiple worksheet cells is no different, except that you have to loop through the range of cells, calling the validation procedure with each iteration through the loop. The difficulty is in deciding where to put the initial code that sends the user input to the validation procedure. With the proper design, you can give yourself several choices for the validation procedure. Consider the sample spreadsheet shown in Figure 4.2.

This spreadsheet simulates an address database in which the user is allowed to edit records and enter new records. Input validation should be included for every field (name, address, phone number, and so on). For simplicity, we will consider validation of the area code only; however, the techniques discussed can be applied to every field.

The question is: Where should we put the validation sub procedure? There are several possibilities. The most obvious place for the validation procedure is in the Click() event of the Command Button control labeled Update. A click of the

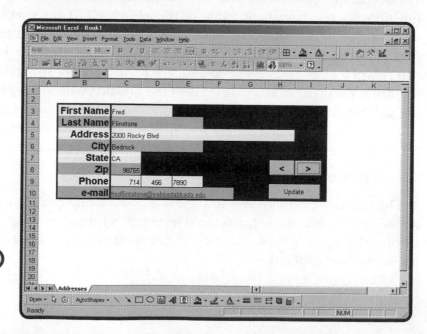

FIGURE 4.2

An address database spreadsheet

Update command button will send code execution to the click() event procedure of that button. Within the Click() event procedure of this Command Button, simply add a call to the validation sub procedure. The validation sub procedure will loop through the cells containing the displayed records information. If all fields pass validation, then the record is updated (stored to a file), if not, then specific information containing the error(s) is output to the user.

Another possible approach to input validation is to call the input validation procedure as each field is entered. For this example, the simplest choice is to use the Worksheet_Change() event procedure of the worksheet. The Worksheet_Change() event procedure is triggered when cells on the worksheet are changed by the user. Consider the following code:

```
Private Sub Worksheet_Change(ByVal Target As Range)
```

The cell range edited by the user is passed to the Worksheet_Change() event procedure and stored in a variable named Target. The variable Target is of type range, which you can think of as using our Cells() property to return a specific cell on a worksheet. So when the user edits a cell on the worksheet, this procedure is called as soon as the user selects another worksheet cell. Again, it is the range of the edited cell that is passed to this procedure.

```
Dim cellContents As String
Dim valLength As Integer
```

The next line is critical to the validation of the input data. First, the innermost VBA function Val() is passed the value of the edited cell. If the user's input was a numerical value, then the Val() function will not change anything except the data type. However, if the user input a non-numerical value, then the Val() function will return 0 or any numerical value that started the input string (for example, if the string 714XYZ is passed to Val() then the function will return 714). The resulting number returned by the Val() function is passed to the Str() function to convert it to a string. Leading and trailing spaces on the string are removed with the Trim() function and the final result is stored in the string variable cellContents.

```
cellContents = Trim(Str(Val(Target.Value)))
```

The length of the cellContents variable is checked for inequality to 3, and if true, a message box is displayed and the selection is returned to the edited cell. Otherwise, the input is validated and cell selection is sent to the next cell in the phone number (cell D9).

```
valLength = Len(cellContents)
If valLength <> 3 Then
```

```
        MsgBox ("Please enter a 3 digit area code.")
        Cells(9, "C").Select
    Else
```

If the user input to cell C9 does not contain exactly three numbers at the start of the input string, then the message above is displayed in the message box. The only non-numerical value that will pass this validation procedure is a string that begins with three numerical values and is followed by something else (for example, 123abc). Since the Val() function returns just the numerical portion of such a string, the line below is used to return that number to the edited cell.

```
        Cells(9, "C").Value = cellContents
        Cells(9, "D").Select
    End If
End Sub
```

This example demonstrates input validation on one specific cell in the simulated database application shown in Figure 4.2. Obviously, the code will depend on the type of information input by the user (numerical, string, date, and so on), so its complexity will vary. The key questions are: when and where do you want the validation procedure to run? and how demanding should the validation procedure be on the user's input? or in other words, how much are you going to let the user get away with?

Arrays

Normally, arrays are not discussed until the end of beginning programming books. However, as you are already familiar with spreadsheet applications, the concept of an array should come easily. An *array* is a variable that can hold multiple values. You should use arrays when a related set of values is to be stored in a variable. Doing so relieves you from having to declare a new variable with a unique name for each value in the set. Arrays are convenient and they simplify program code tremendously.

A spreadsheet column that contains data is basically the same thing as an array—it's a group of related values. Each cell within a spreadsheet column containing the related set of values is referenced by a row and column index. Values in an array are also referenced using indices.

I'm assuming that you organize your spreadsheets in the normal way—by placing data inside columns rather than rows. But the argument is the same whether you equate a spreadsheet column or row to an array.

Before starting with the simplest example of an array (the one-dimensional array), consider a sub procedure that uses a worksheet column much as a programmer would use an array in an application that does not work with a spreadsheet.

In previous chapters, and throughout this chapter, I use the `Cells` **property of the Excel application object in code examples. The** `Cells` **property is straightforward, with a row and column index that corresponds to a single spreadsheet cell. Although discussed in detail in Chapter 5, be aware as you look at the examples in this chapter that the** `Cells` **property acts like a function that returns a Range object consisting of a single spreadsheet cell. I have used the** `Value` **property of the Range object extensively thus far, but the Range object has many other properties for the VBA programmer to use besides the** `Value` **property, and you will see many examples in this chapter and subsequent chapters.**

The `BubbleSort()` procedure sorts a column of integer values from lowest to highest value. Two integer variables and a Boolean variable are all you need.

```
Public Sub BubbleSort()
    Dim tempVar As Integer
    Dim AnotherIteration As Boolean
    Dim I As Integer
```

A `For/Next` loop nested inside a `Do-Loop` will iterate through a column of ten values until the data is sorted from lowest to highest value. The nested `For/Next` loop effectively pushes the largest value from wherever it is located to the last position, much like a bubble rising from the depths to the surface. The `For/Next` loop starts at the beginning and compares two successive values. If the first value in the comparison is larger than the second value, then the position of the two values are swapped with help from the variable `tempVar`. The next two values are then compared, where the first of these values was the second value in the previous comparison (or first if it had been swapped). Note the row index in the `Cells` property uses `I + 1`, so the looping variable in the `For/Next` loop works from 1 to 9, even though the procedure sorts ten values.

```
Do
    anotherIteration = False
    For I = 1 To 9
        If Cells(I, "A").Value > Cells(I + 1, "A").Value Then
            tempVar = Cells(I, "A").Value
            Cells(I, "A").Value = Cells(I + 1, "A").Value
            Cells(I + 1, "A").Value = tempVar
```

If a swap of two values has to be made, then the Boolean variable `anotherIteration` is set to `True` to ensure the outer `Do-Loop` continues with at least one more iteration.

```
            anotherIteration = True
        End If
    Next I
```

Each iteration through the `Do-Loop` moves the next largest value in the set down the column to its correct position. Thus, it will take up to N iterations to sort the data, where N is the number of values in the set. This does not make the `Bubble-Sort()` procedure terribly efficient, but it works well for small data sets. The worksheet shown in Figure 4.3 illustrates what happens to a set of numbers after each iteration through the `Do-Loop`. Note that Figure 4.3 was created for display only; the `BubbleSort()` procedure sorts and copies values within column A only.

```
    Loop While anotherIteration = True
End Sub
```

One-Dimensional Arrays

An *array* is a variable used to hold a group of related values, and it must be declared just as a variable is declared. An array is declared with a single name and the number of elements (values) that can be stored in the array.

```
Dim myArray(number of elements) As Type
```

You may also declare arrays using the `Public` or `Private` keywords to define the scope as you would with a regular variable declaration. If you do not specify a data type, then, like a variable, the array will be a variant type. Arrays may be

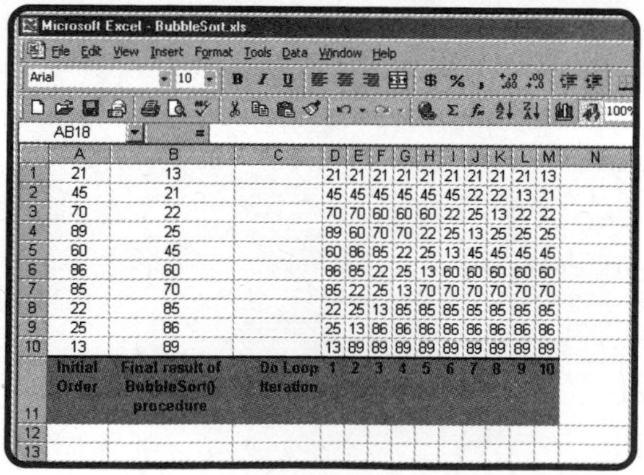

FIGURE 4.3

Worksheet illustration of the `BubbleSort()` sub procedure

declared as any available data type in VBA. All elements in arrays with numerical data types are initialized with the value 0. Elements of string arrays are initialized with an empty string. When specifying the number of elements, you must consider the lower bound of the array. The default lower bound is 0.

```
Dim myArray(10) As Integer
```

When you need multiple array declarations of the same size, use a constant to specify the size of the arrays in the declarations.

```
Const ARRAYSIZE=10
Dim myArray1(ARRAYSIZE) As Integer
Dim myArray2(ARRAYSIZE) As Integer
Dim myArray3(ARRAYSIZE) As Integer
```

This way, if you have to edit the size of your arrays you only need to change the value of the constant.

Thus, the integer array `myArray` declared above has 11 elements accessed with the indices 0 through 10. To override the default, set the lower bound of the array in the declaration.

```
Dim myArray(1 To 10) As Integer
```

The array `myArray` now has just ten elements because the lower bound has been explicitly set to 1.

Use the statement `Option Base 1` **in the general declarations section of a module to change the default lower bound of all arrays declared in the module to 1.**

You can initialize a single element in the array as you would a variable.

```
myArray(5) = 7
```

However, arrays are typically initialized inside a loop. To insert the values of the first ten cells of column A in a spreadsheet into an array, do the following:

```
Dim I As Integer
Dim myArray(10) As Integer
For I = 0 To 9
  myArray(I) = Cells(I + 1, "A").Value
Next I
```

Then use another loop to output the values of the array. The following loop squares the values stored in the array myArray before copying them to column B of the spreadsheet:

```
For I = 0 To 9
    Cells(I + 1, "B").Value = myArray(I)^2
Next I
```

Now let's revisit the BubbleSort() procedure, this time using an array. The sub procedure BubbleSort2() works exactly like the BubbleSort() procedure, except that the tests and swaps are performed on the values in the set after they have been loaded into an array rather than just using the worksheet column.

```
Public Sub BubbleSort2()
    Dim tempVar As Integer
    Dim anotherIteration As Boolean
    Dim I As Integer
    Dim myArray(10) As Integer
```

After variable declarations, the values in column A of the worksheet are loaded into the array with a simple For/Next loop.

```
    For I = 1 To 10
        myArray(I - 1) = Cells(I, "A").Value
    Next I
```

The For/Next loop nested in the Do-Loop is just as it was in the BubbleSort() procedure, except now the Cells property has been replaced with the array named myArray. The looping variable in the For/Next loop now runs from 0 to 8 because the lower bound for the array is 0 not 1.

```
    Do
        anotherIteration = False
        For I = 0 To 8
            If myArray(I) > myArray(I + 1) Then
```

When the first value is greater than the second, the values are swapped.

```
                tempVar = myArray(I)
                myArray(I) = myArray(I + 1)
                myArray(I + 1) = tempVar
                anotherIteration = True
            End If
        Next I
    Loop While anotherIteration = True
```

Finally, the sorted values are copied to column B in the worksheet.

```
    For I = 1 To 10
        Cells(I, "B").Value = myArray(I - 1)
    Next I
End Sub
```

Multi-Dimensional Arrays

If one-dimensional arrays are analogous to a single column in a spreadsheet, then two-dimensional arrays are analogous to multiple columns in a spreadsheet. Three-dimensional arrays are analogous to using multiple worksheets, and higher dimensions than three are a bit difficult to imagine but nevertheless are available. You can declare multi-dimensional arrays in VBA with up to 60 dimensions. Unless you're comfortable imagining multi-dimensional spaces greater than dimension three, I suggest keeping the number of dimensions in an array to three or less.

```
Dim myArray(10, 2) As Integer
```

The above declaration creates a two-dimensional integer array with 11 rows and three columns (remember the lower-bound is 0). Access the individual elements of the array using the row and column indices.

```
myArray(5, 1) = Cells(6, "B").Value
```

This example assigns the value of the spreadsheet cell B6 to the sixth row and second column in the array myArray.

As with one-dimensional arrays, multi-dimensional arrays are typically accessed within loops; however, we need to use nested loops in order to access both indices in a multi-dimensional array.

The sub procedure below transposes the values of a group of cells in a worksheet. This sub procedure takes input from the first ten rows and three columns in a worksheet and transposes the values to the first three rows and ten columns in the same worksheet. See Figure 4.4 and Figure 4.5 for depictions of the initial spreadsheet and the spreadsheet resulting from running the Transpose() sub procedure.

```
Public Sub Transpose()
    Dim I As Integer
    Dim J As Integer
    Dim transArray(9, 2) As Integer
```

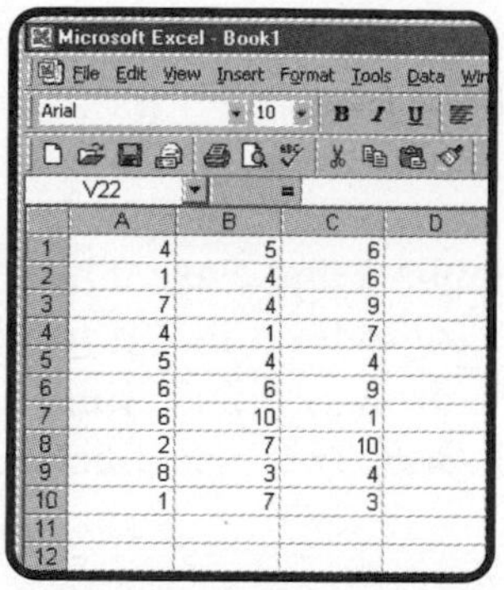

	A	B	C	D
1	4	5	6	
2	1	4	6	
3	7	4	9	
4	4	1	7	
5	5	4	4	
6	6	6	9	
7	6	10	1	
8	2	7	10	
9	8	3	4	
10	1	7	3	
11				
12				

FIGURE 4.4

An Excel spreadsheet prior to running the `Transpose()` sub procedure

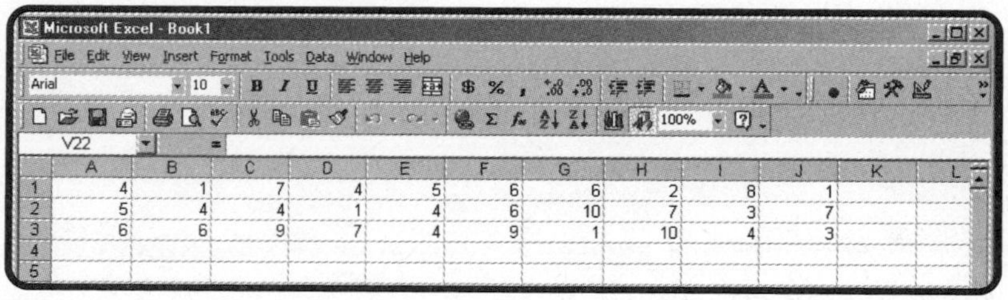

	A	B	C	D	E	F	G	H	I	J	K	L
1	4	1	7	4	5	6	6	2	8	1		
2	5	4	4	1	4	6	10	7	3	7		
3	6	6	9	7	4	9	1	10	4	3		
4												
5												

FIGURE 4.5

An Excel spreadsheet after running the `Transpose()` sub procedure

After variable declarations, the values in the spreadsheet are loaded into the two-dimensional array named `transArray`.

HINT

A three-dimensional array is declared with three values within the parentheses of its declaration (for example, `Dim myArray(9, 2, 2)`**). You could use a three-dimensional array to keep track of rows and columns from multiple worksheets, whereas a two-dimensional array would keep track of rows and columns from a single worksheet.**

As shown in previous examples, the `Chr()` function is used to convert an ASCII value to its corresponding keyboard character to use as the column index in the `Cells` property.

The looping variables in the nested `For/Next` loops are used to access the row and column indices of the array `transArray`. The looping variables `I` and `J` are used as the column and row indices, respectively, in both the array and worksheet.

```
For I = 1 To 3
    For J = 1 To 10
        transArray(J - 1, I - 1) = Cells(J, Chr(I + 64)).Value
    Next J
Next I
```

The contents of the worksheet are cleared. The Range object will be covered in detail in Chapter 5.

```
Range("A1:C10").ClearContents
```

To transpose the values, the looping variables I and J are now used to access the opposite index (that is, I is used for the row index and J is used for the column index) in the Cells property. However, the array transArray uses the indices as in the previous For/Next loop. These nested For/Next loops effectively transpose the values, as shown in Figure 4.5.

```
For I = 1 To 3
    For J = 1 To 10
            Cells(I, Chr(J + 64)).Value = transArray(J - 1, I - 1)
    Next J
    Next I
End Sub
```

Dynamic Arrays

The BubbleSort2() and Transpose() sub procedures used arrays with fixed lengths. The number of values in fixed length arrays cannot be changed while the program is running. This is fine as long as you know the required length of the array before running the program. However, the use of dynamic arrays allows programmers to create a more robust program. Wouldn't the BubbleSort2() procedure be more useful if it sorted data with any number of values rather than just ten values? A similar question can be asked of the Transpose() procedure—wouldn't it be more useful if it worked with any size data set rather than just a set with ten rows and three columns? If we do not want to limit the BubbleSort2() and Transpose() sub procedures to constant-sized data sets, then we must use dynamic arrays.

The size of a dynamic array can be changed (increased or decreased) as necessary while the program runs. To declare a dynamic array, use empty parentheses instead of a value for the bound(s).

```
Dim myArray() As Integer
```

After the required length of the array has been determined the array is re-dimensioned using the ReDim keyword.

HINT

ReDim **can also be used as a declarative statement with arrays, but potential conflicts may arise if there are variables of the same name within your project— even if they are of different scope. Therefore, avoid using** ReDim **as a declarative statement, but use it to resize previously declared arrays.**

```
ReDim myArray(size)
```

The `ReDim` statement will re-initialize (erase) all elements of the array. If you need to preserve the existing values then use the `Preserve` keyword.

```
ReDim Preserve myArray(size)
```

If the new size of the array is smaller than the original size, then the values of the elements at the end of the array are lost. Normally, an array is re-dimensioned with the `Preserve` keyword only when the new size is larger than the previous size of the array. When resizing an array with the `Preserve` keyword, you can only change the size of the last dimension; you cannot change the number of dimensions, and you can only change the value of the upper bound. You'll see an example of using `ReDim Preserve` in the Math Game project at the end of the chapter.

The `BubbleSort2()` and `Transpose()` sub procedures are now rewritten using dynamic arrays.

```
Public Sub DynamicBubble()
    Dim tempVar As Integer
    Dim anotherIteration As Boolean
    Dim I As Integer
    Dim arraySize As Integer
    Dim myArray() As Integer
```

After the dynamic array is declared, you must determine the required size of the array. A `Do-Loop` is used to iterate through the cells in column A of the worksheet until an empty cell is found. By keeping track of the number of iterations with the variable `I`, the number of values in the column—and hence the required size of the array—is discovered. Then the array is re-dimensioned with the appropriate variable and `ReDim` statement.

This is not the best method for learning how many values the user has entered into column A of the worksheet, as the potential for error is high. For example, any text entered into a cell will be counted as a value and the procedure will try to use it as a number. This will eventually generate a type mismatch error. The procedure also limits the sort to data entered into column A of the worksheet. In the next two chapters I'll discuss additional methods for allowing the user more flexibility in terms of where the data can be input, and gathering user input such that ambiguities in the data are minimized.

```
    Do
        arraySize = I
        I = I + 1
```

```
        Loop Until Cells(I, "A").Value = ""
        ReDim myArray(arraySize - 1)
```

The rest of the procedure is the same as the `BubbleSort2()` procedure except the upper limit of all looping variables are set to the same value as the size of the array.

```
        For I = 1 To arraySize
            myArray(I - 1) = Cells(I, "A").Value
        Next I
        Do
            anotherIteration = False
            For I = 0 To arraySize - 2
                If myArray(I) > myArray(I + 1) Then
                    tempVar = myArray(I)
                    myArray(I) = myArray(I + 1)
                    myArray(I + 1) = tempVar
                    anotherIteration = True
                End If
            Next I
        Loop While anotherIteration = True
        '
        For I = 1 To arraySize
            Cells(I, "B").Value = myArray(I - 1)
        Next I
    End Sub
```

The `Transpose()` sub procedure is rewritten using a dynamic array that is re-dimensioned with two dimensions. One dimension is for the number of rows in the grid of values to be transposed and the other dimension is for the number of columns.

```
Public Sub DynamicTranspose()
    Dim I As Integer
    Dim J As Integer
    Dim transArray() As Integer
    Dim numRows As Integer
    Dim numColumns As Integer
```

Once again, `Do-Loops` are used to determine the number of rows and columns holding values in the worksheet. The array `transArray` is then re-dimensioned to the same number of rows and columns. Don't forget that the lower bound on each dimension is 0. The rest of the procedure is the same, with the exception of the upper limit on the looping variables used in the `For/Next` loops.

```
    Do
        numRows = I
        I = I + 1
    Loop Until Cells(I, "A").Value = ""
    '
    I = 0
    Do
        numColumns = I
        I = I + 1
    Loop Until Cells(1, Chr(I + 64)).Value = ""
    ReDim transArray(numRows - 1, numColumns - 1)
    '
    For I = 1 To numColumns
        For J = 1 To numRows
            transArray(J - 1, I - 1) = Cells(J, Chr(I + 64)).Value
        Next J
    Next I
    '
    Range("A1:C10").ClearContents
    '
    For I = 1 To numColumns
        For J = 1 To numRows
            Cells(I, Chr(J + 64)).Value = transArray(J - 1, I - 1)
        Next J
    Next I
End Sub
```

Programming Formulas into Worksheet Cells

If you're going to be an Excel VBA programmer, then it is inevitable that you will have to create programs that enter formulas into worksheet cells. Thankfully, it is a pretty simple thing to do; however, you must decide on the reference style you wish to use—A1 type or R1C1 type.

A1 Style References

The A1 style uses the column and row headings (letters and numbers, respectively) as indices to reference a particular worksheet cell (for example, A1, B5, $C$2). Dollar signs in front of an index denote an absolute reference, and the lack of a dollar sign on an index denotes a relative reference. The A1 style reference is the preferred style of most Excel users.

Creating a formula using VBA is easy. Instead of using the Value property of the range returned by the Cells property, you use the Formula property and assign a string value. The string should be in the form of an Excel formula.

The following example inserts a formula in cell A11 of a worksheet that calculates the sum of the values in the range A2:A10 using the Excel application's SUM function:

```
Dim formulaString As String
formulaString = "=SUM($A$2:$A$10)"
Cells(11, "A").Formula = formulaString
```

If you want to create a set of related formulas in a column, you can use a looping structure to iterate through the cells that receive the formula. The following example uses formulas inserted into the cells of column B in a worksheet to calculate a running sum of column A:

```
Dim formulaString As String
Dim I As Integer
Cells(1, "B").Value = Cells(1, "A").Value
For I = 2 To 10
        formulaString = "=A" & Trim(Str(I)) & "+B" & Trim(Str(I - 1))
        Cells(I, "B").Formula = formulaString
Next I
```

Looping through the cells is not the most efficient method available in VBA for inserting formulas. Using loops to insert formulas can slow your program down considerably, especially if it is running on an older machine with a relatively slow processor. You would not enter individual formulas in the Excel application when it is possible to copy and paste, so why do it with your VBA code? Instead, you can use Copy and Paste or AutoFill functions that run much faster.

```
Dim formulaString As String
Dim I As Integer
Cells(1, "B").Value = Cells(1, "A").Value
formulaString = "=A2+B1"
Cells(2, "B").Formula = formulaString
```

To use the Copy function and Paste method, first insert the formula in the original cell as before, execute the Copy function of the Cells property, select the desired range, and paste the formula.

```
Cells(2, "B").Copy
Range("B2:B10").Select
ActiveSheet.Paste
```

 A *method* **is yet another type of procedure that performs a specific action on a program component or** *object.* **The** `Paste` **method performs its action on an Excel worksheet by pasting the contents of the clipboard onto the worksheet.**

Or, use the `AutoFill` function by specifying the destination range. The term `Destination` is a named argument predefined for the `AutoFill` function in VBA. Named arguments allow the programmer to pass values to a function without having to worry about the order of the arguments or how many commas must be included for optional arguments that are not used. Use the named argument operator (`:=`) to assign the value to the name.

```
Cells(2, "B").AutoFill Destination:=Range("B2:B10")
```

Or, if you prefer, you can still pass the arguments in a list.

```
Cells(2, "B").AutoFill Range("B2:B10")
```

The second line of code using the `AutoFill` function works because `Destination` is the first argument/parameter that must be passed to the function. (As it turns out, the `Destination` argument is the only required parameter of the `AutoFill` function.) Using the named argument with the named argument operator makes the code more readable, so the first example with the `AutoFill` function is probably better. You can use named arguments with any procedure in VBA.

Specifically, the `Copy` and `AutoFill` functions are associated with the range object returned by the `Cells` property, and the `Paste` method is associated with the worksheet object. I'll discuss these objects in detail in the next chapter.

R1C1 Style References

The R1C1 style uses the letters R for row and C for column followed by numbers to reference spreadsheet cells. For example, R[-1]C[2] is a relative reference to the cell one row lower and two columns higher than the cell that contains this formula. To denote an absolute reference, leave off the brackets (for example, R-1C2). The R1C1 reference style can be turned on in the Excel application by clicking on Tools, Options, General, and then clicking on R1C1 reference style as shown in Figure 4.6.

You can use the R1C1 reference style in your VBA code any time. It can be a preferable style to use when dealing with references to columns, as the indices use a

The R1C1
reference style

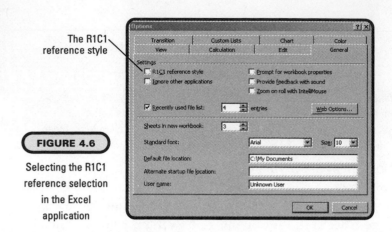

FIGURE 4.6

Selecting the R1C1
reference selection
in the Excel
application

numerical value. The value of the string variable `formulaString` in the previous example can be assigned as shown here:

```
formulaString = "=R[0]C[-1]+ R[-1]C[0]"
Cells(2, "B").FormulaR1C1 = formulaString
```

Although the `Formula` property of the range object returned by the `Cells` property would work just as well, I have used the `FormulaR1C1` property for consistency.

> **Whether you use the A1 style or R1C1 reference style in your VBA code is of no consequence to the user. The user will see whichever style they have set their Excel application to use.**

Chapter Project: Math Game

The Math Game is designed as an exercise in basic math skills suitable for an elementary school child. The game gives the user one minute to correctly answer as many questions as possible with the selected operation (addition, subtraction, multiplication, and division). After the one-minute interval, the user's answers are scored and the result displayed on the worksheet. The game uses several techniques discussed in this chapter, including loops and arrays.

Project Statement

I wish to create a program in VBA that simulates a timed test of the user's basic math skills. The program should continually ask math questions until a one-minute timer runs down to zero. The user's answers should be graded and the results displayed in the worksheet.

Project Tools

The program interface will be through an Excel worksheet in the Excel application. The formatting tools in Excel and the macro-recording tool can be used to create and save most of the interface design. ActiveX controls (option buttons and a command button) can be used to provide the user with a selection of mathematical operations to be tested on, and an easy way to start the program. The program can use several sub procedures, looping code structures, decision structures, and arrays to handle the appearance of the interface, and data input/output to the worksheet. The VBA `OnTime` method can be used to control a timer that displays the number of seconds the user has left to answer questions and stops execution of the program when time runs down to zero.

Recording Macros

Up to this point, all chapter projects have been preformatted with no specific instructions on how it was done. You could certainly type code into a VBA module that formats the worksheet as you want, but this is often a tedious exercise and is not really necessary, as the worksheet is saved to a file. However, there will be occasions when you need to create new worksheets and format them using VBA programs. You will know how you want the worksheet formatted; you just don't want it done until the user has reached a certain stage in your program. This is one example of when recording a macro is very handy. The basic steps for recording a macro are as follows:

1. First turn on Excel's macro recorder.
2. Format the worksheet as desired.
3. Stop the recorder.
4. Proceed to the VBA IDE and find the VBA code you just recorded.
5. Clean the recorded code for readability and add it to your program.

Another situation in which recording macros is useful is when you need to learn how to use a particular VBA function. If you can't find what you need in the online help or get your code to run correctly, simply record a macro that uses the desired function of the Excel application. Of course, you must know how to perform the same task within the Excel application that you are trying to add to your VBA code. Once the task is recorded, return to the VBA IDE and examine the recorded VBA code.

To begin recording a macro, in the Excel application select Tools, Macros, Record New Macro, as shown in Figure 4.7. You can also click the Record Macro button on the Visual Basic toolbar.

The Record
Macro button

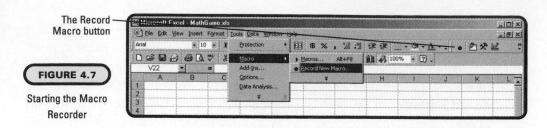

FIGURE 4.7

Starting the Macro
Recorder

A dialog box will appear, as shown in Figure 4.8, asking you to input a name for
your macro, where you want to store the code (a new workbook, the current
workbook, or a personal macro workbook), and for a description of the macro.
You can enter in new values or use the default. I recommend at least changing
the name of the macro to something meaningful. Store the macro in whatever
workbook you want, but keep in mind the macro will be saved with the workbook you choose, and will only be available when this workbook is open.

After selecting the name and location of the macro, a small toolbar with a small
square button will appear, as shown in Figure 4.9. After you are finished recording the macro, click this button to stop the recorder. Until you click the stop button, every action you perform in the Excel application is recorded as VBA code.

After stopping the recorder, you can find the new VBA code stored in a module in
the current project. The module and code window that results from recording a
macro that formats cells A1, B1, and C1 for the Math Game is shown in Figure 4.10.

To record this macro, I followed the procedure above, and then formatted the
cells before stopping the recorder. Specific tasks carried out in the Excel application while the recorder was on were: adding the text to the cells, and specifying

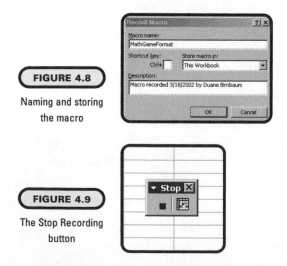

FIGURE 4.8

Naming and storing
the macro

FIGURE 4.9

The Stop Recording
button

Module added by
macro recorder

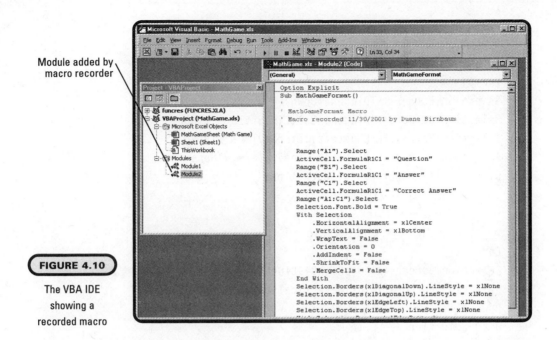

FIGURE 4.10

The VBA IDE
showing a
recorded macro

font size, bold, centered text, word wrapped text, a border, row height, and column widths. The code, exactly as recorded, is as follows:

```
Sub MathGameFormat()
'
' MathGameFormat Macro
' Macro recorded 11/30/2001 by Duane Birnbaum
'


    Range("A1").Select
    ActiveCell.FormulaR1C1 = "Question"
    Range("B1").Select
    ActiveCell.FormulaR1C1 = "Answer"
    Range("C1").Select
    ActiveCell.FormulaR1C1 = "Correct Answer"
    Range("A1:C1").Select
    Selection.Font.Bold = True
    With Selection
        .HorizontalAlignment = xlCenter
        .VerticalAlignment = xlBottom
        .WrapText = False
        .Orientation = 0
```

```vba
        .AddIndent = False
        .ShrinkToFit = False
        .MergeCells = False
    End With
    Selection.Borders(xlDiagonalDown).LineStyle = xlNone
    Selection.Borders(xlDiagonalUp).LineStyle = xlNone
    Selection.Borders(xlEdgeLeft).LineStyle = xlNone
    Selection.Borders(xlEdgeTop).LineStyle = xlNone
    With Selection.Borders(xlEdgeBottom)
        .LineStyle = xlDouble
        .Weight = xlThick
        .ColorIndex = xlAutomatic
    End With
    Selection.Borders(xlEdgeRight).LineStyle = xlNone
    Selection.Borders(xlInsideVertical).LineStyle = xlNone
    Rows("1:1").RowHeight = 31.5
    With Selection
        .HorizontalAlignment = xlCenter
        .VerticalAlignment = xlBottom
        .WrapText = True
        .Orientation = 0
        .AddIndent = False
        .ShrinkToFit = False
        .MergeCells = False
    End With
    With Selection.Font
        .Name = "Arial"
        .Size = 12
        .Strikethrough = False
        .Superscript = False
        .Subscript = False
        .OutlineFont = False
        .Shadow = False
        .Underline = xlUnderlineStyleNone
        .ColorIndex = xlAutomatic
    End With
    Columns("A:A").ColumnWidth = 13.14
    Columns("B:B").ColumnWidth = 12.14
    Columns("C:C").ColumnWidth = 10.29
    Range("A2").Select
End Sub
```

As you can see, recording just a few tasks will generate a considerable amount of code. Because of the volume of code generated by the macro recorder, I do not recommend recording many tasks at any one time. You want to be able to record small pieces, then clean up the recorded code and proceed to the next task.

Much of the recorded code can be eliminated by deleting the setting of default values and compressing multiple statements into one line of code. The macro I just showed you can be quickly reduced to the following:

```
Sub MathGameFormat()
' MathGameFormat Macro
' Macro recorded 11/30/2001 by Duane Birnbaum
'
    Range("A1").FormulaR1C1 = "Question"
    Range("B1").FormulaR1C1 = "Answer"
    Range("C1").FormulaR1C1 = "Correct Answer"
    Range("A1:C1").Select
    With Selection
        .Font.Bold = True
        .Font.Name = "Arial"
        .Font.Size = 12
        .HorizontalAlignment = xlCenter
        .VerticalAlignment = xlBottom
        .WrapText = True
    End With
    With Selection.Borders(xlEdgeBottom)
        .LineStyle = xlDouble
        .Weight = xlThick
    End With
    Rows("1:1").RowHeight = 31.5
    Columns("A:A").ColumnWidth = 13.14
    Columns("B:B").ColumnWidth = 12.14
    Columns("C:C").ColumnWidth = 10.29
    Range("A2").Select
End Sub
```

The macro is public by default and is contained inside a standard module.

 The With/End With **code structure is used to execute a series of statements on the same Excel object. This removes the requirement of constantly qualifying the object before setting one of its properties. The** With/EndWith **programming structure will be covered in Chapter 5.**

To run a recorded macro, in the Excel application select Tools, Macro, Macros, or press Alt+F8. A dialog box displaying a list of available macros will appear, as shown in Figure 4.11.

Select the macro you want and press the Run button to execute the code in the macro.

 Any public procedure (recorded or not) stored in a standard or component module will appear in the list of available macros.

After recording the formatting of the worksheet cells A1 through C1, I record another manageable amount of formatting, clean up the code, and paste it within the previously recorded procedure. After all recording is completed and the code is reduced, it can be copied to any sub procedure necessary to fulfill the algorithm for the program. For example, the recorded code may be needed inside the Click() event procedure of a Command Button control.

The macro-recording tool in Excel was really designed for non-programming users as a method to extend the capabilities of their spreadsheets and eliminate the tedium of repetitive tasks. As it turns out, the macro-recording tool can also serve the VBA programmer as a method of eliminating tedious programming tasks and learning how to carry out specific tasks in Excel with VBA code.

The Forms Toolbar

Along with the macro recorder, Excel comes with a few other controls similar to ActiveX controls that are designed for use with recorded macros. The controls are available from the Forms toolbar and can be accessed through the View menu in the Excel Application (see Figure 4.12).

Most of these controls are the same as the controls on the Control toolbox and their function is basically the same. The difference is in how the controls on the Forms toolbar are used. These controls are designed for non-programmers to use

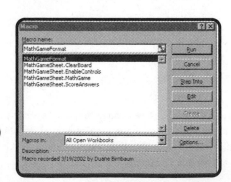

FIGURE 4.11

Selecting an available macro

FIGURE 4.12

The Forms toolbar

with recorded macros, so they don't have code windows other than the module containing the recorded macro. To attach a macro to a control from the Forms toolbar, first draw the control on a worksheet and right click on the control to view its menu, then select Assign Macro. The Assign Macro dialog box, shown in Figure 4.13, will appear with a list of all available procedures (any procedure declared with the Public keyword) currently open in Excel.

Select the procedure that you want executed and click the OK button. The macro will be assigned to the major event of the control (typically a Click() event).

You can use these controls to initiate VBA procedures just as you would with controls from the control toolbox. However, you sacrifice considerable flexibility with respect to properties and events associated with the control. Nevertheless, if all you need is code initiation, the Forms toolbar controls offer a simple set of tools.

Project Algorithm

The Math Game was constructed using the guidance of the following plan. You will notice that the program does not actually follow this algorithm to the letter, nor does the algorithm contain every detail in the program. As a program is written,

FIGURE 4.13

The Assign Macro dialog box

I will inevitably change a few small details or perhaps leave out pieces I originally included in the algorithm. This is normal; however, any major changes to the algorithm are included here to ensure I have a complete plan before I continue writing the program. Figure 4.14 displays the layout of the Math Game worksheet.

Format the worksheet to display the following:

- A timer
- Two numbers and a mathematical operator for the user's question
- Column labels for the question asked, the user's answer, and the correct answer
- ActiveX controls: A command button for starting the program and five option buttons for choosing the mathematical operation.

The program should be constructed such that the user can enter answers quickly. The best way to do this is through the keyboard. The numeric keypad and the enter key should be all the user needs to use once the program begins. The program should start with a click of a button that will trigger a programming sequence to:

1. Start a timer that will countdown from 60 seconds with an update every second.

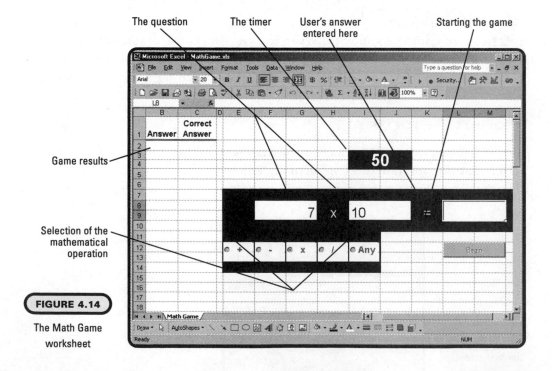

FIGURE 4.14

The Math Game
worksheet

2. Display a mathematical question consisting of two random numbers between 1 and 10 and a mathematical operator selected by the user.

3. Force the user to enter the answer in only one particular worksheet cell. Validate the user's answer for a numerical value (optional).

4. As the user enters his/her answers, the program should store the results (question and user's answer) then display the next question.

5. When the timer runs down to 0, the user's results should be graded and displayed in the worksheet. Wrong answers can be formatted in a different color (red).

The timer is handled best with the OnTime method. This function will call a single procedure for repeated execution at a given timer interval. The most important aspect of this function is that in between procedure calls, the system will yield to other processes. Practically speaking, this means that while the program is running, the user will still be able to enter answers into the worksheet. The procedure called by the timer will check the state of the timer, and if the timer is at zero, then the program will output the results and terminate the program.

The numbers for the questions will be integer values between 1 and 10, chosen randomly with the Rnd function. The user will choose the operator using option buttons, so the value property of the option buttons will have to be checked when the program first starts. If the user selects the "any" operator, then the operator will be chosen randomly. An integer variable will be used to keep track of the operator (1=addition, 2=subtraction, 3=multiplication, and 4=division). If division is chosen as the operation, then the random numbers will be selected such that the correct answer is also an integer value.

 HINT Option Button controls are very much like Check Box controls except that the user is only allowed one selection.

The Worksheet_SelectionChange() event procedure associated with the worksheet will be used to control the program after it begins. The user will be forced to enter the answer in one specific cell. When the user hits Enter to enter the answer, the Worksheet_SelectionChange() event procedure will be triggered. Code placed in this procedure will store the result and display the next question.

The program will use as many sub and function procedures as necessary to handle the tasks listed above. Small details, such as formatting the output, enabling and disabling controls, and anything else that comes up will be handled as they are encountered while writing the program.

Table 4.3. lists the ActiveX controls used in the Math Game, as well as their properties as set at design time.

Adding the Code

The Math Game program uses a component module and a standard module. The component module (named `MathGameSheet`) contains a majority of the code including all event procedures associated with the ActiveX controls and the worksheet. As the game begins with a click on the `cmdBegin` command button, we will start with its `Click()` event procedure.

Several module level variables are declared, including three dynamic arrays for storing the questions, operators, and the user's answers. The variable `opType` will tell the program what mathematical operation is currently being used in the

TABLE 4.3 SELECTED PROPERTIES OF THE ACTIVEX CONTROLS USED IN THE MATH GAME		
ActiveX Control	**Property**	**Value**
Command Button	Name	cmdBegin
	Caption	Begin
Option Button	Name	optAdd
	Value	True
	Caption	Add
Option Button	Name	optSubtract
	Value	False
	Caption	Subtract
Option Button	Name	optMultiply
	Value	False
	Caption	Multiply
Option Button	Name	optDivide
	Value	False
	Caption	Divide
Option Button	Name	optAny
	Value	False
	Caption	Any

question. The variables `numQuestions`, `num1`, and `num2` store the number of questions asked, and the two values used in the question. These variables are declared at module level because the program needs to access and/or manipulate them in more than one procedure in this module.

```
Option Explicit
Dim mathQuestions() As Integer
Dim mathOperators() As String
Dim userAnswers() As Integer
Dim opType As Integer
Dim numQuestions As Integer
Dim num1 As Integer
Dim num2 As Integer
```

The `Click()` event procedure of the `cmdBegin` Command Button control serves as the main procedure in the Math Game program. This procedure initializes a few variables and gets the worksheet ready for the user before calling the procedure that actually begins the game.

```
Private Sub cmdBegin_Click()
    Dim numCells As Integer
    numQuestions = 0
```

The three lines of code below represent small details and were actually added after the program was written and working as desired. Excel's `COUNTA` function is used to return the number of cells in column A of the worksheet that contains some type of value (text or numerical). The range of cells from A2 through the desired length is then cleared. This removes the results output to the user after playing the game.

```
    numCells = Application.WorksheetFunction.CountA(Range("A:A"))
    If numCells = 1 Then numCells = 2
    Range("A2:C" & (numCells)).ClearContents
```

The mathematical operator chosen by the user is determined by checking the `Value` property of the Option Button controls on the worksheet. Only one option button can be selected, so only one of these conditions will be true. An integer value (1, 2, 3, or 4) is used to code the type of operator used in the question and is stored in the variable `opType`.

```
    Cells(8, "L").Select
    If optAdd.Value = True Then opType = 1
    If optSubtract.Value = True Then opType = 2
    If optMultiply.Value = True Then opType = 3
    If optDivide.Value = True Then opType = 4
```

If the user has selected the Any Option button, then a call to the sub procedure GetRandomOperator() will randomly choose one of the four mathematical operators.

```
If optAny.Value = True Then GetRandomOperator
```

Sending program execution to the DisableControls() sub procedure disables the ActiveX controls while the program runs.

```
DisableControls
```

The GetRandomNumbers() sub procedure generates the numbers used for the questions. The two random integers generated are stored in the module level variables, num1 and num2 and copied to the appropriate worksheet cells.

```
GetRandomNumbers
Cells(8, "F").Value = num1
Cells(8, "I").Value = num2
```

The current date is stored in the public (global) variable curDate using VBA's Now function. This value will be used with the games timer. Finally the MathGame() sub procedure is called to start the timer and begin the game.

```
    curDate = Now
    MathGame
End Sub
```

A standard module is used to hold the MathGame() sub procedure and one public (global) variable, curDate, is declared in its general declarations section.

```
Option Explicit
Public curDate As Date

Public Sub MathGame()
    Dim nextTime As Date
    Dim numSeconds  As Integer
    Const TIMEALLOWED = 61
```

The integer variable numSeconds is used to hold the amount of time left in the game. The length of the game is held in the constant TIMEALLOWED. The number of seconds left in the game is calculated by the VBA function DateDiff() using the current time and the time the program was initiated with the click of the cmdBegin command button. This is why the curDate variable is declared as public in a standard module—to make it visible to both modules used in the program.

```
    numSeconds = DateDiff("s", curDate, Now)
    Cells(3, "I").Value = TIMEALLOWED - numSeconds
```

The variable nextTime is used to store a date one second later than the current time.

```
nextTime = Now + TimeValue("00:00:01")
```

The most interesting statement in the procedure comes next. The OnTime method that belongs to the Application object (more in Chapter 5) is used to repeatedly call the MathGame() sub procedure. The OnTime method takes up to four parameters for input, two of which are required. Because I only need to pass the OnTime method three parameters, I am using named arguments.

```
Application.OnTime EarliestTime:=nextTime, Procedure:="MathGame",
Schedule:=True
```

The EarliestTime parameter represents the next time the system will call the procedure specified by the Procedure parameter, in this case the MathGame() procedure. The EarliestTime and Procedure parameters are required. The other two parameters, both of which are optional, are LatestTime and Schedule. The LatestTime parameter represents the latest time the procedure specified by the Procedure parameter can be called; however, it is not required here. The Schedule parameter is used to schedule a new call to the procedure specified by the Procedure parameter. In this case, Schedule must be used and set to true in order to ensure that the next call to the MathGame() procedure occurs. It is important to point out that in between calls to the MathGame() procedure, the system is allowed to process other events. Thus, the system is not locked up processing code as it would be if you used a looping structure to handle the timer. This allows the user to enter answers into the appropriate worksheet cell.

An If/Then decision structure is used to check the value of the timer. If the timer is less than or equal to zero, then the OnTime method is used to disable the timer by setting the Schedule parameter to False. Thus, the MathGame procedure will no longer be called. Without this statement, the MathGame procedure will be called every second and drastic action (Ctrl+Alt+Break) will have to be taken to stop the program.

```
If (TIMEALLOWED - numSeconds <= 0) Then
    Application.OnTime nextTime, "MathGame", , False
```

After the timer reaches zero, procedure calls are made to enable the ActiveX controls, clear the values in the spreadsheet cells containing the question and answer, and score the results of the game. Because the EnableControls, ClearBoard, and ScoreAnswers sub procedures are contained in a component module, they can only be accessed from a standard module by specifying the entire path. The path to these procedures is through the component module name MathGameSheet. Furthermore, the EnableControls, ClearBoard, and ScoreAnswers sub procedures must be declared public or they will not be visible from the standard module.

```
        MathGameSheet.EnableControls
        MathGameSheet.ClearBoard
        MathGameSheet.ScoreAnswers
    End If
End Sub
```

The remaining procedures in the component module (MathGameSheet) are listed below. The Click() event of the Option Button controls is used to set the value of the opType variable and display the mathematical operator in the worksheet.

```
Private Sub optAdd_Click()
    Cells(8, "H").Value = "+"
    opType = 1
End Sub
Private Sub optAny_Click()
    Cells(8, "H").Value = ""
End Sub
Private Sub optDivide_Click()
    Cells(8, "H").Value = "/"
    opType = 4
End Sub
Private Sub optMultiply_Click()
    Cells(8, "H").Value = "x"
    opType = 3
End Sub
Private Sub optSubtract_Click()
    Cells(8, "H").Value = "-"
    opType = 2
End Sub
```

The Worksheet_Change() event procedure will trigger every time the user enters an answer. The parameter passed to this procedure when an answer is entered in the appropriate worksheet cell is the reference to cell L8.

```
Private Sub Worksheet_Change(ByVal Target As Range)
```

If the user has entered the answer in the correct cell, a series of statements are executed. A modicum of input validation is included in the conditional for the If/Then decision structure. If the user presses Enter without typing in an answer, then no code inside the If/Then decision structure is executed. Thus, the game does not display the next question and the user can reselect cell L8 and enter the answer to the existing question.

```
    If (Target.Address = "$L$8") And (Cells(8, "L").Value <> "") Then
```

If the user does answer an question, then the numQuestions variable is incremented by one, the StoreQuestions() sub procedure is called, and a new question is obtained from calls to the GetRandomOperator() (if required) and GetRandomNumbers() procedures and displayed.

```
        numQuestions = numQuestions + 1
        StoreQuestions
        If optAny.Value = True Then GetRandomOperator
        GetRandomNumbers
        Cells(8, "F").Value = num1
        Cells(8, "I").Value = num2
        Cells(8, "L").Select
        Selection.Value = ""
    End If
End Sub
```

The GetRandomNumbers() sub procedure generates two random integer values for the game's questions. If the mathematical operation is division, the code loops until two values are found that result in a non-fractional answer. The VBA operator Mod is used to test the two random numbers for a remainder of zero. This procedure is called from the cmdBegin_Click() and the Worksheet_Change() event procedures.

```
Private Sub GetRandomNumbers()
    Randomize
    If opType = 4 Then
        Do
            num1 = Int(10 * Rnd) + 1
            num2 = Int(10 * Rnd) + 1
        Loop Until (num1 Mod num2 = 0)
    Else
        num1 = Int(10 * Rnd) + 1
        num2 = Int(10 * Rnd) + 1
    End If
End Sub
```

The sub procedure DisableControls() disables the ActiveX controls on the worksheet by setting their Value property to false. This procedure is called from the cmdBegin_Click() event procedure.

```
Private Sub DisableControls()
    cmdBegin.Enabled = False
    optAdd.Enabled = False
    optSubtract.Enabled = False
```

```
            optDivide.Enabled = False
            optMultiply.Enabled = False
            optAny.Enabled = False
        End Sub
```

The StoreQuestions() sub procedure is called from the Worksheet_Change() event procedure, so the code within is executed every time the user enters an answer to a question. The dynamic variable arrays declared at module level are re-dimensioned to increase their size by one with each call to this procedure. The Preserve keyword is used to ensure that previously stored values are not lost.

The two-dimensional array mathQuestions maintains the same number of dimensions, and only the upper bound of the last dimension changes, as required when using the Preserve keyword. Thus, the mathQuestions array can be thought of as containing two rows (indexed by 0 and 1) and N columns where N is equal to the number of questions asked during the game.

```
Private Sub StoreQuestions()
    ReDim Preserve mathQuestions(1, numQuestions) As Integer
    ReDim Preserve mathOperators(numQuestions) As String
    ReDim Preserve userAnswers(numQuestions) As Integer
```

The first (cell F8) and second (cell I8) values for each question are stored in rows 0 and 1 of the mathQuestions array, respectively. The mathematical operator used and the user's answers are stored in the arrays mathOperators and userAnswers, respectively. The index value in the arrays used to store the mathematical operators and the user's answers is identical to the index value in the array used to store the corresponding question. This is critical for outputting these values to the correct worksheet cells later in the program.

```
            mathQuestions(0, numQuestions - 1) = Cells(8, "F").Value
            mathQuestions(1, numQuestions - 1) = Cells(8, "I").Value
            mathOperators(numQuestions - 1) = Cells(8, "H").Value
```

The user's answer is passed to the Val() function before storing in the array. This serves as more input validation. If the user enters a non-numerical string, then the answer will usually be set to zero depending on the string, as discussed earlier in this chapter.

```
            userAnswers(numQuestions - 1) = Val(Cells(8, "L").Value)
        End Sub
```

The GetRandomOperator() sub procedure is called only if the user selects the Any Option Button control. When the Any Option button is selected, the program will randomly choose an operator with each question. The GetRandomOperator() sub procedure uses the Rnd function to choose an integer value between 1 and 4. A Select/Case decision structure is used to display the operator in the appropriate cell on the worksheet. The operator is stored when the StoreQuestions() sub procedure is called.

```
Private Sub GetRandomOperator()
    Randomize
    opType = Int(4 * Rnd) + 1
    Select Case opType
        Case Is = 1
            Cells(8, "H").Value = "+"
        Case Is = 2
            Cells(8, "H").Value = "-"
        Case Is = 3
            Cells(8, "H").Value = "x"
        Case Is = 4
            Cells(8, "H").Value = "/"
        Case Else
            Cells(8, "H").Value = "+"
    End Select
End Sub
```

The EnableControls() and ClearBoard() sub procedures are called at the end of the game from the MathGame() procedure. They must be public or they will not be visible from the standard module containing the Mathgame() procedure. Their content is straightforward, as they are simply used to reset controls and cells on the worksheet.

```
Public Sub EnableControls()
    cmdBegin.Enabled = True
    optAdd.Enabled = True
    optSubtract.Enabled = True
    optDivide.Enabled = True
    optMultiply.Enabled = True
    optAny.Enabled = True
End Sub
Public Sub ClearBoard()
    Cells(8, "F").Value = ""
    Cells(8, "I").Value = ""
    Cells(8, "L").Value = ""
End Sub
```

The ScoreAnswers() sub procedure called at the end of the game from the MathGame() procedure reads the questions asked during the game from variable arrays and then displays them on the worksheet. This procedure also checks the user's answers and outputs the score as a percentage of questions answered correctly.

```
Public Sub ScoreAnswers()
    Dim I As Integer
    Dim numWrong As Integer
```

A For/Next loop is used to iterate through the arrays holding the questions and answers, because we know the number of questions that were asked. The lower bound on the arrays are zero, so the looping variable ranges from zero to the number of questions less one.

```
For I = 0 To numQuestions - 1
```

String concatenation is used to output the questions asked during the game to column A on the worksheet. The user's answers are output to column B on the worksheet. Using the looping variable as the indices for the arrays guarantees that the questions match their corresponding answer.

```
        Cells(I + 2, "A").Value = mathQuestions(0, I) & mathOperators(I) &
mathQuestions(1, I)
        Cells(I + 2, "B").Value = userAnswers(I)
```

To display the correct answer in column C of the worksheet, a formula string is created and copied to the appropriate cell using the formula property of the cell range. Since a × was used as the display for multiplication, an If/Then decision structure is used to replace it with an * for those questions that used the multiplication operator.

```
        If mathOperators(I) = "x" Then
            Cells(I + 2, "C").Formula = "=" & mathQuestions(0, I) & "*" &
mathQuestions(1, I)
            Cells(I + 2, "B").Font.Color = RGB(0, 0, 0)
        Else
            Cells(I + 2, "C").Formula = "=" & mathQuestions(0, I) &
mathOperators(I) & mathQuestions(1, I)
            Cells(I + 2, "B").Font.Color = RGB(0, 0, 0)
        End If
```

If the user entered a wrong answer, the answer is displayed in red and the integer variable numWrong is incremented by one.

```
        If Cells(I + 2, "B").Value <> Cells(I + 2, "C").Value Then
            Cells(I + 2, "B").Font.Color = RGB(255, 0, 0)
            numWrong = numWrong + 1
        End If
    Next I
```

Finally, the user's score is calculated and output to the end of column B on the worksheet as a formula.

```
    Cells(I + 2, "A").Value = "Score (%)"
    Cells(I + 2, "B").Font.Color = RGB(0, 0, 0)
    Cells(I + 2, "B").Formula = "=" & (numQuestions - numWrong) /
numQuestions & "*100"
End Sub
```

This concludes the Math Game program. I wrote the program following the algorithm described earlier. I added small details usually related to formatting the spreadsheet to the appropriate procedures after the program was working to satisfaction. Although no procedure is included to process all of the worksheet formatting, one could easily be recorded. In fact, I recorded and added small pieces of code for the Math Game program (and the previous chapter projects) to the appropriate procedures.

I wrote the Math Game program using two modules, one component and one standard. This adds complexity to the program but serves as a good example for demonstrating interaction between variables and procedures in two separate modules. The Math Game program could have easily been contained within the MathGameSheet component module. This would have eliminated the need for the public variable and some of the public procedures. Changing the Math Game program such that it is contained entirely within a component module is left up to you for an exercise.

Chapter Summary

You covered a significant number of topics concerning VBA programs in this chapter. The looping code structures (Do-Loop and For/Next) and variable arrays provide enormous power by allowing you write more efficient and significantly shorter code.

You also examined a number of methods used for interaction with an Excel worksheet including input validation, entering formulas in spreadsheet cells, and using the Worksheet_Change event procedures of a worksheet.

The Math Game used all of these tools plus a special method (OnTime) of the application object to repeatedly call a procedure at a specified time interval.

You also examined macro recorder and Forms toolbar controls.

The next chapter introduces the Excel object model concentrating on the objects at the top of the hierarchy. You have seen many examples of Excel objects in the first four chapters of this book. Now it is time to take an in depth look at these objects, their properties, and their methods.

CHALLENGES

1. Write a procedure that outputs a random number to the first 100 cells in column A of an Excel worksheet.

2. Add a statement to the procedure from the previous question that inserts a formula into cell A101 that calculates the sum of the first 100 cells. If you can't get it on your own, record a macro and examine the code.

3. Write a VBA procedure that uses a For/Next loop to store the contents of the first 10 cells in row 1 of an Excel worksheet to a variable array.

4. Write a VBA procedure that uses nested For/Next loops to store the contents of the range A1:E5 in an Excel worksheet to a two-dimensional array.

5. Write a VBA procedure that uses nested For/Next loops to store the contents of the range A1:E5 in each of three Excel worksheets to a three-dimensional array.

6. Change the procedures above using an input box to ask the user for the number of rows and/or columns and/or worksheets in which to retrieve values for storage in the same arrays. Use Do-Loops and dynamic arrays. Add validation to the input box.

7. Record a macro that formats a worksheet to look like the worksheet in the Math Game, less the ActiveX controls.

8. Change the Math Game program such that it uses only one component module. Hint: copy the MathGame() procedure and curDate variable to the MathGameSheet module. In the OnTime method, you will have to specify the entire path to the MathGame() procedure in the parameter list. Reduce the scope of as many variables and procedures as possible.

Basic Excel Objects

T he preceding chapters concentrated on fundamental programming constructs common to all languages. Now it is time to introduce some VBA- and Excel-specific programming concepts and capabilities. You will be using programming tools referred to as *objects*, specifically some of the objects available in VBA and Excel.

In this chapter you will learn about:

- **Objects**

- **VBA Collection Objects**

- **The Object Browser**

- **Application and Workbook Objects**

- **The Range object**

- **Working with objects**

- **Chapter project: Battlecell**

Project: Battlecell

The Battlecell program will familiarize you with many of Excel's top level and most common objects, as well as reinforce code and data structures previously discussed. You will also become familiar with the Object Browser, in order to access all of the objects in the available libraries, not just in the Excel library. The Battlecell program relies heavily on Excel's Application, Workbook, Worksheet, and Range objects. The program is a computer simulation of the classic Battleship game you may have played as a kid, and a natural choice for a spreadsheet application. Figure 5.1 shows the Battlecell game board designed from an Excel worksheet.

VBA and OOP

If VBA or Visual Basic is your first programming language, then chances are you have not heard of object-oriented programming (OOP for short). Don't worry if you haven't heard of it, because neither Visual Basic (version 6 or earlier) nor VBA qualifies as an OOP language. There are some technicalities that disqualify VBA from calling itself OOP, but VBA still shares many of the same concepts as genuine OOP languages. Mainly, OOP languages share with VBA the existence of objects and some of the tools used to manipulate these objects. These tools include properties, events, and methods (other languages may call these tools something different, but they are really the same thing).

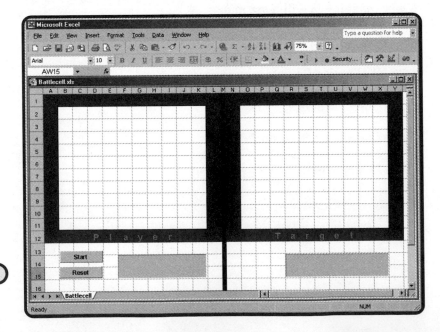

FIGURE 5.1

The Battlecell
game sheet

You have already seen several VBA objects in action. For example, in Chapter 1 the project code contained many references to Excel objects and some of their properties. Objects must be discussed in VBA at a relatively early stage. Objects show up early, often, and everywhere in your VBA code. This is a good thing, because your programs can't really do much without them.

Objects Defined

There is no need to get too abstract here with the definition of an object. It really is a pretty simple thing to understand. You can think of objects as separate computer programs with specific (and often common) functions that are available for repeated use in your programs. Objects are dynamic in that they can be easily manipulated in code with the various parameters used to define them.

In one common analogy, objects are equated to nouns in the English language. A programming object can be described with adjectives (properties), be capable of performing different actions (methods), and be built out of other objects. As an example, consider a bicycle. A bicycle can be described by its size, color, and type

---

IN THE REAL WORLD

Although C++ has been around for a few years, most object-oriented languages are relatively new. Java is an object-oriented language that gained popularity with the rise in popularity of the World Wide Web. Other languages, such as Visual Basic (version 6.0 and earlier), VBA, and some Web-based languages (for example, Javascript and Perl) are also fairly new but do not satisfy all the definitions required for the object-oriented label. However, all of these languages use objects extensively and thus serve as a good introduction to object-based programming, if they aren't totally object-oriented.

Program objects, such as ActiveX controls in VBA, allow greater flexibility and power in software development because they can be developed by one group of programmers and used by other groups in virtually any application. It is this ability to re-use program objects and the time savings it creates that make objects so popular among programmers.

The requirements for a language to be designated as object-oriented are really quite strict. The new version of Visual Basic (VB.net), and the new development language C# satisfy object-orientation requirements. The popularity of object-oriented languages is likely to continue and the migration of object-based languages to true object-oriented status is also probable (if they survive). However, it appears that for the time being, VBA will remain object-based, and not object-oriented.

(among other things). For example, it might be a 26" blue ten-speed. The color, size, and type are all adjectives that describe the bicycle. Thus, they are all *properties* of the bicycle. A bicycle can also perform various actions; it can move straight or turn when ridden. Moving and turning are actions that tell us what tasks the bicycle can perform. Moving and turning are *methods* of the bicycle. Finally, the bicycle is built out of other objects such as a frame, wheels, handlebars, and pedals. These objects, in turn, have their own properties and methods. For example, a bicycle wheel is of a certain diameter, is built out of aluminum or titanium alloys, and it turns or rolls. The diameter and type of material are properties of the wheel object, and to turn or roll would be two of its methods. So you see, there is sort of a hierarchy to the objects in your bicycle and the bicycle object itself sits at the top of the hierarchy.

I could take it further. For example, a wheel is built from a tire, rim, and spoke objects. The tires are built from organic polymers, and so on, and so on. The description continues until eventually you will get to the objects at the very bottom of the hierarchy. These objects may have properties and methods but they are not built out of any other objects. It may take you a while to get to this level if you really think about your bicycle. Eventually you could break the bicycle down to its subatomic components and then you would have to stop because you have reached the limit of human knowledge. Fortunately, in any program the object hierarchy does not extend that far and is well defined by the programmer. In this case, you get help from Excel and VBA in defining the objects, but it is still up to you to choose which objects you want or need to use in your program.

Now there is one more attribute of an object that has not yet been mentioned (at least not here; it was discussed in Chapter 3). Consider what happens when a tire on your bicycle goes flat, or when the rider pedals the bicycle, or when the rider turns the handlebars on the bicycle. These are all *events* that occur when some action is carried out. Don't be confused with the method of the bicycle turning and the event of the rider turning the handlebars. They are not the same—one depends on the other. In this particular case, the bicycle turns when the rider turns the handlebars. Events are actions triggered by an external stimulus of the object. You write code using the turn_bicycle method when the rider triggers the handlebar_turn event. The code that is executed (invoking the turn_bicycle method) is a coded response to the user's stimulus (handlebar_turn event).

Object events are very powerful programming tools, as they allow for a much more interactive experience between the program and the user. Think about what a program would be like without events. Once you started the program running, you would not do anything else except maybe type in some information when prompted by the program. That is, the programmer would completely dictate the flow of the program. If you remember computers prior to GUI's then you may remember this kind of programming. You have already seen some of the events associated with a couple of Excel's objects in previous chapters. Now you should have a little better understanding as to why events exist.

Now let's consider some of the objects in Excel. If you are a regular user of Excel or any spreadsheet program, then you are already familiar with many of its objects. For example, there are workbook objects, worksheet objects, range objects, chart objects, and many more. The rest of this chapter is devoted to showing you how to use a few of Excel's objects, and in particular, some of its top-level objects.

VBA Collection Objects

Collection objects in VBA are fairly straightforward—they are exactly what the name implies: a group or collection of the same object types. Using the bicycle example again, consider a collection of bicycles. The bicycle objects in your bicycle collection can be different sizes, colors, and types, but they are all bicycles.

Collection objects allow you to work with objects as a group rather than just working with a single object. In VBA, the objects that have Collection objects (not all do) are typically denoted with the plural form of the object word. For example, any Workbook object belongs to a Workbooks Collection object. The Workbooks Collection object contains all open Workbook objects. The Excel window shown in Figure 5.2 contains three open Workbook objects (Book1, Book2, and Book3).

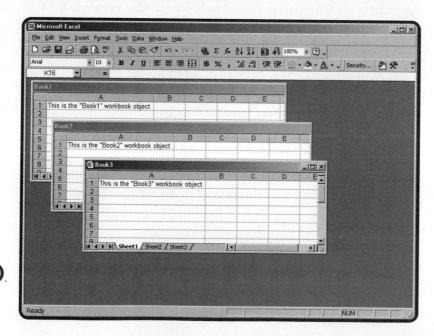

FIGURE 5.2

Excel Workbook objects

To select a Workbook object from the Workbooks Collection object, the code would look like this:

```
Workbooks(2).Activate
```

This line of code uses the Workbooks property of the Application object (more on this later) to return a single Workbook object from the Workbooks Collection object and then uses the Activate method of the Workbook object to select the desired object.

The required syntax when addressing objects in VBA is object.property **or** object.method. **You may also specify more than one object to reach the desired property or method. For example,** ActiveSheet.Range("A1"). Font.Bold = True **is of the form** object.object.object.property **because** ActiveSheet, Range("A1"), **and** Font **all represent objects.** Bold **is a Boolean property of the Font object and its value is set to true. As you may have guessed, this line of code turns on bold formatting in cell A1 of the current worksheet.**

So, from the collection of Workbook objects shown in Figure 5.2, which Workbook object does the above line of code return? If you answered Book2, you'd be wrong, although that is the intuitive answer. The number in parentheses refers to a relative index number for each workbook as it was created (in this case, Book1 was created first, Book2 second, and Book3 third). The confusing part is that an index value of 1 is reserved for the currently selected Workbook object, regardless of when that Workbook object was created. So to select Book2 you would actually have to use an index value of 3 in the above line of code. An index value of 2 would return Book1 and an index value of 1 or 4 would return Book3.

There will always be two choices of an index for the currently selected Workbook object, the value 1 because it is reserved for the currently selected object, and the value corresponding to its sequence in being created. The behavior of the Workbooks Collection object can be confusing, but with practice, patience, and above all, testing, I'm sure you can figure it out.

To avoid confusion, you can select a workbook unambiguously— if you know the name of the desired Workbook object—using the following line of code:

```
Workbooks("Book2").Activate
```

Here you simply include the name of the object as a string in place of the index number. Obviously, this is much less confusing and makes your code easier to read, so I recommend doing it this way whenever possible.

TRICK **When you need to step through several objects in a collection, use a loop and a looping variable to represent the index of the object to be returned.**

```
For I = 1 To 3
     If Workbooks(I).Saved = True Then Workbooks(I).Close
Next I
```

Other examples of Collection objects include Worksheets, Windows, and Charts. For example, each of the Workbook objects in Figure 5.2 contains three Worksheet objects that belong to separate Worksheets Collection objects. There are three Worksheets Collection objects in this example because they are lower in the object hierarchy than the Workbook object.

The Object Browser

The VBA IDE includes a convenient and very useful tool for browsing through all available objects for a project and viewing their properties, methods, and events. It is called the Object Browser, and you'll use it to view Excel's object model and learn about what objects are available for you to use in your programs. You can also view all procedures and constants from your current project.

To open the Object Browser, select Tools, View, Object Browser, as shown in Figure 5.3, or simply hit F2. Figure 5.4 shows the Object Browser window.

To use the Object Browser, first select the library from which you need to view the desired object, or select All Libraries (see Figure 5.5).

An object library is a collection of objects provided by a specific application. You may notice libraries for Excel, Office, VBA, and VBAProject. You may see others as well, but it is these specific libraries that are of the most interest to you now.

FIGURE 5.3

Selecting the Object Browser from the VBA IDE

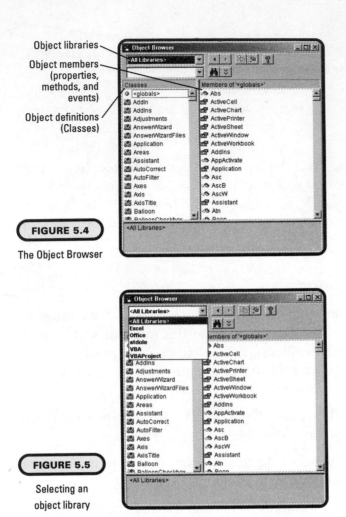

Object libraries

Object members (properties, methods, and events)

Object definitions (Classes)

FIGURE 5.4

The Object Browser

FIGURE 5.5

Selecting an object library

As you might have guessed, the Excel library contains objects specific to Excel and the Office library contains objects common to all MS Office applications (Word, PowerPoint, Excel, etc.). The VBA library adds a few objects specific to the VBA programming language, and the VBAProject library represents objects in the project currently open in Excel (that is, a workbook). In this chapter, it is the Excel library that is of the most interest to you because it's the library that contains specific objects that will allow you to interact with and extend Excel's capabilities.

After selecting the Excel library you'll see a list of all available objects within Excel in the bottom left window of the Object Browser (refer to Figure 5.4 or 5.5). The window is labeled Classes, but don't let that confuse you. A class is just an object definition. A class definition is used to create an instance of the object it defines. This is all just technical jargon that you don't need to worry about right now—just remember that when you see the word *class*, you should immediately think "object." Also, remember that the class/object list represents all objects available for you to use in your program. After selecting an object from the list, the available properties, methods, and events of the selected object will be displayed in the window on the bottom right side of the Object Browser (refer to Figure 5.4). This window is labeled Members, because these items belong to or are members of the selected object. When you select an item in the Members list, information about that member—the member type, required syntax, and data type—will be displayed at the very bottom of the Object Browser. Once you become more familiar with the Object Browser, and VBA in general, you should find this information more helpful.

TRICK To learn more about a specific object or one of its members, simply select an item in the Object Browser and press F1. The Help window will appear, displaying the result for the selected item in much more detail than what you see in the Object Browser.

If you prefer a more graphical representation of the Excel object model, look for the Object Model chart in the Help window under Microsoft Excel Objects. The chart, shown in Figure 5.6, displays the object hierarchy and provides links to documentation on the entire Excel object model.

Whatever tool you prefer (the Object Browser or Object Model chart), keep in mind that there is a hierarchy of objects that must be followed. You should think

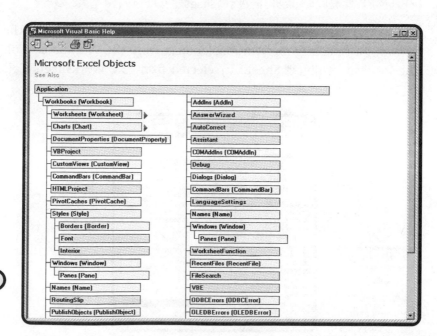

FIGURE 5.6

The Excel
object model

of the object hierarchy as a path to the object of interest much like a file path in a computer's operating system. It is a good idea to use these tools to set a specific object property or invoke an object's method when you're having difficulty navigating through the object hierarchy.

Consider a simple example. How do you insert the string `"VBA is fun!"` into cell A4 of Sheet2 in Book2 from the project shown in Figure 5.2? From examples in previous chapters, you know that you can use the `Cells` property of the Range object.

```
Cells(4, "A").Value = "VBA is fun!"
```

However, the line of code above will insert the string into the current or active worksheet, and this may not be your target worksheet. To ensure the string finds the correct target, first select the desired workbook.

```
Workbooks("Book2").Activate
```

To find the next object in the desired path to cell A4 of Sheet2 of Book2, look at the Object Browser. Since the above line of code gets you to the Workbook object, start by selecting the Excel object library and Workbook from the list of objects. Immediately, the members of the Workbook object are displayed on the right. If you scroll through this list you will eventually come to a property called `Worksheets`, as shown in Figure 5.7.

To select Sheet2, use the following code.

```
Workbooks("Book2").Worksheets("Sheet2").Activate
```

The second part of this statement (`Worksheets("Sheet2")`) is really the same code as written for selecting the Workbook object from the Workbooks Collection object. The Worksheet object Sheet2 is selected from the Worksheets Collection object.

FIGURE 5.7

Viewing the
`Worksheets`
property of the
Workbook object

This code uses the `Worksheets` property of the Workbook object to return a Worksheet object from the Worksheets Collection object. Since the Worksheet object is lower in the object hierarchy than the Workbook object, it follows it in the line of code above. Finally, the `Activate` method of the Worksheet object selects Sheet2 within the Workbook Book2. That was a mouthful, but if you work through the hierarchy slowly, and view each of these components through the Object Browser, it will make sense.

To add the string `"VBA is fun!"` to cell A4, use the following code:

```
Workbooks("Book2").Sheets("Sheet2").Range("A4").Value = "VBA is fun!"
```

TRICK It is often easier to read code containing a long object path from right to left. For example, the previous statement can be read as follows: Assign the string, `"VBA is fun!"` to the value in range A4 of the sheet named Sheet2 located within the workbook named Book2.

The `Range` property is found in the list of members for the Worksheet object, as shown in Figure 5.8. Note that the `Cells` property could have also been used.

```
Workbooks("Book2").Sheets("Sheet2").Cells(4, "A").Value = "VBA is fun!"
```

The `Range` property returns a Range object that represents one or more cells in a continuous block on a worksheet. In this case, the `Range` property returns the Range object that represents cell A4. Next, the `Value` property of the Range object is used to set the contents of cell A4 to the desired string `"VBA is fun!"`, as shown in Figure 5.9.

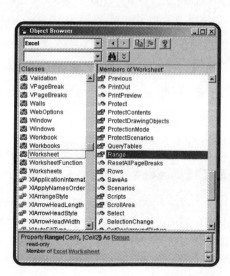

FIGURE 5.8

Viewing the `Range` property of the Worksheet object

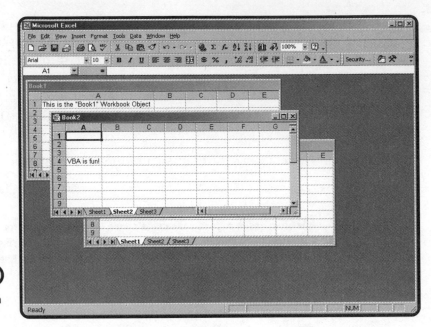

FIGURE 5.9

Inserting a string in
a worksheet cell

You may be wondering if you really need to work your way through the entire
object hierarchy to set one property. The answer is yes, but only if each object referenced in the code needs to be identified out of a collection of objects. For example, if there is only one Workbook object open, then

```
Sheets("Sheet2").Range("A4").Value = "VBA is fun!"
```

works just as well as the previous code. Actually, this code will execute regardless
of how many Workbook objects are open, but it will put the string in the currently selected, or active, workbook. Likewise,

```
Range("A4").Value = "VBA is fun!"
```

executes, but it will put the string in the active worksheet. Thus, each object
qualifier is necessary only as long as it is needed to identify one specific object
out of several possibilities.

Top-Level Excel Objects

I will start at the top of the hierarchy in the Excel object model and work my
way through the first few objects. There are too many objects in the model to
cover them all, but the goal of this chapter is to get you comfortable navigating
through the object model and learning how to use new objects on your own.

The Application Object

The Application object is the top-level object in Excel's object model. It represents the entirety of the Excel application (see Figure 5.6). As the top-level object it is unique, and thus seldom needs to be addressed in code. However, there are a few occasions when you must use the Application object's qualifier in code. One example is the `OnTime` method used in the Math Game program in Chapter 4. Other examples where the Application object must be explicitly referenced in code include the `Width` and `Height` properties used to set the size of the application window, and the `DisplayFormulaBar` property used to show or hide the formula bar.

```
Application.Width = 600
Application.Height = 450
Application.DisplayFormulaBar = True
```

For the most part, you need to use the Application object qualifier to set properties pertaining to the appearance of the Excel window, such as shown above, or the overall behavior of Excel, as shown below.

```
Application.Calculation = xlManual
Application.EditDirectlyInCell = False
Application.DefaultFilePath = "C:\My Documents"
```

However, if you just need to set properties of lower-level objects, then the Application object qualifier is not needed.

```
ActiveCell.Formula = "=SUM(A1:A10)"
```

The line of code above uses the `ActiveCell` property of the Application object to return a Range object. The Range object returned by this line of code is the currently selected spreadsheet cell. The `Formula` property of the Range object is then set with the given string. The formula is then entered into the cell and the result calculated as normal by Excel. To view all the Application object's properties, methods, and events, select it from the Classes list in the Object Browser, as shown in Figure 5.10.

The Workbook and Window Objects

You have already seen in action, in some of the examples in this chapter, the Workbooks and Worksheets Collection objects, as well as the Workbook and Worksheet objects. The difference between Collection objects and regular objects was discussed earlier. When working with these objects, keep in mind that the Workbook object is higher in the hierarchy than the Worksheet object. If you are familiar with Excel, this makes sense to you because a single workbook can hold multiple worksheets.

FIGURE 5.10

The Application object as viewed through the Object Browser

However, the Window object may be unfamiliar and/or a bit confusing. Window objects refer to instances of windows within either the same workbook, or the application. Within the Application object, the Windows Collection object contains all Window objects currently opened; this includes all workbooks and copies of any workbooks. The Window objects are indexed according to their layering. For example, in Figure 5.2, you could retrieve Book2 with the following code:

```
Application.Windows(2).Activate
```

because Book2 is the center window in a total of three Window objects. After Book2 is retrieved and thus brought to the top layer its index would change to 1 when using the Windows Collection object. This is different from accessing Book2 using the Workbooks Collection object. As stated previously, Workbook objects are indexed according to the order of their creation after the value of 1, which is reserved for the selected, or top-level Workbook object.

You may be thinking that the Windows Collection object within the Application object is essentially the same as the Workbooks Collection. This may or may not be true depending whether or not the user creates a new window by selecting New Window from the Window menu in the Excel application. This effectively makes a copy of the currently selected workbook. You may also use the NewWindow method of either the Window or Workbook object in your code to accomplish the same task.

```
Application.Windows(1).NewWindow
```

When a new window is created, the caption in the title bar from the original window is concatenated with a colon and an index number. For example, MyWorkbook.xls becomes MyWorkbook.xls:1, and MyWorkbook.xls:2 when a new window is created (These captions can be changed in code by manipulating the Caption property of the Window object). Do not confuse the creation of a new window from the Window menu with that of a new workbook. New workbooks are created when the user selects New from the File menu, or by using the Add method of the Workbooks Collection object. Of course, creating a new workbook also creates a new window, but the reverse is not true. If a new Window object is created through the use of the Window menu in Excel (or NewWindow method in VBA), then this window does not belong to the Workbooks Collection object and thus cannot be accessed in code by using the following:

```
Application.Workbooks("MyWorkbook.xls:2").Activate
```

This code fails because "MyWorkbook.xls:2" does not belong to the Workbooks collection but to the Windows collection of either the Application object or the Workbook object named MyWorkbook.xls. It could be accessed with either of the following lines of code:

```
Workbooks("MyWorkbook.xls").Windows("MyWorkbook.xls:2").Activate
```

Or

```
Application.Windows("MyWorkbook.xls:2").Activate
```

These examples and the above descriptions demonstrate that there may be more than one path to retrieving an object of interest in your code, and that differences between some objects may be quite subtle. I recommend that you play with these examples and create instances of new windows and new workbooks in your code. Then access these objects through as many paths as you can think of. You will find that it doesn't take long to get comfortable working with the Workbooks collection, Windows collection, Workbook, and Window objects.

All properties, methods, and events for these objects can be viewed in the Object Browser. Let's take a closer look at a few of them via an example, starting with the Workbooks Collection object, shown in Figure 5.4.

The ability of the properties and methods of the Workbooks Collection object are straightforward. Add the following procedure to a standard module in a workbook.

```
Public Sub AddWorkbooks()
    Dim I As Integer
    For I = 1 To 3
        Workbooks.Add
```

```
     Next I
End Sub
```

If you execute this procedure by selecting AddWorkbooks from the Macro menu in Excel, you will immediately see three new workbooks opened in Excel. To select a specific workbook, insert the following line of code at the end of the AddWorkbooks() sub procedure:

```
Workbooks(Workbooks.Count).Activate
```

This is another example of nesting, and it will activate the last workbook to be opened in Excel. The statement Workbooks.Count returns the number of open workbooks in Excel and is then used as the index to activate the last workbook added. If you prefer, edit the above code to make it more readable:

```
Dim numWorkbooks as Integer
NumWorkbooks = Workbooks.Count
Workbooks(NumWorkbooks).Activate
```

Through the Object Browser, you will notice that the Workbooks Collection object only has a few members. They are relatively straightforward to use, and you have already seen a couple of them (the Add method and Count property). You may find the Open and Close methods and Item property useful as well. Some of these members will be addressed later, albeit with different objects. You will find that many of the collection objects share the same properties and methods. This is not unusual, but be aware that depending on the object you use, the parameters that are either available or required for these members may vary. Figure 5.11 shows that the Workbooks Collection object and the Workbook object both have Close methods.

If you look at the bottom of the Object Browser windows displayed in Figure 5.11, you will see that the Close method of the Workbooks Collection object does not accept any parameters, but the Close method of the Workbook object can accept up to three parameters, all of which are optional (denoted by the brackets).

Consider the following VBA procedure illustrating the use of the Close method of the Workbook object. The code can be placed in a standard or component module.

```
Public Sub CloseFirstLast()
    Workbooks(Workbooks.Count).Close (False)
    Workbooks(1).Close (False)
End Sub
```

This procedure will close the first and last workbooks opened in Excel without prompting the user to save changes. However, if this procedure is contained somewhere in the component module of the last workbook to be opened, then

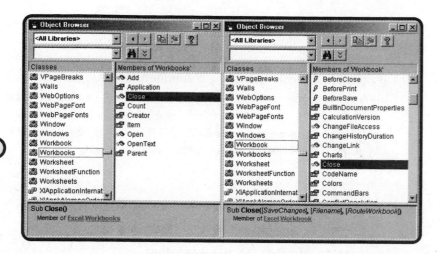

FIGURE 5.11

The Close
methods of the
Workbooks
Collection and
Workbook objects

only the last workbook will be closed. This is because the module containing this code will close before the last line (Workbooks(1).Close (False)) is executed. In the example above, the Close method of the Workbook object is used, not the Close method of the Workbooks Collection object. This must be the case because an index value was specified, and therefore only the Workbook object designated by an index of 1 is available. Because the Workbook object is used, optional arguments can be used with the method. In this case, the prompt to the user for saving changes to the workbook is set to false (the default is true), so the workbook closes immediately. If you want to close all workbooks simultaneously, then use the Close method of the Workbooks Collection object.

```
Workbooks.Close
```

In this case, there are no optional arguments allowed, so the user will be prompted to save the currently selected workbook. All open workbooks will be closed using the line of code above. There is no way to close a single workbook using the Workbooks Collection object. To close just one workbook, you need to use the Close method for a Workbook object.

Now consider an example that sizes and centers the application in the middle of the user's screen such that one-fourth of the screen on every side is unused by Excel. In addition, the workbook is sized so that it just fits inside the available space provided by the application window.

The following code was added to a workbook component module and saved as Center.xls on this book's CD-ROM:

```
Option Explicit
```

Explicit variable declaration is turned on, as usual, in the general declarations section of the code window. The code is contained within the `Workbook_Open()` event procedure to ensure that the program is executed immediately after the workbook is opened. You can access the component module for the workbook through the ThisWorkbook selection in the Project Explorer, as shown in Figure 5.12.

 HINT The name of the module ThisWorkbook can be changed via the `Name` property in the Properties window for the Workbook object.

```
Private Sub Workbook_Open()
    Dim maxWidth As Integer
    Dim maxHeight As Integer
    Application.WindowState = xlMaximized
    maxWidth = Application.Width
    maxHeight = Application.Height
    Call CenterApp(maxWidth, maxHeight)
    Call CenterBook
End Sub
```

After a couple of variable declarations, maximize the application window (fill the user's screen) by using the `WindowState` property (`xlMaximized` is a constant defined by the property) of the Application object. The application window is set to fill the

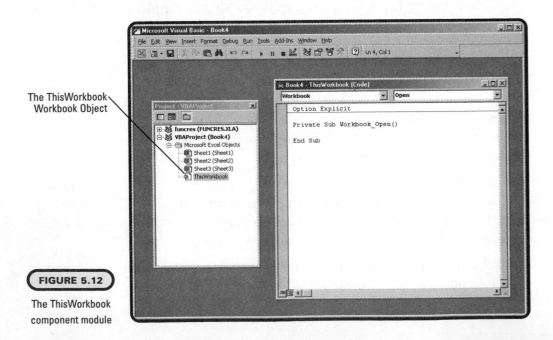

The ThisWorkbook
Workbook Object

FIGURE 5.12

The ThisWorkbook
component module

user's screen so that its maximum size can be determined. The variables maxWidth and maxHeight are used to hold the integer values that represent the maximized width and height of the application window

 Different users will have different monitor resolution settings, so to ensure consistency from one machine to another you must first learn the dimensions of the user's screen. Most languages provide a Screen object from which to determine these properties. VBA has no Screen object, therefore you have to be a bit less elegant about getting the desired width and height.

The rest of the procedure contains two calls to sub procedures. The Call keyword is used for calls to both procedures, however, it is only required when passing parameters. The Call keyword is used with the CenterBook() procedure only for consistency.

The first procedure called from the Workbook_Open() event procedure is to the CenterApp() sub procedure. This procedure receives two parameters, maxWidth and maxHeight. The function of the CenterApp() procedure is to center the application window within the user's screen, leaving one fourth of the screen (on all sides) unoccupied by Excel.

```
Private Sub CenterApp(maxWidth As Integer, maxHeight As Integer)
    Dim appLeft As Integer
    Dim appTop As Integer
    Dim appWidth As Integer
    Dim appHeight As Integer
```

After variable declarations, the state of the application window is returned to normal. This is the equivalent of the user clicking the middle window icon at the top right corner of the workbook window. The application window must be returned to a normal state because you cannot move a maximized window. Thus, trying to set the Left property of the Application object in the subsequent statement will cause an error and the program will crash.

```
    Application.WindowState = xlNormal
```

After returning the window state to normal, the application window is resized according to your specifications.

```
    appLeft = maxWidth / 4
    appTop = maxHeight / 4
    appWidth = maxWidth / 2
    appHeight = maxHeight / 2
    Application.Left = appLeft
```

```
        Application.Top = appTop
        Application.Width = appWidth
        Application.Height = appHeight
End Sub
```

Next, the `Workbook_Open()` event procedure calls the `CenterBook()` sub procedure without passing parameters. The `CenterBook()` procedure is called for the purpose of filling the workbook within the Excel application window.

```
Private Sub CenterBook()
        Dim bookWidth As Integer
        Dim bookHeight As Integer
```

After variable declarations, the `UsableWidth` and `UsableHeight` properties of the Application object are used to retrieve the values for the width and height of the workbook window.

```
        bookWidth = Application.UsableWidth
        bookHeight = Application.UsableHeight
```

The workbook window is set to a normal state just like the application window so that it may be resized.

```
        ActiveWindow.WindowState = xlNormal
```

Next, the `Windows` property of the Workbook object is used to return the top-level window (`Windows(1)`). The size (`Width` and `Height`) properties of the window are set to the usable width and height of the application window via the `bookWidth` and `bookHeight` variables. Finally, the position (`Left`, `Top`) properties of the window are set to the upper-left corner of the application window (0,0).

```
        Workbooks("Center.xls").Windows(1).Width = bookWidth
        Workbooks("Center.xls").Windows(1).Height = bookHeight
        Workbooks("Center.xls").Windows(1).Left = 0
        Workbooks("Center.xls").Windows(1).Top = 0
End Sub
```

It is not necessary to use `Workbooks("Center.xls")` in the code shown above. I did this only to illustrate the path to the desired object. If the reference to the Workbook Object Center.xls were to be omitted, then VBA would simply use the default object path. The default object path is to the active window of the current workbook. Since this code is run immediately after opening Center.xls, it is the current workbook. An index of 1 is used to select the active or top-level window. As there is only one window in Center.xls, you don't have to worry about getting to the desired window. However, if you created multiple windows in the

Center.xls workbook, then you might want to use the Window object's `Caption` property instead of an index number.

The Worksheet Object

The Worksheet object falls just under the Workbook object in Excel's object hierarchy. To investigate some of the events of the Worksheet Object, the following code has been added to the `SelectionChange()` event procedure of Sheet1 in the Center.xls workbook.

```
Private Sub Worksheet_SelectionChange(ByVal Target As Range)
    Dim msgOutput As String
    msgOutput = "The name of this worksheet is " & Worlsheets(1).Name
    MsgBox (msgOutput)
    Worksheets(2).Select
End Sub
```

The `SelectionChange()` event procedure was first introduced in Chapter 2, and is found in the component module of a worksheet. The `SelectionChange()` event procedure is triggered whenever the user changes the current selection in the worksheet. The `Target` parameter passed to the `SelectionChange()` event procedure is of type Range and represents the range of cells selected by the user. I will discuss the Range object shortly; for right now ignore it, because the current example does not use the passed parameter.

The code in the `SelectionChange()` event procedure is straightforward. First, a string variable is created and assigned a value (`"The name of this worksheet is"`) that is then concatenated with the name of the worksheet obtained from the `Name` property of the Worksheet object. The full object path is not used to return the name of the worksheet, as this code will only be executed when the user changes the selection in the first worksheet of the Worksheets Collection object (Sheet1). Therefore, the object path travels through the current Workbook object. This is why index numbers can be used with the `Worksheets` property of the Workbook object without returning the wrong sheet. After displaying the concatenated string in a message box, the `Select` method of the Worksheet object is used to select the second worksheet in the Worksheets Collection object. (This will generate an error if only one worksheet exists in the collection.)

Next, code is added to the `Worksheet_Activate()` event procedure of Sheet2. The `Worksheet_Activate()` event procedure is triggered when a worksheet is first selected by the user or, in this case, by selecting the worksheet using program code (`Worksheets(2).Select`). The code is essentially the same as the previous example.

```
Private Sub Worksheet_Activate()
    Dim msgOutput As String
    msgOutput = "This worksheet is " &  Workheets(2).Name
    MsgBox (msgOutput)
End Sub
```

TRICK The Worksheet_Activate() event procedure is not triggered when a workbook is first opened, so it is not a good place for initialization routines intended to run as soon as a workbook is opened. These procedures should be placed in the Workbook_Open() event procedure.

HINT You may have noticed in the object browser an object called *Sheets*. The Sheets Collection object is nearly identical to the Worksheets Collection object and the two objects can often be used interchangeably (as is the case in the previous two examples). The difference between these two objects is that the Sheets Collection object will also contain any chart sheets open in the active workbook. So if you expect chart sheets to be open in the workbook of interest, you should access worksheets using the Sheets Collection object; otherwise, either Collection object will suffice.

The Range Object

The Range object represents a group of one or more contiguous cells in an Excel worksheet. The Range object is one level beneath the Worksheet object in Excel's object hierarchy, and is extremely useful, as it allows you to manipulate the properties of an individual cell or groups of cells in a worksheet. You will probably find yourself using the Range object in every program you write using VBA for Excel.

Consider the following code examples that use properties of the Range object:

```
Range("A1").Value="Column A"
Range("A1:G1").Columns.AutoFit
Range("A1:C1", "E1:F1").Font.Bold = True
```

First, note that a long object path is omitted from the examples above. Thus, these lines of code will operate on the currently selected worksheet. The first line inserts the text "Column A" into cell A1 by setting its Value property. The Range object was used to return a single cell (A1) in this example. You have already seen several examples of the Value property in this book. Although the Value property exists for several objects, it is the Range object for which it is most commonly used. The second line of code above uses the AutoFit method of the Range object to adjust the width of columns A through G such that the contents of row 1 will just fit into their corresponding cells without overlapping into adjacent columns. This is equivalent to the user selecting Format, Column, AutoFit Selection from the Excel application menu.

Entries in other rows that are longer than the entries in row 1 will still run into the next column. To automatically adjust the width of these columns such that the contents of every cell in the columns fit within cell boundaries, use the range A:G instead of A1:G1. The third and last example demonstrates setting the Bold property of the Font object to true for two distinct ranges in the active worksheet. The two ranges are A1:C1 and E1:F1. You are allowed to return a maximum of two ranges, so adding a third range to the arguments in the parentheses would generate a run-time error.

The examples above demonstrate just a couple of formatting methods and properties belonging to the Range object (AutoFit, Columns, and Font). If you are a regular user of Excel, then you have probably surmised that there are numerous other properties and methods related to formatting spreadsheet cells. You can either search the Object Browser or the online help for more examples on how to use formatting options of interest. However, when you know what formatting options you want to include in your VBA program, record a macro. It is a quick and easy way to generate the code you need without having to search the documentation for descriptions of the desired objects, properties, and methods. After you have recorded the macro in a separate module, you can clean up the recorded code and then cut and paste into your program as needed.

You may have noticed that the range arguments used in the examples above (A1, A1:G1, etc.) are of the same form used with cell references in the Excel application. The identical syntax is highly convenient because of its familiarity.

Finally, it is time to take a closer look at the Cells property, specifically the Cells property of the Application, Range, and Worksheet objects.

Using the Cells Property

The Cells property returns a Range object containing all (no indices used) or one (row and column indices are specified) of the cells in the active worksheet. When returning all of the cells in a worksheet you should only use the Cells property with the Application and Worksheet objects, as it would be redundant, and thus confusing, to use it with the Range object. For example,

```
Range("A1:A10").Cells
```

returns cells A1 through A10, thus making the use of the Cells property unnecessary.

The Cells **property will fail when used with the Application object, unless the active document is a worksheet.**

To return a single cell from a Worksheet object you must specify an index. The index can be a single value beginning with the upper-left most cell in the worksheet (for example, Cells(5) returns cell E1) or the index can contain a reference to the row and column index (recommended), as shown below.

```
Cells(1, 4).Value=5
Cells(1, "D").Value =5
```

This is the familiar notation used throughout this book. Both lines of code will enter the value 5 into cell D1 of the active worksheet. You can either use numerical or string values for the column reference. You should note that the column reference comes second in both examples and is separated from the row reference by a comma. I recommend using the second example above, as there is no ambiguity in the cell reference—though on occasion it is convenient to use a numerical reference for the column index.

Now consider some examples using the Cells property of the Range object.

```
Range("C5:E7").Cells(2, 2).Value = 50
Range("C5:E7").Cells(2, "A").Value = 50
```

The above two lines of code may confuse you, because they appear to be trying to return two different ranges within the same line of code. That is not the case, but you can use these examples to more carefully illustrate how the Cells property works.

Before reading on, guess in what worksheet cell each of these lines places the value 50. If you guessed cells B2 and A2 respectively, you're wrong. Instead, the value 50 is entered in cells D6 and A6, respectively, when using the above lines of code. Why? It's because the Cells property uses references relative to the selected range. Without the reference to the Range object in each statement (Range("C5:E7")), the current range is the entire worksheet, thus Cells(2,2) returns the range B2. However, when the selected range is C5:E7, Cells(2,2) will return the second row from this range (row 6) and the second column (column D). Using a string in the Cells property to index the column forces the selection of that column regardless of the range selected. The row index is still relative. Therefore, the second example above returns the range A6.

Working with Objects

You have now seen numerous examples of objects and how to set their properties and invoke their methods and events. But there are a couple of more tools that can be of tremendous use when working with objects: the With/End With code structure that, although never required, works well to simplify code, and the Object data type, which allows the VBA programmer to reference existing objects or even create new objects. The Object data type is not as easy to use as the numerical and string data types you're now familiar with, but it is an essential tool for the creation of useful and powerful VBA programs.

The With/End With Structure

VBA includes a programming structure designed to reduce the number of object qualifiers required in your code. Although the With/End With structure discussed in this section is not required under any circumstances, its use is often recommended because it makes your programs more readable. Also you will often see the With/End With structure in recorded macros. Consider the programming project from Chapter 1 as an example.

This is the Click() event procedure of a command button named cmdInsertText placed on the worksheet. You may remember that this program takes the value from the Text property of a Textbox control and inserts it into cell D1. After inserting the text in the cell, several formatting tools are used to visually enhance the text.

```
Private Sub cmdInsertText_Click()
```

Start at the beginning of the procedure, where the value of the Text property of the Textbox control txtName is inserted into cell D1 using the Cells property of the Worksheet object (not explicitly referenced, so the current worksheet is used).

```
Cells(1, "D").Value = txtName.Text
```

The worksheet cell D1 is then selected with the Select method of the Range object. The Select method applies to several objects, including the Worksheet and Chart objects. You will notice that using the Select method with the Range object will cause the selected range to be highlighted in the worksheet, just as if the user used the mouse to make the selection.

```
Cells(1, "D").Select
```

Immediately after you invoke the Select method, the With/End With structure appears. The With statement requires an object qualifier to immediately follow.

In this case, the Selection property is used to return the selected object (a Range object). The statement could have just as easily been written without the Select method and Selection property and entered using the Cells property to return the desired Range object (for example, With Cells(1, "D")).

```
With Selection
```

Once inside the structure, any property of the object can be set without having to qualify the object in each line of code. Subordinate objects and their properties can also be accessed. Each line within the structure must begin with the dot operator followed by the property or object name, then the method or assignment.

```
.Font.Bold = True
.Font.Name = "Arial"
.Font.Size = 72
.Font.Color = RGB(0, 0, 255)
.Columns.AutoFit
.Interior.Color = RGB(0, 255, 255)
.Borders.Weight = xlThick
.Borders.Color = RGB(0, 0, 255)
```

After all desired properties and/or methods have been invoked for the given object, the structure closes with End With.

```
End With
```

The Textbox control is activated (selected) before the procedure ends.

```
txtname.Activate
```

```
End Sub
```

The With/End With structure is straightforward and particularly useful when a large number of properties or methods of one object are to be addressed sequentially in a program.

The same procedure, written without the With/End With structure, follows:

```
Private Sub cmdInsertText_Click()
    Cells(1, "D").Value = txtName.Text
    Cells(1, "D").Select
    Cells(1, "D").Font.Bold = True
    Cells(1, "D").Font.Name = "Arial"
    Cells(1, "D").Font.Size = 72
    Cells(1, "D").Font.Color = RGB(0, 0, 255)
    Cells(1, "D").Columns.AutoFit
```

```
        Cells(1, "D").Interior.Color = RGB(0, 255, 255)
        Cells(1, "D").Borders.Weight = xlThick
        Cells(1, "D").Borders.Color = RGB(0, 0, 255)
        txtname.Activate
End Sub
```

Clearly, the use of the With/End With code structure makes the procedure neater and easier to read.

The Object Data Type

A chapter on Excel objects would not be complete without a discussion of the Object data type. If you find multiple instances of the same object in your program, then you can use an object variable to handle the reference rather than constantly retyping the qualifiers. Also, variables can be assigned meaningful names, making the program easier to interpret. Object variables are similar to other VBA data types in that they must be declared in code. For example,

```
Dim myObject as Object
```

declares an object variable named myObject. However, assigning a value to an object variable differs from assignments to more common data types. The Set keyword must be used to assign an object reference to a variable.

```
Set myObject = Range("A1:A15")
```

This will assign the Range object representing cells A1 through A15 to the variable myObject. Properties of the object can then be initialized in the usual way.

```
myObject.Font.Bold = True
```

This will set the values in cells A1 through A15 to be displayed in boldface type. Declaring variables using the general Object data type is not recommended because the object will not be bound to the variable until run-time. If VBA has trouble resolving references to various properties and methods when checking them at run-time, it can significantly slow down execution of a program. I recommend that you use object-specific data types whenever possible. Any object type can be used—just consult the Object Browser for a list of available types. Using the Range object, the above example can be rewritten thusly:

```
Dim myRange as Excel.Range
Set myRange=Range("A1:A15")
myRange.Font.Bold = True
```

You may also include the library (Excel) in your declaration to avoid any ambiguity. However, it is the object type (Range) that is important. Now the object will be referenced at compile time and VBA will have no trouble working out references to the properties and methods of the object, as the type of object and the library to which it belongs have been explicitly declared. You will see more examples of object variable types in the next section, in subsequent chapters, and in the Battlecell program.

For/Each and Looping through a Range

As stated at the beginning of this chapter, objects are often built from other objects. For example, a Workbook object may contain several Worksheet objects, which in turn contain multiple Range objects. It may be necessary, on occasion, to select individual objects contained within other objects. For example, you may want to access each individual Worksheet object in a Worksheets collection in order to set certain properties. If you're thinking *loops* then you are right on track, but you're not going to use any of the looping structures previously discussed. Instead, you'll use a looping structure specifically designed to iterate through collections. This is the For/Each loop, and its use is illustrated in the example that follows.

In this example, the background of a group of cells is changed to all different colors. To accomplish this, each cell is accessed individually as a Range object before setting the Color property of the Interior object. The For/Each loop is used for this purpose.

A few variable declarations are required to use with the For/Each loop. The object variable myRange will represent a collection of cells, while the object variable myCell will be used to represent each individual cell within myRange.

```
Dim myRange As Excel.Range
Dim myCell As Excel.Range
Dim I As Integer
```

The reference to the object variable myRange is set to cells A1 through A15.

```
Set myRange = Range("A1:A15")
```

The loop begins with the keywords For Each, followed by the variable that is to represent the individual elements in the collection—myCell, in this example. The keyword In is followed by the name of the collection—myRange, in this example.

```
For Each myCell In myRange
```

Inside the loop, properties and methods of the individual elements can be addressed. In this case, the Color property of the Interior object is changed using the QBColor() function. The QBColor() function accepts a value between 0 and 15 to return one of 16 standard color values. The variable I is used to change the color returned by the QBColor() function with each iteration through the loop. The variable I does not serve the function of the loop in any capacity whatsoever. Instead, the variable I is used to ensure that a different value is passed to the QBColor() function with each iteration through the loop. Once each statement within the loop is executed, the Next keyword is used to continue the loop.

```
        myCell.Interior.Color = QBColor(I)
        I = I + 1
Next
```

When all elements of the collection have been accessed and each statement executed, program execution resumes at the end of the loop as normal. The above code was added to a standard module in a sub procedure named CellColors() and executed. Figure 5.13 shows the result.

This a common technique for iterating through a group of spreadsheet cells. You will see more examples of this technique in the Battlecell program.

Chapter Project: Battlecell

The Battlecell game is a computer simulation of the classic board game Battleship. It is a natural choice for a game program using Excel because of the grid-like layout used in the game.

Project Statement

I want to create a computerized version of Battleship. A single Excel worksheet will serve as the game board. The game should begin with each player (the user

FIGURE 5.13

Using the QBColor() function in a For/Each loop

and the computer) setting five ships of varying size on a 10 × 10 grid. Then the players take turns "firing" at individual grid elements in hopes of striking an area occupied by a ship. Different ships can take a different number of hits before they are sunk. The game ends when one player manages to sink all of his or her opponent's ships.

Project Tools

A single worksheet in Excel can be formatted prior to any programming such that its appearance simulates a Battlecell game board. If you want, formatting code can be generated using the macro recorder. ActiveX controls (command buttons and labels) can be used with the interface. The program will require the use of event procedures belonging to the Workbook and Worksheet objects, as well as additional sub and function procedures. I expect the program to require extensive use of the Range object, various looping and decision code structures, and arrays. The code should reside in two component modules (one workbook and one worksheet). You can also use Standard modules, but they may not be necessary.

Project Algorithm

The Battlecell game programming will follow these rules:

1. The game board will be pre-formatted on a single Excel Worksheet.

2. The worksheet will clearly define two 10 × 10 grids, one for the player to place ships and one for the player to fire upon.

3. The worksheet will contain two Command Button controls for starting and resetting the game and two Label controls for displaying messages to the player.

4. The program will begin upon loading with a procedure that centers the application window, fills the application window with the workbook, and sets the display such that the entire game board is visible. The Workbook_Open() event procedure and the sub procedures created earlier in this chapter should work well for these tasks.

5. The worksheet will be protected to prevent the player from accidentally changing its appearance. Properties of the Worksheet object can be used to toggle the protection on and off when the game requires a change in the appearance of the worksheet.

6. To start the game, the player clicks on a Command Button control. The click event procedure of this control will contain code that initializes the necessary variables and displays instructions for the player on how to begin.

7. A Label control is used to tell the player to select a pre-defined number of cells that will simulate the placement of ships. With the placement of each ship on the grid, the program calls a validation procedure to ensure a legal selection has been made.

8. The validation procedures for the player's ship placements will test the selection for correct length, being within the proper grid or cell range, being either a single row or single column (no diagonals), and for no overlap with a previous selection.

9. The location of the player's ships will be displayed in blue.

10. After the player finishes placing ships, the click of a Command Button control will trigger the program to place the computer's ships in the appropriate grid following the same rules as stated above. The computer's ships must be marked without being visible to the player.

11. A message will be displayed via Label control to begin the game.

12. The player will begin by selecting a cell from the target grid. Validation procedures will test the selection for being within the correct range, correct length (one cell only), end of the game, and whether or not the cell has been selected previously.

13. For the player, the color of each selected cell will change to blue for a miss and red for a hit.

14. The computer's turn will occur automatically after each turn of the player's following the same rules. For now the selection of the cell by the computer will occur randomly within the proper grid or cell range. Intelligence will be added later.

15. For the computer, the color of each selected cell will change to red for a hit and green for a miss.

16. Label controls will be used to display messages for a hit or a miss and when the game is over.

17. A Command Button control will be available to the player at all times for resetting the game.

18. When a game ends the program will disable all functionality until the player selects the reset button.

19. When the player closes the workbook, the worksheet should be initialized to a startup appearance.

Adding the Code

The worksheet was formatted as shown in Figure 5.1. The formatting was recorded and stored in a standard module with the rest of the Battlecell project. The code from the recorded macro will not have to be executed unless the formatting on the worksheet is changed. The Name property of the ActiveX controls will have to be changed to the original values in design time.

First handle centering the application window and displaying the workbook such that the entire game board can be seen. As with Center.xls, the Workbook_Open() event procedure is used to trigger the code that centers the application window.

```
Private Sub Workbook_Open()
    Dim bookWidth As Integer
    Dim bookHeight As Integer
    Dim gameWidth As Integer
    Dim gameHeight As Integer
    Dim maxWidth As Integer
    Dim maxHeight As Integer
    Dim percentChangeW As Single
    Dim percentChangeH As Single
```

The player's screen width and height are obtained using the Width and Height properties of the Application object after the Excel window has been maximized.

```
    Application.WindowState = xlMaximized
    maxWidth = Application.Width
    maxHeight = Application.Height
```

The size of the application window is set to 600 × 450 points, which equates to 800 × 600 pixels. Program execution is then sent to the CenterApp() and CenterBook() sub procedures.

```
    Application.WindowState = xlNormal
    Application.Width = 600
    Application.Height = 450
    bookWidth = Application.UsableWidth
    bookHeight = Application.UsableHeight
    Call CenterApp(maxWidth, maxHeight)
    Call CenterBook(bookWidth, bookHeight)
```

The state of the current window is set to normal, and its Zoom property is set to 100%. This causes the worksheet to be displayed such that the game board is partially obscured behind the application window, as shown in Figure 5.14.

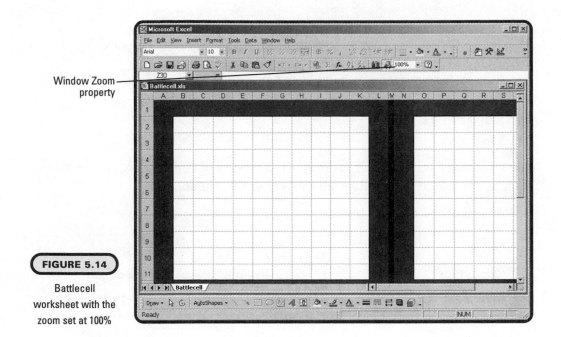

Window Zoom property

FIGURE 5.14

Battlecell worksheet with the zoom set at 100%

`ActiveWindow` is a property of the Application object and returns a Window object.

```
ActiveWindow.WindowState = xlNormal
ActiveWindow.Zoom = 100
```

The dimensions of the game board are obtained from the `Width` and `Height` properties of the Range objects (returned by the Range property of the Application object) that define the number of columns and rows used in the worksheet for the game's layout. To account for the width of the borders (title bar, scroll bars, and row numbers) along the workbook window, the Range objects were defined with a couple of extra columns and rows. As there is only one Worksheet object, the path to these Range objects does not have to be specified. The Range objects are obtained from the current or active worksheet, which must be the Battlecell worksheet, as it has just been opened.

```
gameWidth = Range("A1:AA1").Width
gameHeight = Range("A1:A18").Height
```

The fraction that represents the difference between the size of the window and the currently oversized game board is calculated for both dimensions. The larger of these two values is used to decrease the `Zoom` property on the Window object that is obtained using the `ActiveWindow` property of the Application object.

```
percentChangeW = 1 - bookWidth / gameWidth
percentChangeH = 1 - bookHeight / gameHeight
```

```
    If percentChangeH >= percentChangeW Then
        ActiveWindow.Zoom = ActiveWindow.Zoom - percentChangeH *
ActiveWindow.Zoom
    Else
        ActiveWindow.Zoom = ActiveWindow.Zoom - percentChangeW *
ActiveWindow.Zoom
    End If
```

The scroll bars are set such that row 1 is at the top of the window and column 1 (A) is at the left of the window (all the way to the top and left).

```
    ActiveWindow.ScrollRow = 1
    ActiveWindow.ScrollColumn = 1
End Sub
```

The CenterApp() and CenterBook() sub procedures are essentially the same as in the Center.xls application. The application is centered in the player's screen because the width and height of the Application object is 600 × 450 points.

```
Private Sub CenterApp(maxWidth As Integer, maxHeight As Integer)
    Dim appLeft As Integer
    Dim appTop As Integer
    appLeft = maxWidth / 2 - 300
    appTop = maxHeight / 2 - 225
    Application.Left = appLeft
    Application.Top = appTop
End Sub
```

Figure 5.15 illustrates the result of setting some of the properties of the Application object listed in this program.

You can use the the ActiveWindow property of the Application object throughout these procedures without having to worry about the wrong object being returned. This is because these procedures will only be executed when the Battlecell application is first opened. Thus, the ActiveWindow property will always return the newly opened Battlecell.xls Window object.

```
Private Sub CenterBook(bookWidth As Integer, bookHeight As Integer)
    ActiveWindow.WindowState = xlNormal
    ActiveWindow.Width = bookWidth
    ActiveWindow.Height = bookHeight
    ActiveWindow.Left = 0
    ActiveWindow.Top = 0
End Sub
```

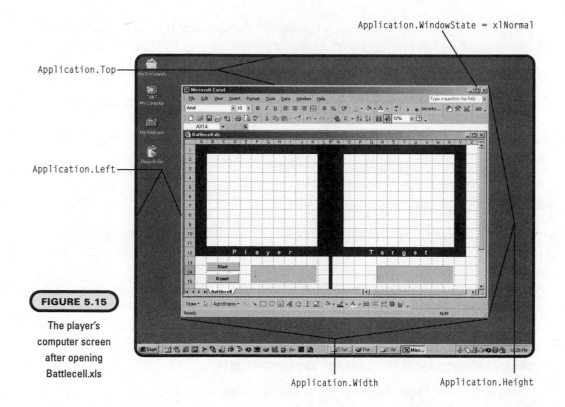

Application.Top

Application.Left

Application.WindowState = xlNormal

Application.Width

Application.Height

FIGURE 5.15

The player's
computer screen
after opening
Battlecell.xls

You can use the full object path if you prefer. For example, Application.Windows ("Battlecell.xls").Top = 0 leaves no ambiguity as to the Window object that will be altered.

The rest of the code is contained in the component module belonging to the Battlecell worksheet. Several module-level variables are declared in the general declarations section of the module. The function of these variables will be discussed as they are used in the program.

```
Option Explicit
Dim playerRange As Range
Dim targetRange As Range
Dim allowSelection As Boolean
Dim totalCells
Dim numCellsInShip As Integer
Dim shipType
Dim nextShip As Integer
Dim bombsAway As Boolean
Dim numPlayerHits As Integer
Dim numTargetHits As Integer
```

The Click() event procedure of a Command Button control is used to begin the game. The Caption property of the control is initially set to "Start" but after the player's ships are placed, the Caption property is set to "Done." If the game is just starting, then code execution is sent to the BeginGame() sub procedure. The variable numCellsInShip is used to keep track of the number of worksheet cells that must be selected by the player for each ship placed.

```
Private Sub cmdPlaceShips_Click()
    If cmdPlaceShips.Caption = "Start" Then
        numCellsInShip = 5
        BeginGame
```

After the player's ships are placed, the same Command Button control is used to initialize variables and send program execution to the next phase of the game. First, the Command Button control is disabled and the Caption properties of the Label controls are set to tell the player to begin firing at the computer's ships. The variable bombsAway is used to tell the program that the game is in the active phase—when the player and computer are firing at each other's ships. The decision structure ends with a call to the TargetShips() sub procedure that is used to place the computer's ships on the appropriate grid.

```
    ElseIf cmdPlaceShips.Caption = "Done" Then
        cmdPlaceShips.Enabled = False
        lblDefense.Caption = ""
        lblOffense.Caption = "You may begin."
        bombsAway = True
        TargetShips
    End If
End Sub
```

The BeginGame() sub procedure is used to initialize several variables for starting the game. The shipType variable declared in the general declarations section of the module as a variant is converted to an array using the Array() function and initialized with five strings. These strings represent the type of ship that is to be placed on the game board by the player. The Array() function is also used to initialize the totalCells variable with integer values that represent the number of cells in each type of ship. It is a bit unusual to create variable arrays in this manner. However, when the array is small and the values the array must hold are unordered (in the sense that they cannot be easily initialized with a loop), then the Array() function is a good choice.

```
Private Sub BeginGame()
    shipType = Array("Carrier", "Destroyer", "Battleship", "Submarine",
```

```
"Patrol Boat")
    totalCells = Array(5, 4, 3, 3, 2)
```

The Command Button control is disabled and its caption removed to prevent the player from triggering the click event procedure during the wrong phase of the game.

```
cmdPlaceShips.Enabled = False
cmdPlaceShips.Caption = ""
```

A message is displayed using the Caption property of a Label control. String concatenation is used to build a string out of the appropriate variables that tells the player how many cells to select for placement of the first ship.

```
lblDefense.Caption = "Place the " & shipType(0) & Chr(13) & "Choose "
& numCellsInShip & _

                    " Contiguous Cells"
```

The variable allowSelection is used throughout the program to toggle player interaction with the game board (worksheet) on and off.

```
allowSelection = True
numPlayerHits = 0
numTargetHits = 0
End Sub
```

The game now enters a phase in which the player must place his/her ships on the game board. There are a total of five ships to be placed. The size of these ships varies from five cells (simulating an aircraft carrier) to two cells (simulating a patrol boat). Highlighting worksheet cells of the correct length within the Player section of the game board places the ships. This will require input from the player and, thus, validation sub procedures. The Worksheet_SelectionChange() event procedure is used to capture the player's selection. The Worksheet_SelectionChange() event procedure is triggered whenever the player selects a new range on the worksheet. Excel passes the range of cells selected by the player to this event procedure.

```
Private Sub Worksheet_SelectionChange(ByVal Target As Range)
    Dim inRange As Boolean
```

First, the value of the allowSelection variable is checked to see if the game is in a phase where player interaction with the worksheet is turned on. If the value of the allowSelection variable is false, then the program exits this procedure immediately, otherwise program execution proceeds through the rest of the procedure.

```
If allowSelection = False Then Exit Sub
```

If the game is to the point where the player and computer are firing at each other's ships, then the bombsAway variable is true and the code inside this decision structure is executed. The If/Then decision structure listed below tests a Boolean variable (bombsAway), therefore the rest of the conditional expression (for example, If bombsAway = True) can be omitted.

```
If bombsAway  Then
```

The function procedure CheckTarget() is used to validate the player's selection. If the player's selection is valid, then the CheckTarget() function procedure returns true and the program calls two more sub procedures. The sub procedure HitOrMiss() will check the player's selection for a hit or miss on the computer's ships. The sub procedure ComputerFire() will simulate the computer's counterattack.

```
inRange = CheckTarget(Target)
If Not inRange Then Exit Sub
Call HitOrMiss(Target)
ComputerFire
```

If the player and computer are not firing at each other, then the player is placing ships on the game board. Since the requirements of the player's selection differ, a different validation procedure, CheckRange(), is used to test the selection. If the selection is valid, then the sub procedure AssignShip() is called to change the color of the selected cells, increment the necessary variables, and display the message that tells the player to place the next ship on the board.

```
Else
    inRange = CheckRange(Target)

    If inRange Then
        Call AssignShip(Target)
    End If
End If
End Sub
```

The CheckRange() function procedure is used to validate the player's selection for placing a ship on the game board. The cell range representing the player's selection is passed to the procedure as a range variable named userSelection. The selection must be tested for length, being within the correct range, being within one row or one column, and to make sure there's no overlap with a previous selection.

```
Private Function CheckRange(userSelection As Range) As Boolean
    Dim col1 As String
```

```
Dim col2 As String
Dim row1 As Integer
Dim row2 As Integer
Dim c As Range
```

Checking for proper length is easy. The `Count` property of the Range object representing the player's selection is compared to the value stored in the `numCellsInShip` variable. If these two values are not equivalent, then the function procedure is assigned the value false and the function is immediately exited.

```
If userSelection.Count = numCellsInShip Then
    CheckRange = True
Else
    MsgBox ("Please select " & numCellsInShip & " cells")
    CheckRange = False
    Exit Function
End If
```

After the player's selection passes the test for length it must be tested for being within the proper range of cells on the game board. First the column and row indices are extracted from the selected range using VBA string functions (`Mid()` and `Instr()`) and the `Address` property of the Range object. The `Address` property returns a string representation of the Range object (for example, "$C$4:$E$4").

```
col1 = Mid(userSelection.Address, 2, 1)
col2 = Mid(userSelection.Address, InStr(1, userSelection.Address, ":",
1) + 2, 1)
row1 = userSelection.Row
row2 = Val(Mid(userSelection.Address, InStr(4, userSelection.Address,
col2, 1) + 2, 2))
```

The values extracted above are tested to see if they fall between rows 2 and 11 and between columns B and K. If the test fails, the function procedure is assigned the value false and the function is immediately exited.

```
If ((row1 > 1) And (row2 < 12)) And ((col1 > "A") And (col2 < "L"))
Then
    CheckRange = True
Else
    MsgBox ("Selection out of range")
    CheckRange = False
    Exit Function
End If
```

Next, the selection is tested to make sure it falls within a single row or column. This test really only applies to the placement of the destroyer (4 cells), as the test for length will rule out any other combination (that is, you can't select an odd number of cells across more than one column or row). Again, if the test fails, the function procedure is assigned the value false and the function is immediately exited.

```
If (col1 <> col2) And (row1 <> row2) Then
    MsgBox ("Selection must be within the same row or column")
    CheckRange = False
    Exit Function
End If
```

Finally, the selection is tested to see if it overlaps a previous selection. To accomplish this task, a For/Each loop is used to compare the color of the cells in the selected range to the value returned for the color blue. The range variable c is used to represent each element in the range variable userSelection. Essentially, the color of each individual cell in the selected range is tested, and if any of them are blue then the function is assigned the value false. The Color property of the Interior object subordinate to the Range object is used to return the long integer used to represent color. This is compared to the long integer returned by VBA's RGB() function. The RGB() function receives three integer values between 0 and 255. The three parameters represent the red, green, and blue components of the desired color. The larger the value of the parameter the larger the contribution from that color to the final color returned by the function. The values 0, 0, and 255 are used in the RGB() function because these are the values used to set the color in the AssignShip() sub procedure.

```
For Each c In userSelection
    If c.Interior.Color = RGB(0, 0, 255) Then
        MsgBox ("Selection cannot overlap another ship!")
        CheckRange = False
    End If
Next
End Function
```

The sub procedure AssignShip() is called from the Worksheet_SelectionChange() event procedure after the player's selection has been validated. The range of cells is passed to this procedure as a Range object and stored in the range variable named Target.

```
Private Sub AssignShip(Target As Range)
```

The protection on the worksheet is turned off so that the color of the selected range can be changed to blue. The RGB() function is used to select the color. The color is changed by altering the Color property of the Interior object subordinate to the Range object in the Excel object model. After altering the color, the worksheet protection is turned back on using the Protect method of the Worksheet object. No arguments are passed to the Unprotect and Protect methods, because the default behavior is all that is needed (that is, no password is required and the contents of the worksheet will be protected).

```
ActiveSheet.Unprotect
Target.Interior.Color = RGB(0, 0, 255)
ActiveSheet.Protect
```

The module-level variable nextShip which is used to determine the type and length of the ship to be placed on the game board, is incremented by one. When the value of nextShip reaches 5 the player has placed all ships and you're ready to start the game.

```
nextShip = nextShip + 1
If nextShip = 5 Then
    lblDefense.Caption = "All ships are Placed"
```

After all the player's ships have been placed, the Command Button control used to start the game is enabled and its Caption property set to "Done." The allowSelection variable is set to false to disable the code in the Worksheet_SelectionChange() event procedure. This forces the player to click on a Command Button control to continue program execution.

```
        cmdPlaceShips.Enabled = True
        cmdPlaceShips.Caption = "Done"
        allowSelection = False
Else
```

If there are more ships to be placed, then the variable numCellsInShip is set to the value stored in the variable array totalCells at index value nextShip. Thus, if the previous ship required five cells, then the next ship requires four cells, followed by three cells, and finally two cells. The length of the next ship to be placed is then passed on to the player via the Caption property of a Label control.

```
        numCellsInShip = totalCells(nextShip)
        lblDefense.Caption = "Place the " & shipType(nextShip) & Chr(13) &
"Choose " & numCellsInShip & _
                        " Contiguous Cells"
```

```
        End If
    End Sub
```

At this point in the program the game board appears, as shown in Figure 5.16.

After the player's ships are placed, the Command Button control with its Caption property set to "Done" must be selected by the player to continue the game. The activated code is in the cmdPlaceShips_Click() event procedure listed previously. The sub procedure called from this sequence of events is TargetShips(). The TargetShips() sub procedure is used to randomly place the computer's ships on the game board within the target grid.

```
Private Sub TargetShips()
    Dim randomCol As Integer
    Dim randomRow As Integer
    Dim randomRowOrCol As Integer
    Dim rangeStr As String
    Dim tempStr As String
    Dim upperBoundCol As Integer
    Dim lowerBoundCol As Integer
    Dim upperBoundRow As Integer
    Dim lowerBoundRow As Integer
    Dim compSelection As Range
```

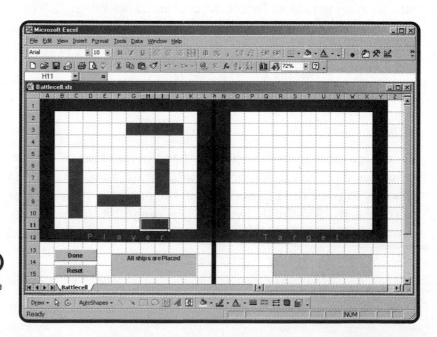

FIGURE 5.16

The Battlecell game board after player ship placement

The random number generator is initialized and the `nextShip` variable is set to 0 so it can be used to set the length of the computer's ships.

```
Randomize
nextShip = 0
```

A `Do-Loop` is used to iterate through the code that places the computer's ships on the game board. A `For/Next` loop is not a good choice here because even though the program must place exactly five ships on the game board, it may take more than five iterations through the loop to place these ships.

```
Do
    numCellsInShip = totalCells(nextShip)
```

Four variables are used to set the lower and upper bounds for ship placement. The range of allowed rows is between row 2 and 7 if the ship to be placed is the carrier (5 cells). The range of allowed columns is between column O and column T for placement of the carrier. Since ships will be placed starting from the lower bound to the upper bound, the upper bound in the cell range is dependent on the number of cells in the ship.

```
upperBoundRow = 11 - numCellsInShip + 1
lowerBoundRow = 2
upperBoundCol = 24 - numCellsInShip + 1
lowerBoundCol = 15
```

Whether a ship is placed inside a column or row is chosen randomly along with the row or column that will contain the computer's ship. Since the `Rnd` function returns a number between 0 and 1, the `Int()` function is used to convert the result to an integer.

```
randomRowOrCol = Int(2 * Rnd)
```

The random numbers returned to represent the row or column fall between the lower and upper bounds defined above.

```
randomRow = Int((upperBoundRow - lowerBoundRow + 1) * Rnd + lowerBoundRow)
randomCol = Int((upperBoundCol - lowerBoundCol + 1) * Rnd + lowerBoundCol)
```

Once the lower and upper bounds are determined, a string representing the range of cells containing the computer's ship is constructed. Concatenation and several string functions are used to construct the strings. For example, if the ship that requires five cells is to be placed in column 15 ("O"), and the lower bound on the row is 2, then the resultant string stored in the variable `rangeStr` is "O2:O6."

```
        If randomRowOrCol = 1 Then
            rangeStr = Chr(randomCol + 64) & Trim(Str(randomRow)) & ":" &
Chr(randomCol + 64) & _
                        Trim(Str(randomRow + numCellsInShip - 1))
        Else
            rangeStr = Chr(randomCol + 64) & Trim(Str(randomRow)) & ":" &
Chr(randomCol + 64 + numCellsInShip - 1) _
                        & Trim(Str(randomRow))
        End If
```

The `Range` property of the Worksheet object is used to convert the string variable `rangeStr` to a Range object and store it in the range variable `compSelection`.

```
        Set compSelection = Range(rangeStr)
```

The range variable `compSelection` is passed to the validation function procedure `CheckRangeComp()` to test for a previous selection. If the range passes validation, then the sub procedure `AssignShipComp()` is called to set the ship on the game board. If the range fails validation, then it will take another iteration through the loop to place the ship.

```
        If CheckRangeComp(compSelection) = True Then
            Call AssignShipComp(compSelection)
```

The variable `nextShip` is incremented so that the next ship to be placed can be selected for the next iteration through the `Do-Loop`.

```
            nextShip = nextShip + 1
        End If
    Loop While (nextShip < 5)
End Sub
```

The function procedure `CheckRangeComp()` is used to test the computer-generated range variable `compSelection` from the `TargetShips()` sub procedure for overlap with a previous selection. Cells that hold a computer's ship have a `Value` property of "X" as set by the `AssignShipComp()` sub procedure. (The cells in the target grid have been preformatted such that the background and foreground colors are equivalent, thus the X is not visible to the player.)

HINT It is possible for the player to cheat by highlighting all cells in the target range. This will make the X visible for as long as the cells are highlighted. A better choice of strings to use in place of X would be a space. However, this is hard to illustrate in text, so stick with the X.

The `CheckRangeComp()` function procedure uses a simple `For/Each` loop to test each element in the range variable `compSelection` for a `Value` property of `"X"`. If an `"X"` is found within the selected range, then the function returns false and the computer must select another location to place its ship.

```
Private Function CheckRangeComp(compSelection As Range) As Boolean
    Dim c As Range
    CheckRangeComp = True
    For Each c In compSelection
        If c.Value = "X" Then
            CheckRangeComp = False
        End If
    Next
End Function
```

The `AssignShipComp()` sub procedure is used to set the `Value` property of each cell in the range selected by the computer to `"X"`. The protection must be toggled off before changing the `Value` property of the cells.

```
Private Sub AssignShipComp(compSelection As Range)
    Dim c As Range
    ActiveSheet.Unprotect
    For Each c In compSelection
        c.Value = "X"
    Next
    ActiveSheet.Protect
End Sub
```

After all ships are placed and the message to the player to begin the game is displayed, the game board appears as shown in Figure 5.17.

At this point, the player can begin the game by firing at the computer's ships in the target region of the game board. When the player makes a selection in the target region, the `Worksheet_SelectionChange()` event procedure listed earlier is triggered. Re-examination of the code in the `Worksheet_SelectionChange()` event procedure will tell you that, at this phase of the program, execution proceeds to the `CheckTarget()` function procedure. The range selected by the player is passed to the function as a range variable that is stored in another range variable named `playerSelection`. The `CheckTarget()` function procedure validates the player's selection for length (one cell), being within the correct range of cells, and equivalence to a previous selection.

```
Private Function CheckTarget(playerSelection As Range) As Boolean
```

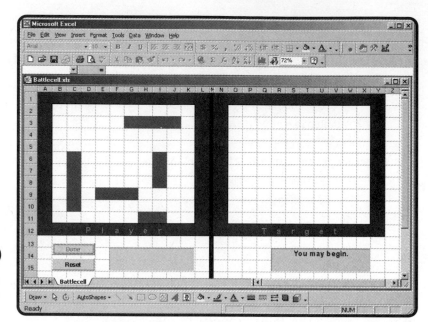

FIGURE 5.17

The Battlecell game
board after all ships
are placed

The variable c should be familiar by now. It will be used in a For/Each loop to iterate through a range of cells. Using the Range property of the Worksheet object,
the module-level variable targetRange is set to the range of cells representing the
target grid that holds the computer's ships.

```
Dim c As Range
Set targetRange = Range("O2:X11")
```

If the Count property of the Range object representing the player's selection
returns a value greater than one, then an error message is displayed in a message
box and the function is exited.

```
If playerSelection.Count > 1 Then
        MsgBox ("You can only fire at one cell!")
        CheckTarget = False
        Exit Function
End If
```

A For/Each loop iterates through the range of cells representing the target grid
on the game board. First, the Address property of each element is checked for
equality with the Address property of the player's selection. If the two strings are
equal, then the player's selection is validated for proper range and the function
is assigned the value true. If the player selects a cell outside the required range,
then nothing happens and the function procedure returns its default value of
false and the player must make another selection.

```
    For Each c In targetRange
        If c.Address = playerSelection.Address Then
            CheckTarget = True
```

If the player's selection is within the required range, then the value returned by the Color property of the Interior object of the selected cell is tested for equality to the value returned by the RGB() function for the color red (used to denote a hit) or blue (used to denote a miss). If the conditional evaluates as true, then the cell was selected previously and the appropriate error message is sent to the player via a message box.

```
            If c.Interior.Color = RGB(0, 0, 255) Or c.Interior.Color =
RGB(255, 0, 0) Then
                MsgBox ("You have already selected that cell!")
                CheckTarget = False
            End If
        End If
    Next
End Function
```

If the player's selection is valid, then the code in the Worksheet_Selection-Change() event procedure next sends program execution to the HitOrMiss() sub procedure. Again the player's selection is passed in a range variable. As the name indicates, the HitOrMiss() sub procedure tests the player's selection for a hit or miss on one of the computer's ships.

```
Private Sub HitOrMiss(Target As Range)
```

Basically, if the cell selected by the player contains an X, then the player scores a hit. The color of the cell is set to red, the result of the selection is displayed for the player via the Caption property of a Label control, and the module-level variable numTargetHits is incremented by one.

```
    If Target.Value = "X" Then
        ActiveSheet.Unprotect
        Target.Interior.Color = RGB(255, 0, 0)
        ActiveSheet.Protect
        lblOffense.Caption = "HIT!"
        lblDefense.Caption = ""
        numTargetHits = numTargetHits + 1
```

The variable numTargetHits is tested to see if the player has sunk all the computer's ships (the total number of cells occupied by all five ships is 17). If all ships have been sunk, then the game is over and the appropriate message is displayed.

The variables `bombsAway` and `allowSelection` are set to `False` to effectively turn off the `Worksheet_SelectionChange()` event procedure and end the game.

```
If (numTargetHits = 17) Then
    lblOffense.Caption = "All Ships Sunk! YOU WIN!"
    bombsAway = False
    allowSelection = False
End If
Exit Sub
End If
```

If the cell selected by the player does not contain an X, then the player is informed of the miss and the color of the cell is changed to blue.

```
lblOffense.Caption = "You Missed!"
ActiveSheet.Unprotect
Target.Interior.Color = RGB(0, 0, 255)
ActiveSheet.Protect
End Sub
```

Immediately after the player's selection is evaluated with the `CheckTarget()` and `HitOrMiss()` procedures, the `Worksheet_SelectionChange()` event procedure sends program execution to the `ComputerFire()` sub procedure. The `ComputerFire()` sub procedure simulates the computer's turn at firing upon the player's ships.

```
Private Sub ComputerFire()
    Dim colIndex As String
    Dim rowIndex As String
    Dim targetCell As String
    Dim targetRange As Range
    Dim tryAgain As Boolean
```

The computer will fire at the player's ships randomly with no consideration of previous hits and/or misses. This makes the Battlecell game pretty easy for the player to win. In the next chapter, some intelligence will be added to the program to make the game a bit more challenging. The code in this procedure runs inside of a `Do-Loop` until a valid cell is randomly obtained.

```
Randomize
Do
```

First, a string is constructed representing a single cell within the desired range and converted to a range variable. This is the same method used to randomly construct range variables representing the location of the computer's ships in the `TargetShips()` sub procedure.

```
colIndex = Chr(Int(10 * Rnd + 2) + 64)
rowIndex = Trim(Str(Int(10 * Rnd + 2)))
targetCell = colIndex & rowIndex
Set targetRange = Range(targetCell)
```

The random selection must be tested to see if it has been selected previously. If the selection was used previously, then the variable used to continue the Do-Loop is set to true and it will require at least one more iteration through the Do-Loop to select a cell.

```
If targetRange.Interior.Color = RGB(255, 0, 0) Or
targetRange.Interior.Color = RGB(0, 255, 0) Then
        tryAgain = True
    End If
```

If the color of the selected cell is blue, then it contains one of the player's ships. A message signifying the hit is displayed in a Label control, the cell color is changed to red, and the module-level variable numPlayerHits is incremented by one.

```
If targetRange.Interior.Color = RGB(0, 0, 255) Then
    lblDefense.Caption = "HIT!"
    ActiveSheet.Unprotect
    targetRange.Interior.Color = RGB(255, 0, 0)
    ActiveSheet.Protect
    numPlayerHits = numPlayerHits + 1
    tryAgain = False
```

After the Do-Loop conditional variable tryAgain is set to false, the numPlayerHits variable is tested to see if the game is over, this time with the computer winning.

```
If (numPlayerHits = 17) Then
    lblDefense.Caption = "All Ships Sunk! COMPUTER WINS!"
    allowSelection = False
    bombsAway = False
    Exit Sub
End If
```

The first part of the decision structure tested the selection for the color blue. The next part of the decision structure tests if the selection is green or red. If the selected cell is not green or red, then its color is changed to green, signifying a miss by the computer. The Do-Loop conditional variable is set to false, and a message is displayed in a Label control.

```
      ElseIf targetRange.Interior.Color <> RGB(0, 255, 0) And _
            targetRange.Interior.Color <> RGB(255, 0, 0) Then
        ActiveSheet.Unprotect
        targetRange.Interior.Color = RGB(0, 255, 0)
        ActiveSheet.Protect
        tryAgain = False
        lblDefense.Caption = "A Miss!"
      End If
  Loop While (tryAgain = True)
End Sub
```

After a valid selection is made by the computer and the results displayed, it is again the player's turn and play proceeds until a winner is declared. Figure 5.18 shows the appearance of the game board after the player has won a game.

The player always has the option of restarting the game with a click on the Command Button control with the Caption property of "Reset". This triggers the Click() event procedure of the Command Button control that is listed below.

The cmdReset_Click() event procedure is used to re-initialize some of the variables described earlier. The procedure also calls the ClearBoard() sub procedure that is used to reset the game board.

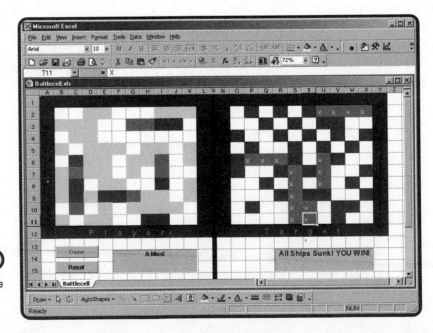

FIGURE 5.18

The Battlecell game board after a win by the player

```
Private Sub cmdReset_Click()
    cmdPlaceShips.Caption = "Start"
    cmdPlaceShips.Enabled = True
    ClearBoard
    allowSelection = False
    bombsAway = False
End Sub
```

The sub procedure `ClearBoard()` resets the game board by removing the color from both the target range and player range. Also cleared are the cells in the target range containing an X that were used to set the location of the computer's ships.

```
Public Sub ClearBoard()
    Dim c As Range
    Set playerRange = Range("B2:K11")
    Set targetRange = Range("O2:X11")
    ActiveSheet.Unprotect
    playerRange.Interior.ColorIndex = xlNone
    targetRange.Clear
```

The `ColorIndex` property of the Interior object is used to reset the color of the cells. The `ColorIndex` property accepts integer values between 1 and 56 or two constants (`xlNone` and `xlAutomatic`). The `RGB()` function could have been used with the `Color` property instead of the `ColorIndex` property.

```
    targetRange.Interior.ColorIndex = xlNone
```

Although pre-formatted this way, the color of the font is set to white to ensure that any text entered in these cells remains invisible.

```
    targetRange.Font.ColorIndex = 2
```

Finally, the `Caption` properties of the Label controls and a couple of module-level variables are re-initialized.

```
    lblOffense.Caption = ""
    lblDefense.Caption = ""
    ActiveSheet.Protect
    numCellsInShip = 5
    nextShip = 0
End Sub
```

The last procedure to be examined in the Battlecell game is contained back in the component module representing the Workbook object. The `Workbook_BeforeClose()`

event procedure is used to trigger code that resets the game board before the workbook is closed. This procedure was added just in case the player does not reset the game board with the Command Button control before closing the workbook.

```
Private Sub Workbook_BeforeClose(Cancel As Boolean)
```

The ClearBoard() procedure contained in the component module representing the Worksheet object containing the game is called via its full path (Battlebook is the Name property of the project, Battlesheet is the Name property of the worksheet).

```
    Battlebook.Battlesheet.ClearBoard
```

To alter a property of an ActiveX control, the Object property of the OLEObjects Collection object (discussed in Chapter 10), subordinate to the Worksheet object, is used to return the ActiveX object.

```
    ActiveSheet.OLEObjects("cmdPlaceShips").Object.Enabled = True
    ActiveSheet.OLEObjects("cmdPlaceShips").Object.Caption = "Start"
```

The next line saves the workbook to prevent a prompt to the player asking whether or not changes should be saved. This is a bit dangerous since it is possible for a player to alter the workbook in such a way that the game won't work if the changes are saved. However, to do so the player would have to remove the protection from the worksheet and/or edit the code for the program from the VBA IDE.

```
    ActiveWorkbook.Save
End Sub
```

This concludes the Battlecell program. The program is not terribly long or even that complex, but is starting to approach a level of programming that makes the game fun even for adults. The intention of the program is to help you get comfortable using VBA objects and navigating through Excel's object hierarchy. The Range object is used extensively in the Battlecell program, and that will be typical of the VBA programs you write. The use of Workbook and Worksheet object event procedures is also prevalent in the Battlecell program. To take full advantage of the power of VBA, you should get comfortable identifying and using these procedures.

Chapter Summary

This chapter represents a critical phase in your development as a VBA programmer. Understanding objects and their role in creating dynamic and powerful applications is critical in any programming language including VBA.

In this chapter you learned how to use several of Excel's top-level objects and how to navigate through its object model. Specifically, you looked at the Application,

Workbook, Window, Worksheet, and Range objects in detail. Some of the event procedures, methods, and properties of these objects were also introduced.

Next you learned about some of the tools available in VBA for working with objects. This included the Object Browser for navigating through the object hierarchy and getting fast help to an object of interest. The With/End With code structure, object data type, and For/Each loop were also introduced.

Finally, the Battlecell program illustrated a practical and fun programming example that relied heavily on Excel's top-level objects. As there is a tendency for such things to occur, a few subordinate objects also appeared in the program.

CHALLENGES

1. Write a VBA procedure that outputs a range after being selected by the user (one statement will do it).

2. Write a VBA procedure that firsts asks the user to input some text and then changes the caption of the current window to the text value input by the user.

3. Write a VBA procedure that adds three additional workbooks to the application and ten additional worksheets to each workbook added. Hint: Use object variables and nested For/Each loops.

4. Write a VBA procedure that deletes all but one worksheet in all workbooks currently open in the Excel application. Again use nested For/Each loops. To turn off prompts to the user, use the DisplayAlerts property of the Application object.

5. Open a workbook with more than one worksheet. Write a procedure that inserts a string in each cell in the range A1:E5 in every worksheet. Make the string a concatenation of the worksheet name and cell address (for example, Sheet1:$A$3).

6. Use the Worksheet_Change() event procedure to alter the properties of the Font object (Bold, Size, Color, etc.) after the user enters text into a cell. Use a With/End With code structure.

7. Create a spreadsheet that contains several names in multiple rows and columns.

8. Write a VBA procedure that finds a specific name within a highlighted range on the spreadsheet. Use the Find method of the Range object and the Worksheet_SelectionChange() event procedure of the Worksheet object. Refer to the Object Browser or online help for syntactic requirements. Then record a macro with a similar function and compare the recorded procedure to your own.

Enhancing VBA Programs: Adding Multimedia and Intelligence

The Battlecell program from Chapter 5 is a challenging and fun project for a beginning programmer. However, the game may not be much fun for the player because it is rather plain and very easy to win. This chapter will examine methods that make a program more visually and intellectually stimulating by adding intelligence and multimedia elements to the Battlecell program from Chapter 5. Multimedia elements will include adding animation and sound to a VBA program.

This chapter will cover

- **Multimedia (animation and sound)**

- **Artificial intelligence**

- **Chapter project: Enhanced Battlecell**

Project: Enhanced Battlecell

The Battlecell program from Chapter 5 will be enhanced to add intelligence on the computer's side in an effort to make the game more challenging for the player. The Battlecell program will also be made more aesthetically appealing using animation and sound. Figure 6.1 shows an example of the enhanced Battlecell game in progress.

Adding Multimedia to a Program

Multimedia is the use of multiple forms of communication. In programming, there are basically three methods for communicating with the player: text, sound, and graphics. There are a number of choices available to the programmer for delivering each form of communication, ranging from very simple methods of displaying text (font type, size, and color) to more complex methods of presenting audio and visual elements (hand-drawn animations, movies, interactive graphics, and so on). This chapter will take a look at some relatively simple methods available in VBA for including animation and sound in a program.

Animation in VBA

Most people think of animation as the presentation of a sequence of images at a rate fast enough that the elements within the image appear to be moving in a

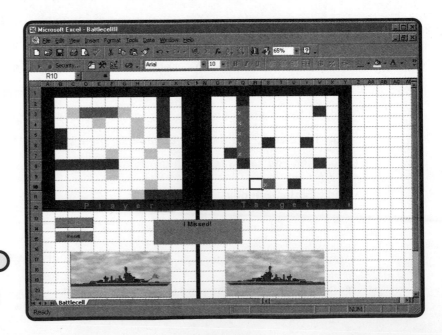

FIGURE 6.1

The enhanced
Battlecell game
(in progress)

realistic fashion. You've probably seen one of those little books containing a sequence of images that, when flipped through very quickly with a thumb, give the illusion of movement. This is one form of animation and you'll see examples of this type later in the chapter. However, if you define animation as any "visual dynamic," then you have more choices available.

There are a number of simple techniques you can use in VBA and Excel to include animation in a program. Some of these techniques are

- Changing cell formatting, such as color and borders.
- Animating text with a number of possible techniques.
- Altering the properties of ActiveX controls such that they move around the screen.
- Displaying a sequence of images within a single Image control.

Regardless of the type, your animation will certainly involve the use of a timed sequence of events. Typically, this means the program will have to access the system clock. You may recall that the Math Game project from Chapter 3 used the OnTime method of the Application object to repeatedly execute a specified procedure at a set interval (one second). The basic syntax of the OnTime method follows:

```
Application.OnTime(EarliestTime, Procedure, LatestTime, Schedule)
```

The Math Game can be considered an example of animation, as it displays a visual dynamic with the timer used to count down from 60 seconds. Although the OnTime method of the Application object could be an excellent tool for creating animations in VBA, it is severely limited by the minimum time interval (one second) in which it works. Unfortunately, the EarliestTime argument requires a specified time in date format, and it is not possible to format the Date data type with fractional values for the second. This limits the OnTime method to timers and clocks, or other examples in which the visual dynamic (animation) in the program can be relatively slow (that is, does not have to be updated more frequently than once per second). Another programming example illustrating the use of the OnTime method is included with the source code for this chapter (AnimationDemos.xls).

To create an interesting animation you must be able to access the system clock at intervals smaller than one second. The only way to access the system clock using tools provided within VBA is with the Timer function. The Timer function takes no arguments and returns a value of type Single representing the number of seconds passed since midnight.

 On the Macintosh, the resolution of the Timer function is one second.

The following code example, when executed, will display in a message box the number of seconds passed since midnight. It is important to note that the precision of the number returned by the Timer function is to two decimal places, as shown in Figure 6.2.

```
Dim seconds As Single
seconds = Timer
MsgBox (seconds)
```

To use the Timer function with animation, create a procedure that delays program execution by a specified interval of time.

```
Private Sub Delay(pauseTime As Single)
    Dim begin As Single
    begin = Timer
    Do While Timer < (begin + pauseTime)
        DoEvents
    Loop
End Sub
```

FIGURE 6.2

Message box displayed from the code example illustrating the use of the Timer function

This procedure accepts one parameter (pauseTime) that is used to set the length of the delay in program execution when called. The delay is caused by the Do-Loop that will execute as long as its condition is true. The condition Timer <(begin + pauseTime) will only be true for the time increment specified by the variable pauseTime. The value of pauseTime can be any number within the range of allowed values for the Single data type. However, the variable pauseTime will typically be set to a value less than one. Since the precision of the Timer function extends to two decimal places, the pauseTime variable should not be set to a value less than 0.01.

The DoEvents function yields program execution to the operating system, thus allowing other events to be processed. The DoEvents function is placed inside the Do-Loop to prevent the loop from tying up the operating system while it executes. Without DoEvents, the user will be unable to interact with your program while code execution proceeds through the loop. This can have the dangerous effect of locking up the operating system, forcing the user to either exit the application in an undesirable way or even to reboot his or her machine.

Animation Using Cell Formatting

Let's consider some examples using the Delay() sub procedure to animate various elements of Excel. The following program animates the interior color of a range of cells representing a framed area on the worksheet. The cells alternate color from red to black in a continuous fashion. The workbook containing the code is called AnimationDemos.xls. The worksheet containing the program is called AnimateCells, and the code is contained in a component module of the worksheet shown in Figure 6.3.

HINT The source code for all the animation demos in this chapter can be found with the AnimationDemos.xls file on the CD that comes with this book. Accompanying image files are also included. If you copy the Excel file to your hard drive, then you must copy the image files to preserve the path to these files. Alternatively, you can open the Excel file directly from the CD and the image files will be loaded as needed by the programs.

Notice that a scroll bar has been added to the worksheet shown in Figure 6.3. The scroll bar is another ActiveX control available from the Control Toolbox, shown again in Figure 6.4.

Table 6.1 summarizes the properties of the Scroll Bar control that are typically changed at design time.

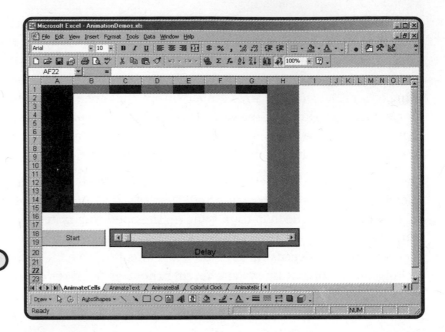

FIGURE 6.3

Using color to animate a worksheet

The Scroll Bar control

FIGURE 6.4

The Scroll Bar control on the Control Toolbox

TABLE 6.1 SELECTED PROPERTIES OF THE SCROLL BAR CONTROL

Property	Function
Name	Sets the name of the control for referencing in code
Min	Sets the minimum value allowed for the Value property
Max	Sets the maximum value allowed for the Value property
Value	Holds the current value of the scroll bar
LargeChange	Sets the increment the scroll box moves when the user clicks between the box and the arrow
SmallChange	Sets the increment the scroll box moves when the user clicks on the arrow

The AnimateCells program does not contain any unfamiliar code structures or references to new objects other than the Scroll Bar control. The program contains a total of five procedures, four of which are listed below; the fifth is the Delay() procedure listed earlier in this chapter.

Two module-level variables are used to toggle the animation on and off and to set the delay time passed to the Delay() procedure.

```
Option Explicit
Dim animationOn As Boolean
Dim cellDelay As Integer
```

The Click() event of the Command Button control named cmdAnimate (labeled Start), and shown in Figure 6.3, is used to initiate the animation.

```
Private Sub cmdAnimate_Click()
```

The Value property of the Scroll Bar control named scrDelay is used to set the delay time for the animation. The variable cellDelay will later be divided by 100 and passed to the Delay() sub procedure.

```
    cellDelay = scrDelay.Value
```

The Command Button control cmdAnimate is used to both start and stop the animation; thus, a decision structure is used to dictate program action.

```
    If cmdAnimate.Caption = "Start" Then
        animationOn = True
        cmdAnimate.Caption = "Stop"
```

If the caption displays Start, then the module-level Boolean variable animationOn is set to true and the Caption property of the Command Button control is updated. Next, the sub procedure AnimateCells() is called to begin the animation.

```
        AnimateCells
    Else
```

If the caption displays Stop, the looping variable animationOn is set to false, which will serve to stop the animation in the AnimateCells() procedure. The Caption property of the Command Button control is also updated.

```
        animationOn = False
        cmdAnimate.Caption = "Start"
    End If
End Sub
```

The Change() event procedure of the Scroll Bar control named scrDelay is triggered when the user moves the scroll box and changes its Value property. The variable cellDelay is used to catch the user's action.

```
Private Sub scrDelay_Change()
    cellDelay = scrDelay.Value
End Sub
```

The AnimateCells() sub procedure contains the looping structure used to control the animation.

```
Private Sub AnimateCells()
    Dim frameRange As Range
    Dim c As Range
    Dim colorVal As Integer
    Dim prevColor As Integer
    Set frameRange = Range("A1:H15")
    colorVal = 0
```

A Do-Loop is used to control the animation. The loop will continue as long as the variable animationOn holds the value true.

```
    Do
```

A For/Each loop is used to iterate through each cell contained within the range of cells specified in the frameRange variable set earlier.

```
    For Each c In frameRange
```

If the cell is in column A or H, or in row 1 or 15, then its interior color is set to either black or red using the QBColor() function (0=black, 12=light red; see the online help for remaining colors).

 HINT

The QBColor() function is a holdover from the old QBasic programming language. In those days, 16 colors was about all a programmer had to work with. The QBColor() function is used here because I'm not concerned with the number of colors available, and I want to illustrate that there are always several functions available for selecting colors (remember RGB() and ColorIndex).

The variable prevColor is used to hold the current value of the color so that it can be used to change the cell color with the next iteration through the For/Each loop.

```
        If (c.Column = 1 Or c.Column = 8) Or (c.Row = 1 Or c.Row = 15) Then
            c.Interior.Color = QBColor(colorVal)
            prevColor = colorVal
```

After the cell color is changed, the `Delay()` sub procedure is called to pause code execution within the `For/Each` loop. The length of the delay will vary between approximately ten milliseconds (0.01 seconds) and one second, as the `Min` and `Max` properties of the Scroll Bar control are set to 1 and 100, respectively.

```
            Delay (cellDelay / 100)
        End If
        If prevColor = 0 Then colorVal = 12
        If prevColor = 12 Then colorVal = 0
    Next
```

The following `If/Else` structure ensures that the cell colors will alternate between black and red with each iteration through the `Do-Loop`.

```
        If colorVal = 12 Then
            colorVal = 0
        Else
            colorVal = 12
        End If
    Loop While animationOn = True
End Sub
```

Finally, a call to the `AnimateCells()` sub procedure is placed in the `SelectionChange()` event procedure of the Worksheet object in order to ensure that the animation continues when the user edits the worksheet. Without the `Worksheet_SelectionChange()` procedure, code execution will be directed out of the `AnimateCells()` sub procedure when the user edits the worksheet. Without a directive to send execution back to the `AnimateCells()` sub procedure, the program effectively quits.

```
Private Sub Worksheet_SelectionChange(ByVal Target As Range)
    If animationOn = True Then AnimateCells
End Sub
```

The program above may not be all that useful in your applications, but it does illustrate how you can use cell formatting to create an animation that users may find appealing. You don't have to limit your animations to the alteration of cell colors. With the creative use of borders and text, you can create some visually appealing animations. A very short and simple example of animated text (in the form of a scrolling text box) is included on the CD-ROM in the source code with this chapter.

Animation Using Properties of Controls

The next example animates an image of a ball by moving an Image control around a worksheet via the `Left` and `Top` properties of the control. Again, a component module of a worksheet contains the code. Figure 6.5 displays the worksheet.

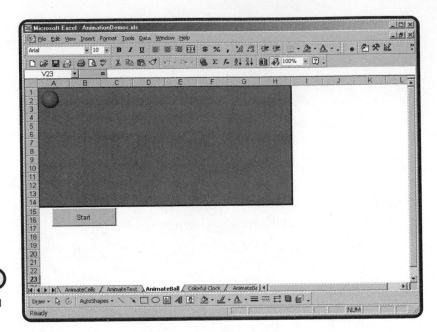

FIGURE 6.5

The Animated Ball
worksheet

An Image control named imgBall is added to the worksheet with its AutoSize property set to true and Picture property set to hold the image stored as Ball.gif. The BackStyle and BorderStyle properties of the Image control are set to transparent and none, respectively. A Command Button control name cmdAnimateBall is used to start and stop the animation. The code is very similar to that of the AnimateCells program, and it uses the same Delay() sub procedure. The most significant difference from the AnimateCells program is in the sub procedure that controls the movement of the Image control.

```
Option Explicit
Dim animationOn As Boolean
Private Sub cmdAnimateBall_Click()
    If cmdAnimateBall.Caption = "Start" Then
        animationOn = True
        cmdAnimateBall.Caption = "Stop"
        AnimateBall
    Else
        animationOn = False
        cmdAnimateBall.Caption = "Start"
        imgBall.Left = 0
        imgBall.Top = 0
    End If
End Sub
```

The AnimateBall() sub procedure controls the animation by altering the Left and Top properties of the Image control inside a Do-Loop. The variables xInc and yInc are used to increment or decrement the value of the Top and Left properties of the Image control. The upper left corner of the worksheet (or upper left corner of cell A1) represents the position where Top=0 and Left =0.

```
Private Sub AnimateBall()
    Dim yInc As Integer
    Dim xInc As Integer
```

The values of xInc and yInc are set to give a reasonable illusion of a bouncing ball. Increasing or decreasing the values of the xInc and yInc variables can adjust the perceived speed of the ball. However, as the values of these variables increase, the animation will degrade, because the user will begin to see the skip of the Image control from one location to the next. Large increments of xInc and yInc will give the animation a "choppy" look.

```
    xInc = 3
    yInc = 7
```

The ball is contained within the range A1:H14 by using the Height and Width properties of both the Range object and Image control. When the ball travels to the right or bottom edge of the range A1:H14, the sign is reversed for the xInc and yInc variables, respectively. Reversing the sign of these variables effectively sends the ball in the opposite direction, with respect to the axis variable altered. For example, yInc is positive if the ball is moving in a downward direction and negative if the ball is moving in an upward direction.

```
    Do
        If imgBall.Top > (Range("A1:A14").Height - imgBall.Height) Or
imgBall.Top < 1 Then yInc = -yInc
        If imgBall.Left > (Range("A1:H1").Width - imgBall.Width) Or
imgBall.Left < 1 Then xInc = -xInc
        imgBall.Left = imgBall.Left + xInc
        imgBall.Top = imgBall.Top + yInc
```

The delay is set to 10 milliseconds with our familiar call to the Delay() sub procedure. The speed of the ball is partially defined by the value passed to the Delay() procedure. Typically, a variable would be used to hold the value of the delay time, as it would allow the programmer to change the speed of the ball during the course of program execution.

The delay time is currently set to the smallest possible value that can be used with the Delay() procedure. To make the ball travel faster you can remove the call to the Delay() procedure, but be sure to add DoEvents to prevent the creation of an infinite loop. The speed of the ball without the call to the Delay() sub procedure will vary from one computer to another, depending on the speed of the processor. For a consistent animation, you must use a well-defined delay time in your animation loop.

```
Delay (0.01)
```

Another click of the Command Button control changes the value of the animationOn variable and program execution exits the loop.

```
    Loop While animationOn = True
End Sub
```

Images such as Ball.gif (found on the CD) can be created with any image processing software that can handle transparency. Without transparency, the background color of the image would have to match the background color of the application in which the file is animated in order to create a realistic animation.

Reducing the size of the image also helps the appearance of the animation. The human eye will more easily perceive jumping of the Image control from one location to the next as the area of the Image control increases.

The previous two examples are simple and somewhat crude examples of animations in Excel. Animations such as these should only be executed for brief periods of time. These animations should not be run continuously because processor control is being toggled between the program and the Excel application with each call to the Delay() sub procedure. The toggling of processor control back and forth between Excel and the program is noticeable to the user in a couple of ways. First, the animation may appear a bit jittery when the Image control moves position, and second, the mouse icon will transition between the pointer and the hourglass at the same rate the Delay() sub procedure is being called. This makes for a less elegant animation, and can be distracting to the user.

Animation Using Image Frames

The final example of animation is probably more familiar. It involves giving the illusion of movement by showing a sequence of images in rapid succession. This is the equivalent of thumbing through the pages of an animated book very quickly.

The first requirement in building an animation from a series of images is, of course, the creation of the images. This can be easy or difficult depending on the software and your artistic ability. Regardless of ability, you can at least use something like MS Paint to create a few simple images for testing in a program. As this is not a book about graphic arts, creating the images will be left up to you.

The next animation gives the illusion of a ball rolling toward you across a floor. The worksheet is named AnimateBallonOnFloor in the AnimationDemos.xls workbook. There are ten images in the sequence; they are shown in Figure 6.6.

The idea is to quickly display the sequence of images in an Image control to give the illusion of a ball rolling across a floor. The techniques used to do this are not difficult and involve little code.

 Images can be optimized for animation by eliminating those sections of the image that do not change from one frame to the next. This can significantly reduce file size, saving system resources. Animated gifs commonly found on Web pages use this technique.

The animation procedure is really quite simple. An image array is created to load all images into the computer's memory. The image data type is a specific form of the object data type. After object variable declaration, each image to be stored in the array must be assigned a reference to the variable array using the Set statement. A For/Next loop is used to set the reference for each Image object and the LoadPicture method is used to load all ten images into the array. From there it is easy to animate the images using another For/Next loop and a call to the Delay() sub procedure listed earlier.

```
Private Sub cmdAnimate_Click()
    Dim I As Integer
    Dim filePath As String
    Dim myImages(9) As Image
    For I = 0 To 9
        Set myImages(I) = New Image
```

The Path property of the workbook object is used to return a string containing the file path to the AnimationDemos.xls workbook. Therefore, the Ball_Animation _Images folder containing the images of the ball must be in the same directory as the workbook.

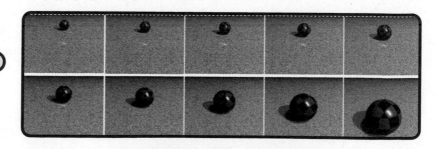

FIGURE 6.6

The sequence of images used to simulate a rolling ball

```
        filePath = ActiveWorkbook.Path & "\Ball_Animation_Images\ball" &
Trim(Str(I)) & ".bmp"
        myImages(I).Picture = LoadPicture(filePath)
    Next I
```

To animate the ball, copy the picture from the image array myImages to the Image control named imgBall.

```
    For I = 0 To 9
        imgBall.Picture = myImages(I).Picture
        Delay (0.1)
    Next I
End Sub
```

This concludes the animation section of this chapter. However, this section certainly does not cover every tool available for animation in your VBA project. You may be able to find third-party ActiveX controls, or create your own ActiveX controls using Visual Basic (6.0 or earlier). Multimedia and animation controls do exist, but they usually have very specific requirements for the media to be delivered (for example, Microsoft's Animation control requires .avi files).

Sound in VBA

Earlier versions of Excel (Excel 95) offered the ability to add sound to a VBA program via the SoundNote property of the Range object. However, support for playing sound files has since been removed from VBA. This leaves two choices for playing sounds in Excel applications with VBA: ActiveX controls and the Windows API (application programming interface).

There are numerous ActiveX controls available for playing sound in VBA applications. However, many of these controls are either expensive or lack documentation. Whether or not to use these controls depends on the sound requirements of your project as well as financial resources and licensing. Even if an ActiveX control is freely available, it may be difficult to get it to work in a VBA program because of a lack of documentation and/or serious bugs in its source code.

As there are no ActiveX controls for playing sound that currently ship with VBA, the Windows API will be used for adding sound to the VBA programs in this book.

The Windows API

The Windows Application Programming Interface (API) is the interface used to programmatically control the Windows operating system. The Windows API is comprised of numerous procedures that provide programmatic access to the features of the Windows operating system (for example, windows functions, file functions, and so on). The API procedures are stored in the system directory of Windows as .dll (dynamic link library) files. There can be dozens of procedures stored within a single .dll file. The API procedures are conceptually the same as procedures used in any programming language, including VBA. However, because the API procedures are written in C/C++, accessing them via the VBA programming environment can be difficult and in some cases impossible.

Normally, the Windows API is left as an advanced programming topic for some very good reasons. Using the Windows API can be dangerous, as it bypasses all of the safety features built into VBA to prevent the misuse of system resources and the subsequent system crashes they usually cause (but nothing that can't be fixed by turning your computer off and back on). However, the API can greatly extend the ability and therefore, the power of a program.

Fortunately, tapping into the Windows API to play a .wav file (Wave Form Audio) is about as easy as it gets. This section of the book will only show you how to play .wav files using the Windows API and will not discuss the Windows API in any detail. Instead, the Windows API is left as an advanced topic for you to consider after becoming comfortable with VBA. The Windows API is the best (and probably easiest) tool available to all VBA programmers for adding sound to a program, but it should not be used extensively by beginning programmers; therefore, I will only show you how to use it to add sound to a VBA program.

To use a function from the Windows API in VBA, open a standard module and use a Declare statement in the general declarations section to create a reference to the external procedure (Windows API function). Note that that line continuation character has been used in the declaration below due to its length.

```
Public Declare Function sndPlaySoundA Lib "winmm.dll" _
(ByVal lpszSoundName As String, ByVal uFlags As Long) As Long
```

In reality, this is a relatively short API call. This declaration creates a reference to the sndPlaySoundA() function found in the file winmm.dll. It looks a lot like a function call in VBA, but it is only a declaration; the call to the function will come later. Capitalization is important and will not be corrected automatically if typed incorrectly. Although the function can take more, only two parameters are included in the declaration. The argument lpszSoundName is the named parameter (type String) for the .wav file to be played, and the argument uFlags is the named parameter (type Long) used to denote whether or not program execution should proceed immediately or wait until after the file is done playing. The `sndPlaySoundA()` function returns a value of type Long that may be discarded. Hence, calls to the `sndPlaySoundA()` function from a VBA procedure can appear as follows:

```
sndPlaySoundA "Path to .wav file", 1
returnVal = sndPlaySoundA("Path to .wav file", 0)
```

Playing .Wav files via the Windows API

The Sounds worksheet included in the AnimationDemos.xls workbook uses the Windows API to play .wav files simulating a cannon firing and an explosion. The sound files are courtesy of http://www.a1freesoundeffects.com. Two Button controls are used to play the files. The source code, which can be found in the Modules folder contained in the AnimationDemos.xls project file, is listed below.

```
Option Explicit
Public Declare Function sndPlaySoundA Lib "winmm.dll" _

(ByVal lpszSoundName As String, ByVal uFlags As Long) As Long
```

The `PlayWav()` sub procedure is used to call the Windows API function declared above. The parameter, `WavFile`, is a string variable and holds the path to the desired .wav file.

```
Public Sub PlayWav(WavFile As String)
```

The `CanPlaySounds` property of the Application object is used to test the user's computer for the ability to play sounds. If the user's machine does not have the ability to play sounds (for instance, it has no sound card), then the appropriate message is displayed and the procedure is immediately exited.

```
If Application.CanPlaySounds = False Then
    MsgBox "Sorry, sound is not supported on your system."
    Exit Sub
End If
```

The `Dir()` function is used to test the input path to the .wav file. If an empty string is returned by the `Dir()` function, then the file was not found and the procedure is exited after displaying an error message.

```
If Dir(WavFile) = "" Then
    MsgBox ("Wave file not found")
    Exit Sub
End If
```

Finally, the call to the Windows API function `sndPlaySoundA` is made, passing the string containing the path to the .wav file, and the value 1 is passed to the `uFlags` parameter so that program execution will not wait for the sound file to finish playing (use 0 for `uFlags` to halt program execution until the sound file finishes playing).

```
    sndPlaySoundA WavFile, 1
End Sub
```

Two public procedures linked to Button controls are used to initiate the playing of each sound file. The files must be in a directory labeled Sounds, found within the same directory as the AnimationDemos.xls workbook file. Each of these procedures simply calls the `PlayWav()` sub procedure listed above, while passing it the string variable containing the path to the desired sound file.

```
Public Sub TestPlayWav1()
    Dim filePath As String
    filePath = ActiveWorkbook.Path
    PlayWav (filePath & "\Sounds\cannon.wav")
End Sub
Public Sub TestPlayWav2()
    Dim filePath As String
    filePath = ActiveWorkbook.Path
    PlayWav (filePath & "\Sounds\explode.wav")
End Sub
```

You can see how easy it is to play sound files using the Windows API. Although programming via the Windows API is an advanced technique, there really is nothing simpler for the VBA programmer to use for playing sound files.

Simulating Intelligence in Programs

Even if you have been out of touch with the computer industry, you have probably heard or read about artificial intelligence. Artificial intelligence (AI) is a topic that has been covered extensively in the mainstream media, and, of course, Hollywood has been using it as a subject in television shows and movies for decades.

AI refers to the ability of a computer program to simulate human intellectual thought processes. Artificial intelligence is a popular research subject in the field of computer science for both intellectual and economic reasons. The benefits of AI in software applications are enormous and have been used for years. The obvious example is in the computer gaming industry (remember IBM's Deep Blue Supercomputer and its defeat of the chess master Gary Kasparov?).

There are more subtle examples of AI in commercial software. For instance, I'm writing this chapter using Microsoft Word 2000, which checks my spelling and grammar as I type and will suggest corrections if asked. The ability of MS Word to check a document for mistakes and offer corrections is a relatively simple example of AI, in terms of what we as humans consider intelligence. However, I doubt it seemed so simple a task for the programmers who wrote the code that simulates these features in MS Word.

If you have used the last several versions of MS Word (or any other word processor with these features), then you have noticed the improvement in these AI features, and have probably also thought that there is still plenty of room for more improvement. This describes the status of AI in the computer industry: plenty of room for improvement. We are a long way from creating a program that can fully mimic human intellectual thought, so don't be fooled by Hollywood and media hype that tends to focus on the negative sides of the issue. Creating AI in a program is a difficult task. You will get a taste of just how difficult it is by using a relatively simple example—the Battlecell program from the last chapter.

Incorporating AI into a program does not involve additional code structures or objects that I have not already discussed. The code used to simulate AI will typically involve numerous decision structures and the program branches that result from these structures. The most difficult step in adding AI to a program is the algorithm development. Without a detailed plan of what is to be accomplished by the AI added to a program, the code can be exceedingly difficult and frustrating to write. Let's move along with the example for adding AI to the Battlecell program from Chapter 5.

Chapter Project: Enhanced Battlecell

The enhanced version of Battlecell contains a modicum of AI that may be enough to allow the computer to win a game once in a while, if the user isn't careful. Animation and sound have also been added to make the game more appealing to the user.

 The enhanced version of Battlecell and all associated image and sound files can be found on the accompanying CD-ROM. The Excel file is stored as BattlecellII.xls.

Project Statement

I want to create animations in the Battlecell program that simulate the following:

- Entrance of the player and computer's ships onto the game board.

- The firing of a cannon from each ship.
- The hitting of an opponents ship via cannon fire.
- The destruction of a ship when all ships have been sunk and the game has ended.

In addition to the animations, the Battlecell program should play sound files that simulate a cannon firing and an explosion. The playing of the sound files should be synchronized to the appropriate animation.

Finally, I wish to add intelligence to the Battlecell program so that the computer can more easily locate the player's ships once they have been hit.

Project Tools

Animation images can be created with any reasonable image creation and editing software (I used the GIMP), and can be presented in the program using Image controls and a frame-by-frame technique (just like the rolling ball example discussed earlier in this chapter). Sound can be added to the program at the appropriate time during the animation with calls to the Windows API function sndPlaySoundA(). Intelligence can be added to the program using standard coding structures and techniques and by carefully following an appropriate algorithm.

Project Algorithm

There are basically three animation sequences to add. The first animation will simply show a battleship moving to the center of an image and will run after the player's ships are placed. Figure 6.7 shows the first animation is a sequence of the 14 images. A sub procedure called from the cmdPlaceShips_Click() event procedure will handle the first animation.

The second animation will simulate the ship firing one of its big guns and will run immediately after the player or computer fires. Figure 6.8 shows the second animation is a sequence of 13 images. A sub procedure called from the Worksheet _SelectionChange() event procedure and the ComputerFire() sub procedures will handle the second animation.

The third animation will simulate a hit of an opponent's ship and, if appropriate, the sinking of that ship. Figure 6.9 shows the sequence of 16 images used for the third animation. When a player scores a hit but has not yet won the game, only the first four images in the sequence are used. A sub procedure called from the HitOrMiss() sub procedure and the ComputerFire() sub procedure will handle the third animation.

FIGURE 6.7

The images used in the first animation for the enhanced version of Battlecell

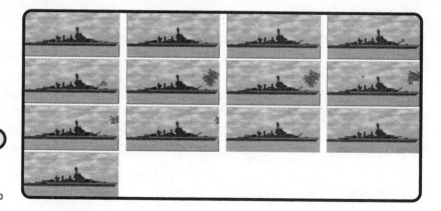

FIGURE 6.8

The sequence of images used to display a firing ship

FIGURE 6.9

The sequence of images used to display a sinking ship

Sound files simulating cannon fire and an explosion will be played when the player's and the computer's ships fire at each other and score a hit. Calls to sub procedures from the Worksheet_SelectionChange() event procedure, the ComputerFire()

sub procedure, and the `HitOrMiss()` sub procedure that use a call to the Windows API will handle the playing of the appropriate sound file.

Intelligence will be added to the program and used by the computer when looking for a cell location to select for the firing simulation. To search for a cell location on the player's grid to serve as a target, do the following:

1. Search the player's grid for all red colored cells.

2. If there are no red-colored cells in the player's grid, then select a cell randomly to use as the target cell.

3. For each red-colored cell found, determine potential target cells. Store the cell location of all potential target cells in a variable array.

4. To find potential target cells, test for sequential red cells in a worksheet column or row.

5. If sequential red cells exist, add two target cells to the list (array) located at the beginning and end of the row or column of red cells discovered.

6. If an isolated red cell is found, then add four target cells to the list (one cell above, below, to the right and left of the red cell discovered).

7. Remove potential target cells that do not fall within the player's grid.

8. When firing, loop through the array holding the cell locations of the target cells, testing each cell for a previous selection.

9. The first cell not selected previously will be used as the target cell.

10. If all cells in the target list have been previously selected, then choose a target randomly.

After reading this list of requirements you can see that there will be a number of `If/Then` statements used to handle the selection of a target cell for the computer. As more requirements are added to the list, more decisions have to be made and it doesn't take very long before the list becomes difficult to manage. Therefore, it is best to encapsulate the problem starting at the top of the list and solving small manageable pieces of the algorithm one at a time until the entire problem is solved.

The list of requirements above will double the length of the Battlecell program, but only allow the computer to find the player's ship once one has been hit. The initial targeting is still done randomly. This means that it will still be fairly easy to defeat the computer.

Adding targeting selection that chooses the next cell logically rather than randomly when there is no target list will further improve the algorithm. Constructing procedures that recognize when individual ships have been sunk would also aid in the selection of target cells and bring the skill level of the computer up to a point where it might actually win a few games. The addition of the last two elements does not require any special programming structures or objects that have not been previously discussed. Careful planning and implementation are the most important skills you need, because these exercises are left for you. Good luck!

Adding the Code

Only the procedures that have undergone significant editing are included here, along with the new procedures added to the Battlecell program. The workbook with all the source code can be found in the Excel file stored as BattlecellIII.xls.

The first procedure to be altered is the Click() event procedure of the Command Button control name cmdPlaceShips. There are only a couple of changes in this procedure. First, there is now just one Label control in the enhanced version of Battlecell, named lblOutput, and its Caption property is changed. Second, a call to the first animation sub procedure AnimateShips_Place(), is used to display the computer's and player's ships.

```
Private Sub cmdPlaceShips_Click()
    If cmdPlaceShips.Caption = "Start" Then
        numCellsInShip = 5
        BeginGame
    ElseIf cmdPlaceShips.Caption = "Done" Then
        cmdPlaceShips.Enabled = False
        lblOutput.Caption = "Please wait while I place my ships."
        AnimateShips_Place
        TargetShips
        lblOutput.Caption = "You may begin."
        allowSelection = True
        bombsAway = True
    End If
End Sub
```

Two Image controls named imgPlayer and imgComputer are used to display all animations. The first animation simply displays a ship moving into the center of the Image control and represents the placement of the player's ships. Then, the mirror image of the first animation is used in the second Image control to represent the placement of the computer's ships. The image sequence used for each animation totals 14 images (see Figure 6.7).

```
Private Sub AnimateShips_Place()
    Dim I As Integer
```

```
Dim filePath As String
Dim shipImages(12) As Image
Dim imagePath As String
Dim J As Integer
```

I created two sets of images that are identical, except that one set has been flipped 180 degrees horizontally. The image names are identical, but the files are stored in two different directories—one each for the player's and computer's ships. Nested For/Next loops are used to load and display the images.

```
For J = 0 To 1
    If J = 0 Then imagePath = ActiveWorkbook.Path & "\playerAnimation\"
    If J = 1 Then imagePath = ActiveWorkbook.Path & "\compAnimation\"
```

A For/Next loop is used to load the images into the image array variable shipImages. The first iteration loads the images of the player's ship (J = 0) and the second iteration loads the images of the computer's ship (J = 1). The file path is constructed from the Path property of the Workbook object, and a string representing the remainder of the file path. The LoadPicture() function is used to load the images into the Picture property of each Image object in the shipImages array.

```
For I = 0 To 12
    If J = 0 Then Set shipImages(I) = New Image
    filePath = imagePath & Trim(Str(I)) & ".jpg"
    shipImages(I).Picture = LoadPicture(filePath)
Next I
```

Next, another For/Next loop is used to display the images in sequence with a 150 millisecond delay between images. The Delay() sub procedure called here is the same procedure used throughout this chapter.

```
For I = 0 To 12
    Call Delay(0.15)
    If J = 0 Then imgPlayer.Picture = shipImages(I).Picture
    If J = 1 Then imgComputer.Picture = shipImages(I).Picture
Next I
Call Delay(1)
Next J
End Sub
```

The player begins the action by selecting a cell within the target grid. You may recall that the Worksheet_SelectionChange() event procedure was used to capture the cell selected by the player. This procedure has been lengthened to include a call to another animation sub procedure. Otherwise it is essentially the same.

```
Private Sub Worksheet_SelectionChange(ByVal target As Range)
    Dim inRange As Boolean
    If allowSelection = False Then Exit Sub
    '
    If bombsAway Then
        inRange = CheckTarget(target)
        If Not inRange Then Exit Sub
```

The variables allowSelection and bombsAway are temporarily set to false while the animation plays to prevent the player from selecting more than one cell. The sub procedure AnimateShips_Fire() is used to animate the player's and the computer's ships firing at each other. A string parameter is passed to this procedure to specify which competitor is firing.

```
        allowSelection = False
        bombsAway = False
        Call AnimateShips_Fire("player")
        Call HitOrMiss(target)
        If numTargetHits < 17 Then
            ComputerFire
```

If the computer has not sunk all of the player's ships, then the allowSelection and bombsAway variables must be set to true so the player will be allowed to make another selection. The remainder of the procedure is the same as in the previous version of the game. It includes the validation procedure CheckRange() and the sub procedure AssignShip() used to set the player's cell selection when placing his/her ships.

```
            If numPlayerHits < 17 Then
                allowSelection = True
                bombsAway = True
            End If
        End If
    Else
        rangeStatus = CheckRange(target)
        If  inRange Then
            Call AssignShip(target)
        End If
    End If
End Sub
```

The HitOrMiss() sub procedure is still used to check whether or not the player has scored a hit on the computer's ships and test for the end of the game. This procedure is essentially the same as before, with the exception of the Boolean variable sinkShip and the call to the sub procedure AnimateHit().

```
Private Sub HitOrMiss(target As Range)
    Dim sinkShip As Boolean
    sinkShip = False
    If target.Value = "X" Then
        ActiveSheet.Unprotect
        target.Interior.Color = RGB(255, 0, 0)
        ActiveSheet.Protect
        lblOutput.Caption = "You Hit My Ship!"
        numTargetHits = numTargetHits + 1
        If (numTargetHits = 17) Then
            bombsAway = False
            lblOutput.Caption = "All Ships Sunk! YOU WIN!"
            allowSelection = False
            sinkShip = True
        End If
```

The AnimateHit() sub procedure is used to animate a hit on an opponent's ship and, if the game is over (sinkShip = True), to animate the sinking of the ship.

```
        Call AnimateHit("player", sinkShip)
        Exit Sub
    End If
    lblOutput.Caption = "You Missed!"
    ActiveSheet.Unprotect
    target.Interior.Color = RGB(0, 0, 255)
    ActiveSheet.Protect
End Sub
```

The ComputerFire() sub procedure is used to simulate the computer's return fire at the player's ships. This procedure also checks for a hit and the end of the game. However, there are a few more modifications that need to be carried out with this procedure.

```
Private Sub ComputerFire()
    Dim randomGuess As Boolean
    Dim I As Integer
    Dim targetCell As String
    Dim targetRange As Range
    Dim sinkShip As Boolean
```

Again, the Boolean variable sinkShip will be passed to an animation procedure for signaling whether or not to display the images of a sinking ship.

```
sinkShip = False
Delay (2)
```

The AnimateShips_Fire() sub procedure is used to display the animations that simulate the firing of the player's and the computer's ships.

```
AnimateShips_Fire ("computer")
```

The module-level variable array targetCells holds the list of cell locations representing possible targets for the computer to fire upon. This array is re-initialized at the beginning of the procedure with a ReDim statement. The function procedure CountRedCells scans the player's grid for cells previously hit by the computer and returns the number of red cells to the integer variable numRedCells.

```
ReDim targetCells(0)
numRedCells = CountRedCells
randomGuess = True
```

If at least one red cell is found, then the sub procedure FindTargets() is called to locate potential target cells and load their locations into the variable array targetCells.

```
If numRedCells > 0 Then
    FindTargets
```

A For/Next loop is used to iterate through each potential target cell listed in the variable array targetCells until a candidate is found that has not been previously used. For the upper bound in the For/Next loop I used the UBound() function to return the largest available index for an array. Then I subtract one from this index because the program is working in Option Base 0. If all cell locations have been previously used, then a target cell will be chosen randomly.

```
For I = 0 To UBound(targetCells) - 1
    targetCell = targetCells(I)
    Set targetRange = Range(targetCell)
    If targetRange.Interior.Color <> RGB(255, 0, 0) And _
        targetRange.Interior.Color <> RGB(0, 255, 0) Then
        randomGuess = False
        Exit For
    Else
        randomGuess = True
    End If
Next I
End If
```

A Do-Loop is used to run the code that randomly selects a target cell. A loop is used in case the random selection has been previously used.

```
If randomGuess = True Then
    Randomize
    ReDim targetCells(0)
    Do
```

A string is built to represent the address of a single cell for the randomly selected target. The column reference is built from a random number between 66 and 75 that is converted to an uppercase letter between B and K by the Chr() function. The row reference is built from a random number between 2 and 12. The resulting string is passed to the Range property of the Application object and returns a reference to a Range object that is stored in the variable targetRange.

```
        targetCells(0) = "$" & Chr(Int(10 * Rnd + 66)) & "$" &
Trim(Str(Int(10 * Rnd + 2)))
        targetCell = targetCells(0)
        Set targetRange = Range(targetCell)
    Loop While (targetRange.Interior.Color = RGB(255, 0, 0) Or
targetRange.Interior.Color = RGB(0, 255, 0))
    End If
```

The target range is tested to see if it has hit the player's ship (true if the cell's color is blue). If the computer scores a hit, then the cell is colored red, the integer variable numPlayerHits is incremented, and the game is tested for its end. Next the AnimateHit() sub procedure is called and passed the appropriate parameters. If the computer's shot missed the player's ship, then a message is displayed in the Label control and the game continues.

```
If targetRange.Interior.Color = RGB(0, 0, 255) Then
    lblOutput.Caption = "I Hit Your Ship!"
    ActiveSheet.Unprotect
    targetRange.Interior.Color = RGB(255, 0, 0)
    ActiveSheet.Protect
    numPlayerHits = numPlayerHits + 1
    If (numPlayerHits = 17) Then
        lblOutput.Caption = "All Ships Sunk! I WIN!"
        allowSelection = False
        bombsAway = False
        sinkShip = True
    End If
    Delay (1)
```

```
                Call AnimateHit("computer", sinkShip)
        Else
                ActiveSheet.Unprotect
                targetRange.Interior.Color = RGB(0, 255, 0)
                ActiveSheet.Protect
                lblOutput.Caption = "I Missed!"
        End If
End Sub
```

The AnimateShips_Fire() and AnimateHit() sub procedures control animations for both the player and computer. They simulate the ships firing at their opponent, direct hits, and the sinking of the ships. These procedures are essentially the same as those for the rolling ball animation and the first animation (AnimateShips _Place()) sub procedure used for the enhanced version of Battlecell.

```
Private Sub AnimateShips_Fire(player As String)
    Dim I As Integer
    Dim filePath As String
    Dim shipImages(11) As Image
    Dim imagePath As String
    If player = "player" Then imagePath = ActiveWorkbook.Path &
"\playerAnimation\"
    If player = "computer" Then imagePath = ActiveWorkbook.Path &
"\compAnimation\"
```

The looping variable I is set to iterate from 13 to 24, because these are the numbers used in the filenames of the images needed for the animations.

```
    For I = 13 To 24
        Set shipImages(I - 13) = New Image
        filePath = imagePath & Trim(Str(I)) & ".jpg"
        shipImages(I - 13).Picture = LoadPicture(filePath)
    Next I
    For I = 13 To 24
        Delay (0.15)
        If I = 16 Then
```

The PlayCannon() sub procedure is called to play the sound file simulating cannon fire. The sound file is timed to begin playing when the fourth image (file 16.jpg) is being displayed in the animation.

```
            PlayCannon
        End If
```

```
      If player = "player" Then imgPlayer.Picture = shipImages(I -
13).Picture
      If player = "computer" Then imgComputer.Picture = shipImages(I -
13).Picture
   Next I
End Sub
```

The `AnimateHit()` sub procedure will display from 4 to 16 images depending on whether or not the game is at an end and the animation of a sinking ship needs to be executed.

```
Private Sub AnimateHit(player As String, sinkShip As Boolean)
   Dim I As Integer
   Dim filePath As String
   Dim shipImages(15) As Image
   Dim imagePath As String
   Dim endLoop As Integer
```

The integer variable `endLoop` sets the number of images to be used in the animation and is used as the upper bound in the `For/Next` loops.

```
   If sinkShip = True Then endLoop = 40
   If sinkShip = False Then endLoop = 28
   If player = "computer" Then imagePath = ActiveWorkbook.Path &
"\playerAnimation\"
   If player = "player" Then imagePath = ActiveWorkbook.Path &
"\compAnimation\"
   For I = 25 To endLoop
      Set shipImages(I - 25) = New Image
      filePath = imagePath & Trim(Str(I)) & ".jpg"
      shipImages(I - 25).Picture = LoadPicture(filePath)
   Next I
   For I = 25 To endLoop
      If sinkShip = False Then Delay (0.05)
      If sinkShip = True Then Delay (0.2)
      If I = 26 Then
```

The `PlayExplode()` sub procedure plays the sound file used to simulate an explosion when either player scores a hit on the other's ship.

```
         PlayExplode
      End If
```

```
        If player = "player" Then imgComputer.Picture = shipImages(I -
25).Picture
        If player = "computer" Then imgPlayer.Picture = shipImages(I -
25).Picture
    Next I
    If sinkShip = False Then
        Delay (1)
```

If the game has not ended and the animation only displays a hit on an opponent's ship, then the animation is extended by replaying the same four images in reverse sequence.

```
        For I = endLoop To 25 Step -1
            Delay (0.3)
            If player = "player" Then imgComputer.Picture = shipImages(I
- 25).Picture
            If player = "computer" Then imgPlayer.Picture = shipImages(I
- 25).Picture
        Next I
    End If
End Sub
```

The sub procedures PlayWav(), PlayCannon(), and PlayExplode() are used to play the sound files cannon.wav and explode.wav. The code statements in these procedures were discussed previously in this chapter.

```
Private Sub PlayWav(WavFile As String)
    If Dir(WavFile) = "" Then Exit Sub
    sndPlaySound WavFile, 1
End Sub
Private Sub PlayCannon()
    Dim filePath As String
    filePath = ActiveWorkbook.Path
    PlayWav (filePath & "\Sounds\cannon.wav")
End Sub
Private Sub PlayExplode()
    Dim filePath As String
    filePath = ActiveWorkbook.Path
    PlayWav (filePath & "\Sounds\explode.wav")
End Sub
```

Don't forget to add the API declaration to the Windows .dll file used to play sounds to the general declarations section of a standard module.

```
Public Declare Function sndPlaySoundA Lib "winmm.dll" _

(ByVal lpszsoundname As String, ByVal uflags As Long) As Long
```

The remaining procedures added to enhance the Battlecell game are used to help the computer locate potential target cells when firing at the player's ships. The CountRedCells() function procedure counts the number of red cells in the cell range used for holding the player's ships, stores the location of each red cell found in the variable array redCells, and returns the integer number of red cells found. Remember that a cell is colored red if the computer has previously scored a hit on that cell.

```
Private Function CountRedCells() As Integer
    Dim I As Integer
    Dim c As Range
    I = 0
    numRedCells = 0
    Set playerRange = Range("B2:K11")
```

A For/Each loop is used to iterate through the 100 individual cells in the range representing the grid that holds the player's ships.

```
    For Each c In playerRange
        If c.Interior.Color = RGB(255, 0, 0) Then
            numRedCells = numRedCells + 1
```

When a red cell is found, the dynamic variable array redCells is re-dimensioned and the Address property of the Range object representing the location of that red cell is used to store the cell location in the array.

```
            ReDim Preserve redCells(numRedCells)
            redCells(I) = c.Address
            I = I + 1
        End If
    Next
    CountRedCells = numRedCells
End Function
```

The sub procedure FindTargets() looks for potential targets on the player's grid based on the cells already identified as hit.

```
Private Sub FindTargets()
    Dim isColumn As Boolean
    Dim isRow As Boolean
    Dim testCell As String
    Dim startCell As String
```

```
    Dim endCell As String
    Dim I As Integer
    isColumn = False
    isRow = False
```

A For/Next loop is used to iterate through each red-colored cell whose locations are stored in the variable array redCells.

```
    For I = 0 To numRedCells - 1
        testCell = redCells(I)
```

Each red cell is tested for its presence in a column or row of adjacent red cells using the CheckForCol() and CheckForRow() function procedures. The procedures are passed a string value representing the address of a red-colored cell and return a Boolean value (true if the cell is in a row or column, false if not).

```
        isColumn = CheckForCol(testCell)
        isRow = CheckForRow(testCell)
```

The FindBegin(), FindEnd(), and FindNeighbors() procedures are called to locate the beginning and ending cells of a row or column of red cells and the adjacent cells to a row or column of red cells, respectively. The values of the parameters passed to these procedures are based on the return values of the CheckForCol() and CheckForRow() function procedures.

```
        If isColumn = True And isRow = False Then
            startCell = FindBegin(testCell, "col")
            endCell = FindEnd(testCell, "col")
            Call FindNeighbors("col", startCell, endCell)
        End If
        If isRow = True And isColumn = False Then
            startCell = FindBegin(testCell, "row")
            endCell = FindEnd(testCell, "row")
            Call FindNeighbors("row", startCell, endCell)
        End If
        If isColumn = False And isRow = False Then
            startCell = testCell
            endCell = testCell
            Call FindNeighbors("onecell", startCell, endCell)
        End If
        isColumn = False
        isRow = False
    Next I
End Sub
```

Figure 6.10 shows the shot order the computer will take at a player's ship after scoring a single hit. In this example, the computer will fire seven more shots before random shot selection resumes.

The CheckForCol() function procedure takes the address of a red-colored cell as input and tests its two adjacent cells within the column for their presence within the variable array redCells. For example, if the address of cell C5 is passed to the CheckForCol() function procedure, then the addresses of cells C4 and C6 are tested for their presence in the array redCells. If either of the addresses of cells C4 or C6 are found in the array, then the red-colored cell C5 must be within a column of red cells. The AlterIndex() function procedure is used to increment and decrement the row index for the variables testCell1 and testCell2.

```
Private Function CheckForCol(testCell As String) As Boolean
    Dim I As Integer
    Dim testCell1 As String
    Dim testCell2 As String
    testCell1 = AlterIndex(testCell, "col", False)
    testCell2 = AlterIndex(testCell, "col", True)
    For I = 0 To UBound(redCells) - 1
        If testCell1 = redCells(I) Or testCell2 = redCells(I) Then
            CheckForCol = True
        End If
    Next I
End Function
```

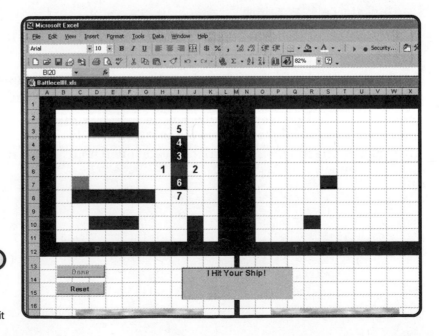

FIGURE 6.10

Computer's shot
selection after
scoring an initial hit

The CheckForRow() function procedure works just like the CheckForCol() procedure, except that the column index is incremented and decremented by the AlterIndex() function procedure so the test cell can be checked for its presence within a row of red-colored cells.

```
Private Function CheckForRow(testCell As String) As Boolean
    Dim I As Integer
    Dim testCell1 As String
    Dim testCell2 As String
    testCell1 = AlterIndex(testCell, "row", False)
    testCell2 = AlterIndex(testCell, "row", True)
    For I = 0 To UBound(redCells) - 1
        If testCell1 = redCells(I) Or testCell2 = redCells(I) Then
            CheckForRow = True
        End If
    Next I
End Function
```

The AlterIndex() function simply adds or subtracts one unit from a row or column index of a cell address passed in as a string. The string "row" or the string "col" is passed to the function to use as an indicator for altering either the column or row index.

```
Private Function AlterIndex(testCell As String, rowOrCol As String, incre-
ment As Boolean) As String       Dim lowCell As String
    Dim highCell As String
    Dim rowIndex As Integer
    Dim colIndex As Integer
```

Basically, the address passed to the function is ripped apart using string functions to find either its row or column index. The row or column index is then decremented and incremented and two new strings are created (lowCell and highCell) using the altered indices. If the string "$C$10" and string value "col" are passed to the function, the variable lowCell will hold "$C$9" and the variable highCell will hold "$C$11".

```
    If rowOrCol = "col" Then
        rowIndex = Val(Right(testCell, 2))
        lowCell = Left(testCell, 3) & Trim(Str(rowIndex - 1))
        highCell = Left(testCell, 3) & Trim(Str(rowIndex + 1))
        If rowIndex = 0 Then
            rowIndex = Val(Right(testCell, 1))
            lowCell = Left(testCell, 3) & Trim(Str(rowIndex - 1))
```

```
          highCell = Left(testCell, 3) & Trim(Str(rowIndex + 1))
      End If
  ElseIf rowOrCol = "row" Then
    colIndex = Asc(Mid(testCell, 2, 1))
    lowCell = "$" & Chr(colIndex - 1) & Right(testCell, Len(testCell) - 2)
    highCell = "$" & Chr(colIndex + 1) & Right(testCell, Len(testCell) - 2)
  Else
    MsgBox ("Error! Row or column not specified!")
  End If
```

A Boolean value is also passed to the AlterIndex() function to tell it which value to return. The AlterIndex() function then has to be called twice (see the Check-ForCol() and CheckForRow() procedures) in order to get both the decremented and incremented cell addresses.

```
  If increment = True Then
      AlterIndex = highCell
  Else
      AlterIndex = lowCell
  End If
End Function
```

The function procedures FindBegin() and FindEnd() loop through the list of red-colored cells comparing the address of a test cell to each cell address in the list. The column or row index of the test cell is either decremented or incremented, depending on the procedure to which it is sent. Thus, if the altered test cell is found within the list of red-colored cells, the outer Do-Loop continues. This effectively finds the beginning or ending red-colored cell contained within a row or column of red-colored cells.

```
Private Function FindBegin(testCell As String, rowOrCol As String) As String
    Dim I As Integer
    Dim firstCell As String
    Dim foundOne As Boolean
    foundOne = False
    firstCell = testCell
```

The outer Do-Loop will continue as long as the cell address altered by the AlterIndex() function procedure is found within the list of red-colored cells. This means that the test cell is not at the beginning of a row or column so the loop must continue.

```
    Do
        foundOne = False
```

A nested For/Next loop is used to compare the altered cell address to the list of red-colored cells contained in the variable array redCells.

```
For I = 0 To UBound(redCells) - 1
    If (AlterIndex(testCell, rowOrCol, False)) = redCells(I) Then
        firstCell = redCells(I)
        foundOne = True
    End If
Next I
```

If the comparison of the altered cell address to the list of red-colored cells is true, then the variable testCell is assigned the string value of the red-colored cell stored in the variable firstCell for use in the next iteration of the Do-Loop. The process continues until the altered cell address is not found within the list of red-colored cells.

```
        If foundOne = True Then testCell = firstCell
    Loop While (foundOne = True)
    FindBegin = firstCell
End Function
```

The FindEnd() function procedure works exactly like the FindBegin() function procedure, except that the altered cell address is incremented rather than decremented.

```
Private Function FindEnd(testCell As String, rowOrCol As String) As String
    Dim I As Integer
    Dim lastCell As String
    Dim foundOne As Boolean
    foundOne = False
    lastCell = testCell
    Do
        foundOne = False
        For I = 0 To UBound(redCells) - 1
            If (AlterIndex(testCell, rowOrCol, True)) = redCells(I) Then
                lastCell = redCells(I)
                foundOne = True
            End If
        Next I
        If foundOne = True Then testCell = lastCell
    Loop While (foundOne = True)
    FindEnd = lastCell
End Function
```

The last procedure added to the enhanced Battlecell program is `FindNeighbors()`. This sub procedure is used to find the nearest neighbors to an isolated red-colored cell, and a row or column of red-colored cells. The neighboring cells represent potential targets for the computer. The parameters passed to the `FindNeighbors()` sub procedure are all strings representing the beginning and ending cells in a row or column of red-colored cells.

```
Private Sub FindNeighbors(rowOrCol As String, startCell As String, endCell
As String)
    Dim target(3) As String
    Dim I As Integer
    Dim J As Integer
    For I = 0 To 3
        target(I) = "$A$1"
    Next I
```

If the beginning and ending cells are in a row or column, then there are only two potential targets that need to be considered. If the cell is isolated, then there are four potential targets: above, below, and to either side. The `AlterIndex()` function procedure is used to produce the strings representing the targets.

```
If rowOrCol = "col" Then
    target(0) = AlterIndex(startCell, "col", False)
    target(1) = AlterIndex(endCell, "col", True)
ElseIf rowOrCol = "row" Then
    target(0) = AlterIndex(startCell, "row", False)
    target(1) = AlterIndex(endCell, "row", True)
ElseIf rowOrCol = "onecell" Then
    target(0) = AlterIndex(startCell, "row", False)
    target(1) = AlterIndex(endCell, "row", True)
    target(2) = AlterIndex(startCell, "col", False)
    target(3) = AlterIndex(endCell, "col", True)
End If
```

The potential target cells just saved to the variable array target are first tested for their location within the player's grid. The value of the target cell is changed to the string literal `"$A$1"` if the potential target cell is outside the desired range.

```
For I = 0 To 3
 If (Range(target(I)).Column < 2) Or (Range(target(I)).Column > 11) Or _
        (Range(target(I)).Row < 2) Or (Range(target(I)).Row > 11) Then
target(I) = "$A$1"
```

Next, potential target cells are tested to see if they have already been added to the list of target cells the computer will use in the `ComputerFire()` sub procedure. The value of the target cell is changed to the string literal `"$A$1"` if it has already been recorded as a target.

```
For J = 0 To UBound(targetCells) - 1
    If target(I) = targetCells(J) Then target(I) = "$A$1"
Next J
```

Finally, the potential target cells are added to the list of targets the computer will use in the `ComputerFire()` sub procedure unless their value is `"$A$1"`.

```
If target(I) <> "$A$1" Then
    targetCells(UBound(targetCells)) = target(I)
    ReDim Preserve targetCells(1 + UBound(targetCells))
End If
    Next I
End Sub
```

I made other minor adjustments to the program, but they make no significant contribution to these enhancements. They are included on the CD-ROM in the source code for your perusal.

Although the enhancements to the intelligence of the Battlecell program are significant, they are still not enough to make the computer competitive. Furthermore, if the additional enhancements discussed earlier are to be added to the Battlecell program, then I would suggest considering a different algorithm for finding potential target cells. The above procedures work fairly well for finding targets once a player's ship has been hit, but significant room for improvement still exists. The important thing to note here is that the larger problem of finding potential targets for the computer was encapsulated in the algorithim into a list of smaller problems that were much easier to solve.

Chapter Summary

This has been one of the more fun chapters to write, and I expect it was one of the most fun for you to read. Multimedia events in a program are what make a program fun, both for the player and the programmer.

In this chapter you learned how to add simple animations to your VBA/Excel programs using a number of techniques, all involving the use of a `Delay()` sub procedure and the `Timer` function. You also learned how to play sound files using the Windows API. Finally, you considered the problem of adding intelligence to a program and learned that it doesn't necessarily involve special programming techniques but, instead, careful planning and implementation of the plan.

CHALLENGES

1. Create an animation in Excel using cell formatting to spell your first name. Use borders and color along with the `width` and `height` properties of the Range object to create the animation.

2. Use any image creation software application to create a few images for animation. Then, using the procedures from the rolling ball animation demo, animate your images. If you are artistically challenged, then do something simple, such as changing an expression on a face from a frown to a smile. You can also animate text by creating images with the text placed in different positions.

3. Add a scroll bar to the rolling ball animation to use for controlling the speed of the ball.

4. Create a tic-tac-toe game in Excel that cannot be beaten. Use either worksheet cells and the `Worksheet_SelectionChange()` event procedure or nine Command Button controls and the `Click()` event procedure to mark the squares with X's and O's. Add sound to the game when an X or an O is played (you can find hundreds of sound files on the Internet).

5. Add further intelligence enhancements to the Battlecell II program to make it more difficult to defeat the computer.

UserForms and Additional Controls

UserForms enable you to build customized windows that can be added to an application. UserForms serve as containers for ActiveX controls that are typically added to create custom dialog boxes used for gathering specific input from the user.

In this chapter I will specifically examine:

- **UserForms**

- **The Frame control**

- **The ListBox and ComboBox controls**

- **Modal and modeless UserForms**

- **Chapter project: Blackjack**

Project: Blackjack

Blackjack is a standard on most computers. You can find numerous versions of this game in Windows, Java, and JavaScript. This chapter reproduces the game using VBA UserForms with Excel, which is something you probably have not seen before. Figure 7.1 shows the Blackjack game in the Excel application.

UserForms

If you have ever programmed in Visual Basic (even as a novice), then UserForms will be very familiar, because they will remind you of Visual Basic forms. If you have never used Visual Basic, then UserForms will probably look just like another window. However, UserForms are not quite VB forms or regular windows, because they don't have as many features. For example, there are no minimize and maximize buttons in the upper-right corner. Also, there are fewer properties and methods that can be used to alter the appearance and behavior of the UserForm.

UserForms are included in VBA to allow programmers to build custom dialog boxes with their office applications. Up to this point, input from the user via dialog boxes has been limited to the use of the InputBox() and MsgBox() functions. Because UserForms can be customized using a number of ActiveX controls, they greatly extend the abilities of VBA programmers to collect user input.

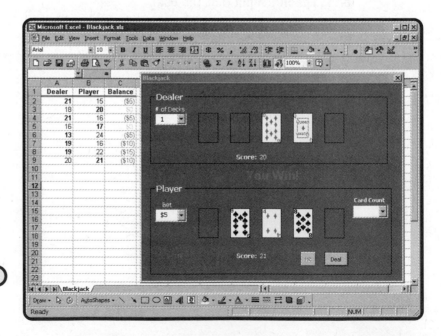

FIGURE 7.1

The Blackjack game

Adding a UserForm to a Project

To add a UserForm to a VBA project, select Insert/UserForm from the menu bar in the VBA IDE, as shown in Figure 7.2.

A new folder labeled Forms appears in the Project Explorer window. An example of a UserForm just added to a project is shown in Figure 7.3

Components of the UserForm Object

UserForms are VBA objects that are similar to ActiveX controls. So when a UserForm is selected, its properties will appear in the Properties window in the VBA IDE (see Figure 7.3). Table 7.1 defines a few of the properties of UserForms commonly set at design time.

> **HINT**
>
> The UserForm object has several additional appearance properties besides those listed in Table 7.1. BorderColor, BorderStyle, and SpecialEffect are others that may be used for aesthetic appeal.

FIGURE 7.2

Inserting a
UserForm from
the VBA IDE

The ListBox control
The ComboBox control
The Frame control
The Forms folder in the Project Explorer
Properties of the UserForm object
The Toolbox containing ActiveX controls

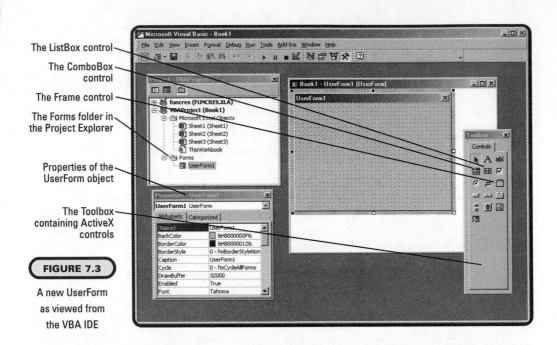

FIGURE 7.3

A new UserForm as viewed from the VBA IDE

TABLE 7.1 SELECTED PROPERTIES OF THE USERFORM

Property	Description
Name	Sets the name of the UserForm for use as a code reference to the object
BackColor	Sets the color of the UserForm
Caption	Sets the text displayed in the title bar
Height	Sets the height of the UserForm
StartUpPosition	Sets the position of the UserForm on the screen when displayed
Width	Sets the width of the UserForm

UserForms represent separate entities in a VBA project and have their own code window. To view the code window (module) associated with the UserForm, select the View Code icon from the Project Explorer, or select View, Code (with the User-Form selected). You can also double-click the UserForm to open its code window. The structure of a UserForm code window (usually referred to as a *form module*) is the same as any other module window. The upper-left corner contains a drop-down list with all objects contained within the form, including the UserForm object. The upper-right corner contains a drop-down list of all event procedures associated with the various objects that may be contained in the UserForm. There is also a general declarations section for making module level declarations in the form module. An example code window for a UserForm is shown in Figure 7.4.

The behavior of the variables and procedures declared with the `Dim`, `Private`, and `Public` keywords in a form module are identical to that of a component module as discussed in Chapter 3, "Procedures and Conditions." Thus, the scope of variables and procedures declared as `Public` in the general declarations section of the module are module-level, not global. Variables and procedures declared as `Public` in a form module can be accessed from procedures in other modules when the full path is specified (`ModuleName.VariableName` or `ModuleName.ProcedureName`).

The UserForm object has several event procedures, including `Click()`, `Activate()`, and `QueryClose()`, among others. To view the full list of event procedures of the UserForm object, select the UserForm object in the object list and then select the event procedure drop-down list from the form module (see Figure 7.4). Some of these event procedures should be familiar, as they are common to several ActiveX controls.

Adding ActiveX Controls to a UserForm

Like the Worksheet object, the UserForm is a container object, which means it can be used to hold other objects. UserForms are specifically used as a container for ActiveX controls. When a UserForm is added to a project, the control toolbox should automatically appear (see Figure 7.3). If the ActiveX control toolbox does not appear, select View/Toolbox from the menu bar. There will be a couple of additional controls displayed in the control toolbox when viewed with a UserForm. Most notable is the Frame control that will be discussed later in this chapter.

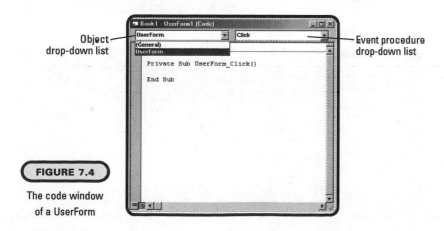

Object drop-down list

Event procedure drop-down list

FIGURE 7.4

The code window of a UserForm

ActiveX controls are added to a UserForm in the same manner that they are added to worksheets. When added to a UserForm, the properties and events of an ActiveX control can be accessed via the Properties and Module windows, respectively. To illustrate the use of ActiveX controls on UserForms, access the frmMessage User-Form from the FormDemo.xls Excel file located on the CD-ROM. The frmMessage UserForm, as viewed at design time, from the VBA IDE is shown in Figure 7.5.

To create this application, a UserForm was inserted into the project, and Label and Command Button controls were added. Properties (Name, Caption, and some appearance properties) were changed at design time by selecting the object and altering the values in the Properties window exactly as is done when using ActiveX controls with an Excel worksheet. The application contains just one line of code contained in the Click() event procedure of the Command Button control.

```
Private Sub cmdHello_Click()
    lblOutput.Caption = "Hello!"
End Sub
```

When the user clicks the Command Button control name cmdHello, the preceding procedure is triggered and the Caption property of the Label control named lblOutput is changed.

To test the application, select the UserForm and click on Run/Sub UserForm from the IDE standard toolbar or menu bar, or press F5 on the keyboard. The UserForm appears

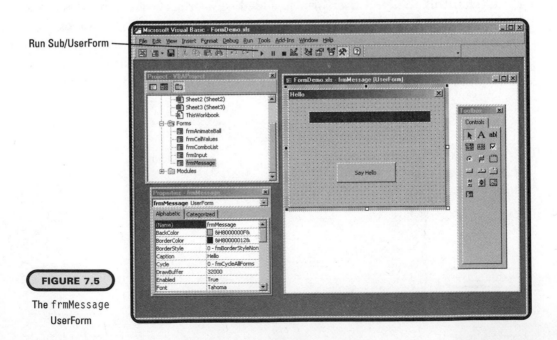

Run Sub/UserForm

FIGURE 7.5

The frmMessage UserForm

as a window above the Excel application. To close the UserForm, click on the X in the upper-right corner of the window.

Showing and Hiding UserForms

To display a UserForm from the Excel application, use the Show method of the UserForm object in a procedure that can be triggered from Excel (a public procedure in a standard module or an event procedure from a component module). The basic syntax follows:

```
UserFormName.Show Modal
```

 To load a UserForm into system memory without displaying it, use the Load **statement.**

```
Load UserFormName
```

 The UserForm object and all its components can be accessed from a VBA program after loading the object into memory.

For example, to display a UserForm named frmMessage when a Click() event procedure of a Command Button control (named cmdShowForm) placed on a worksheet is triggered, use the following code:

```
Private Sub cmdShowForm_Click()
    frmMessage.Show
End Sub
```

To hide a UserForm from the user but retain programmatic control, use the Hide method of the UserForm object.

```
UserFormName.Hide
```

The Hide method does not remove the UserForm object from system memory, so the UserForm and its components can still be accessed from a VBA program. To remove a UserForm from system memory, use the UnLoad statement.

```
UnLoad UserFormName
```

Modal Forms

The Show method of the UserForm object takes an optional Boolean parameter that specifies whether the UserForm is modal. The default value of the modal parameter is true, which creates a modal UserForm. A modal UserForm must be addressed by the user and subsequently closed (by the user or the program) before any other part of the Excel application can be used. If the UserForm is modeless, then the user may select between any open windows in the Excel application.

 Modeless UserForms are only supported in MS Office 2000 and Office XP. Trying to create a modeless UserForm in an earlier version of MS Office will generate a runtime error.

A modal form is safest and should be used unless user interaction with the Excel application is required while the UserForm is displayed. The UserForm can be displayed via the Show method from anywhere in a VBA program. However, be aware that program execution may proceed differently depending on where in a procedure the UserForm is shown and whether the UserForm is modal. For example, the two procedures that follow will yield different results.

In the first example, the Show method is used with a UserForm object to display a modeless UserForm. Next a MsgBox() function is used to display some text. In this example, code execution proceeds through the entire procedure, first displaying the UserForm, then the message box, so both dialogs are displayed to the user at the same time.

```
Private Sub MyProcedure()
    frmMyUserForm.Show False
    MsgBox("The message box is displayed immediately after the UserForm")
End Sub
```

In the second example the UserForm is displayed modally, so code execution within the procedure pauses while the UserForm is displayed. After the user closes the UserForm, program execution proceeds to the next line of code. Thus, when using a modal UserForm, program behavior is identical to the MsgBox() and InputBox() functions.

```
Private Sub MyProcedure()
    frmMyUserForm.Show True
    MsgBox("The message box is displayed after the UserForm is closed.")
End Sub
```

 To determine which version of Excel is running on a user's computer, use the Version property of the Application object. The Version property returns a read-only string containing a number that represents the version of Excel currently running on your computer (8.0 for Excel 97, 9.0 for Excel 2000, and 10.0 for Excel XP/2002).

Now that you know how to display a UserForm in a program, it's time to take a look at the ActiveX controls that can be used with it, as well as how to use User-Forms to interact with the Excel application.

Custom Dialog Boxes with UserForms

As mentioned earlier, UserForms are generally used as dialog boxes to collect user input relevant to the current application. You can use ActiveX controls to expand the capabilities of UserForms well beyond that of the InputBox() and MsgBox() functions. ActiveX controls are the same as those used with an Excel worksheet, so there is no need to spend more time discussing how to use them. Instead, let's look at a couple of ActiveX controls that have not yet been introduced.

The Frame Control

The Frame control is used to group ActiveX controls on the UserForm. The ActiveX controls grouped within a Frame control may be related by content, or in the case of OptionButton controls, be made mutually exclusive. The properties of the Frame control are seldom referenced in code. The Name and Caption properties, along with a couple of appearance properties (BorderStyle, Font, and so on), are typically set at design time.

A sample form using the two Frame controls to group three OptionButton controls is shown in Figure 7.6.

The purpose of the UserForm shown in Figure 7.6 is to give the user a selection of font types and font sizes. The result of the user's selections is displayed in the Label control. The Frame control is used to group the OptionButton controls by content and make each set mutually exclusive. Without at least one Frame control the user would only be allowed to select one of the six option buttons.

In this example, I used the Click() event procedure of each OptionButton control to set the desired property of the Label control. For example, the procedures shown here are used to set the font size to 24 and the font type to Times New Roman.

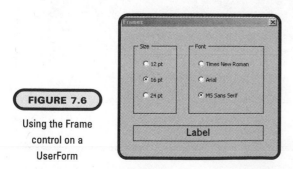

FIGURE 7.6

Using the Frame control on a UserForm

```
Private Sub OptionButton3_Click()
    lblOutput.Font.Size = 24
End Sub
Private Sub OptionButton4_Click()
    lblOutput.Font.Name = "Times New Roman"
End Sub
```

Selecting a Worksheet Range with a Custom Dialog Box

A common requirement for custom dialog boxes is that they allow the user to select a range of cells from the active worksheet before performing a specific task. Prior to modeless forms this was a somewhat tedious programming task that often produced mixed results. The following example uses methods designed to work with modal and modeless forms, allowing the user to easily select a range of cells on a worksheet for the calculation of some simple statistics. The UserForm displayed at runtime is shown in Figure 7.7. To access this UserForm, load the FormDemos.xls workbook file from the CD-ROM and run the ShowForm() sub procedure (select Run Macro from the Visual Basic toolbar) while in Sheet1. The worksheet contains a series of random numbers to use for testing the UserForm's function.

The UserForm contains two Frame controls, one for grouping the controls responsible for selecting the worksheet range and the other for grouping the Label controls used to display the statistics. At the bottom of the UserForm are three Command Button controls, two of which are used for navigating through

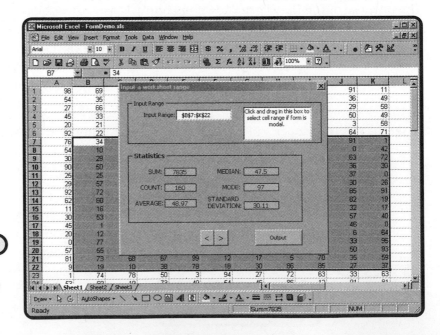

FIGURE 7.7

Selecting a worksheet range with a custom dialog box

the worksheets in the current workbook and the other for outputting the statistical results to a new worksheet.

The form module named `frmInput` contains the following code:

```
Option Explicit
Dim selectCells As Boolean
Dim col1 As String
Dim row1 As Integer
Dim col1Value As Integer
```

After module-level variable declarations, the `Activate()` event procedure of the UserForm will be triggered as soon as the UserForm is loaded and displayed.

 HINT Unlike with other ActiveX controls, changing the `Name` property of the UserForm does not change the name of its event procedures.

The `Activate()` event procedure sends code execution to the `CalcStats()` sub procedure that calculates a few statistical values associated with the currently selected cell(s) on the active worksheet.

```
Private Sub UserForm_Activate()
    CalcStats
End Sub
```

The `CalcStats()` sub procedure uses Excel's built-in functions to do most of the work. These functions are accessed via the `WorksheetFunction` property of the Application object.

```
Public Sub CalcStats()
    Const noValue = "N/A"
```

Because some of the statistical functions used can generate divide-by-zero errors, the next line is used to catch these errors and send code execution to the next line after it. You will learn more about error trapping in Chapter 8, "Data Access and File I/O."

```
    On Error Resume Next
```

The `Address` property of the Range object defined by the currently selected range in the active worksheet is copied to the TextBox control named `txtInput`. This is followed by calls to Excel's worksheet functions that calculate the desired statistics and display the results in various Label controls. If the worksheet function used generates an error, the string constant N/A is displayed in the Label control, and code execution skips to the next line because of the `On Error Resume Next` line of code listed earlier in the procedure.

```
    If txtInput.Text = "" Then txtInput.Text = Selection.Address
    lblSum.Caption =
Application.WorksheetFunction.Sum(Range(txtInput.Text))
    lblCount.Caption =
Application.WorksheetFunction.Count(Range(txtInput.Text))
    lblAverage.Caption = noValue
    lblAverage.Caption =
Format(Application.WorksheetFunction.Average(Range(txtInput.Text)), "#.##")
    lblMedian.Caption =
Application.WorksheetFunction.Median(Range(txtInput.Text))
    lblMode.Caption = noValue
    lblMode.Caption =
Application.WorksheetFunction.Mode(Range(txtInput.Text))
    lblStanDev.Caption = noValue
    lblStanDev.Caption =
Format(Application.WorksheetFunction.StDev(Range(txtInput.Text)), "#.##")
End Sub
```

The next three sub procedures use mouse events of a Label control to allow the user to select a range of cells in the active worksheet. These procedures are designed to work with modal forms that do not allow the user to select other windows in the Excel application while a UserForm is displayed. This makes these procedures more useful with versions of Excel prior to Office 2000.

The location of the mouse pointer, when the mouse button is initially pressed by the user, is sent to the MouseDown() event procedure of the Label control and stored in the variables X and Y. The values of the variables X and Y will range between the minimum and maximum values of the Width and Height properties of the Label control, respectively. In this example, the Width and Height properties of the Label control are set to 104 and 50, respectively.

```
Private Sub lblCellSelect_MouseDown(ByVal Button As Integer, ByVal Shift
As Integer, ByVal X As Single, ByVal Y As Single)
    If X < 104 And X > 0 And Y > 0 And Y < 51 Then
        selectCells = True
```

The module-level variable selectCells is set to true for later use in the MouseMove() event procedure. The range of cells the user has to choose from is limited to approximately the first 100 rows and first 25 columns by multiplying and dividing the values of the variables X and Y by integers, then storing the results in two module-level variables named col1 and row1. The values of col1 and row1 are used to set a reference cell to the range of cells that will be selected by the user.

```
col1 = Chr(65 + Int(X / 4))
row1 = Int(Y * 2)
col1Value = Int(X / 4)
```

The values of `col1` and `row1` are converted to a string and copied to the `Text` property of `txtInput`, which is then converted to a Range object. The referenced cell is then selected on the active worksheet via the `Select` method of the Range object.

```
        txtInput.Text = "$" & col1 & "$" & row1
        Range(txtInput.Text).Select
        lblCellSelect.Caption = ""
    End If
End Sub
```

The `MouseMove()` event procedure is used to catch the user's movement of the mouse through the Label control.

```
Private Sub lblCellSelect_MouseMove(ByVal Button As Integer, ByVal Shift
As Integer, ByVal X As Single, ByVal Y As Single)
    Dim col2 As String
    Dim row2 As Integer
    Dim col2Value As Integer
```

Again the location of the mouse within the Label control is captured and stored in two new variables, `col2` and `row2`.

```
    col2 = Chr(65 + Int(X / 4))
    row2 = Int(Y * 2)
    col2Value = Int(X / 4)
```

The module-level variable `selectCells` is tested to ensure that cells are selected while the user holds down the mouse. The value of the second reference cell in the selected range is set as with the `MouseDown()` event procedure. The values of both reference cells are then tested such that the range displayed in the text box is of the proper form (for example, $A$1:$B$5 instead of $B$5:$A$1).

```
If selectCells = True And X < 104 And X > 0 And Y > 0 And Y < 51 Then
    If (col1Value <= col2Value) And (row1 <= row2) Then
        txtInput.Text = "$" & col1 & "$" & row1 & ":$" & col2 & "$" & row2
    ElseIf (col2Value <= col1Value) And (row2 <= row1) Then
        txtInput.Text = "$" & col2 & "$" & row2 & ":$" & col1 & "$" & row1
    ElseIf (col2Value <= col1Value) And (row1 <= row2) Then
        txtInput.Text = "$" & col2 & "$" & row1 & ":$" & col1 & "$" & row2
    ElseIf (col1Value <= col2Value) And (row2 <= row1) Then
```

```
        txtInput.Text = "$" & col1 & "$" & row2 & ":$" & col2 & "$" & row1
      End If
      Range(txtInput.Text).Select
  End If
End Sub
```

The `MouseUp()` event procedure is used to set the user's selected range and call the `CalcStats()` sub procedure listed earlier.

```
Private Sub lblCellSelect_MouseUp(ByVal Button As Integer, ByVal Shift As
Integer, ByVal X As Single, ByVal Y As Single)
    selectCells = False
    Range(txtInput.Text).Select
    CalcStats
    lblCellSelect.Caption = "Click and drag in this box to select cell
range if form is modal."
End Sub
```

The process of collecting a user-selected range with a modal form is not trivial. Even though the preceding procedures are relatively simple to code, the user will find the process a bit frustrating. To improve the process, a control with a larger area can be used for the selection of the range, perhaps with some type of grid displayed so the user knows approximately where to start the selection (for example, a Frame control containing numerous Label controls stacked in rows and columns). Of course, the user can also just enter the range directly into the TextBox control.

The `Click()` event procedures of two Command Button controls (`cmdNext` and `cmdPrev`) are used to navigate through all open worksheets in the current workbook.

```
Private Sub cmdNext_Click()
    Dim wkIndex As Integer
```

The `Index` property of the Worksheet object is used to determine the currently selected worksheet. If the currently selected worksheet is not the last worksheet in the workbook, then the value of the index is incremented by one and the next worksheet is made active with the `Select` method.

```
    wkIndex = ActiveSheet.Index
```

The `Count` property of the Worksheet object returns the number of Worksheet objects in the active workbook. This effectively tells you the index of the last worksheet in the collection. This procedure appears to do nothing when the last worksheet in the current workbook is selected.

```
        If wkIndex >= Worksheets.Count Then
            wkIndex = Worksheets.Count
        Else
            wkIndex = wkIndex + 1
        End If
        Worksheets(wkIndex).Select
        ActiveSheet.Range(txtInput.Text).Select
        CalcStats
End Sub
```

The Click() event procedure of cmdPrev uses the same code, except that now the first worksheet in the collection has an index value of 1. This procedure appears to do nothing when the first worksheet in the current workbook is selected.

```
Private Sub cmdPrev_Click()
    Dim wkIndex As Integer
    wkIndex = ActiveSheet.Index
    If wkIndex <= 1 Then
        wkIndex = 1   'Worksheets.Count + 1
    Else
        wkIndex = wkIndex - 1
    End If
    Worksheets(wkIndex).Select
    ActiveSheet.Range(txtInput.Text).Select
    CalcStats
End Sub
```

Outputting to a worksheet data that has been manipulated within form-module procedures is easy and really no different than previous methods discussed. The following Click() event procedure outputs the statistical results calculated in the sub procedure CalcStats() to a new worksheet added to the current workbook. To output data to a workbook other than the one currently selected, specify the full path in code.

Most of this procedure is simple formatting of the cells used to hold the statistical results and the corresponding labels. The Add method of the Worksheet object is used to create a new worksheet. The Add method can take several optional parameters that are used to specify the location, type, and number of worksheets to be added. If these parameters are omitted, then one worksheet is inserted before the active sheet and the new worksheet becomes the active sheet.

```
Private Sub cmdOutput_Click()
    Worksheets.Add
```

```vba
    Range("A1").Value = Worksheets(ActiveSheet.Index + 1).Name & ":"
    ActiveSheet.Name = Worksheets(ActiveSheet.Index + 1).Name & " Stats"
    Range("A1").HorizontalAlignment = xlRight
    Range("B1").Value = txtInput.Text
    Range("A2").Value = "Statistic"
    Range("B2").Value = "Value"
    Range("A2:B2").Font.Bold = True
    Range("A2:B2").Borders(xlEdgeBottom).Weight = xlThick
    Range("A2:B2").HorizontalAlignment = xlCenter
    Range("A3").Value = "Sum"
    Range("A4").Value = "Count"
    Range("A5").Value = "Average"
    Range("A6").Value = "Median"
    Range("A7").Value = "Mode"
    Range("A8").Value = "Stan. Dev."
    Range("A3:A8").HorizontalAlignment = xlRight
    Range("B3:B8").HorizontalAlignment = xlCenter
    Range("A:B").Columns.AutoFit
    Range("B3").Value = lblSum.Caption
    Range("B4").Value = lblCount.Caption
    Range("B5").Value = lblAverage.Caption
    Range("B6").Value = lblMedian.Caption
    Range("B7").Value = lblMode.Caption
    Range("B8").Value = lblStanDev.Caption
End Sub
```

The resulting worksheet created from the previous procedure is shown in Figure 7.8.

The QueryClose() event procedure is used to capture the user's action when the UserForm is closed by clicking the X in the upper-right corner of the UserForm. The keyword Me sets a reference to the current active object, in this case the User-Form named frmInput. If preferred, the name of the object can also be used.

```vba
Private Sub UserForm_QueryClose(Cancel As Integer, CloseMode As Integer)
    Unload Me
End Sub
```

If the UserForm is modeless, then the SelectionChange() event procedure of the Worksheet object can be used to capture the range selected by the user. If a program must run on a new worksheet that does not contain code, then the Click() event of a Command Button control will work just as well. You can test this by selecting a range in Sheet1 of FormDemos.xls and then running the ShowForm() sub procedure.

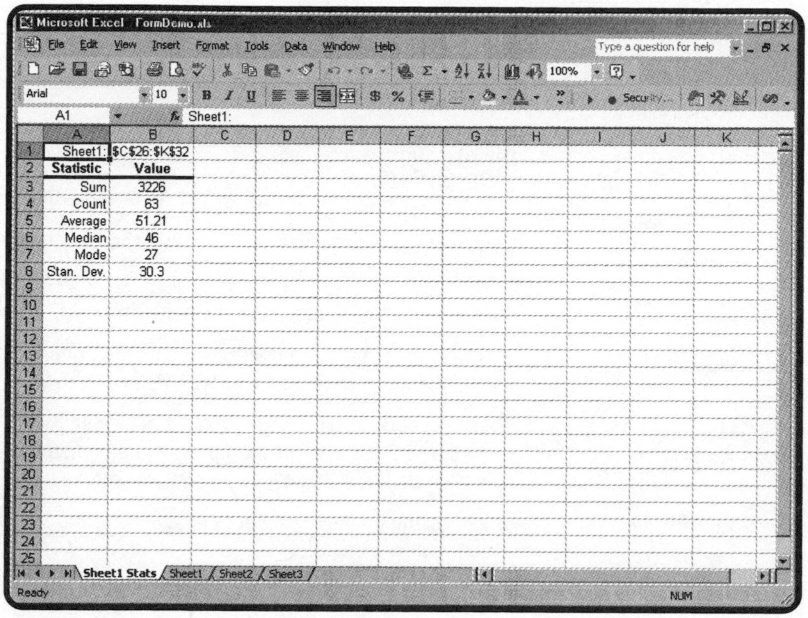

FIGURE 7.8

New worksheet
created from the
frmInput
UserForm

```
Private Sub Worksheet_SelectionChange(ByVal Target As Range)
    frmInput.txtInput.Text = Target.Address
```

The CalcStats() procedure has public scope, so it can be accessed from the component module of the worksheet.

```
    frmInput.CalcStats
End Sub
```

Finally, a public procedure in a standard module is used to give the user access to the program from the Tools menu or from the Visual Basic toolbar in the Excel application.

```
Public Sub ShowForm()
    frmInput.Show False
End Sub
```

The ListBox and ComboBox Controls

The ListBox control (refer to Figure 7.3) is used to display data in a list from which the user may select one or more items. The ComboBox control combines the features of a ListBox control with a TextBox control, allowing the user to enter a new value if desired. Properties of the ListBox and ComboBox controls commonly set at design time and runtime are listed in Table 7.2.

TABLE 7.2 SELECTED PROPERTIES OF THE LISTBOX AND COMBOBOX CONTROLS

Property	Description
Name	Sets the name of the control for use as a code reference to the object
MultiSelect	ListBox control only. Indicates whether the user will be able to select multiple items in the list.
ColumnCount	Sets the number of data columns to be displayed in the list
ListStyle	Indicates whether option buttons (single selection) or check boxes (multi selection) should appear with items in the list
Value	Holds the current selection in the list. If a multi-select ListBox control is used, the BoundColumn property must be used to identify the column from which the value property is set.
BoundColumn	Identifies the column that sets the source of the Value property in a multi-select ListBox
List	Runtime only. Used to access the items in the control.
ListCount	Runtime only. Returns the number of entries in the control.
ListIndex	Runtime only. Identifies the currently selected item in the control.
Style	ComboBox control only. Specifies the behavior of the control as a combo box or a drop-down list box.

The ListBox control may be drawn on the UserForm with varying height and width such that it displays one or multiple items in the list. If there are more items in the list than can be displayed in the area provided, the scroll bars will automatically appear. Normally, the ListBox control is drawn with the Height property set to a value large enough for several values to be displayed, because it is difficult to see the scroll bar when the control is at a minimum height. If space on the UserForm is at a premium, use the ComboBox control and set the Style property to drop-down list.

Data is added to the ListBox and ComboBox controls at runtime using the AddItem method.

```
ControlName.Additem (item)
```

The AddItem method must be used for every row of data added to the list. A looping code structure will often work well to complete this task. The example User-Form frmComboList (FormDemo.xls), shown in Figure 7.9, is used to display the values of individual rows and columns in a worksheet.

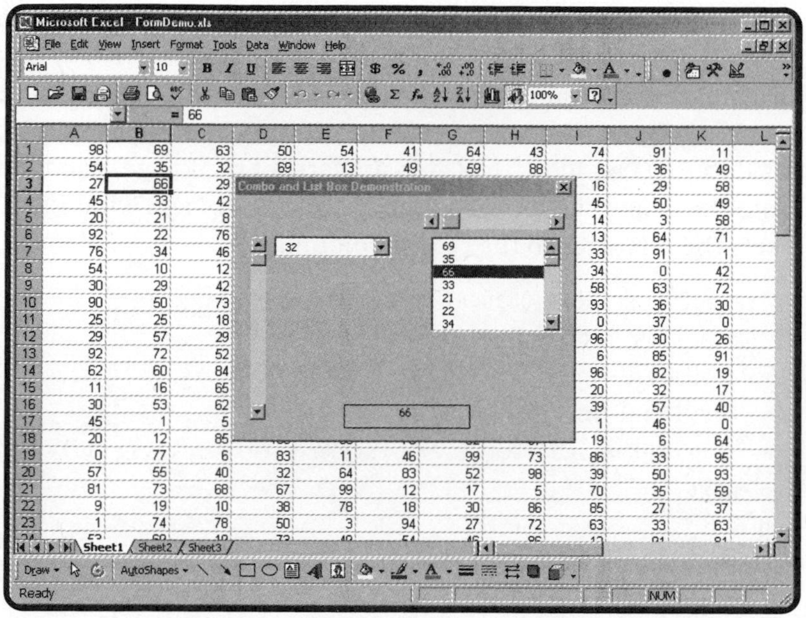

FIGURE 7.9

Using the ListBox and ComboBox controls on a UserForm

The UserForm contains a ComboBox control, a ListBox control, two ScrollBar controls, and a Label control. The vertical scroll bar (scrRows) is used to set the row number to be displayed in the ComboBox control. The horizontal scroll bar (scrColumns) is used to set the column number to be displayed in the ListBox control. The Label control displays the user's selection from either the ComboBox or ListBox control.

The code contained in the form module is minimal and straightforward. The Change() event procedure of the ComboBox control (cmbRows) and Click() event procedure of the ListBox control (lstColumns) are used to display the currently selected item in the Label control (lblDisplay). The choice of the Click() event procedure or the Change() event procedure for the ComboBox and ListBox controls is arbitrary.

```
Private Sub cmbRows_Change()
    lblDisplay.Caption = cmbRows.Value
End Sub
Private Sub lstColumns_Click()
    lblDisplay.Caption = lstColumns.Value
End Sub
```

The ScrollBar control (scrColumns) is used to set the column from which the List-Box control will receive its data. The Min and Max properties of scrColumns are set to 1 and 26, respectively. The ScrollBar control (scrRows) sets the row from which the ComboBox control receives data. The Min and Max properties of scrRows are set to 1 and 100, respectively. The Change() event procedures of each scroll bar control are used to clear any items in the list before adding the data from the newly selected column. The AddItem method of the ComboBox or ListBox control is used inside a For/Next loop. The Cells property of the Range object returns each value from the respective row or column in the worksheet where the looping variable I sets the reference to the row or column.

```
Private Sub scrRows_Change()
    Dim I As Integer
    cmbRows.Clear
    For I = 1 To 26
        cmbRows.AddItem (Cells(scrRows.Value, I).Value)
    Next I
End Sub
Private Sub scrColumns_Change()
    Dim I As Integer
    lstColumns.Clear
    For I = 1 To 100
        lstColumns.AddItem (Cells(I, scrColumns.Value).Value)
    Next I
End Sub
```

Again, the QueryClose() event procedure of the UserForm object is used to clear the object from system memory.

```
Private Sub UserForm_QueryClose(Cancel As Integer, CloseMode As Integer)
    Unload Me
End Sub
```

 TRICK Use the Me keyword to access all controls associated with the current object, including their properties and methods. For example, Me.scrColumns.Value = 3 will set the Scroll Bar control in the previous example to the value of 3, which changes the items in the ListBox control to the values in column 3 of the worksheet.

Chapter Project: Blackjack

Blackjack is a favorite for beginning programmers because it is relatively straightforward programming and can be a lot of fun to customize. The game is saved as Blackjack.xls on the CD-ROM accompanying this book. I added some sound to the game, but it also could easily be dressed up with features such as animation or odd rule twists.

- A ComboBox control for the player to enter or select an amount to bet.
- A ComboBox control (used as a drop-down list) so the player can view previously used cards.
- A Label control for displaying the player's score.
- A Label control for displaying the player's current balance.
- A Command Button control for beginning and selecting a new game.
- A Command Button control for selecting another draw from the deck.

A single Label control is also used to display the result of each hand. Figure 7.10 shows the Blackjack UserForm (named frmTable) in design time after I added ActiveX controls listed above.

After the player starts the game, the UserForm described previously is displayed. A single Command Button control is used to begin the game, deal each hand, and offer the player the choice to stand on the current hand.

When a game first begins, the images of the deck are loaded into a variable array of type image. The image array should only contain 52 elements regardless of the number of decks selected by the player to minimize memory usage. A second UserForm appears to tell the player that the deck is being shuffled. The code module for the second UserForm contains the procedure that shuffles the deck. To shuffle a deck, a dynamic integer array is dimensioned to the proper size by multiplying the number of decks by 52. This dynamic array holds integer values between 0 and 51 that will serve as the index for the image array when displaying the images of the cards on the UserForm. The deck is shuffled randomly by generating integer random numbers between 0 and the number of elements in

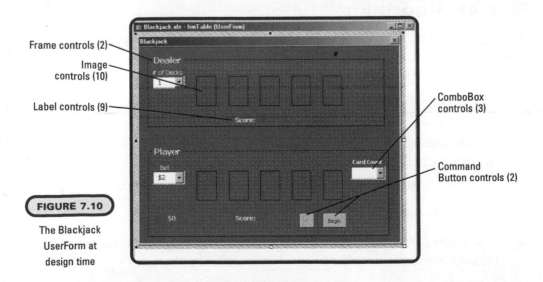

FIGURE 7.10

The Blackjack
UserForm at
design time

This particular version of Blackjack uses an Excel UserForm and various ActiveX controls to simulate the card game. There are two players, the user and the computer, and the game follows most of the standard rules of Blackjack. The idea is to draw as many as five cards with a total value that comes as close to 21 as possible without going over. Face cards are worth 10 and aces are 1 or 11. All other cards are face value. The game begins with two cards dealt to each player. One of the computer's cards is dealt face down so it is unknown to the player. The player draws cards until the sum of the cards' value exceeds 21 or the player decides to stop. After the player is finished, the computer takes its turn.

Project Statement

I want to create a Blackjack game using VBA UserForms and ActiveX controls. The computer will act as the dealer and play against a single player. The game should follow most of the standard rules for Blackjack. Some additional features, such as sound and card counting, should be added to make the game more interesting. Finally, there should be some data exchange between the game and an Excel worksheet.

Project Tools

This project uses many of the tools discussed in previous chapters of this book, including various code structures and common ActiveX controls. In particular, the project includes additional tools discussed in this chapter. These tools are UserForms and their code modules, along with Frame, ComboBox, and ListBox controls.

Project Algorithm

The Blackjack game runs from a VBA UserForm that contains several ActiveX controls. The UserForm is separated into a Dealer area and a Player area using Frame controls. The dealer frame contains the following controls:

- Five Image controls for displaying images of cards representing the dealer's hand.
- A ComboBox control (used as a drop-down list) so the player can choose the number of card decks to be used before reshuffling.
- A Label control for displaying the score of the dealer's hand.

The player frame contains the following controls:

- Five Image controls for displaying images of cards representing the player's hand.

the array. Then two elements in the array (chosen randomly) representing two cards in the deck are swapped. The process of choosing a random number and swapping two elements in the array is contained within a loop such that it may be repeated. Figure 7.11 illustrates the process of swapping two values in an array. When this process is repeated many times the deck is effectively shuffled.

The value of each card is stored in another array of the same length as the deck, and these elements are swapped inside the same loop to ensure that the value of each card can be easily tracked. The UserForm displaying the message to the player that the deck is being shuffled is hidden, using code, after the deck is shuffled.

The game is then played by incrementing a variable from 0 to the number of elements in the deck. This variable serves as the index for the arrays representing the deck and the value of each card. The appropriate images are displayed and the scores of each hand calculated. The player is given the choice of standing or drawing another card by selecting different Command Button controls. The player's score must be checked after each draw. If the player's score exceeds 21, then the game is over and the appropriate UserForm controls are updated to display the result of the hand and give the option to start another hand (Label and Command Button controls).

If the player stands on a hand that scores less than 21, then a procedure will be called that simulates the computer drawing cards based on the criterion that the computer must draw if its score is less than 16, otherwise it must stand on the current hand.

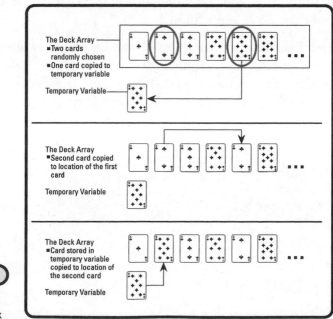

FIGURE 7.11

Swapping two cards in the deck

When the game is over, the winner is declared using a Label control. The player's balance is updated and the Command Button caption is reset for another hand.

The start of a new hand triggers a sub procedure that resets the necessary variables and controls, such as the Image controls and the scores. With the start of each hand the number of cards left in the simulated deck will be checked, and if there are fewer than 10 the deck will be reshuffled and the additional variable representing the place in the deck is reset to 0.

A couple of additional items not really necessary for the game will be added to enhance the player's experience. Sounds simulating the shuffling and drawing of cards will be added at the proper time. A ComboBox control will be used to keep track of the number and value of cards already played from the deck in case the player wants to practice card counting skills. The ComboBox control will be updated with the drawing of each card and reset when the deck is re-shuffled. Finally, the result of each hand (the player's and computer's score and the current balance) will be output to the active worksheet.

Adding the Code

Most of the code is contained within the form module for the UserForm representing the card table (frmTable). Additional procedures will be held within the formmodule of the UserForm displayed when the deck is reshuffled (frmShuffle). A standard module contains the API call for the sound along with the procedures used to play the sound files and the public procedure that can be used to show the UserForm from the Excel application.

The code contained in the form module for the UserForm named frmTable is listed first. Several module-level variables are used to hold the images of the cards and to keep track of the current place in the deck, the dealer's hidden card, the number of dealer and player hits (cannot exceed 3), and the scores of each card in the dealer's and player's hands.

```
Option Explicit
Dim theDeck(51) As Image
Dim numCard As Integer
Dim hiddenCard As Integer
Dim numPlayerHits As Integer
Dim numDlrHits As Integer
Dim dlrScores(4) As Integer
Dim plyrScores(4) As Integer
```

The Command Button control named cmdDeal has three functions identified by three captions ("Begin", "Deal", and "Stand") and basically controls the flow of the game. The procedure-level variables filePath1 and filePath hold the strings that specify the path to the card images and the sound files, respectively. The variables playerBet and numDecks hold the values selected in the two ComboBox controls named cmbBet and cmbNumDecks.

```
Private Sub cmdDeal_Click()
    Dim filePath1 As String
    Dim filePath As String
    filePath1 = ActiveWorkbook.Path & "\Cards\"
    filePath = ActiveWorkbook.Path & "\Sounds\"
```

A new hand will begin if the Caption property of cmdDeal reads "Deal". A call to the sub procedure ResetVariables() is used to reset several variables and controls on the UserForm between hands. The module-level variable numCard represents the location of the next draw in the deck. If the value of numCard is within ten cards from the end of the deck, then the deck is reshuffled by displaying the UserForm frmShuffle. After the deck is shuffled, the sub procedure InitForm() is used to reset controls on the UserForm that must be reset between shuffles of the deck.

```
If cmdDeal.Caption = "Deal" Then
    ResetVariables
    If (numCard >= UBound(shuffledDeck) - 10) Then
        numCard = 0
        frmShuffle.Show
        InitForm
    End If
```

The variable hiddenCard holds the reference to the dealer's card not immediately displayed to the player. Next, four cards are drawn from the deck (two each to the dealer and the player) and their values stored in the variable arrays dlrScores and plyrScores. The value of numCard is incremented with each draw and the appropriate card images are loaded into the Picture property of the Image controls. The value of the card is also counted and the list of cards in cmbCardsPlayed is updated with a call to the ListValue() sub procedure. A sound file is played with each draw from the deck, using the same techniques covered in the previous chapter. A small delay is also added between draws from the deck to give the sound file time to play. Finally, the player's score is calculated with a call to the sub procedure CalcScore().

```
hiddenCard = numCard
dlrScores(0) = cardValues(numCard)
```

```
imgDlr1.Picture = LoadPicture(filePath1 & "Back.bmp")
PlayWav (filePath & "\draw.wav")
Call Delay(Timer, 0.5)
numCard = numCard + 1
imgDlr2.Picture = theDeck(shuffledDeck(numCard)).Picture
dlrScores(1) = cardValues(numCard)
ListValue (cardValues(numCard))
PlayWav (filePath & "\draw.wav")
Call Delay(Timer, 0.5)
numCard = numCard + 1
imgPlayer1.Picture = theDeck(shuffledDeck(numCard)).Picture
plyrScores(0) = cardValues(numCard)
ListValue (cardValues(numCard))
PlayWav (filePath & "\draw.wav")
Call Delay(Timer, 0.5)
numCard = numCard + 1
imgPlayer2.Picture = theDeck(shuffledDeck(numCard)).Picture
plyrScores(1) = cardValues(numCard)
ListValue (cardValues(numCard))
CalcScore ("Plyr")
PlayWav (filePath & "\draw.wav")
numCard = numCard + 1
```

The Caption property of cmdDeal is changed to "Stand", and the Command Button
control cmdHit is enabled. Figure 7.12 shows these controls immediately after a
new hand is dealt.

```
cmdDeal.Caption = "Stand"
cmdHit.Enabled = True
```

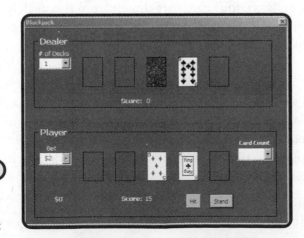

FIGURE 7.12

The Blackjack
UserForm after a
new hand is dealt

The Caption property of cmdDeal is set to "Begin" at design time, so this will be the caption when the UserForm is first shown (see Figure 7.10). When the player clicks this Command Button several sub procedures are called that serve to initialize variables and controls, load the images of the deck into an image array, and shuffle the deck. This section of the If/Then code structure will run only when the game is first started as the Caption property of cmdDeal is set to "Deal" at the end.

```
ElseIf cmdDeal.Caption = "Begin" Then
    Range("A:B").Font.Bold = False
    InitCombos
    InitForm
    LoadDeck
    frmShuffle.Show
    cmdDeal.Caption = "Deal"
Else
```

The last block of code in the If/Then code structure will be triggered when the Caption property of cmdDeal reads "Stand". When this block of code is triggered, the ability of the player to take another draw from the deck is disabled (see the Command Button in Figure 7.1), the dealer's hidden card is displayed, and the score is calculated. The dealer's turn at drawing cards is then taken and the game ends with calls to the DealerDraw() and GameOver() sub procedures.

```
    cmdHit.Enabled = False
    imgDlr1.Picture = theDeck(shuffledDeck(hiddenCard)).Picture
    ListValue (dlrScores(0))
    CalcScore ("Dlr")
    DealerDraw
    GameOver
    End If
End Sub
```

The InitForm() and IntiCombos sub procedures are used to initialize some of the controls on the UserForm. The InitForm() sub procedure must be called after every shuffle. The InitCombos() sub procedure need only be called when the game begins.

The InitForm() sub procedure initializes the ComboBox control named cmbCardsPlayed.

```
Private Sub InitForm()
    Dim I As Integer
    lblResult.Caption = ""
```

```
lblDlrScore.Caption = "0"
lblPlyrScore.Caption = "0"
```

Items listed in a ComboBox or ListBox control must be added in code. First, the contents of the ComboBox controls are cleared before the desired values are added.

```
cmbCardsPlayed.Clear
cmbCardsPlayed.AddItem ("Aces")
cmbCardsPlayed.AddItem ("10's")
cmbCardsPlayed.AddItem ("9's")
cmbCardsPlayed.AddItem ("8's")
cmbCardsPlayed.AddItem ("7's")
cmbCardsPlayed.AddItem ("6's")
cmbCardsPlayed.AddItem ("5's")
cmbCardsPlayed.AddItem ("4's")
cmbCardsPlayed.AddItem ("3's")
cmbCardsPlayed.AddItem ("2's")
```

The ColumnCount property of the ComboBox control used to count the cards played during the game (cmbCardsPlayed) was set to 2 at design time. The List property is used to access the second column in the list. The List property takes two integer parameters used to specify the row and column in the list. Indices for the row and column parameters begin with zero. A For/Next loop is used to set all the values of the second column (index value of 1) in cmbCardsPlayed to zero.

```
For I = 0 To 9
    cmbCardsPlayed.List(I, 1) = "0"
Next I
End Sub
```

The only call to the InitCombos() sub procedure is when the game first begins. However, this code cannot be placed in the Activate() event procedure of the UserForm because this event procedure is called every time the UserForm is made active. With the use of another UserForm for signaling to the player when the deck is being shuffled, the Activate() event procedure of frmTable will be called after each shuffling of the deck (when the UserForm frmTable is again made active). If the following code is run at an inappropriate time the program could crash, because this code will reset the Value properties of the ComboBox controls. The Value properties of these ComboBox controls are used later in the program and must contain data.

```
Private Sub InitCombos()
    cmbNumDecks.Clear
```

```
    cmbNumDecks.AddItem ("1")
    cmbNumDecks.AddItem ("2")
    cmbNumDecks.AddItem ("3")
    cmbBet.Clear
    cmbBet.AddItem ("$2")
    cmbBet.AddItem ("$5")
    cmbBet.AddItem ("$10")
    cmbBet.AddItem ("$25")
    cmbBet.AddItem ("$50")
    cmbBet.AddItem ("$100")
End Sub
```

The LoadDeck() sub procedure loads the 52 images representing the deck into an image variable array. The value of these cards is loaded into another array called theValues.

```
Private Sub LoadDeck()
    Dim I As Integer
    Dim K As Integer
    Dim imagePath As String
    Dim cardStr As String
```

The variable array theDeck is module-level. Each element of the array must be assigned an object reference using the Set statement, as the image data type is a specific form of the object data type.

```
    For I = 0 To 51
        Set theDeck(I) = New Image
    Next I
    imagePath = ActiveWorkbook.Path + "\Cards\"
```

The image files are conveniently named (for example, 1Clubs.bmp, 2Clubs.bmp, etc.) so a nested For/Next loop can be used to load the images and assign the value of the card to the variable arrays theDeck and theValues. These nested For/Next loops load the images in order from ace to king starting with clubs, then hearts, spades, and diamonds.

```
    For K = 0 To 3
        For I = 0 To 12
            If (K = 0) Then cardStr = (I + 1) & "Clubs.bmp"
            If (K = 1) Then cardStr = (I + 1) & "Hearts.bmp"
            If (K = 2) Then cardStr = (I + 1) & "Spades.bmp"
            If (K = 3) Then cardStr = (I + 1) & "Diamonds.bmp"
```

```
            theDeck(I + 13* K).Picture = LoadPicture(imagePath & cardStr)
            If (I + 1) < 10 Then
                theValues(I + 13* K) = I + 1
            Else
                theValues(I + 13* K) = 10
            End If
        Next I
    Next K
End Sub
```

The ResetVariables() sub procedure is called from the Click() event procedure listed immediately above when its caption reads "Deal". The function of this procedure is to reset several variables and controls between hands. Multiple hands are played from a single shuffling of the deck, so not all the variables and controls need to be reset.

```
Private Sub ResetVariables()
    Dim I As Integer
```

The most interesting part of this procedure is how the images are removed from the Image controls. First a variable is declared of type control, then a For/Each loop is used to iterate through each control contained within the Controls collection. The Controls collection is made up of all the controls contained in the UserForm frmTable, because the name of the UserForm is used to qualify the collection for the looping code structure. This is identical to previous methods in which we used For/Each loops to iterate through each cell in a collection of Cells (Range object). As the loop iterates through each control on the form, the Name property of each control is tested to see if it begins with "img". Because the only controls on the form whose Name property begins with "img" are Image controls, it is relatively simple to remove the images from these controls by passing an empty string to the LoadPicture function.

```
    Dim imgCtrl As Control
    For Each imgCtrl In frmTable.Controls
        If Left(imgCtrl.Name, 3) = "img" Then
            imgCtrl.Picture = LoadPicture("")
        End If
    Next
```

The variables numPlayerHits and numDlrHits keep track of the number of draws made from the deck in each hand and must be reset to zero. The arrays used to hold the values of the cards in the dealer's and player's hands (dlrScores and plyrScores) must also be reset to zero.

```
    numPlayerHits = 0
    numDlrHits = 0
    lblDlrScore.Caption = "0"
    lblResult.Caption = ""
    For I = 0 To 4
        dlrScores(I) = 0
        plyrScores(I) = 0
    Next I
```

The ComboBox control used for selecting the amount to bet must be disabled to prevent the player from betting after drawing cards.

```
    cmbBet.Enabled = False
End Sub
```

When the Command Button control cmdHit is enabled, the player has the choice of selecting another card from the deck. The code that handles the drawing of another card by the player is contained in the Click() event procedure of cmdHit.

```
Private Sub cmdHit_Click()
    Dim filePath As String
    filePath = ActiveWorkbook.Path
    PlayWav (filePath & "\Sounds\draw.wav")
    numPlayerHits = numPlayerHits + 1
```

After a sound file is played, the image of the drawn card is displayed by using the integer array shuffledDeck that is used to hold an index value between 0 and 51. This value is then used as the index for the image array, theDeck. A maximum of three hits is allowed to each player.

```
    If (numPlayerHits = 1) Then imgPlayer3.Picture =
theDeck(shuffledDeck(numCard)).Picture
    If (numPlayerHits = 2) Then imgPlayer4.Picture =
theDeck(shuffledDeck(numCard)).Picture
    If (numPlayerHits = 3) Then imgPlayer5.Picture =
theDeck(shuffledDeck(numCard)).Picture
```

The array that stores the values of the player's cards (plyrScores) is updated along with the card count before the score is calculated and the variable numCard is incremented.

```
    plyrScores(numPlayerHits + 1) = cardValues(numCard)
    ListValue (cardValues(numCard))
    CalcScore ("Plyr")
    numCard = numCard + 1
```

If the player has drawn the maximum three cards, then the game is turned over to the computer. If the player's score exceeds 21 then the game is over.

```
    If numPlayerHits > 2 Then
        cmdHit.Enabled = False
        CalcScore ("Dlr")
    End If
    If lblPlyrScore.Caption > 21 Then
        imgDlr1.Picture = theDeck(shuffledDeck(hiddenCard)).Picture
        CalcScore ("Dlr")
        GameOver
    End If
End Sub
```

The DealerDraw() sub procedure is called from the Click() event procedure of cmdDeal when its Caption property reads "Stand". The DealerDraw() sub procedure serves the same purpose as the Click() event procedure for cmdHit and uses much of the same code. This procedure forces the computer to hit on any score less than 16 and stand on scores 16 or greater.

```
Private Sub DealerDraw()
    Dim filePath As String
    filePath = ActiveWorkbook.Path
```

A Do-Loop is used to iterate through draws by the computer while the score of its hand is less than 16. After the third draw, the procedure is exited and returned to the Click() event procedure of cmdDeal, where the game will end.

```
    Do While (lblDlrScore.Caption < 16)
        If (numDlrHits = 3) Then Exit Sub
        numDlrHits = numDlrHits + 1
        If (numDlrHits = 1) Then imgDlr3.Picture =
theDeck(shuffledDeck(numCard)).Picture
        If (numDlrHits = 2) Then imgDlr4.Picture =
theDeck(shuffledDeck(numCard)).Picture
        If (numDlrHits = 3) Then imgDlr5.Picture =
theDeck(shuffledDeck(numCard)).Picture
        PlayWav (filePath & "\Sounds\draw.wav")
        Call Delay(Timer, 0.5)
        dlrScores(numDlrHits + 1) = cardValues(numCard)
        ListValue (cardValues(numCard))
        CalcScore ("Dlr")
        numCard = numCard + 1
```

```
    Loop
End Sub
```

The `CalcScore()` sub procedure is called after each draw of a card from the player and the computer. This procedure takes a string parameter used to indicate which players' score is to be calculated.

```
Private Sub CalcScore(player As String)
    Dim I As Integer
    Dim numAces As Integer
    Dim score As Integer
```

The values of the cards in each hand are stored in variable arrays (`dlrScores` and `plyrScores`) as the cards are drawn from the deck. This makes it very simple to calculate the score by summing the values in these arrays. Aces are stored with the value one and require special treatment.

```
    If player = "Dlr" Then
        For I = 0 To 4
            score = score + dlrScores(I)
            If dlrScores(I) = 1 Then numAces = numAces + 1
        Next I
```

If there are aces held in the hand, then they are counted as 11 as long as the total score is less than 22; otherwise their value remains at 1. This is accomplished by first adding an additional value of 10 to the score for each ace (remember that the value 1 has already been counted for each ace). Second, a `For/Next` loop is used to remove 10 points from the score for each ace that keeps the total score over 21. Thus, if a hand has two or more aces in it, the values of these aces may be a mix of 1 and 11 depending on the total score of the hand.

```
        If (numAces > 0) Then
            score = score + 10 * numAces
            For I = 1 To numAces
                If (score > 21) Then score = score - 10
            Next I
        End If
        lblDlrScore.Caption = score
    Else
```

An identical process is used to calculate the player's score.

```
        For I = 0 To 4
            score = score + plyrScores(I)
```

```
                If plyrScores(I) = 1 Then numAces = numAces + 1
            Next I
            If (numAces > 0) Then
                score = score + 10 * numAces
                For I = 1 To numAces
                    If (score > 21) Then score = score - 10
                Next I
            End If
            lblPlyrScore.Caption = score
        End If
End Sub
```

The `GameOver()` sub procedure is called from the `Click()` event procedures of `cmdHit` and `cmdDeal` and is used to update the UserForm just before the game ends.

```
Private Sub GameOver()
    Dim earningsLength As Integer
    Dim betLength As Integer
    earningsLength = Len(lblEarnings.Caption)
    betLength = Len(cmbBet.Value)
```

If the scores of both hands are equivalent, then the game is a tie and the `Caption` property of `lblResult` is updated.

```
    If (lblDlrScore = lblPlyrScore) Then
        lblResult.Caption = "Push"
    End If
```

If the player's score is higher and does not exceed 21, or the computer's score exceeds 21, then the player wins the hand. The `Caption` properties of `lblResult` and `lblEarnings` are updated.

```
    If ((Val(lblDlrScore.Caption) < Val(lblPlyrScore.Caption)) _
        And (Val(lblPlyrScore.Caption) < 22)) Or _
        ((Val(lblPlyrScore.Caption) < 22) And (Val(lblDlrScore.Caption) >
21)) Then
        lblResult.Caption = "You Win!"
        lblEarnings.Caption = "$" & Val(Right(lblEarnings.Caption,
earningsLength - 1)) + Val(Right(cmbBet.Value, betLength - 1))
    End If
```

Another `If/Then` decision structure tests for a computer win and updates the `Caption` properties of `lblResult` and `lblEarnings` accordingly.

```
    If ((Val(lblDlrScore.Caption) > Val(lblPlyrScore.Caption)) And
(Val(lblDlrScore.Caption) < 22) _
        Or (Val(lblDlrScore.Caption) < 22) And (Val(lblPlyrScore.Caption) >
21)) Then
        lblResult.Caption = "Dealer Wins!"
        lblEarnings.Caption = "$" & Val(Right(lblEarnings.Caption,
earningsLength - 1)) - Val(Right(cmbBet.Value, betLength - 1))
    End If
```

The rest of the procedure formats some of the controls on the UserForm to select the color of the dollar amount displayed in lblEarnings, and gets the UserForm ready for the next hand.

```
    earningsLength = Len(lblEarnings.Caption)
    If Val(Right(lblEarnings.Caption, earningsLength - 1)) < 0 Then
        lblEarnings.ForeColor = RGB(255, 0, 0)
    Else
        lblEarnings.ForeColor = RGB(0, 255, 255)
    End If
    WorksheetOutput
    cmdHit.Enabled = False
    cmdDeal.Caption = "Deal"
    cmbBet.Enabled = True
End Sub
```

The ListValue() sub procedure is called whenever a card is drawn by the player or the computer and is used to update the ComboBox control that keeps track of the cards that have been played from the deck. The value of the drawn card is passed to this procedure and a Select/Case decision structure uses this passed parameter (cardValue) to make short work of the problem. The List property of the ComboBox control is used to update the current value of the second column (index value of 1) displayed.

```
Private Sub ListValue(cardValue As Integer)
    Select Case cardValue
        Case 1
            cmbCardsPlayed.List(0, 1) = cmbCardsPlayed.List(0, 1) + 1
        Case 11
            cmbCardsPlayed.List(0, 1) = cmbCardsPlayed.List(0, 1) + 1
        Case 10
            cmbCardsPlayed.List(1, 1) = cmbCardsPlayed.List(1, 1) + 1
        Case 9
```

```
                cmbCardsPlayed.List(2, 1) = cmbCardsPlayed.List(2, 1) + 1
        Case 8
                cmbCardsPlayed.List(3, 1) = cmbCardsPlayed.List(3, 1) + 1
        Case 7
                cmbCardsPlayed.List(4, 1) = cmbCardsPlayed.List(4, 1) + 1
        Case 6
                cmbCardsPlayed.List(5, 1) = cmbCardsPlayed.List(5, 1) + 1
        Case 5
                cmbCardsPlayed.List(6, 1) = cmbCardsPlayed.List(6, 1) + 1
        Case 4
                cmbCardsPlayed.List(7, 1) = cmbCardsPlayed.List(7, 1) + 1
        Case 3
                cmbCardsPlayed.List(8, 1) = cmbCardsPlayed.List(8, 1) + 1
        Case 2
                cmbCardsPlayed.List(9, 1) = cmbCardsPlayed.List(9, 1) + 1
    End Select
End Sub
```

Figure 7.13 shows the UserForm frmTable after one hand has been played. The ComboBox control cmbCardsPlayed shows the list of cards played thus far from the deck. The first column labels the cards and the second column represents the number of times a card with the specified value has been played from the current deck. The value of the second column is updated in the ListValue() sub procedure. Since only one hand has been played, the ComboBox lists two cards played with a face value of 10 (jack of diamonds and king of clubs) and one card each with face values of 7 and 8. As more hands are played the list will be updated until the deck is reshuffled and the numbers in the second column are reset to 0.

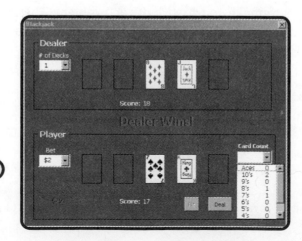

FIGURE 7.13

The Blackjack game listing the played cards

One of the last sub procedures in the form module for the UserForm `frmTable` outputs the result of each hand to a worksheet.

```
Private Sub WorksheetOutput()
    Dim c As Range
    Dim nextRow As Integer
```

A `For/Each` loop is used to find the first empty cell, a technique previously discussed in Chapter 5. The `Row` property of the Range object returns an integer value stored in the variable `nextRow` that represents the next available row in the worksheet.

```
    For Each c In Range("A:A")
        If c.Value = "" Then
            nextRow = c.Row
            Exit For
        End If
    Next
```

Next, the scores for the computer and player are output to the worksheet and formatted before the player's current balance is copied to column C of the worksheet.

```
    Range("A" & nextRow).Value = lblDlrScore.Caption
    Range("B" & nextRow).Value = lblPlyrScore.Caption
    Range("C" & nextRow).Value = lblEarnings.Caption
    If lblResult.Caption = "Dealer Wins!" Then
        Range("A" & nextRow).Font.Bold = True
    ElseIf lblResult.Caption = "You Win!" Then
        Range("B" & nextRow).Font.Bold = True
    End If
    Range("C" & nextRow).Font.Color = lblEarnings.ForeColor
End Sub
```

Finally, the `QueryClose()` event procedure is used to remove the UserForms from system memory when the player exits the program.

```
Private Sub UserForm_QueryClose(Cancel As Integer, CloseMode As Integer)
    Unload frmTable
    Unload frmShuffle
End Sub
```

The form module for the UserForm named `frmShuffle` uses the `Activate()` event procedure of the UserForm to hold the code that simulates the shuffling of the deck. Figure 7.14 shows what the game looks like when the UserForm `frmShuffle` appears. This UserForm is programmed to be displayed for at least one second, and is added to send the player a message that the deck is being shuffled.

```
Option Explicit
Private Sub UserForm_Activate()
    Dim I As Integer
    Dim K As Integer
    Dim tempInt As Integer
    Dim tempInt2 As Integer
    Dim ranNum As Integer
    Dim filePath As String
    Dim curTime As Single
    Randomize
    filePath = ActiveWorkbook.Path
```

The dynamic variable arrays cardValues and shuffledDeck are of global scope and are re-dimensioned to the size of the deck chosen by the player with the ComboBox control named cmbNumDecks.

```
ReDim cardValues(52 * frmTable.cmbNumDecks.Value - 1)
curTime = Timer
ReDim shuffledDeck(52 * frmTable.cmbNumDecks.Value - 1)
```

The variable array shuffledDeck holds integer values between 0 and 51 representing the index number of a card stored in the image array theDeck. The sequence of numbers 0 through 51 is repeated for the number of decks chosen by the player. For example, if there are three decks the sequence 0 through 51 is repeated in the array shuffledDeck three times. Likewise, the values of the cards are copied to the array cardValues repetitively using the nested For/Next loops that follow.

FIGURE 7.14

The Blackjack
game during
card reshuffling

```
For K = 0 To frmTable.cmbNumDecks.Value - 1
    For I = 0 To 51
        shuffledDeck(I + K * 52) = I
        cardValues(I + K * 52) = theValues(I)
    Next I
Next K
PlayWav (filePath & "\Sounds\shuffle.wav")
```

The shuffledDeck and cardValues arrays that were just redimensioned and initialized will now be shuffled using nested For/Next loops. The choice for the upper limit of the outer looping variable is subjective. With more iterations through the outer loop the deck will become more randomized. However, if the loop uses too many iterations it may take a considerable amount of time (this is highly dependent on the machine on which the code runs) and annoy the player.

```
For K = 1 To 50
```

The inner loop does the shuffling by swapping two values in both the shuffledDeck and cardValues arrays with each iteration (see Figure 7.11). A random number is used to determine the element in the array that will be swapped. It is important to note that the same random number is used to swap values in both arrays. This ensures that the value of the card can be determined by accessing the cardValues array with the same index value used to access the shuffledDeck array.

```
    For I = 0 To UBound(shuffledDeck)
        ranNum = Int(Rnd * UBound(shuffledDeck))
        tempInt = shuffledDeck(I)
        tempInt2 = cardValues(I)
        shuffledDeck(I) = shuffledDeck(ranNum)
        cardValues(I) = cardValues(ranNum)
        shuffledDeck(ranNum) = tempInt
        cardValues(ranNum) = tempInt2
    Next I
Next K
```

A delay of one second is used in case the preceding For/Next loops run too fast and the player never sees the UserForm appear and disappear. The variable curTime was initialized before the For/Next loops, so there is no additional delay if the loops take more than one second to run.

```
    Call Delay(curTime, 1)
    frmShuffle.Hide
End Sub
```

A standard module is used to hold the public procedures for playing sound files and the API declarations. The three arrays shuffledDeck, cardValues, and theValues are global because they must be accessed in both form modules.

```
Option Explicit
Public shuffledDeck() As Integer
Public theValues(51) As Integer
Public cardValues() As Integer
Public Declare Function sndPlaySoundA Lib "winmm.dll" _
(ByVal lpszSoundName As String, ByVal uFlags As Long) As Long
```

The public procedure Blackjack() gives access to the frmTable UserForm from the Excel application. The Blackjack() sub procedure can be accessed via the Macro selection on the Tools menu or through an event procedure of an ActiveX control (for example, the Click() event of a Command Button) placed on a worksheet. You will find a Button control on the Forms toolbar on a worksheet in the CD-ROM's Blackjack.xls project.

```
Public Sub Blackjack()
    frmTable.Show
End Sub
```

The last two procedures listed (PlayWav() and Delay()) were discussed in detail in Chapter 6. They are used to play sound files via the Windows API and to delay program execution by a specified number of seconds.

```
Public Sub PlayWav(WavFile As String)
    If Application.CanPlaySounds = False Or Dir(WavFile) = "" Then
        Exit Sub
    End If
    sndPlaySoundA WavFile, 1
End Sub
Public Sub Delay(curTime As Single, pauseTime As Single)
    Do While Timer < pauseTime + curTime
        DoEvents
    Loop
End Sub
```

That's it for the Blackjack program. Take the code, play with it, change it, add to it, learn from it, and enjoy. If you are having trouble, then focus on just a small piece of the program until you figure it out before moving on to the next problem.

Chapter Summary

This chapter introduced VBA UserForms and a few new ActiveX controls. Specifically, you learned how to add UserForms to a VBA project and show them in a program. This chapter discussed adding ActiveX controls to a UserForm, including the Frame, ComboBox, and ListBox controls, and how to use the code window of a UserForm. The use of modal and modeless UserForms was also discussed.

CHALLENGES

1. Add a modeless UserForm (ShowModal property) to a VBA project, then use the Click() event procedures of two Command Button controls placed on an Excel worksheet to show and hide the UserForm.

2. Add a TextBox control to the UserForm created in the previous challenge that displays the range selected on the active Excel worksheet. Show the UserForm as modeless (Office 2000 or later) so the user can select a new range on the worksheet. Update the range displayed in the TextBox control via the Click() event procedure of a Command Button control placed on the UserForm.

3. Create a UserForm that contains a ListBox control. Use the AddItem method of the ListBox control to display the contents of column A of the active worksheet in the ListBox. Hint: A For/Each loop in the Activate() event procedure of the UserForm will work well.

4. Add a Command Button control to the UserForm from the previous challenge and change the MultiSelect property of the ListBox control to allow multiple selections. Add code to the Click() event procedure of the Command Button control that will copy the selected values of the ListBox control to column B of the worksheet. Hint: Use the Selected property of the ListBox control to return an array of Boolean values that can be used to determine which items displayed in the control have been selected by the user. The ListCount and List properties of the ListBox control used with a For/Next loop can return the values if the Selected property is true.

5. Alter the Blackjack game to display the used cards on an Excel worksheet.

6. Alter the Blackjack game such that the program knows when the player or dealer get blackjack (21 with first two cards) so the player does not have to select Stand and the hand immediately ends.

7. Alter the Blackjack game to display the used cards on another UserForm that can be toggled on and off (Show and Hide methods) from a Command Button control on the UserForm frmTable.

Data Access, File I/O, Error Handling, and Debugging

The ability to read and write data to a computer's disk drives is fundamental to most programming languages. This chapter examines the different tools available in VBA and Excel that allow the programmer to read and write data to a disk. Additional tools used for error handling and debugging your VBA programs are also discussed.

This chapter discusses:

- File input and output (I/O)

- Error handling

- Debugging

- Chapter project: Word Find

Project: Word Find

The Word Find program allows the user to enter lists of words associated with various topics into a simple database. The program can also access this database to create word find puzzles that can be for the user's enjoyment. The program is shown in Figure 8.1.

File Input and Output (I/O)

VBA includes several objects, methods, and functions that can be used for file I/O. You have probably surmised that one possibility for file I/O involves the Workbook object and its methods for saving and opening files. However, there are other tools available in VBA, some of which will be discussed in this chapter.

When a VBA application requires file I/O, it often involves a relatively small amount of data stored in program variables and not in a worksheet or document. With Excel, the programmer has the choice of copying the data to a worksheet so the user can save the data in the usual way (File/Save menu item) or saving the content of the variables directly to a file. It is often more convenient to simply write the data directly to a file on the hard drive so the user does not have to be concerned with the task. In fact, it may be undesirable to give the user access to the data, as he or she might alter it before saving. In this case, reading and writing simple text files within the program code offers an attractive solution.

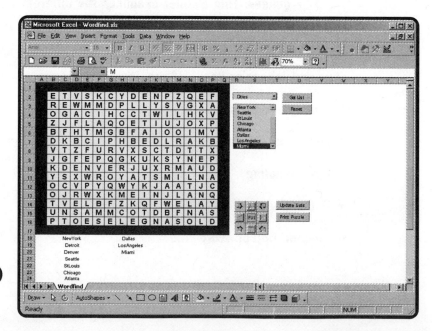

FIGURE 8.1

The Word Find program

Using VBA File I/O Methods

The file I/O methods discussed in this chapter are not associated with any VBA or
Excel objects, although such methods do exist. The Excel object library contains
several file I/O methods found with the Application and Workbook objects. Also,
VBA includes several I/O objects, such as the FileSystem and FileSystemObject
objects, the TextStream object, and the Drive object (among other associated
objects and methods). These objects are conceptually somewhat more difficult to
use than what will be discussed in this chapter. Coupled with the sheer number
of objects involved and space limitations in this book, their use is left up to you
as an exercise.

TABLE 8.1 FILE ACCESS MODES WITH VBA

Access Type	Writing Data	Reading Data
Sequential	Print#, Write#	Input#, Input
Random	Put	Get

The Open Statement

The Open statement is used to read or write data to a file. Table 8.1 summarizes the type of access, and modes or functions available for reading and writing data to a file with VBA.

 There is also a Binary access type for reading and writing to any byte position in a file as might be done with an image. However, this technique is beyond the scope of this book.

The Open statement requires several arguments, including a string used to designate the path to a specified file. If the file does not exist, then one will be created. The Open statement also requires an access mode (Append, Binary, Input, Output, or Random) and a file number. Optional parameters include an access parameter (Read, Write, or Read Write), lock (used to restrict operations on the file from other programs), and record length (specifies the length of the buffer or record).

```
Open "c:\data\Test.txt" For Input As #1
```

The preceding line opens a file named Test.txt, found at the path "c:\data\" for input, and assigns the file to the file number 1. If the file is not found, then one will be created at the designated location with the name Test.txt.

 Multiple files can be opened in a VBA program, but they must be assigned a unique file number.

Sequential Access Files

Writing information to a sequential access file is sort of like recording music to a cassette tape. The songs vary in length and are recorded one after the other. Because it is hard to know the location of each song on the tape, it is difficult to quickly access a particular song. When information is written to a sequential file, the individual pieces of data (usually stored in variables) vary in length and are written to the file one after the other. For example, a sequential file containing names and phone numbers may look something like what's shown here:

"John Smith", "111-2222"

"Joe James", "123-4567"

"Jane Johnson", "456-7890"

The names and phone numbers were all written to the file as strings so they are enclosed in quotes. Numerical values written to a sequential access file will not contain the quotes. The strings containing the names vary in length and will require different amounts of memory for storage. If access to a part of the sequential file is desired at a later time (say we want Jane Johnson's phone number), the entire file must be read into memory because it is not possible to know the location of the desired component within the file. After loading the file, the content must be searched for the desired value. This makes sequential access inefficient with very large files, because it will take too long to access the desired information. However, with smaller files that do not take long to read, sequential access will work well. A VBA sub procedure used to write textual information to a sequential access file is listed here.

```
Public Sub CreateSeqFile()
    Dim filePath As String
    Dim I As Integer
    filePath = ActiveWorkbook.Path & "\SeqPhone.txt"
    Open filePath For Output As #1
        For I = 1 To 3
            Write #1, Cells(I, "A").Value, Cells(I, "B").Value
        Next I
    Close #1
End Sub
```

The preceding procedure uses a For/Next loop to write the contents of the first three cells of columns A and B to a file called SeqPhone.txt. The I/O operation is terminated with the Close statement. The resulting file as viewed from Notepad is shown in Figure 8.2.

Using Write # places quotes around each string value written to the file. The file contains three lines of data because Write # adds a new line character to the end of the last value written to the file; because the For/Next loop iterates three times, the Write # statement was executed three times, resulting in three lines of data.

Because the structure of the file is known, it is a simple task to alter the previous procedure to create a new procedure that reads the data.

FIGURE 8.2

Using Notepad to view a sequential file created using VBA code

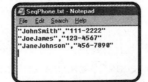

```
Public Sub ReadSeqFile()
    Dim filePath As String
    Dim I As Integer
    Dim theName As String
    Dim theNumber As String
    I = 1
    filePath = ActiveWorkbook.Path & "\SeqPhone.txt"
    Open filePath For Input As #1
    Do While Not EOF(1)
        Input #1, theName, theNumber
        Cells(I, "A").Value = theName
        Cells(I, "B").Value = theNumber
        I = I + 1
    Loop
    Close #1
End Sub
```

The Open statement in the preceding procedure was changed to allow for data input, and Input # replaces Write #. A Do-Loop replaces the For/Next loop and uses the EOF() function in the conditional. The EOF() function accepts the file number as an argument and returns true when the end of the file is reached. Therefore, the loop continues as long as the EOF() function returns false (Do While NOT False equates to Do While True). Variables must be used to hold the strings returned from the file. Two variables (theName and theNumber) are used to match the structure of the procedure that wrote the data to the file.

Random Access Files

Random access files allow the programmer to access specific values within the file without having to load the entire file into memory. This is accomplished by ensuring that the individual data elements are of the same length before writing to the file. Again, consider the example of a phone book. Instead of storing the information as variable-length strings, the name and phone number can be stored with fixed length strings. The combination of the two fixed length strings that follow require the same amount of memory for every line written to the file. This makes it easy to locate a particular line in the file when the data is input.

```
Dim theName As String*20
Dim theNumber As String*8
```

If the name to be stored is fewer than 20 characters, then spaces are added to match the defined length. If the string exceeds 20 characters, only the first 20 characters of the string are stored. Therefore, it is important to define the length of the string so that it will be long enough to contain any possible value, yet not so long that too much memory is wasted by saving lots of spaces. The resulting data file might then look something like this:

"John Smith   ", "111-2222"

"Joe James   ", "123-4567"

"Jane Johnson   ", "456-7890"

Each line in the file requires the same amount of memory to store and is referred to as a record. Records can be represented by one or more values of the same or different data type (string, integer, and so on). Because the length of each record is identical, finding a specific record in the file without loading the entire file into memory is relatively easy (as you will see shortly).

Rather than declare the individual elements of a record as separate variables, it is useful to define a new data type that can be used in a variable declaration. The variable of the newly defined type can include all the desired elements of the record. To define a phone record for the previous example, a user-defined data type that includes both string elements must be declared in the general declarations section of a module.

```
Private Type Phone
            theName As String*20
            theNumber As String*8
End Type
```

With the new data type definition, any variable can now be declared in a procedure as type Phone.

```
Dim phoneRec As Phone
```

Individual elements of the phoneRec variable are accessed using the dot operator.

```
phoneRec.theName = "John Smith"
phoneRec.theNumber = "111-2222"
```

To take full advantage of the user-defined data type, writing the phoneRec variable to a file should be done using random access.

```
Open filePath For Random As #1 Len = Len(Phone)
phoneRec.theName = "John Smith"
phoneRec.theNumber = "111-2222"
Put #1, recNum, phoneRec
Close #1
```

The length of the record is specified using the Len() function. The data is written to the file using Put and read with Get. An integer variable indicating the record number (recNum) must also be included with the user-defined variable in the Put statement so VBA knows where to insert the value within the file.

The Word List program section provides a more in-depth look at using random access files in VBA.

The Word List Program

The Word List program maintains a file containing a list of words and their associated topics, and will be used with the Word Find program described later in this chapter. The program can be found on the accompanying CD-ROM stored as the Excel workbook WordList.xls. The idea is to keep a file that contains several topics, and a list of words associated with each topic, for use in the creation of Word Find puzzles. A random access file is used with each record containing two string variables, one for the topic and another for the word. The code is contained within a form module of a UserForm that is shown in Figure 8.3.

The UserForm contains a ComboBox control (named cmbTopics) and ListBox control (named lstWords) to display the list of topics and associated words. The Style property of the ComboBox control is set to drop-down list at design time. Two TextBox controls (named txtTopic and txtWord) are available for the user to add new topics and words to the file when a Command Button control (cmdAddRec) is selected. Finally, a Label control is used to display the number of the current, or next available record.

The program begins with a few module-level variable declarations including a user-defined data type.

```
Option Explicit
Dim recNum As Integer
Private Type WordList
    topic As String * 15
    word As String * 15
End Type
Dim currentTopic As Integer
Dim myWords() As String
Dim myTopics() As String
```

The integer variable recNum keeps track of the record number when accessing the file used to store the word lists (Wordfind.txt). The user-defined type WordList is built from two string variables (topic and word) that are used to hold a word from the list and its associated topic. The variable currentTopic holds the value of the

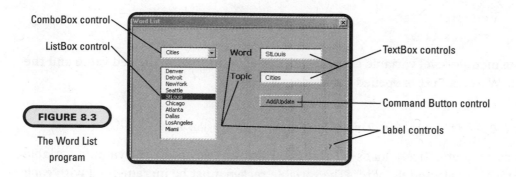

ComboBox control

ListBox control

FIGURE 8.3

The Word List program

Word List

Cities

Denver
Detroit
NewYork
Seattle
StLouis
Chicago
Atlanta
Dallas
LosAngeles
Miami

Word   StLouis

Topic   Cities

Add/Update

TextBox controls

Command Button control

Label controls

ComboBox control. The dynamic variable arrays `myWords` and `myTopics` hold the entire contents of the file for listing in the ListBox and ComboBox controls.

The `Activate()` event procedure is triggered when the UserForm is loaded and shown. From this procedure, code execution proceeds through two other sub procedures before the `Caption` property of the Label control `lblRecNum` is updated with the currently displayed or next available record.

```
Private Sub UserForm_Activate()
    Dim myWord As WordList
    GetAllRecords
    GetUniqueTopics
    lblRecNum.Caption = recNum
End Sub
```

The `GetAllRecords()` sub procedure is the first procedure called from the `Activate()` event procedure of the UserForm. This procedure loads the records contained in the file Wordfind.txt and copies their values to the dynamic arrays `myWords` and `myTopics`. The required procedure-level variables include the string variable `filePath` for holding the path to the file Wordfind.txt, and the user-defined type variable `myWord` for holding the two values (`word` and `topic`) in each record.

```
Private Sub GetAllRecords ()
    Dim filePath As String
    Dim myWord As WordList
    filePath = ActiveWorkbook.Path & "\Wordfind.txt"
```

The contents of the ComboBox and ListBox controls must be cleared before they are updated to avoid displaying the same lists of words and topics repetitively. This has the unfortunate consequence of triggering the `Change()` event procedure of the ComboBox control, which is used later in the program. Additional Boolean variables could be added to prevent this, but as doing so is not critical, it is left as a reader exercise.

```
cmbTopics.Clear
lstWords.Clear
```

The module-level variable recNum is initialized to its lowest allowed value and the file Wordfind.txt is opened for random access.

```
recNum = 1
Open filePath For Random As #1 Len = Len(myWord)
```

A Do-Loop effectively loads all records from the file into the dynamic variable arrays myWords and myTopics. The variable recNum must be incremented with each iteration through the loop to ensure that the Get statement retrieves successive records from the file.

```
Do While Not EOF(1)
    Get #1, recNum, myWord
    ReDim Preserve myWords(recNum - 1)
    myWords(recNum - 1) = myWord.word
    ReDim Preserve myTopics(recNum - 1)
    myTopics(recNum - 1) = myWord.topic
    recNum = recNum + 1
Loop
Close #1
```

The preceding Do-Loop will iterate one more time than is required before the condition Not EOF(1) evaluates as false, because the variable recNum is incremented at the end of the loop. Therefore, the variable recNum is decremented by one so it will hold the value of the next available record before code execution exits this procedure.

```
    recNum = recNum - 1
End Sub
```

After code execution returns to the Activate() event procedure of the UserForm, the GetUniqueTopics() sub procedure is called. The purpose of this procedure is to pick out unique values stored in the myTopics array and display them in the ComboBox control cmbTopics.

```
Private Sub GetUniqueTopics()
    Dim I As Integer
    Dim K As Integer
    Dim addTopic As Boolean
    Dim uniqueTopics() As String
```

Another dynamic variable array is used to hold unique values stored in myTopics.

Obviously, the first value in the array myTopics can be added to the list of unique topics.

```
ReDim uniqueTopics(0)
uniqueTopics(0) = myTopics(0)
```

Nested For/Next loops are used to compare the entire list of topics contained in the array uniqueTopics to each value in the array myTopics (note the different index variables in the inner loop). If there is even one instance of equality found while comparing the strings, then the topic has already been added to the list stored in uniqueTopics and should not be added again.

```
For I = 1 To UBound(myTopics) - 1
    For K = 0 To UBound(uniqueTopics)
        If myTopics(I) <> uniqueTopics(K) Then
            addTopic = True
        Else
            addTopic = False
```

When an identical topic is found, the inner loop must be exited immediately to prevent the Boolean variable addTopic from being reset to true.

```
            Exit For
        End If
    Next K
```

With each iteration through the outer loop, the value of the Boolean variable addTopic is checked to see if a unique topic was found.

```
    If addTopic = True Then
        ReDim Preserve uniqueTopics(UBound(uniqueTopics) + 1)
        uniqueTopics(UBound(uniqueTopics)) = myTopics(I)
    End If
Next I
```

Next, the ComboBox control cmbTopics is updated to display the list of unique topics.

```
For I = 0 To UBound(uniqueTopics)
    cmbTopics.AddItem uniqueTopics(I)
Next I
```

The ListIndex property of cmbTopics is set to the value stored in the module-level variable currentTopic. When the program is first activated, the value of current-Topic is zero, and therefore the Value property of cmbTopics is set to the first item in its list. This is done to prevent the value displayed in the ComboBox control from changing when a new record is added to the list and these controls are updated. This will also trigger the Change() event procedure of cmbTopics. Finally, the Text properties of the TextBox controls are updated.

```
    cmbTopics.ListIndex = currentTopic
    txtTopic.Text = cmbTopics.Text
    txtWord.Text = ""
End Sub
```

The Change() event procedure of cmbTopics is triggered more often than desired, but is useful for updating the other controls on the UserForm when the user selects a new topic. First, the Text properties of the TextBox controls are updated to display the new selection in cmbTopics. The sub procedure GetRecNum() is called to update the variable recNum to the next available record (number of records in the file plus one), and this value is copied to the Caption property of lblRecNum. The GetWords() sub procedure is called to display the list of words associated with the currently selected topic in the ListBox control lstWords.

```
Private Sub cmbTopics_Change()
    txtTopic.Text = cmbTopics.Text
    txtWord.Text = ""
    GetRecNum
    lblRecNum.Caption = recNum
    GetWords
End Sub
```

The sub procedure GetRecNum() searches through each record in the file Wordfind.txt until it finds the values for the word and topic that matches the user's selection. If there is no match, then GetRecNum() returns the number of the next available record for storage.

```
Private Sub GetRecNum()
    Dim filePath As String
    Dim myWord As WordList
    filePath = ActiveWorkbook.Path & "\Wordfind.txt"
    recNum = 1
    Open filePath For Random As #1 Len = Len(myWord)
    Do While Not EOF(1)
        Get #1, recNum, myWord
```

An If/Then decision structure is used to test the values of the currently loaded record to the Text properties of the TextBox controls. If both values match, then the sub procedure is immediately exited while the variable recNum holds the number of the currently displayed record.

```
        If myWord.topic = txtTopic.Text And myWord.word = txtWord.Text
Then
            Close #1
            Exit Sub
        End If
        recNum = recNum + 1
    Loop
    Close #1
    recNum = recNum - 1
End Sub
```

The sub procedure GetWords() is used to copy the list of words stored in the variable array myWords to the ListBox control. An If/Then decision structure is used to display just those words associated with the currently selected topic in cmbTopics.

```
Private Sub GetWords()
    Dim I As Integer
    lstWords.Clear
    For I = 0 To UBound(myWords)
        If myTopics(I) = cmbTopics.Value Then
            lstWords.AddItem myWords(I)
        End If
    Next I
End Sub
```

The Click() event procedure of the ListBox control lstWords is triggered whenever the user selects an item displayed in the control. The idea here is to immediately display the selected word in the TextBox control for editing. The code updates the Text property of the TextBox control txtWord before sending code execution to the sub procedure GetRecNum(). Recall from earlier in the chapter that GetRecNum() determines the record number of the currently displayed values in the TextBox controls.

```
Private Sub lstWords_Click()
    txtWord.Text = lstWords.Text
    GetRecNum
    lblRecNum.Caption = recNum
End Sub
```

The `Click()` event procedure of the Command Button control `cmdAddRec` either adds a new record to the file entered by the user, or updates the existing record displayed in the TextBox controls.

```
Private Sub cmdAddRec_Click()
    currentTopic = cmbTopics.ListIndex
```

After the topic displayed in `cmbTopics` is copied to the module-level variable `currentTopic`, the procedure makes several calls to previously listed sub procedures. The sub procedure `SaveFile()` writes the currently displayed record to the file Wordfind.txt. The other procedures listed below are called to update the controls on the UserForm to include the record that was just added or updated.

```
    SaveFile
    GetAllRecords
    GetUniqueTopics
    GetWords
End Sub
```

The `SaveFile()` sub procedure saves the currently displayed record to the file Wordfind.txt. The record number is tracked throughout program execution so that when this procedure is called, the record is written to the proper location in the file. If the user enters a new record, then it is written to the end of the file. If the user updates an existing record, then it is written to its original location in the file.

```
Private Sub SaveFile()
    Dim filePath As String
    Dim myWord As WordList
    filePath = ActiveWorkbook.Path & "\Wordfind.txt"
    If recNum = 0 Then recNum = 1
    Open filePath For Random As #1 Len = Len(myWord)
    myWord.topic = txtTopic.Text
    myWord.word = txtWord.Text
    Put #1, recNum, myWord
    Close #1
    recNum = recNum + 1
    txtWord.Text = ""
    txtWord.SetFocus
End Sub
```

Finally, the UserForm is removed from memory when the user closes it.

```
Private Sub UserForm_QueryClose(Cancel As Integer, CloseMode As Integer)
    Unload Me
End Sub
```

The Word List program is made available to the user in the Word Find project listed at the end of this chapter. Not all the code will be listed again, and some of it will be altered slightly to include error handling.

Error Handling

All programs contain errors (often called *bugs*). Syntax errors occur when the programmer violates the rules of the language (for example, misspelled keywords, missing components of a code structure, or improper declaration of a variable), preventing the program from compiling. Syntax errors are relatively easy to fix because the VBA debugger sends you right to the source of the problem. Logic errors occur when the code contains errors that result in improper program behavior (for example, infinite loop or wrong variable initialization). Logic errors do not prevent the program from compiling and executing. Therefore, logic errors can be difficult to find. However, with proper debugging, the number of errors in a program can be significantly reduced.

Besides syntax and logic errors, programs may contain errors that can only be anticipated. Examples might include a divide by zero error (as seen in Chapter 7) or a file not found error. Left unchecked, these errors will cause the program to crash. Furthermore, errors of this type cannot be fixed by altering the logic of the program. In situations such as these, the program requires additional error handling code and procedures. Error handling code should be included whenever the program interacts with the user or other components of the computer. Validation procedures are examples of error handling procedures and are relatively easy to add to the code (see Chapter 4) This section focuses on special statements and objects available in VBA for handling anticipated errors.

Using the On Error Statement

In the FormDemo project from Chapter 7, the CalcStats() sub procedure contained the statement

```
On Error Resume Next
```

The On Error statement enables error handling in a VBA program. The On Error statement must be followed with instructions to VBA for deciding a course of action when a runtime error is encountered. The course of action to be taken depends on the type of error anticipated.

HINT

The On Error **statement must precede the code that is anticipated to generate the runtime error. The** On Error **statement is normally placed near the beginning of a procedure.**

In the case of the CalcStats() sub procedure, a divide by zero error was anticipated for the AVERAGE, MODE, MEDIAN, and STANDEV worksheet functions. Because the divide by zero error will only occur under special circumstances, it was handled by using the Resume Next clause. To inform the user of the error, the Caption properties of the Label controls meant to display the return values from these functions were set to "N/A" for not applicable. The CalcStats() sub procedure is listed below.

```
Public Sub CalcStats()
    Const noValue = "N/A"
    '
    On Error Resume Next
    If txtInput.Text = "" Then txtInput.Text = Selection.Address
    lblSum.Caption =
Application.WorksheetFunction.Sum(Range(txtInput.Text))
    lblCount.Caption =
Application.WorksheetFunction.Count(Range(txtInput.Text))
```

In anticipation of an error the Caption property of the Label control lblAverage is set to "N/A".

```
    lblAverage.Caption = noValue
```

The next line will generate a run-time error if the Average() function tries to divide by 0. If an error is generated, then program execution proceeds to the next line of code and the Caption property of lblAverage remains "N/A". If no error is generated and the Average() function returns a value, then the Caption property of lblAverage is updated with the desired statistical result.

```
    lblAverage.Caption =
Format(Application.WorksheetFunction.Average(Range(txtInput.Text)), "#.##")
    lblMedian.Caption =
Application.WorksheetFunction.Median(Range(txtInput.Text))
    lblMode.Caption = noValue
    lblMode.Caption =
Application.WorksheetFunction.Mode(Range(txtInput.Text))
    lblStanDev.Caption = noValue
    lblStanDev.Caption =
Format(Application.WorksheetFunction.StDev(Range(txtInput.Text)), "#.##")
End Sub
```

The Resume Next clause sends program execution to the next line of code following the line that generated the error. It is the simplest solution for handling runtime errors and works well in the case of the CalcStats() sub procedure. However, it is not always the best solution.

When an anticipated error requires execution of a special block of code, use the GoTo statement after On Error.

On Error GoTo ErrorHandler

The term ErrorHandler refers to a line label used to direct program execution to the block of code specifically created for handling the runtime error. Line labels must start at the leftmost position in the editor window and end with a colon. The error handling code follows the line label.

The use of the GoTo statement goes all the way back to the earliest versions of Basic and a few other programming languages. The GoTo statement is rarely seen anymore because when overused, the order of execution of programming statements can be very difficult to follow and results in what is termed "spaghetti code." Spaghetti code is very hard to debug, and for that reason the use of the GoTo statement in VBA should be limited to error handling routines.

An illustration of the use of an error handling routine apppears in Figure 8.4.

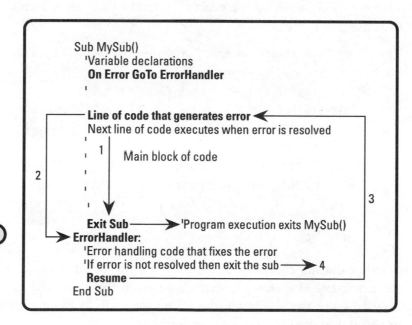

FIGURE 8.4

Order of program execution in a procedure with error handling

The figure shows the order of program execution in a sub procedure that contains error handling code. The order of program execution proceeds as follows:

1. If no error is generated, the main block of code executes but program execution exits the sub procedure before reaching the ErrorHandler.

2. An error is generated and code execution proceeds to the ErrorHandler.

3. The error is resolved in the ErrorHandler and code execution proceeds back to the original line of code that generated the error. Then the main block of code executes before program execution exits the sub procedure.

4. If the error is not resolved, then program execution should exit the sub without executing the main block of code.

Now consider the ReadSeqFile() sub procedure listed earlier in the chapter. Trying to open a file for sequential access will generate a runtime error if the file cannot be found at the specified location.

```
Public Sub ReadSeqFile()
    Dim filePath As String
    Dim I As Integer
    Dim theName As String
    Dim theNumber As String
    Dim msgReturn As Integer
```

The error handler must be "turned on" with the On Error statement and a reference to the line label.

```
    On Error GoTo ErrorHandler
    I = 1
    filePath = ActiveWorkbook.Path & "\SeqPhone.txt"
    Open filePath For Input As #1
    Do While Not EOF(1)
        Input #1, theName, theNumber
        Cells(I, "A").Value = theName
        Cells(I, "B").Value = theNumber
        I = I + 1
    Loop
    Close #1
```

The error handling code is not a separate procedure but a block of code isolated by the line label. Therefore, an exit statement is used near the end of the procedure just before the line label to prevent the code in the error-handling block from being executed if no error is generated.

```
    Exit Sub
```

The error handling code follows the line label, and due to the structure of the sub procedure, will only be executed when a runtime error occurs. In this example, the error handling code is only one line. A message box with a description of the error is displayed to the user. The description is obtained from the Description property of the Err object. The Err object stores information about runtime errors and is intrinsic to VBA. The properties of the Err object are initialized when a runtime error occurs with an error handling routine enabled.

```
ErrorHandler:
   msgReturn = MsgBox(filePath & " " & Err.Description, vbCritical, "Error")
   'Additional error handling code
   'Resume
End Sub
```

Error handling routines are typically longer than the preceding example. Additional code in this example might include showing a UserForm with code and ActiveX controls designed to display the file structure of the computer (techniques that are beyond the scope of this book). The user could then navigate through his computer's files to find the right file. Another possibility would be to just create the file at the specified path when the file not found error is raised. If the error handler fixes the runtime error, then Resume can be used to send program execution back to the line of code that generated the error.

Warning! If the error handling routine does not fix the error and contains a Resume **statement, code execution will proceed back and forth between the error generating line of code and the error handling code, forcing drastic action to terminate the program.**

Debugging

By now, you have probably encountered numerous errors in your programs and have struggled to correct some of them. Finding bugs in a program can be frustrating. Fortunately, VBA has several tools to help debug a program.

Break Mode

When a runtime error is generated while testing a program, the dialog box shown in Figure 8.5 is displayed.

Selecting the Debug option calls up the VBA IDE and displays the program in break mode. While in break mode, program execution is paused and can be stepped through one line at a time to closely examine factors such as order of code execution and the current values stored within variables. The line of code that generated the error will be highlighted, as shown in Figure 8.6.

To intentionally enter break mode, insert a breakpoint at the desired location in the program using the Debug menu item or Debug toolbar (select from the View menu) in the VBA IDE (refer to Figure 8.6). You can also toggle a breakpoint by clicking the left margin of the code window next to the line of code at which you want program execution to pause, or by pressing F9.

Insert breakpoints at locations in code where bugs are suspected or known to exist and then run the program. Break mode is entered when program execution proceeds to a line of code containing a breakpoint. At this time, you have the option of resetting the program, stepping through the program one line at a time, or continuing normal operation of the program. While in break mode, the value currently stored in a variable can be checked by holding the cursor over the name of that variable. Logic errors are often caused by code that assigns the wrong value to a variable. Break mode can help locate the code that creates these errors.

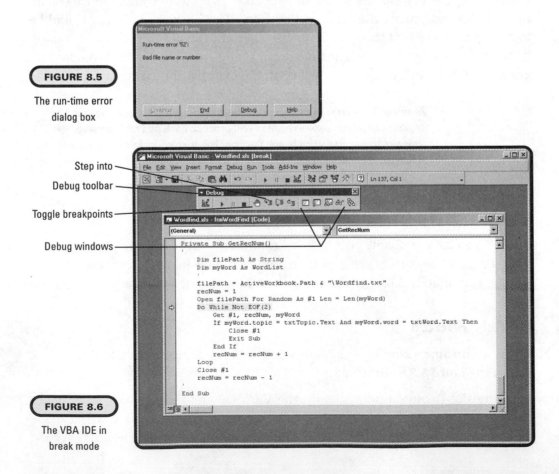

FIGURE 8.5

The run-time error dialog box

FIGURE 8.6

The VBA IDE in break mode

Stepping through code while in break mode is another useful debugging feature. Use Step Into on the Debug toolbar, or press F8, to execute one line of code at a time starting from the location of the break. The order of program execution can be verified, and values stored within variables checked as code execution proceeds one line at a time.

The Immediate Window

Stepping through code one line at a time can be tedious if the error is not found quickly. The Immediate window allows you to test program variables and procedures under normal program execution. The Immediate window can be displayed by selecting it from the View menu or the Debug toolbar in the VBA IDE (refer to Figure 8.6).

The Immediate window is often used to hold the value of a variable or variables written to it with debugging statements located at suspected trouble spots in the program. Debugging statements use the Assert and Print methods of the Debug object. The Assert method can be used to break program execution based on a Boolean expression. The Print method is used to write values to the Immediate window.

 Debugging statements are not compiled and stored in the executable program file, so there is no harm in leaving them in your code.

In the code that follows, the Boolean variable comboOff is used as the expression with the Assert method of the Debug object that breaks program execution. The expression does not have to be a variable of type Boolean, but can be any expression that evaluates as true or false (for example, myVar>5). The Assert method breaks program execution when the Boolean expression evaluates to false. The Print method of the Debug object is used to write the value of the variable recNum to the Immediate window whenever this procedure is called. It is a good idea to include a string identifying the variable, especially if there are more debugging statements elsewhere in the program. After (or during) program execution the Immediate window and its contents can be viewed from the VBA IDE, as shown in Figure 8.7.

```
Private Sub cmbTopics_Change()
    Debug.Assert comboOff
    Debug.Print "Record Number"; recNum
    If comboOff = True Then Exit Sub
    GetWords
End Sub
```

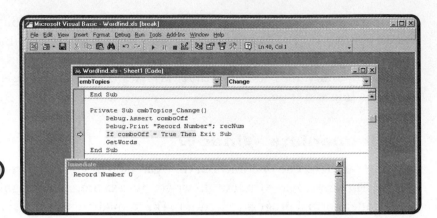

FIGURE 8.7

The Immediate window

The preceding procedure is the Change() event of a ComboBox control. Program execution enters break mode whenever the procedure is called and the value of comboOff is false. The value of the recNum variable is written to the Immediate window each time this procedure is executed. The purpose of these debugging statements is to ensure that the program holds the desired values of comboOff and recNum when the events that trigger this procedure occur.

The Immediate window can also be used to enter code statements while the program is in break mode. Statements that change the value of a variable or the property of an ActiveX control, or call a procedure, can be entered directly into the Immediate window. The statements take effect after the Enter key is pressed. Using the previous example, the value of the variable comboOff can be changed while in break mode by entering comboOff = True in the Immediate window. This is useful for re-directing program execution and testing the results without having to alter code.

The Watch Window

Besides the Immediate window, another useful tool for debugging VBA programs is the Watch window. The Watch window makes it possible to track the value of a variable or expression (property, function call, and so on) from anywhere in a program. Add a watch to an expression from the Debug menu or right click the expression and choose Add Watch from the shortcut menu. The resulting dialog box is shown in Figure 8.8.

Choose either the specific procedure in which you want to watch the expression, or choose all procedures. Next, choose the specific module in which you want to watch the expression or select all modules. Finally, select the type of watch (Watch Expression, Break When Value Is True, or Break When Value Changes).

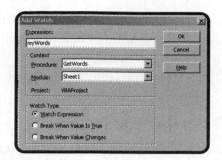

FIGURE 8.8

The Add Watch
dialog box

The watch type selected will be displayed in the Watch window only when the program enters break mode. Therefore, if the watch type Watch Expression is selected, a breakpoint will have to be inserted in the procedure(s) containing the expression before running the program. The other two watch types automatically pause the program at the specified location. A Watch window showing the value of an expression while the program is in break mode is shown in Figure 8.9.

The Locals Window

The Locals window (see Figure 8.10) is used to display the value of the declared variables local to the procedure in which program execution has been paused with a breakpoint. Module-level variables are also listed under the object Me in the Locals window. Display the Locals window by selecting it from the View menu or Debug toolbar.

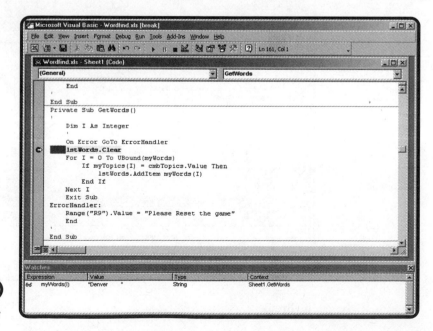

FIGURE 8.9

The Watch window

When you suspect a procedure contains an error, insert a breakpoint in the procedure, run the program, and display the Locals window before stepping through the procedure's code. This is a handy tool for debugging a procedure, as it allows you to view the values of all local variables while stepping through the code.

Chapter Project: Word Find

The Word Find project can be used to create standard word find puzzles. The topics and words used in a puzzle can be added to a file using the program discussed earlier in this chapter. The file containing the word lists is accessed and displayed by the Word Find program. The user can then select individual words and place them within a 15 × 15 grid running in any direction. After placing the words, the puzzle is filled with random letters before printing the puzzle. The Word Find program can be found on the accompanying CD-ROM stored as Wordfind.xls.

Project Statement

In VBA using an Excel worksheet, I want to create a program that makes it easy for the user to create word find puzzles. The program should allow the user to place words selected from a list within a 15 × 15 grid. The capability to add new word lists to the file used by the program should also be included.

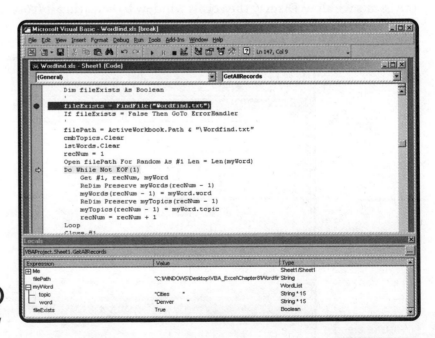

FIGURE 8.10

The Locals window

Project Tools

The tools used to create this program include most of the components studied to this point in the book. This includes the Excel worksheet and its associated objects, ActiveX controls, UserForms, and all associated programming modules. Error handling routines should be included in the code to handle any anticipated errors that might cause the program to fail.

Project Algorithm

The Word Find program will be built following the approach listed here.

1. Format an Excel worksheet to isolate a range of cells that includes 15 rows and 15 columns for holding the letters in the puzzle.

2. Format the worksheet to include an area below the puzzle grid that will be used to list the words added to the puzzle. A sequence of four to five cells will have to be merged for each word to ensure the word will fit within the target cell when displayed.

3. Format the worksheet to include an area of merged cells that will be used to display helpful messages to the user.

The preformatted worksheet is shown in Figure 8.11

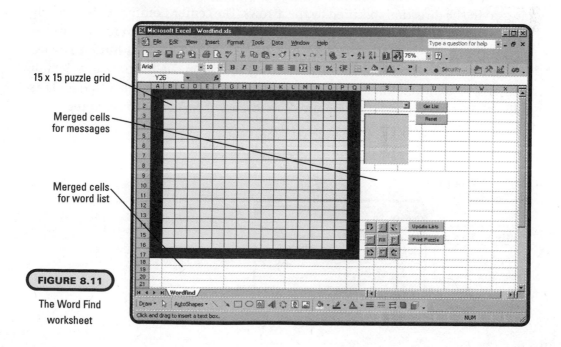

FIGURE 8.11

The Word Find worksheet

Several ActiveX controls are added to the worksheet to handle adding the following:

- A ComboBox control for selecting the puzzle's topic.
- A ListBox control for displaying the words associated with the selected topic.
- A Command Button control for loading the topics and lists.
- A Command Button control for resetting the worksheet.
- Command Button controls for choosing the direction of the word.
- A Command Button control for filling in the puzzle with randomly selected letters.
- A Command Button control for accessing the UserForm that maintains the word list file.
- A Command Button control for printing the puzzle.

Figure 8.12 shows the ActiveX controls used to display the topics and word list to the user for selecting a word to add to the puzzle. The Command Button labeled Get List will retrieve the records from the file Wordfind.txt and display them in the ComboBox and ListBox controls when clicked. The Command Button labeled Reset will clear the worksheet of words (puzzle grid and controls) when clicked.

The remaining ActiveX controls placed on the worksheet are shown in Figure 8.13. The 3 × 3 grid of Command Button controls are used to write the word to the puzzle grid in the direction specified by the arrows. The center Command Button control in the 3 × 3 grid of controls labeled Fill will randomly fill empty cells in the puzzle grid with uppercase letters when clicked. The Command Button labeled Print prints the puzzle and list of words used in the puzzle to the user's default printer when clicked. Finally, the Command Button control labeled Update Lists calls the Word List UserForm and program discussed earlier in the chapter.

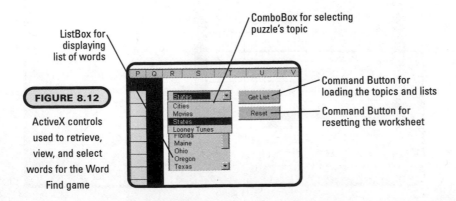

FIGURE 8.12

ActiveX controls used to retrieve, view, and select words for the Word Find game

ListBox for displaying list of words

ComboBox for selecting puzzle's topic

Command Button for loading the topics and lists

Command Button for resetting the worksheet

FIGURE 8.13

ActiveX controls
used to place a
word on the puzzle,
print the puzzle,
and call the Word
List UserForm for
updating the
Wordfind.txt file

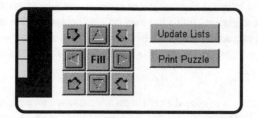

As the program proceeds, the following will be true:

- The program will begin from the Click() event procedure of a Command Button control that loads the topics and word list into the ComboBox and ListBox controls, respectively.

- When the user selects a word from the ListBox control and then clicks on one of eight different Command Button controls, the word will be added to the grid running in the direction indicated by the image of an arrow displayed in the Command Button control.

- When the user clicks the Command Button control labeled Fill, the empty cells in the puzzle grid will be filled with randomly selected letters.

- When the user clicks the Command Button control labeled Print, the area containing the puzzle grid and the list of words contained in the puzzle will be printed to the user's default printer.

- The option of resetting the worksheet will be provided via the Click() event procedure of a Command Button control. The procedure should clear the puzzle grid, and the ComboBox and ListBox controls.

- The user can maintain the word lists via the program created and listed earlier in this chapter. The UserForm that contains the code for this maintenance program will be shown modally from the Click() event procedure of a Command Button control.

- A validation procedure will be added to ensure the user has properly selected a cell within the puzzle grid for the start of a word. The word must fit within the puzzle grid.

- A validation procedure will be added to ensure the user has selected a word from the list before trying to place it in the grid.

- When validation procedures fail, help messages will be displayed to the user via the Value property of a merged range of cells.

- Error handling routines will be added to the program wherever errors are anticipated or discovered via testing and debugging.

HINT

Depending on the combination of Windows operating system (98, 2000, XP) and Excel version (97, 2000, 2002) running on your computer, the Word Find program (and perhaps others in this book) may generate runtime errors specifying "Can't find project or library." If this happens on your computer, then the simplest solution is to create a new project in Excel and copy and paste the code from the loaded project file into the new file (select Move or Copy Sheet from the Edit menu in Excel).

You will also have to copy the code from any modules not contained in the component module of the worksheet that was copied into the new project. Any ActiveX controls will have to be renamed to their original names before the program will execute. The error is the result of a missing reference to the needed VBA libraries and was probably caused by a change in a file path or file name. The code itself is error-free and the reference error will be resolved when a new project is created and the code is copied into the new project rather than loaded into Excel.

Adding the Code

Before writing the program, a few properties of the ActiveX controls placed on the worksheet were changed from their default values. The Caption properties of the Command Button controls were changed to the values shown in Figure 8.1. For the Command Button controls displaying the arrows, the Picture property was used to load an image file. The Style property of the ComboBox control was set to drop-down list and all controls were given meaningful values for the Name property.

The code listed next is from the component module of the worksheet and begins with a few module-level variable declarations that include one user-defined type. These are essentially the same variables used in the program listed earlier in the chapter that maintained the random access file. A Boolean variable comboOff is used to toggle the Change() event procedure of the ComboBox control to prevent it from executing all its code when not required. The variable, puzzleGrid, is used to define the 15 × 15 grid of worksheet cells that contain the letters of the word find puzzle.

```
Option Explicit
Dim recNum As Integer
Private Type WordList
    topic As String * 15
    word As String * 15
End Type
Dim myWords() As String
```

```
Dim myTopics() As String
Dim currentTopic As Integer
Dim comboOff As Boolean
Dim puzzleGrid As Range
```

The program begins from the `Click()` event procedure of the Command Button control named `cmdGetList`. This procedure calls the same sub procedures listed earlier in the chapter used to copy the records from the Wordfind.txt file to the ComboBox and ListBox controls (`cmbTopics` and `lstWords`).

```
Private Sub cmdGetList_Click()
    GetAllRecords
    GetUniqueTopics
    GetWords
    comboOff = True
End Sub
```

The `GetAllRecords()`, `GetWords()`, and `GetUniqueTopics()` sub procedures have been modified slightly to include error handling. The error handling code is discussed for the `GetAllRecords()` and `GetWords()` sub procedures, which are listed here. The `GetUniqueTopics()` sub procedure is not listed again here but can be viewed from the listing described earlier in the chapter.

```
Private Sub GetAllRecords()
    Dim filePath As String
    Dim myWord As WordList
    Dim fileExists As Boolean
```

When opening a file for random access, if the file does not exist then a new file will be created and no runtime error is generated. The Word Find program depends on the records contained in the Wordfind.txt file, so it's preferable to send program execution to an error handler if the file does not exist.

A call to the function procedure `FindFile()` is used to return a Boolean value indicating whether the Wordfind.txt file exists in the required directory. If the file is not found, then code execution proceeds immediately to the `ErrorHandler()` line label. The error message `"Word list file not found"` is displayed to the user and the program is terminated with the `End` statement.

```
    fileExists = FindFile("Wordfind.txt")
    If fileExists = False Then GoTo ErrorHandler
    filePath = ActiveWorkbook.Path & "\Wordfind.txt"
    cmbTopics.Clear
    lstWords.Clear
```

```
        recNum = 1
        Open filePath For Random As #1 Len = Len(myWord)
        Do While Not EOF(1)
            Get #1, recNum, myWord
            ReDim Preserve myWords(recNum - 1)
            myWords(recNum - 1) = myWord.word
            ReDim Preserve myTopics(recNum - 1)
            myTopics(recNum - 1) = myWord.topic
            recNum = recNum + 1
        Loop
        Close #1
        recNum = recNum - 1
        Exit Sub
ErrorHandler:
        Range("R9").Value = "Word list file not found"
        End
End Sub
```

The `FindFile()` function procedure uses the properties of the FileSearch object to search for the Wordfind.txt file. This procedure could easily be omitted and replaced with an `On Error Goto ErrorHandler` statement in the `GetAllRecords()` sub procedure. The error handler could then send the `Description` property of the Err object to cell R9 (`Range("R9").Value = Err.Description`).

```
Private Function FindFile(wordFile As String) As Boolean
    Dim I As Integer
```

The `NewSearch` method resets the FileSearch object to its default property values, essentially getting it ready to begin a new search. The `LookIn` property sets the path to the top-level directory that will be searched. The `SearchSubFolders`, `MatchTextExactly`, and `FileType` properties are intuitive and are set accordingly before the `Execute` method is used to begin the search. Based on the search criteria specified, if the `Count` property of the FoundFiles object is greater than zero, then the Wordfind.txt file was found by the search. Next, the value of the `FindFile()` function procedure is set to true before code execution is sent back to the calling procedure.

```
    With Application.FileSearch
        .NewSearch
        .LookIn = ActiveWorkbook.Path
        .SearchSubFolders = False
        .Filename = wordFile
```

```
            .MatchTextExactly = True
            .FileType = msoFileTypeAllFiles
            .Execute
            If .FoundFiles.Count > 0 Then
                FindFile = True
            Else
                FindFile = False
            End If
        End With
End Function
```

An error handler was added to the GetWords() and GetUniqueTopics() sub procedures in case the user resets (stops) the program. Unlike the case of the form
module of a UserForm, the user's actions can stop a program contained in a component module of a worksheet inadvertently (for example, by toggling the Design
Mode button on the Visual Basic toolbar). Once program execution is stopped,
memory used to hold variables is released and the myWords and myTopics arrays no
longer exist. If the user triggers the Change() event procedure of the ComboBox
control (which calls the GetWords() sub procedure) before the records from the
Wordfind.txt file are loaded again, then a runtime error will be generated from
the code that follows. Specifically, the UBound() function cannot return an upper
index value on an array that does not exist.

```
Private Sub GetWords()
    Dim I As Integer
    On Error GoTo ErrorHandler
    lstWords.Clear
    For I = 0 To UBound(myWords)
        If myTopics(I) = cmbTopics.Value Then
            lstWords.AddItem myWords(I)
        End If
    Next I
    Exit Sub
ErrorHandler:
    Range("R9").Value = "Please Reset the game"
    End
End Sub
```

After the file is loaded and its contents are copied to the ComboBox and ListBox
controls, the user selects a word from the list. The selected word is placed on the
puzzle grid by clicking one of the Command Button controls containing an
image of an arrow.

The `Click()` event procedures of the Command Button controls containing an image of an arrow sends program execution to the `PlaceWord()` sub procedure. The `PlaceWord()` sub procedure accepts a string parameter used to indicate the direction in which to place the word (N, NE, E, SE, S, SW, W, and NW). There are a total of eight `Click()` event procedures that look like the one listed here, albeit with different string parameters in the argument list.

```
Private Sub cmdSE_Click()
    PlaceWord ("SE")
End Sub
```

The `PlaceWord()` sub procedure writes the selected word to the specified cells on the worksheet. For example, if the user clicks on the Command Button control named cmdSE (bottom right control in the 3 × 3 grid), then the selected word will be written on a diagonal proceeding down and to the right on the puzzle grid, as shown in Figure 8.14.

```
Private Sub PlaceWord(wordDirection As String)
    Dim selectionOK As Boolean
    Dim wordSelection As String
    Dim wordLength As Integer
    Dim I As Integer
    Dim cellRow As Integer
    Dim cellCol As Integer
```

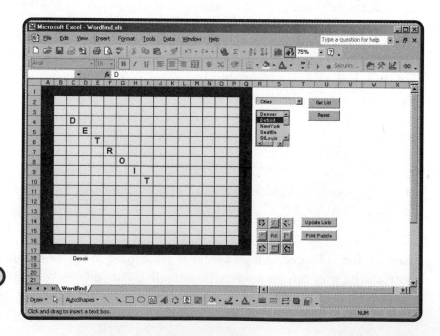

FIGURE 8.14

Placing a word on
the puzzle grid

An error handler is used to ensure that the user has selected a word from the list displayed in the ListBox control (lstWords) before trying to place it on the puzzle grid. Next, the Value property of the Range object that represents the set of merged cells used to display help messages to the user is reset. The cell reference R9 is the upper-leftmost cell of the merged range. The next line trims the selected word of its spaces (remember it was stored as a user-defined type with 15 characters), converts it to all uppercase, and copies it to the wordSelection variable.

```
On Error GoTo ErrorHandler
Range("R9").Value = ""
wordSelection = UCase(Trim(lstWords.Value))
```

The number of characters in the selected word will be needed later, as will the row and column index of the cell selected by the user to hold the first letter.

```
wordLength = Len(wordSelection)
cellRow = Selection.Row
cellCol = Selection.Column
```

A validation sub procedure (ValidateStartCell()) is called to verify that the user selected only one cell in the puzzle grid and that the selected word will fit in the defined puzzle area. If the user's selection is validated, then code execution proceeds to the Select/Case decision structure.

```
selectionOK = ValidateStartCell(wordDirection)
If selectionOK  Then
```

The Select/Case decision structure operates on the string variable wordDirection that was passed to this procedure. A Do-Loop and the string manipulation function Mid() is used to select individual characters from the selected word and write that character to the appropriate cell on the worksheet. For example, the direction NW indicates that the word should be written to the grid on a diagonal starting from the lower right cell and proceeding to the upper left cell. Therefore, the row index variable and column index variable are both decremented by one with every iteration through the Do-Loop. The remaining cases used for the other directions follow the same logic. The only difference is whether or not the column and row index variables are decremented, incremented, or left unchanged.

```
Select Case wordDirection
    Case Is = "NW"
        Do
            cells(cellRow, cellCol).Value = Mid(wordSelection, I + 1, 1)
            I = I + 1
            cellRow = cellRow - 1
```

```vba
                    cellCol = cellCol - 1
            Loop While (I < wordLength)
        Case Is = "N"
            Do
                cells(cellRow, cellCol).Value = Mid(wordSelection, I + 1, 1)
                I = I + 1
                cellRow = cellRow - 1
            Loop While (I < wordLength)
        Case Is = "NE"
            Do
                cells(cellRow, cellCol).Value = Mid(wordSelection, I + 1, 1)
                I = I + 1
                cellRow = cellRow - 1
                cellCol = cellCol + 1
            Loop While (I < wordLength)
        Case Is = "E"
            Do
                cells(cellRow, cellCol).Value = Mid(wordSelection, I + 1, 1)
                I = I + 1
                cellCol = cellCol + 1
            Loop While (I < wordLength)
        Case "SE"
            Do
                cells(cellRow, cellCol).Value = Mid(wordSelection, I + 1, 1)
                I = I + 1
                cellRow = cellRow + 1
                cellCol = cellCol + 1
            Loop While (I < wordLength)
        Case "S"
            Do
                cells(cellRow, cellCol).Value = Mid(wordSelection, I + 1, 1)
                I = I + 1
                cellRow = cellRow + 1
            Loop While (I < wordLength)
        Case "SW"
            Do
                cells(cellRow, cellCol).Value = Mid(wordSelection, I + 1, 1)
                I = I + 1
                cellRow = cellRow + 1
                    cellCol = cellCol - 1
```

```
                    Loop While (I < wordLength)
          Case "W"
              Do
                cells(cellRow, cellCol).Value = Mid(wordSelection, I + 1, 1)
                I = I + 1
                cellCol = cellCol - 1
              Loop While (I < wordLength)
       End Select
       WordToGrid
       Range("R9").Value = ""
   End If
   Exit Sub
```

The error handler uses the Number property of the Err object to catch "Invalid use of Null" runtime errors generated by the Trim() function when it is passed a null string because the user did not make a selection from the list of words.

```
ErrorHandler:
   If Err.Number = 94 Then
       Range("R9").Value = "Please select a word from the list!"
   End If
End Sub
```

The ValidateStartCell() function procedure is called from PlaceWord() sub procedure and is used to validate the user's selection of a worksheet cell for holding the first character in the selected word.

```
Private Function ValidateStartCell(wordDirection As String) As Boolean
   Dim wordSelection As String
   Dim wordLength As Integer
   Dim maxCells As Integer
   wordSelection = Trim(lstWords.Value)
   wordLength = Len(wordSelection)
```

After the number of characters in the selected word is stored for later use, the Count property of the Range object representing the cells selected by the user is tested. The user is required to select only one cell, and if this is the case, the function is assigned the value true (this assignment may change later in the procedure). If more than one cell is selected, then the function is assigned the value false, an error message is displayed to the user, and the procedure is immediately exited.

```
   If Selection.Count = 1 Then
       ValidateStartCell = True
```

```
    Else
        ValidateStartCell = False
        Range("R9").Value = "Improper cell selection!"
        Exit Function
    End If
```

The selection for a starting cell must also fall within the defined puzzle area, which is between rows 2 and 16 and columns 2 and 16 (columns B to P). If the selection is outside the defined area, then the function is assigned the value false and exited.

```
    If (Selection.Row > 2 And Selection.Row < 16) And (Selection.Column > 2
And Selection.Column < 16) Then
        ValidateStartCell = True
    Else
        ValidateStartCell = False
        Range("R9").Value = "Improper cell selection!"
        Exit Function
    End If
```

Next, the selection of a starting cell is tested to ensure that the selected word will fit in the puzzle grid. The number of available cells in the puzzle grid is determined using the CountCells() function procedure. If there are not enough available cells, then the function is assigned the value false and an error message is displayed to the user.

```
  maxCells = CountCells(wordDirection)
  If wordLength > maxCells Then
      Range("R9").Value = "The selection does not fit in the target area."
      ValidateStartCell = False
  End If
End Function
```

The CountCells() function procedure is used by the ValidateStartCell() function procedure to calculate the maximum number of cells available for a word. The calculation is based on the location of the cell used to hold the first character in the word, and the direction in which the word will be written to the grid. Consider an example wherein the user selects the word Denver from the ListBox control and cell D16 on the puzzle grid, as shown in Figure 8.15.

If the user tries to place the word so that it runs from right to left by clicking on the Command Button control named cmdWest, then the CountCells() function

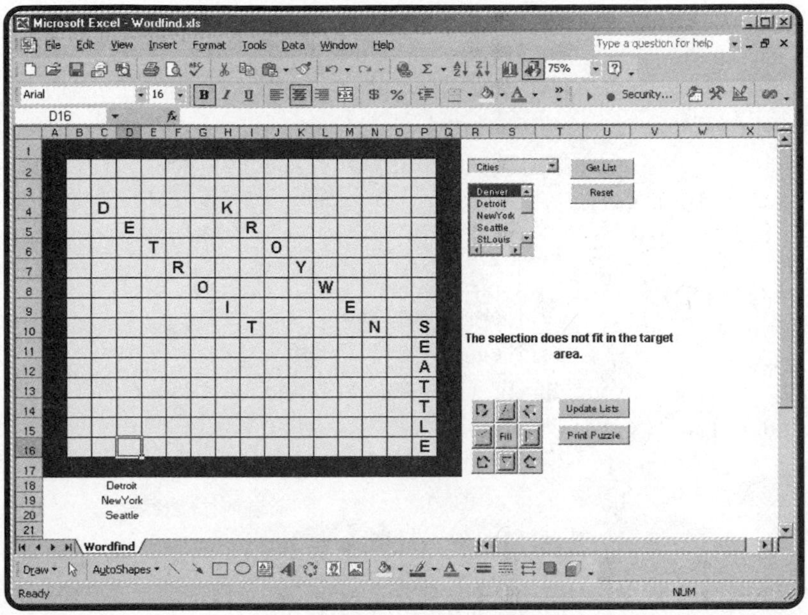

FIGURE 8.15

Placing a word on
the puzzle grid

will calculate a total of three available cells. The number 3 is returned to the
ValidateStartCell() procedure, where it is compared to the number of letters in
the word Denver (6). In this case the user's selection is invalid because at least
six cells were needed. A message is output to the worksheet telling the user that
the selection does not fit in the grid.

The structure and logic of the CountCells() function procedure is very similar to
that of the PlaceWord() sub procedure. A Select/Case decision structure is used to
distinguish the direction of the word, and a Do-Loop is used to count the number
of available cells. Again, the row and column indexes are initialized via the Row
and Column properties of the Range object (Selection.Row and Selection.Column).
Then the row and column indexes are incremented, decremented, or left
unchanged inside the Do-Loop as the numbers of available cells are counted and
stored in the variable cellCount.

```
Private Function CountCells(wordDirection As String) As Integer
    Dim cellRow As Integer
    Dim cellCol As Integer
    Dim cellCount As Integer
    cellRow = Selection.Row
    cellCol = Selection.Column
    Select Case wordDirection
        Case Is = "NW"
```

```
                    Do
                        cellRow = cellRow - 1
                        cellCol = cellCol - 1
                        cellCount = cellCount + 1
                    Loop While (cellRow > 1 And cellRow < 17) And (cellCol > 1
          And cellCol < 17)
                Case Is = "N"
                    Do
                        cellRow = cellRow - 1
                        cellCount = cellCount + 1
                    Loop While (cellRow > 1 And cellRow < 17) And (cellCol > 1
          And cellCol < 17)
                Case Is = "NE"
                    Do
                        cellRow = cellRow - 1
                        cellCol = cellCol + 1
                        cellCount = cellCount + 1
                    Loop While (cellRow > 1 And cellRow < 17) And (cellCol > 1
          And cellCol < 17)
                Case Is = "E"
                    Do
                        cellCol = cellCol + 1
                        cellCount = cellCount + 1
                    Loop While (cellRow > 1 And cellRow < 17) And (cellCol > 1
          And cellCol < 17)
                Case "SE"
                    Do
                        cellRow = cellRow + 1
                        cellCol = cellCol + 1
                        cellCount = cellCount + 1
                    Loop While (cellRow > 1 And cellRow < 17) And (cellCol > 1
          And cellCol < 17)
                Case "S"
                    Do
                        cellRow = cellRow + 1
                        cellCount = cellCount + 1
                    Loop While (cellRow > 1 And cellRow < 17) And (cellCol > 1
          And cellCol < 17)
                Case "SW"
                    Do
```

```
                    cellRow = cellRow + 1
                    cellCol = cellCol - 1
                    cellCount = cellCount + 1
                Loop While (cellRow > 1 And cellRow < 17) And (cellCol > 1
And cellCol < 17)
            Case "W"
                Do
                    cellCol = cellCol - 1
                    cellCount = cellCount + 1
                Loop While (cellRow > 1 And cellRow < 17) And (cellCol > 1
And cellCol < 17)
        End Select
        CountCells = cellCount
End Function
```

The region of cells below the puzzle grid is used to display the words selected and copied to the puzzle by the user. The size of the region is 8 × 15 cells, with five cells merged into one cell across the rows. Therefore, there are only three available cells within each of the eight rows, for a total capacity of 24 words.

```
Private Sub WordToGrid()
    Dim I As Integer
    Dim K As Integer
```

Nested For/Next loops iterate through the cells starting with the upper-leftmost cell (B18) and proceeding down a column, then to the next column until reaching the last cell (L25). The selected word is copied to the first empty cell encountered in the nested loop. The looping variable K represents the column index, and I the row index.

```
    For K = 2 To 12 Step 5
        For I = 18 To 25
            If cells(I, K).Value = "" Then
                cells(I, K).Value = 1stWords.Value
                Exit Sub
            End If
        Next I
    Next K
End Sub
```

The Click() event procedure of the Command Button control named cmdFill is used to fill empty cells in the puzzle grid with uppercase letters. A For/Each loop and a random number between 65 and 90 easily solve the problem.

```
Private Sub cmdFill_Click()
    Dim c As Range
    Dim ranNum As Integer
    Randomize
    Set puzzleGrid = Range("B2:P16")
    For Each c In puzzleGrid
```

The ASCII characters A through Z are represented by decimal values 65 through 90. The Chr() function returns the randomly selected character.

```
        ranNum = Int(26 * Rnd + 65)
        If c.Value = "" Then c.Value = Chr(ranNum)
    Next
    Range("R9").Value = ""
End Sub
```

The puzzle is printed via the Click() event procedure of the Command Button control named cmdPrint.

```
Private Sub cmdPrint_Click()
    Dim rt As Integer
    On Error GoTo ErrorHandler
```

The borders are removed from the area of cells that define the puzzle so they won't show on the printout.

```
    Range("B2:P16").Select
    Selection.Borders(xlEdgeLeft).LineStyle = xlNone
    Selection.Borders(xlEdgeTop).LineStyle = xlNone
    Selection.Borders(xlEdgeBottom).LineStyle = xlNone
    Selection.Borders(xlEdgeRight).LineStyle = xlNone
    Selection.Borders(xlInsideVertical).LineStyle = xlNone
    Selection.Borders(xlInsideHorizontal).LineStyle = xlNone
    Selection.Interior.ColorIndex = xlNone
```

The print area is defined as the cells containing the puzzle and the list of words contained within the puzzle before the puzzle is printed.

```
    ActiveSheet.PageSetup.PrintArea = "$A$1:$Q$25"
    ActiveWindow.SelectedSheets.PrintOut Copies:=1, Collate:=True
```

The borders and interior color of the puzzle grid are returned to their original settings.

```
    Selection.Borders(xlEdgeLeft).LineStyle = xlContinuous
    Selection.Borders(xlEdgeTop).LineStyle = xlContinuous
```

```
    Selection.Borders(xlEdgeBottom).LineStyle = xlContinuous
    Selection.Borders(xlEdgeRight).LineStyle = xlContinuous
    Selection.Borders(xlInsideVertical).LineStyle = xlContinuous
    Selection.Borders(xlInsideHorizontal).LineStyle = xlContinuous
    Selection.Interior.ColorIndex = 34
    Exit Sub
```

An error handler is used to display any runtime errors generated by trying to print the puzzle (for example, No printer available).

```
ErrorHandler:
    rt = MsgBox(Err.Description, vbCritical, "Error")
End Sub
```

The game is reset from the `Click()` event procedure of the Command Button control named `cmdReset` by clearing the puzzle grid, word list, message cell, ComboBox control, and ListBox control. This forces the user to start building another puzzle from the `Click()` event procedure of `cmdGetList`, which calls the procedure used to load the records from the Wordfind.txt file. It also initializes all the necessary variables and controls required for building a puzzle.

```
Private Sub cmdReset_Click()
    Range("B18:P25").ClearContents
    Set puzzleGrid = Range("B2:P16")
    puzzleGrid.ClearContents
    comboOff = True
    cmbTopics.Clear
    lstWords.Clear
    Range("R9").Value = ""
End Sub
```

When the user selects a new topic, the list of words in the ListBox control named `lstWords` is updated with the appropriate values by a call to the `GetWords()` sub procedure listed earlier. The Boolean variable `comboOff` forces program execution to exit this procedure if set to true.

```
Private Sub cmbTopics_Change()
    If comboOff = True Then Exit Sub
    GetWords
End Sub
```

The `DropButtonClick()` event procedure is triggered when the user selects the drop button on a ComboBox control. This event procedure is used to set the variable `comboOff` to false so that the entire contents of the `Change()` event procedure of cmbTopics (listed just above) is executed. This ensures that the GetWords() sub procedure is called only when the user chooses a new topic, and is not called when the control is cleared.

```
Private Sub cmbTopics_DropButtonClick()
    comboOff = False
End Sub
```

The last two procedures listed are the Click() event procedures of the ListBox and Command Button controls (lstWords and cmdUpdateLists). Selecting a word from the list displayed in lstWords will display a help message on the worksheet. The control cmdUpdateLists will show the UserForm frmWordFind used to maintain the Wordfind.txt file, as discussed earlier in the chapter.

```
Private Sub lstWords_Click()
    Range("R9").Value = "Select a location in the puzzle grid and click on
an arrow to specify the words direction."
End Sub
Private Sub cmdUpdateLists_Click()
    frmWordFind.Show
End Sub
```

This concludes the Word Find program. If you know someone who likes these word puzzles, you can now create a few for him or her. Add the features described in the Challenges section at the end of the chapter to more easily create puzzles with this program.

Chapter Summary

In this chapter, you learned how to create and access text files using sequential and random methods. VBA includes a number of additional methods for file I/O not covered in this chapter. However, learning how to read and write text files is a good first step and often comes in handy with applications that only require access to small amounts of data. You also learned how to create error-handling routines in VBA procedures that prevent the program from crashing because of a runtime error. Finally, you learned how to use some of the debugging tools available from the VBA IDE to help write nearly error-free code.

This chapter introduced the last of the fundamental programming concepts covered in this book. The remaining chapters are concerned with programming specific objects in the Excel object model. Chapter 9 examines the Chart object, which is a rather substantial object in Excel.

CHALLENGES

1. Create a program that stores the string "VBA is Fun" to a sequential access text file.

2. Extend the previous program to read the contents of the file into a worksheet cell.

3. Extend the previous program to write the contents of a selected area on a worksheet to a sequential access file. The program should also be able to read the contents of the file into a worksheet. Be sure to include an error handler for file not found errors.

4. Create a program that writes the contents of a worksheet to a random access file. Don't use more than five columns and create a user-defined data type with a component for each column. Add a UserForm that can be used to display and update individual records stored in the file.

5. Enhance the Word Find program to include a validation procedure that ensures that the user's placement of a word does not overwrite words or parts of a word previously placed on the puzzle grid.

6. Enhance the Word Find program to include an option for placing an entire list of words randomly on the puzzle grid with the click of a Command Button control.

CHAPTER 9

Excel Charts

C harts are valuable tools for data analysis and presentation in Excel or in any spreadsheet application. Unfortunately, the learning curve for creating charts is typically a bit longer and steeper than for other spreadsheet components. This is also true with regard to programming charts in Excel, because the Chart object is a rather substantial component of the Excel object model. Before attempting to program with Excel's Chart object, a good understanding of the common chart types and their components is required.

This chapter discusses the following topics:

- **The Chart object**

- **Chart sheets and embedded charts**

- **Creating and Manipulating charts**

- **Chart events**

- **Chapter project: The Alienated Game**

Project: The Alienated Game

The Alienated program is similar to a number of games that can be found on the Internet. The game is played with a bubble chart and interacts with the user via the mouse. The object of the game is to continuously swap two images to create a group of three or more aliens in a row or column (please forgive the images—I'm artistically challenged). The Alienated worksheet with an embedded bubble chart is shown in Figure 9.1.

The Chart Object

A graphical representation of the Charts collection object and Chart object is shown in Figure 9.2. The figure shows the objects and collections that are subordinate to the Chart object. Many of these components also have numerous subordinate objects, so Figure 9.2 does not illustrate the breadth of the Chart object. You should not be intimidated, though, because programming the Chart object involves many of the same techniques that have been discussed throughout this book. The goal of this chapter is to point out major components and some of the unique properties involved with programming the Chart object.

Accessing Existing Charts

When creating a chart in Excel you have the choice of embedding the chart in an existing worksheet or creating a new worksheet to hold the chart. When a chart is created and placed in a new worksheet it is referred to as a *chart sheet*. Chart sheets are special because their only function is to hold a single chart; they cannot be used for holding any other data. Embedded charts are contained in worksheets and there are no limits (other than system memory) to the number of

---

IN THE REAL WORLD

Charts are used in spreadsheet applications as a tool for interpreting data. The analysis may be as simple as a visual inspection of the charted numerical data or as complex as a multidimensional curve-fit to the data.

Complex data analyses involving searches for parameter minima through multidimensional space often required customized software that ran on mainframe (or larger) computers. With the incredible advances in computer technology in recent years, the same analysis can now often be done on a desktop computer using ordinary software such as Excel.

embedded charts a worksheet can hold. Using VBA to programmatically control chart sheets and embedded charts involves the use of different objects that, at first, can be a little confusing. However, when you follow the object model, the differences make sense.

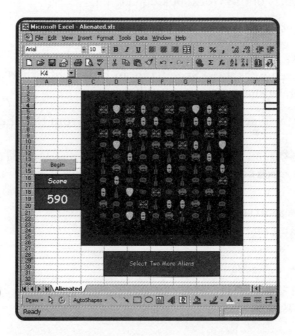

FIGURE 9.1

The Alienated game

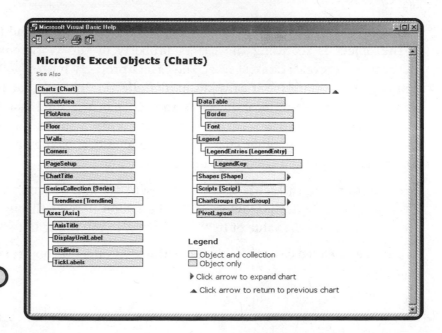

FIGURE 9.2

The Charts
collection object

Chart Sheets and Embedded Charts

Chart sheets are members of the Sheets Collection object, and as such must be accessed via the Sheets Collection object. For example, consider a workbook that contains multiple worksheets and chart sheets. To access a particular chart sheet, use the Charts property of the Workbook object.

```
ActiveWorkbook.Charts(1).Select
```

The Charts property returns the Charts Collection object containing all chart sheets in the specified workbook. Specifying an index with the Charts property returns a specific chart sheet from the collection.

The code listed here will access only the chart sheets from the Sheets collection.

 The ChartDemo.xls workbook contained on the accompanying CD-ROM contains the sample code and worksheets discussed in this chapter.

```
Public Sub GetChartSheets()
    Dim myCharts As Sheets
    Dim chSheet As Chart
    Set myCharts = ActiveWorkbook.Charts
    For Each chSheet In myCharts
        Debug.Print chSheet.Name
    Next
End Sub
```

The variable myCharts is declared as a Sheets Collection object and the reference to the object is set using the Charts property of the Workbook object (Set myCharts = ActiveWorkbook.Charts). The Charts property returns a Sheets Collection object (or, more specifically, a Charts Collection object) that represents all chart sheets (excluding worksheets) in the active or specified workbook. It may seem confusing to use the Charts property to return a Sheets Collection object, although remembering that chart sheets are members of the Sheets Collection object makes the choice of names more understandable.

Next, the variable chSheet is used to represent a single chart sheet within the myCharts Sheets Collection object. A For/Next loop iterates through each chart sheet and outputs the value of its Name property to the Immediate window.

To access embedded charts, use the ChartObjects Collection object and the ChartObject object.

```
ActiveSheet.ChartObjects(1).Select
```

The ChartObjects Collection object represents all ChartObjects in a single worksheet. The ChartObject object is a container object for a single Chart object, so accessing the actual chart is slightly different from the preceding code listing. Confusion between the ChartObject object and the Chart object will probably be a common source of error in your VBA code when programming charts. Consider the procedure listed here:

```
Public Sub GetEmbeddedCharts()
    Dim myChart As ChartObject
    Dim myCharts As ChartObjects
    Set myCharts = ActiveSheet.ChartObjects
    For Each myChart In myCharts
        Debug.Print myChart.Chart.Name
    Next
End Sub
```

The variable myChart is declared as a ChartObject object and is used to access each embedded chart in the active worksheet. The variable myCharts represents a Chart-Objects collection referenced to the ChartObjects contained in the active worksheet. Again, a For/Each loop iterates through each ChartObject object. However, to access the actual chart object and not just the container object, the Chart property must be used (myChart.Chart.Name). Without the reference to the Chart object, the preceding procedure would output the value of the Name property of a Chart-Object object, which is not the same as the Name property of the Chart object.

Table 9.1 summarizes the objects in VBA used to access Excel charts.

TABLE 9.1 VBA OBJECTS USED TO ACCESS EXCEL CHARTS

Object	Function
Sheets Collection	A collection of all sheets in the specified workbook, including chart sheets and worksheets
Charts Collection	A collection of all chart sheets in the specified workbook
Chart	Represents a single chart (embedded or as a chart sheet)
ChartObjects Collection	A collection of all ChartObject objects in the specified worksheet
ChartObject	Represents the container object for an embedded chart

Manipulating Charts

You can create several different types of charts in Excel, including the common column and pie charts and the not-so-common doughnut and radar charts. Table 9.2 summarizes the more common chart types available in Excel and their functions.

The Chart object has numerous properties that can be used in your VBA code to alter the appearance and behavior of an Excel chart. The Excel application file ChartDemos.xls contains several examples of manipulating charts using VBA programs. The worksheet named Chart Type is shown in Figure 9.3.

The Chart Type worksheet contains a column of arbitrary data charted in a column chart. Several ActiveX controls are used to change the properties of the embedded chart. Option buttons are used to select one of four chart types (Column, Bar, Area, or Line). Another set of option buttons, along with a scroll bar, is used to change the color of the chart area, plot area, and data series.

 TRICK To learn how to manipulate properties of a chart using VBA, record a macro while changing the desired properties from the Excel application.

To change the type of chart, the integer constant representing the chart type is passed to the sub procedure SetChartType() where the ChartType property of the Chart object is set. The constants used to specify the chart type were found in the online help.

```
Private Sub optArea_Click()
    SetChartType (xlArea)
End Sub
'
Private Sub optBar_Click()
    SetChartType (xlBarClustered)
End Sub
'
Private Sub optColumn_Click()
    SetChartType (xlColumnClustered)
End Sub
'
Private Sub optLine_Click()
    SetChartType (xlLine)
End Sub
'
Private Sub SetChartType(myType As Integer)
    Dim myChart As Chart
```

TABLE 9.2   COMMON EXCEL CHART TYPES

Chart Type	Function
Column	Compares categorized values by charting the data as vertical columns running from 0 to the charted value. There is one column for each value and all columns in the same category share the same color.
Bar	The same as a column chart, except that the columns now run in a horizontal direction and are called bars
Line	Similar to column and bar charts, except that the values are charted as points connected by a line.
Pie	Charts each value in a data series according to its contribution to the whole
Area	Combines a line chart with a pie chart. Shows the contribution to the whole for several data series over time or categories.
Scatter	Plots x,y coordinate pairs as a series of points
Bubble	Same as a scatter, except that a third variable can be included that is represented by the size of the data marker

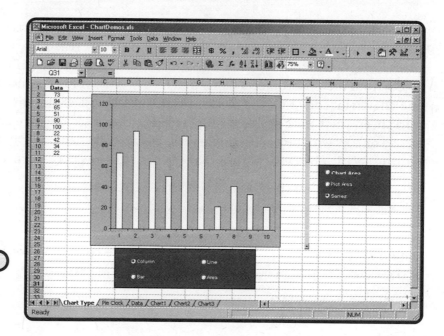

FIGURE 9.3

The Chart Type worksheet with a column chart

For example, selecting the Option Button labeled Bar in Figure 9.3 changes the chart to type bar, as is shown in Figure 9.4.

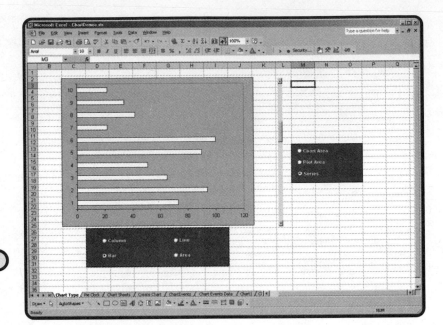

FIGURE 9.4

The Chart Type
worksheet with
a bar chart

The path to the chart traverses the Worksheet object, the ChartObjects Collection object, and the ChartObject object before finally reaching the destination Chart object. An index value of one is used to return the specific ChartObject object from the ChartObjects Collection object. This works because there is only one chart embedded on the worksheet. If subsequent charts are added to the worksheet, their index values will proceed in the order they are added (2, 3, 4, and so on). As with any collection object, be careful when using index values to return specific objects to ensure that the desired object is returned.

```
    Set myChart = ActiveSheet.ChartObjects(1).Chart
    myChart.ChartType = myType
End Sub
```

Option buttons and a scroll bar are used to set the color of various components of the chart. The action occurs in the sub procedure ChangeColor.

```
Private Sub optChartArea_Click()
    ChangeColor
End Sub
'
Private Sub optPlotArea_Click()
    ChangeColor
End Sub
'
```

```
Private Sub optSeries_Click()
    ChangeColor
End Sub
'
Private Sub scrColor_Change()
    ChangeColor
End Sub
```

A reference to the chart is set with the variable myChart using the same object path in the SetChartType() sub procedure. A simple test for the value of the Option Button controls (optChartArea, optPlotArea, and optSeries) sets the variable used as the conditional in a Select/Case decision structure. In the Select/Case structure, the ColorIndex property of the ChartArea, PlotArea, and Series objects is assigned to the Value property of the ScrollBar control (scrColor). The ChartArea object generally represents the background, axes, titles and legend in a chart, but this depends on the chart type. The PlotArea object represents the area on a chart where the data is plotted (data markers, data labels, gridlines, and so on). The Series object represents an individual data series and is returned from the SeriesCollection Collection object.

```
Private Sub ChangeColor()
    Dim component As Integer
    Dim myChart As Chart
    Set myChart = ActiveSheet.ChartObjects(1).Chart
    If optChartArea.Value = True Then component = 1
    If optPlotArea.Value = True Then component = 2
    If optSeries.Value = True Then component = 3
    Select Case component
        Case 1
            myChart.ChartArea.Interior.ColorIndex = scrColor.Value
        Case 2
            myChart.PlotArea.Interior.ColorIndex = scrColor.Value
        Case 3
            If optLine.Value <> True Then
                myChart.SeriesCollection(1).Interior.ColorIndex =
scrColor.Value
            End If
        Case Else
            MsgBox ("Please select a chart component")
    End Select
End Sub
```

The available objects and properties of a Chart object will vary somewhat with chart type. Therefore, it is very important that you have a good understanding of the type of chart you are trying to manipulate.

For example, unlike the area, column, and bar charts, a line chart does not have an Interior object subordinate to its Series object. As a result, you cannot set the `ColorIndex` property of the Interior object of the Series object for a line chart.

For a refresher on charts, I recommend *Microsoft Excel 2002 Fast & Easy,* by Faithe Wempen.

Although the Chart Type worksheet illustrates the manipulation of a few Chart object properties, it is not a practical example of a good VBA application because it is just as easy for the user to manipulate these properties from the Excel application.

Typically, properties of a Chart object are set from VBA code when the chart must be added to the workbook or worksheet programmatically.

See the ChartDemo.xls workbook for another example of chart manipulation where a clock is fashioned out of a pie chart. The pie chart displaying the hour and minute is only updated when the seconds read "00".

Creating Charts

To write a VBA procedure that creates a chart, you must decide whether to create a chart sheet or embed the chart in an existing worksheet. The difference between creating a chart sheet and embedding a chart is subtle; it is presented in the code listings that follow. These procedures can also be found in the Chart-Demo.xls file and activated from the worksheet named Create Chart.

The sub procedure `AddChartSheet()` creates a new chart sheet and a column chart of sample data selected from a worksheet by the user.

```
Public Sub AddChartSheet()
    Dim dataRange As Range
    Set dataRange = Range(frmDataRange.txtDataRange.Text)
    frmDataRange.Hide
```

The worksheet range that contains the data is selected via a custom dialog box using methods discussed in Chapter 7. The `Add` method of the Charts Collection object is used to create a new chart sheet. Remember, the Charts Collection object represents a collection of chart sheets in a workbook (refer to Table 9.1). After the chart sheet is added, the chart it contains is automatically made active because it is the only component of the sheet. Next, a `With/End With` structure is used to modify the properties of the Chart object. Many of these subordinate objects and properties have common sense names, so their function is intuitive. To learn more about any of the listed objects and properties, see the online help.

```
Charts.Add
With ActiveChart
    .ChartType = xlColumnClustered
    .HasLegend = True
    .Legend.Position = xlRight
```

A specific Axis object is returned from the Axes Collection object by passing a defined constant (for example, `xlCategory` or `xlValue`) with the Axes method. The Axes method returns a specific Axis object and takes up to two parameters: one for the axis type (`xlCategory`, `xlSeries`, or `xlValue`) and another for the axis group (`xlPrimary` or `xlSecondary`). The axis type `xlCategory` represents the x-axis on the chart, and `xlValue` represents the y-axis. The axis type `xlSeries` applies only to 3D charts and represents the z-axis. The axis group is either `xlPrimary` (default) or `xlSecondary` (applies to charts containing multiple Series objects).

The rest of the objects and properties set via the Axis object are fairly straight-forward and include setting tick marks and chart labels. The upper limit of the y-axis scale is set using Excel worksheet functions that return the maximum value from the `dataRange` range variable (defined at the beginning of the procedure) rounded up to single-digit precision.

```
    .Axes(xlCategory).MinorTickMark = xlOutside
    .Axes(xlValue).MinorTickMark = xlOutside
    .Axes(xlValue).MaximumScale =
Application.WorksheetFunction.RoundUp(Application.WorksheetFunction.Max(data_
Range), -1)
    .Axes(xlCategory).HasTitle = True
    .Axes(xlCategory).AxisTitle.Characters.Text = "X-axis Labels"
    .Axes(xlValue).HasTitle = True
    .Axes(xlValue).AxisTitle.Characters.Text = "Y-axis"
```

The data is finally added to the chart by setting the `Values` property of the Series object (returned from the SeriesCollection collection object) to the range variable `dataRange`.

```
    .SeriesCollection(1).Name = "Sample Data"
    .SeriesCollection(1).Values = dataRange
    End With
End Sub
```

Figure 9.5 shows the components specifically added to the chart by the preceding code. The chart also contains components created from default properties of the various chart related objects. For example, the gridlines in the figure are the major gridlines on the y-axis and are displayed by default. To prevent them from being displayed, I could have added a statement such as `ActiveChart.Axes(xlValue).Major Gridlines = False`.

To add an embedded chart to a worksheet, use the `Add` method of the ChartObjects collection object.

```
Public Sub AddEmbeddedChart()
    Dim dataRange As Range
    Set dataRange = Range(frmDataRange.txtDataRange.Text)
    frmDataRange.Hide
```

When adding an embedded chart, the `Add` method accepts four parameters that define the position of the upper-left corner of the chart on the worksheet, as well as the chart width and height. The position properties of the `Add` method (`Left` and `Top`) are relative to the upper-left corner of cell A1 and are in units of points. The `Activate` method of the ChartObject object is equivalent to selecting the chart, because only one Chart object is contained in a ChartObject object.

```
    Sheets("Create Chart").ChartObjects.Add Left:=200, Top:=50, Width:=500,
Height:=350
    Sheets("Create Chart").ChartObjects(1).Activate
    With ActiveChart
        .ChartType = xlColumnClustered
```

Before you set the properties of the Chart object, the chart must contain at least one Series object. Thus, the `NewSeries` method is used to add an empty Series

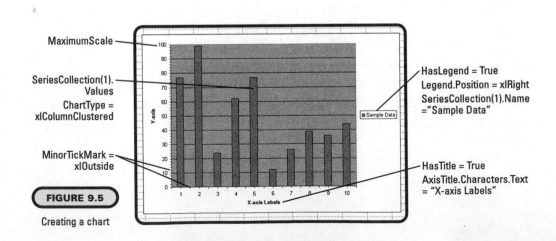

MaximumScale

SeriesCollection(1).
Values

ChartType =
xlColumnClustered

MinorTickMark =
xlOutside

HasLegend = True
Legend.Position = xlRight
SeriesCollection(1).Name
="Sample Data"

HasTitle = True
AxisTitle.Characters.Text
= "X-axis Labels"

FIGURE 9.5

Creating a chart

object to the chart. This is another difference from adding chart sheets, where a Series object is automatically added on creation of the chart sheet. The properties of the Chart object are then set in the same manner as was done with the chart sheet.

```
        .SeriesCollection.NewSeries
        .HasLegend = True
        .Legend.Position = xlRight
        .Axes(xlCategory).MinorTickMark = xlOutside
        .Axes(xlValue).MinorTickMark = xlOutside
        .Axes(xlValue).MaximumScale =
Application.WorksheetFunction.RoundUp(Application.WorksheetFunction.Max(data_
Range), -1)
        .Axes(xlCategory, xlPrimary).HasTitle = True
        .Axes(xlCategory, xlPrimary).AxisTitle.Characters.Text = "X-axis_
Labels"
        .Axes(xlValue, xlPrimary).HasTitle = True
        .Axes(xlValue, xlPrimary).AxisTitle.Characters.Text = "Y-axis"
        .SeriesCollection(1).Name = "Sample Data"
        .SeriesCollection(1).Values = dataRange
    End With
End Sub
```

The preceding examples demonstrate only a small fraction of the objects, properties, and methods available in a Chart object. Don't be intimidated by the breadth of the Chart object and its components! Always remember that a large problem can be broken into many smaller, more manageable problems. Once you learn how to access a chart, setting the properties of any of its component objects is easy. The hard part is learning what objects are available to the specific chart being manipulated. The number of component objects in a Chart object varies with the chart type (column, bar, scatter, and so on) and with the sub-category of chart type (clustered, stacked, 3D, and so on). For example, a 3D column chart has Wall, Floor, and Corners objects, but a clustered column chart does not have these objects.

To learn the differences between chart types, or to just learn what is available for a specific chart type, use recorded macros. First, create the chart from the Excel application, then alter its appearance with the macro recorder turned on. Be careful to record only a small number of actions—say two to three—at one time, because the macro recorder adds a lot of unnecessary code (setting default values). Keep in mind that as you select a component of the chart with the mouse, you are really selecting a component object of the Chart object. The dialog box that appears when the component object is double-clicked or selected from the chart menu sets the properties of that object. For example, the Format Axis dialog box shown in Figure 9.6 appears when the user double-clicks on a chart axis.

Figure 9.6 shows some of the properties of the Axis object. If the macro recorder is on while these properties are altered, the VBA code used to set these properties will be recorded when OK is clicked in the dialog box. After recording a small macro, proceed to the VBA IDE to examine the recorded code. If any of the code needs clarification, select the unknown keyword and press F1 to retrieve its documentation from the online help. This is an extremely helpful tool for learning how to program specific Excel components, and you should exploit the advantage.

Chart Events

The Chart object has several events that are triggered by various user actions. Some of the events are familiar—like `Activate()`, `MouseDown()`, and `MouseUp()`— but a few are unique to the Chart object. Table 9.3 summarizes the unique events associated with the Chart object.

TABLE 9.3   CHART OBJECT EVENTS

Event	Trigger
Calculate	When new or changed data is charted
DragOver	When a range of cells is dragged over a chart
DragPlot	When a range of cells is dragged and dropped on a chart
Resize	When the chart is resized
Select	When a chart element is selected
SeriesChange	When the value of a charted data point changes

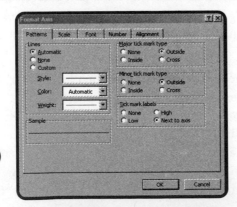

FIGURE 9.6

The Format Axis
dialog box

Chart Sheets

Chart events are automatically enabled with chart sheets. To catch events triggered by the user in a chart sheet, add code to an event procedure contained in the module associated with the chart sheet. The code window can be opened in the same manner as with a worksheet. Figure 9.7 shows the code window of a chart sheet selected from the project explorer. The active project displayed in Figure 9.7 is an Excel workbook containing several chart sheets.

Unfortunately, most of the events unique to the Chart object cannot be used with a chart sheet because there is no manner in which the user can trigger them. For example, the user cannot drag and drop a range of cells over the chart when the data is in another worksheet. However, the other chart events work as expected, and an example using the Select() event procedure of the Chart object is listed here.

```
Private Sub Chart_Select(ByVal ElementID As Long, ByVal Arg1 As Long,
ByVal Arg2 As Long)
    If ElementID = 3 And Arg2 > 0 Then
        ActiveChart.SeriesCollection(Arg1).Points(Arg2).ApplyDataLabels
Type:=xlShowValue
    End If
End Sub
```

The Select() event procedure of the Chart object accepts three parameters: ElementID is a long integer that refers to the component or element selected by

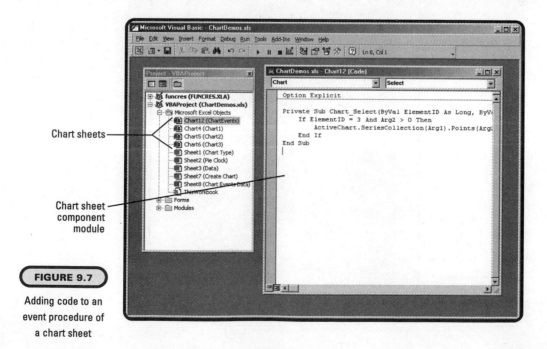

FIGURE 9.7

Adding code to an event procedure of a chart sheet

the user (ChartArea, PlotArea, Series, etc.), and Arg1 and Arg2 are long integers that refer to specific components of the selected object. In the preceding example, when the user selects a single data point on the chart Arg1 holds the index value of the selected Series object (representing a series of values) and Arg2 holds the index value of the selected Point object (representing the individual values in the series). Both Arg1 and Arg2 must be greater than zero.

The purpose of the procedure is to add a label to any point in a data series selected by the user. To accomplish this, the parameter ElementID is tested for equivalence to three because that's the value that represents a Series object. If the user has selected a single point in a data series, the selected point is labeled with its value by using the ApplyDataLabels method and setting the Type parameter to the constant xlShowValue. In this example, Arg2 holds the value −1 if the entire series is selected and will not hold a meaningful value until the user selects an individual point from the data series. When the user does select an individual data point, the value of Arg2 is passed to the Points method, which returns a Point object from the Points Collection object. In this case, the Points method returns the specific data point selected by the user.

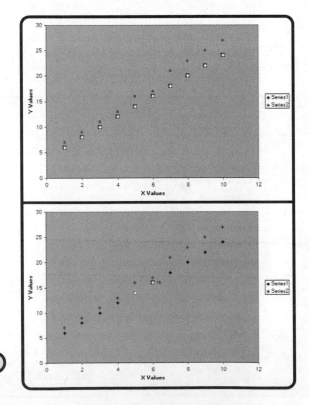

FIGURE 9.8

Chart events

Consider the two identical charts in Figure 9.8, where two data series are plotted in a scatter chart.

The chart is contained in a chart sheet and the Select() event procedure of the Chart object contains the previously listed code. In the first chart the user has selected Series 1 with a single click of the mouse. This triggers the Select() event procedure but the parameters passed to the procedure are ElementID=3, Arg1=1, and Arg2=-1, so the conditional expression in the If/Then statement is false. Therefore, no label is added to the chart. With Series 1 selected, the user then clicks on the sixth data point in Series 1. Again, the Select() event procedure is triggered, but this time the parameters passed to it are ElementID=3, Arg1=1, and Arg2=6. This time the conditional in the If/Then statement is true and the label "16" is added to the chart (bottom chart in Figure 9.8).

TRICK

Before writing the code for the Select() event procedure, I recorded a macro while adding a label to a charted point. This reminded me how to add the label to individual data points using VBA.

To learn how to use the Select() event procedure of the Chart object, I added the statement Debug.Print ElementID; Arg1; Arg2 to the procedure and watched the Immediate window while I clicked on various components of the Chart object.

Embedded Charts

To make use of all the event procedures of the Chart object, the chart must be embedded on a worksheet. Unfortunately, chart events are not automatically enabled for embedded charts. To enable the events of an embedded chart you must insert a class module (Insert menu in VBA IDE) into the project and declare an object of type Chart. The Chart object must be declared with events in the general declarations section of the class module.

```
Public WithEvents myChartClass As Chart
```

After the preceding statement is entered, the myChartClass object appears in the object drop-down list of the class module with the event procedures of a Chart object (see Figure 9.9).

Class modules are used to define a new class. You may remember from Chapter 5 that a class represents an object definition. We are not going to define new objects here, as that is beyond the scope of this book. In this case, there is no need to create a new object because the Chart object is already defined in VBA. All that needs to be done is to enable the events for the embedded chart. After

myChartClass
object selection

Class module
code window

Name property of
class module

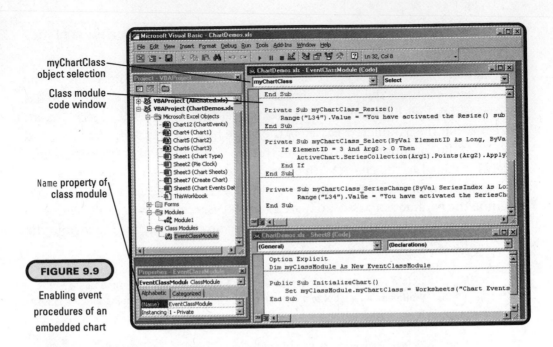

FIGURE 9.9

Enabling event
procedures of an
embedded chart

declaring the Chart object with events in the class module, connect it to the
embedded chart with the following declaration and initialization sub procedure.

```
Dim myClassModule As New EventClassModule
Public Sub InitializeChart()
    Set myClassModule.myChartClass = Worksheets("Chart Events
Data").ChartObjects(1).Chart
End Sub
```

In this example, the class module was named `EventClassModule` using the Properties window. Thus, the preceding declaration creates an instance of an object
variable of type `EventClassModule`, much like any other variable declaration. The
object declaration can be located in the general declarations section of any module. Before the event procedures created in the class module will work, the specific embedded chart must be connected to the `myClassModule` object. This is
accomplished with the `InitializeChart()` sub procedure that contains a single
line of code used to set the object reference. In this case, the object reference is
set to the first chart embedded on the worksheet named Chart Events Data. The
`InitializeChart()` sub procedure must run before the event procedures of the
Chart object defined in the class module will work.

The ChartDemos.xls project contains an embedded chart in the worksheet named
Chart Events Data (see Figure 9.10). A form button is used to call the `InitializeChart()`
sub procedure listed previously.

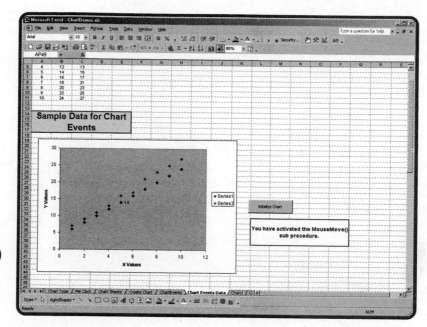

FIGURE 9.10

An embedded chart
with enabled event
procedures

After the `InitializeChart()` sub procedure is executed, the event procedures of the referenced chart object contained in the `EventClassModule` class module are enabled. The event procedures and all the code from the class module are listed here.

```
Option Explicit
Public WithEvents myChartClass As Chart
Private Sub myChartClass_DragOver()
    Range("L34").Value = "You have activated the DragOver() sub procedure."
End Sub
'

Private Sub myChartClass_DragPlot()
    Range("L34").Value = "You have activated the DragPlot() sub procedure."
End Sub
'

Private Sub myChartClass_MouseDown(ByVal Button As Long, ByVal Shift As
Long, ByVal x As Long, ByVal y As Long)
    Range("L34").Value = "You have activated the MouseDown() sub procedure."
End Sub
'

Private Sub myChartClass_MouseMove(ByVal Button As Long, ByVal Shift As
Long, ByVal x As Long, ByVal y As Long)
    Range("L34").Value = "You have activated the MouseMove() sub procedure."
End Sub
'
```

```
Private Sub myChartClass_MouseUp(ByVal Button As Long, ByVal Shift As
Long, ByVal x As Long, ByVal y As Long)
    Range("L34").Value = "You have activated the MouseUp() sub procedure."
End Sub
'
Private Sub myChartClass_Select(ByVal ElementID As Long, ByVal Arg1 As
Long, ByVal Arg2 As Long)
    If ElementID = 3 And Arg2 > 0 Then
        ActiveChart.SeriesCollection(Arg1).Points(Arg2).ApplyDataLabels
Type:=xlShowValue
    End If
End Sub
'
Private Sub myChartClass_Resize()
    Range("L34").Value = "You have activated the Resize() sub procedure."
End Sub
'
Private Sub myChartClass_SeriesChange(ByVal SeriesIndex As Long, ByVal
PointIndex As Long)
        Range("L34").Value = "You have activated the SeriesChange() sub
procedure."
End Sub
```

The DragOver(), DragPlot(), Resize(), SeriesChange(), and mouse activated event procedures contain one line of code that outputs a message to the worksheet when they are executed. The Select() event procedure contains the same code listed for the chart sheet earlier in this chapter. The DragOver() and DragPlot() event procedures are triggered when the user drags and releases selected data over the chart, respectively. The SeriesChange() event procedure is triggered when the user selects and moves a single point on the chart, changing its value. Finally, the Resize() event procedure is triggered when the user resizes the chart. Before using the sample code listed previously, you may want to comment out the MouseMove() event procedure as it interferes with the messages output by the SeriesChange() and Resize() event procedures.

Chapter Project: The Alienated Game

The Alienated program illustrates the use of several VBA objects subordinate to the Chart object. The program uses the less common bubble chart type because the Point objects in a regular scatter chart cannot hold images. A total of ten data series with ten values each are charted and randomly filled with seven different images. The object of the game is to swap two images such that a sequence of three or more identical images in a column or row is created. When a sequence of three or more identical images is created, they are removed from the chart, the images above are moved down, and the empty points at the top of the chart are randomly filled with new images. The player scores ten points for each image removed and the game ends when all possible moves are exhausted.

Project Statement

I want to create a game that illustrates the use of the Chart object and its subordinate objects. The game should also make use of event procedures of the Chart object. The game should display a grid of randomly selected images on a chart, and the object of the game is for the player to continuously swap two images to create a sequence of three or more identical images. The game should have a scoring mechanism, along with validation procedures and help for the player to ensure that it is easily played.

Project Tools

A Chart object and its subordinate objects, events, properties, and methods will be used to create the game. The chart can be embedded or exist as a chart sheet, but an embedded chart must be used if ActiveX controls are needed, because ActiveX controls cannot be placed on chart sheets. To use the event procedures of an embedded chart, a class module must be used to create an instance of the embedded chart object. The worksheet module representing the sheet with the embedded chart, a class module, and a standard module can be used to hold all program code. Images of the aliens can be created using standard image editing and creation software.

Project Algorithm

Write the Alienated program following the general approach listed here.

1. Using an embedded chart, the worksheet will be preformatted to include a range of cells to hold the player's score, and another range for displaying help messages. A bubble chart with all the desired formatting (no axis, titles, legends) will be added to the worksheet. An optional macro will be recorded/written that can add a formatted bubble chart if needed.

2. The game begins with the click of a Command Button control. Initialization procedures are called from the Click() event procedure of this control.

3. Initialization procedures handle the following tasks: Setting module-level and global variables, adding data to a hidden worksheet that will track the images loaded into the chart, adding ten data series to the chart with randomly distributed images of the aliens, and initializing the embedded chart to activate its event procedures. The charted data remains static, therefore it can be added from a worksheet or from within the VBA code.

4. After the data series with random images are displayed, the chart will be scanned for sequences of three or more identical images. The score will be updated as the chart is scanned until there are no more sequences of three or more identical images. The sub procedure that scans the chart for consecutive images will also be called after the player selects two images for swapping.

5. The player will be directed to swap two images by selecting individual data points on the chart.

6. Validation procedures will be written to test the player's selections for the following criteria: The two points selected must be adjacent (within the same row or column) and the result of the swap must create a sequence of three or more identical images. If the player's selection is invalid, a message will be output to the worksheet explaining the problem.

7. The Select() event procedure of the embedded chart will be used to catch the player's selection. The class module will also contain the validation sub procedures. The rest of the program will be held within the component module of the worksheet, except for global variable definitions and the optional procedure used to add a formatted bubble chart to the worksheet.

8. After the player's selection has been validated, the chart will be scanned for sequences of three or more identical images, as done when the game began. Image sequences of the required length will be removed from the chart before the images above them are brought down. Data points at the top of the chart without an image will be filled with new images in a random manner. The chart must be scanned until there are no more sequences of three or more identical images. The score will be updated and the game waits for the next selection.

9. The game ends when there are no more allowed moves. Creating a sub procedure that scans the chart for potential moves is left as an exercise for you to try on your own.

Adding the Code

The Excel worksheet containing the Alienated game is shown in Figure 9.11. As per the algorithm, the game begins from the Click() event procedure of a Command Button control located in the component module of the worksheet.

The Click() event procedure of cmdBegin is used to call several initialization sub procedures (InitData(), AddSeries(), SwapImages(), and InitializeChart()) that will be discussed later. The InitData() sub procedure adds data to a hidden worksheet that will be used to keep track of the positions of the images in the chart.

```
Option Explicit
Dim myClassModule As New EventClassModule
Private Sub cmdBegin_Click()
    InitData
```

Prior to calling procedures that will affect the chart, the ScreenUpdating property of the Application object is set to false. When data is altered, Excel updates the chart's appearance. This can be a slow process, because the updating occurs every time the value of a point is changed. To significantly speed up the code, turn off screen updating. The Excel application automatically turns the screen updating back on when code execution stops.

```
    Application.ScreenUpdating = False
```

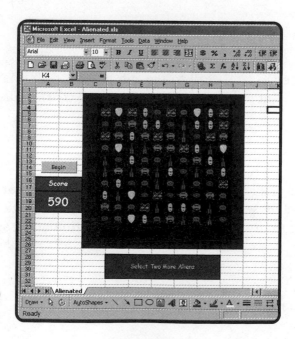

FIGURE 9.11

The Alienated game

TRICK

To disable user interaction through the keyboard and mouse, set the `Interactive` property of the Application object to false. This property must be assigned true before the user may interact with Excel.

This is a handy tool when you have a time-consuming program running that you do not want interrupted by some user action in the Excel application.

The `AddSeries()` sub procedure adds ten data series to the chart and fills each point with an image. The `SwapImages()` sub procedure then randomly fills the points with one of seven images. Each image is assigned a numerical value that is stored in a hidden worksheet named Images. The filenames for the images end with a number between one and seven, making them easy to identify.

```
AddSeries
SwapImages
```

After the images are loaded, the chart is scanned for sequences of three or more identical images. If these sequences are found, the sequential images are removed, the score is updated, and new images are added to the chart with a call to the `ScanImages()` sub procedure. This process is repeated in a `Do-Loop` for as long as image sequences of the proper length are found.

```
Do
    scanAgain = False
    ScanImages
Loop While scanAgain = True
Worksheets("Alienated").Range("F34").Select
```

After the chart is deselected, a call to the sub procedure `InitializeChart()` is used to activate the event procedures of the embedded chart, as discussed earlier in this chapter.

```
    InitializeChart
End Sub
```

The `InitData()` sub procedure is called from the `Click()` event procedure of `cmdBegin` and is used for variable initialization and writing data to the Images worksheet that will be used to keep track of the position of the seven different images in the chart.

```
Private Sub InitData()
    Dim I As Integer
    Dim K As Integer
```

The global variable filePath must be initialized immediately, because it is used to set the path to the image files that are loaded throughout the program.

```
filePath = ActiveWorkbook.Path & "\AlienImages\alien"
Worksheets("Alienated").Range("A16").Value = "Score"
```

The merged cells A18:B20 were named "PlayerScore" in the Excel application, allowing the use of the named range in the program. This is entirely optional but may be considered more readable than using A18.

 TRICK **Consult the Names Collection object and the Name object in the online help to learn how to create named ranges dynamically in your VBA programs.**

```
Worksheets("Alienated").Range("PlayerScore").Value = 0
```

Initially, only five images are filled into the series points and only one image is used per series. The values representing the newly added images are stored in the Images worksheet. These values are stored such that their positions in the Images worksheet directly correspond to the representative image position in the chart. For example, if the upper-left cell of the range in the Images worksheet containing the image identification numbers (cell B2) holds the value one, then point one of series one holds the image named alien1.png. Data series one holds the largest y-axis values (9) and therefore is at the top of the chart. See Figure 9.12 for an illustration of the bubble chart and the Images worksheet just prior to the execution of the SwapImages() sub procedure.

Nested For/Next loops are used to write the image identification numbers to the worksheet.

```
With Worksheets("Images")
    For I = 2 To 11
        For K = 2 To 11
            If K < 7 Then
                .Cells(K, I).Value = K - 1
            Else
                .Cells(K, I).Value = K - 6
            End If
        Next K
    Next I
End With
Range("D28").Value = "Select two adjacent aliens to swap. Two single
clicks will select a single alien."
End Sub
```

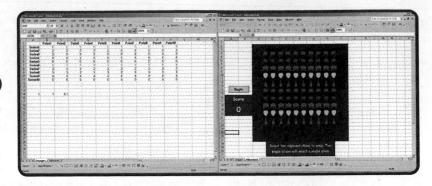

FIGURE 9.12

The Alienated game paused just before execution of the SwapImages() sub procedure

The AddSeries() sub procedure is called from the Click() event procedure of cmdBegin immediately after the InitData() sub procedure. This procedure adds the data to the chart and fills each point with an image.

```
Private Sub AddSeries()
    Dim ms As Integer
    Dim I As Integer
    On Error GoTo ErrorHandler
```

Bubble charts use three values per point, the x,y coordinate pair and a third value representing the relative size of the point. The third variable representing size is not needed for this program, but a regular scatter chart does not allow the plotted points to be filled with images. Consequently, the values of the size of all data points will be set to the same value and the displayed size will be set with the next line of code.

```
ActiveSheet.ChartObjects("Alienated").Chart.ChartGroups(1).BubbleScale = 35
```

The BubbleScale property of the ChartGroup object is assigned a value of 35%, reducing the size of the plotted point—and thus the size of the images—by about two-thirds. The ChartGroup object represents one or more series plotted in a chart with the same format. Because all ten series in the chart have identical formatting, the BubbleScale property applies to all points.

Next, the chart is made active using the Activate method of the ChartObject object and a With/End With structure is used to manipulate the objects and properties of the chart.

```
ActiveSheet.ChartObjects("Alienated").Activate
With ActiveChart
    If .SeriesCollection.count > 0 Then
        For I = .SeriesCollection.count To 1 Step -1
            .SeriesCollection(I).Delete
```

```
        Next I
    End If
```

After all existing data series are deleted from the chart, ten new series are added in the following For/Next loop. The values of the x, y, and size variables are assigned using the Array() function. Each series will have identical x-values and sizes, but the y-values vary from 9 to 0 for series 1 through 10, respectively. The values assigned to each series could just as easily have come from a worksheet. Either way, these values will not change as the program executes; only the images held in each point will change.

```
For I = 1 To 10
    .SeriesCollection.NewSeries
    .SeriesCollection(I).XValues = Array(0, 1, 2, 3, 4, 5, 6, 7, 8, 9)
    .SeriesCollection(I).Values = Array(10 - I, 10 - I, 10 - I, 10 - I,_
10 - I, 10 - I, 10 - I, 10 - I, 10 - I, 10 - I)
    .SeriesCollection(I).BubbleSizes = Array(1, 1, 1, 1, 1, 1, 1, 1, 1, 1)
```

The images are loaded using the UserPicture method of the FillFormat object returned by the Fill property of the Series object. This is a somewhat lengthy voyage through a fairly obscure section of Excel's object hierarchy. The path through the object model leading to the UserPicture method for loading an image into a data point was initially determined from a recorded macro.

As stated earlier, only five different images are initially loaded into the data points. At this stage of the program, the number of images in the chart doesn't really matter, but it is important that every data point contains an image. You will see why in the next procedure.

```
        If I < 6 Then
                .SeriesCollection(I).Fill.UserPicture
PictureFile:=filePath & I & ".png"
        Else
                .SeriesCollection(I).Fill.UserPicture
PictureFile:=filePath & Trim(Str(I - 5)) & ".png"
        End If
    Next I
    End With
    Exit Sub
```

A minimal error handler is used in this procedure in anticipation of problems loading the images.

```
ErrorHandler:
    ms = MsgBox(Err.Description, vbCritical, "Error")
    End
End Sub
```

Immediately after the data is added to the chart, the SwapImages() sub procedure is called from the Click() event procedure of cmdBegin. This procedure randomly adds one of seven images to the data points. All the data points must contain an image before this procedure is called, because there is a chance that some of the points might be missed in the random selection. The game cannot be properly played if any of the data points are missing an image.

```
Private Sub SwapImages()
    Dim ms As Integer
    Dim ranSeries As Integer
    Dim ranPoint As Integer
    Dim ranImage As Integer
    Dim tempInt As Integer
    Dim I As Integer
    Dim K As Integer
    Randomize
    On Error GoTo ErrorHandler
    ActiveSheet.ChartObjects("Alienated").Activate
```

A For/Next loop is used to randomly select a data point from one of the Series objects. The loop iterates 500 times, which may be overkill (5:1 ratio to the number of data points), but the code runs quickly with the screen updating turned off. Without the screen updating turned off it would probably take half an hour for this loop to execute.

```
For I = 1 To 500
    ranSeries = Int(10 * Rnd + 1)
    ranPoint = Int(10 * Rnd + 1)
    ranImage = Int(7 * Rnd + 1)
    ActiveChart.SeriesCollection(ranSeries).Points(ranPoint). _
Fill.UserPicture _
                    PictureFile:=filePath & ranImage & ".png"
```

With each change in the image held in a data point, the corresponding change must be made to the image identification number in the Images worksheet, in order to ensure that these values continue to map directly to the displayed images in the chart.

```
        Worksheets("Images").Cells(ranSeries + 1, ranPoint + 1).Value =
ranImage
    Next I
    Exit Sub
ErrorHandler:
    ms = MsgBox(Err.Description, vbCritical, "Error")
    End
End Sub
```

The ScanImages() sub procedure is called whenever the chart needs to be checked for a sequence of three or more consecutive images (immediately after starting the game and after the player moves two images). The procedure has public scope because it will have to be called from the class module EventClassModule. This procedure iterates, checking for consecutive values, through each column and row containing the image identification numbers in the Images worksheet. The consecutive values found in the rows and columns of the Images worksheet correspond directly to consecutive, identical images in the chart.

```
Public Sub ScanImages()
    Dim c As Range
    Dim curRange As Range
    Dim rangeStr As String
    Dim I As Integer
    Dim count As Integer
    Dim curVal As Integer
    Dim scoreRange1 As String
    Dim scoreRange2 As String
    Dim updateScore As Boolean
```

The procedure works by looping through a series of Range objects representing the rows and columns in the Images worksheet that contains the image identification numbers. A For/Next loop first iterates through the ten columns. Within the For/Next loop, a For/Each loop iterates through each cell in the column, checking for consecutive image identification numbers. When three or more consecutive image identification numbers are found, the string variable scoreRange2 that represents the range of cells holding these values is constructed for later use.

```
    For I = 1 To 10
        rangeStr = Chr(I + 65) & "2:" & Chr(I + 65) & "11"
        Set curRange = Worksheets("Images").Range(rangeStr)
```

The variable curVal holds the image identification number of the current cell in the Images worksheet as the For/Each loop iterates through a column. The variable count keeps track of the number of consecutive image identification numbers found within a column.

```
curVal = 0
count = 1
For Each c In curRange
    If c.Value = curVal Then
        count = count + 1
        If count > 2 Then
            scoreRange2 = scoreRange1 & ":" & c.Address
            updateScore = True
            scanAgain = True
        End If
    Else
        count = 1
        scoreRange1 = c.Address
    End If
    curVal = c.Value
Next
```

When three or more consecutive image identification numbers are found, the Boolean variable updateScore evaluates as true. In this case, calls to the sub procedures CalcScore() and UpdateImages() are made to update the player's score and the images are displayed in the chart.

```
If updateScore Then
    Call CalcScore(scoreRange2)
    Call UpdateImages(scoreRange2, "col")
    updateScore = False
End If
Next I
```

The rows are evaluated for three consecutive image identification numbers using the same logic as in the preceding code. The choice to search columns for three or more identical images before rows was arbitrary.

```
For I = 2 To 11
    rangeStr = "B" & I & ":K" & I
    Set curRange = Worksheets("Images").Range(rangeStr)
    curVal = 0
    count = 1
    For Each c In curRange
        If c.Value = curVal Then
```

```
                count = count + 1
                If count > 2 Then
                    scoreRange2 = scoreRange1 & ":" & c.Address
                    updateScore = True
                    scanAgain = True
                End If
            Else
                count = 1
                scoreRange1 = c.Address
            End If
            curVal = c.Value
        Next
        If updateScore Then
            Call CalcScore(scoreRange2)
            Call UpdateImages(scoreRange2, "row")
            updateScore = False
        End If
    Next I
End Sub
```

The string variable scoreRange representing the worksheet range holding identical image identification numbers is passed to the CalcScore() sub procedure from the ScanImages() sub procedure listed previously. The string is used with the Range property to return a Range object referenced to the variable c. The Count property of the Range object returns the number of cells in the worksheet range, which is used to update the player's score (ten points per image).

```
Private Sub CalcScore(scoreRange As String)
    Dim c As Range
    Set c = Range(scoreRange)
    Worksheets("Alienated").Range("PlayerScore").Value = _
                Worksheets("Alienated").Range("PlayerScore").Value +
c.count * 10
End Sub
```

The sub procedure UpdateImages() is called from ScanImages(); it functions to replace images in the chart that have been scored. The game requires scored images to be removed, and any images appearing above a scored image in a column are moved down. Images at the top of the column are randomly replaced with new images. The string variables scoreRange and rowOrCol pass in the information needed to remove the scored images.

```
Private Sub UpdateImages(scoreRange As String, rowOrCol As String)
    Dim remRange As Range
    Dim c As Range
    Dim mySeries As Integer
    Dim myPoint As Integer
    Dim I As Integer
    Randomize
    Application.ScreenUpdating = False
```

The bubble chart is activated and the range variable holding the image identification numbers (remRange) is used to delete the scored images.

```
ActiveSheet.ChartObjects("Alienated").Activate
Set remRange = Worksheets("Images").Range(scoreRange)
For Each c In remRange
    mySeries = c.Row - 1
    myPoint = c.Column - 1
```

An image is removed from a charted data point by assigning the constant xlNone to the ColorIndex property of the Interior object for the Point object that represents the datum.

```
        ActiveChart.SeriesCollection(mySeries).Points(myPoint).Interior.
ColorIndex = xlNone
    Next
```

If code execution is stopped at this point in the program, then the bubble chart might look something like that shown in Figure 9.13. In this example, a sequence of four identical images was removed from the fourth column.

Next, the images above the removed images must be moved down. This is accomplished with a call to the MoveColumn() sub procedure, which moves a single column down the required number of series. If the scored range is within a single series (that is, row), then the images move down one series, otherwise the images move down three or more series depending on the number of scored images in the column. The information passed to the MoveColumn() sub procedure includes the column reference (remRange.Column) in the Images worksheet containing the image identification number or numbers to be removed, the starting row index (remRange.Row) in the Images worksheet of the scored range, and the length of the scored range (remRange.Count).

```
If rowOrCol = "col" Then
    Call MoveColumn(Chr(remRange.Column + 64), remRange.Row, remRange.count)
Else
```

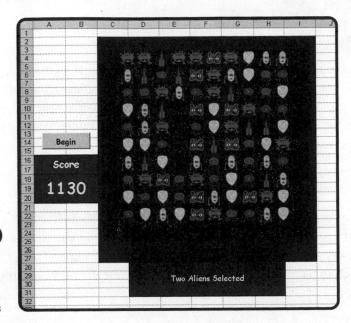

If the scored range represents a row in the chart, then the length of the scored
range is 1, so the `MoveColumn()` sub procedure must be called the same number of
times as there are images to be removed.

```
    For Each c In remRange
        Call MoveColumn(Chr(c.Column + 64), c.Row, 1)
    Next
  End If
End Sub
```

The `MoveColumn()` sub procedure is called from `UpdateImages()` and serves two purposes. First, it updates the image identification numbers in the Images worksheet, and then `MoveColumn()` uses the new image identification numbers to
update the images in the chart.

```
Private Sub MoveColumn(myCol As String, myRow As Integer, delLength As Integer)
    Dim ms As Integer
    Dim rangeStr As String
    Dim colRange As Range
    Dim c As Range
    Dim mySeries As Integer
    Dim myPoint As Integer
    Dim I As Integer
    Randomize
```

```
On Error GoTo ErrorHandler
If myRow > 2 Then
```

If the variable myRow is greater than two, then the scored images were not at the very top of the chart (series index > 1) and image identification numbers will have to be moved down the column. The string variable rangeStr represents the range of cells in a column above the removed image and is used to set a reference to the range variable colRange.

```
rangeStr = myCol & "2:" & myCol & Trim(Str(myRow - 1))
Set colRange = Worksheets("Images").Range(rangeStr)
```

The range of cells in the Images worksheet that lie above the cell representing a removed image is copied to the Clipboard using the Copy method of the Range object. The Copy method takes an optional parameter specifying the destination range, which is set as the first cell in the range of cells representing the removed images.

```
rangeStr = Chr(colRange.Column + 64) & Trim(Str(colRange.Row +
delLength))
colRange.Copy (Worksheets("Images").Range(rangeStr))
```

The cells at the top of the altered column in the Images worksheet that no longer represent an image on the chart are replaced with random integers between 1 and 7. If the scored range is a row, then only one random number will be added to the top of the column. If the scored range is a column, then the number of random numbers added is equivalent to the length of the scored range.

```
rangeStr = Chr(colRange.Column + 64) & "2:" & Chr(colRange.Column
+ 64) & Trim(Str(colRange.Row + delLength - 1))
For Each c In Worksheets("Images").Range(rangeStr)
    c.Value = Int(7 * Rnd + 1)
Next
```

If the variable myRow is equal to 2, then the scored range is contained in, or starts with, series one in the chart (row 2 in the Images worksheet). In this case, nothing has to be moved down, but a random number still must be added to the column.

```
Else
    For I = 0 To delLength - 1
        Worksheets("Images").Range(myCol & (myRow + I)).Value = Int(7
* Rnd + 1)
    Next I
End If
```

Finally, the images in the chart are updated by looping through the Altered column in the Images worksheet to check the new image identification numbers. Using the image identification numbers, the corresponding images are added to the chart in the proper location. The location in the chart is determined using the series and point indices represented by the row and column of the cell holding the image identification number.

Because it's easier, I set the loop to iterate through the entire column holding the image identification numbers. So even if only one number and corresponding image is removed from the column and bubble chart, the loop will still iterate ten times and replace nine image identification numbers and nine images with identical numbers and images. You will not notice a difference in the execution speed with the screen updating turned off.

```
        rangeStr = myCol & "2:" & myCol & "11"
        For Each c In Worksheets("Images").Range(rangeStr)
            mySeries = c.Row - 1
            myPoint = c.Column - 1


ActiveChart.SeriesCollection(mySeries).Points(myPoint).Fill.UserPicture _
                        PictureFile:=filePath & c.Value & ".png"
        Next
        Exit Sub
ErrorHandler:
        ms = MsgBox(Err.Description, vbCritical, "Error")
        End
End Sub
```

After execution of the previous procedure, the bubble chart from Figure 9.13 is updated, and appears as shown in Figure 9.14.

Note that the three images that were at the top of column 4 have each been moved down four rows and the points above filled with randomly selected images. These images have been highlighted in Figure 9.14.

As discussed earlier in this chapter, the InitializeChart() sub procedure is used to set the object reference to the Chart object used for the Alienated game.

```
Private Sub InitializeChart()
    Set myClassModule.myChartClass =
Worksheets("Alienated").ChartObjects("Alienated").Chart
End Sub
```

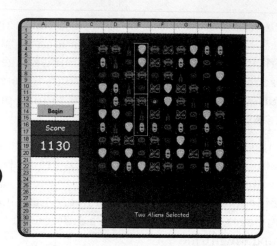

FIGURE 9.14

The Alienated
bubble chart after
updating

The remainder of the Alienated game program is contained in the class module named EventClassModule. This module contains the event procedures of the Chart object used for the game. The event procedures of the Chart object are used to catch the player's selection of images for swapping.

Module level declarations include variables that represent the Chart object and the series and points in the chart selected by the player.

```
Option Explicit
Public WithEvents myChartClass As Chart
Dim pt1Series As Integer
Dim pt2Series As Integer
Dim pt1Point As Integer
Dim pt2Point As Integer
```

The Select() event procedure is used to catch the index values of the Series and Point objects selected by the player. Index values for both Series and Point objects run from 1 to 10 in the chart and are passed to the Select() event procedure by the Excel application as parameters Arg1 and Arg2, respectively. A series is selected from the Chart object with a single click of the mouse on any point. Individual points are selected from a series with a second mouse click on a previously selected series. The index values of the Series and Point objects represent rows and columns in the Images worksheet, respectively. The parameter ElementID represents the component of the chart selected by the player where a value of 3 indicates a Series object.

```
Private Sub myChartClass_Select(ByVal ElementID As Long, ByVal Arg1 As
Long, ByVal Arg2 As Long)
    Dim curScore As Integer
```

The series and point indices are collected for the player's first selection and stored in the module-level variables pt1Series and pt1Point.

```
If ElementID = 3 And Arg2 > 0 Then
    If pt1Series < 1 Or pt1Series > 10 Then
        pt1Series = Arg1
        pt1Point = Arg2
        Worksheets("Alienated").Range("D28").Value = "One Alien Selected"
```

If the first image has already been selected, then the series and point indices are collected for the player's second selection and passed to the ValidatePt2() sub procedure for validation of the game rule requiring the selection of adjacent cells.

```
    ElseIf pt2Series < 1 Or pt2Series > 10 Then
        If Not ValidatePt2(Arg1, Arg2) Then Exit Sub
```

If the player's selection passes the first validation test, the image identification numbers corresponding to the values held in the variables pt1Series, pt1Point, pt2Series, and pt2Point are swapped with a call to the ImageIDSwap() sub procedure.

```
        pt2Series = Arg1
        pt2Point = Arg2
        Worksheets("Alienated").Range("D28").Value = "Two Aliens Selected"
        ImageIDSwap
        curScore = Range("PlayerScore").Value
```

The player's score is stored in the variable curScore before code execution is sent to the ScanImages() sub procedure contained in the component module for the worksheet containing the game chart (listed earlier). If a call to ScanImages() changes the player's score, then the selection is validated for the requirement that any move by the player creates a sequence of at least three identical images.

```
        Sheet1.ScanImages
        If Range("PlayerScore").Value = curScore Then
```

If the player's score does not change, then ScanImages() did not find any sequence of three identical images and the player's selection is invalid. The image identification numbers are swapped back to their original values, a message stating the nature of the error is sent to the worksheet, variables are re-initialized, and the procedure is exited.

```
            ImageIDSwap
            Worksheets("Alienated").Range("D28").Value = "Selection must
create 3 or more sequential aliens."
                pt1Series = 0
```

```
                        pt1Point = 0
                        pt2Series = 0
                        pt2Point = 0
                        Exit Sub
                End If
```

If the selection has passed all validation tests, then the images selected by the player are swapped with a call to the TwoImageSwap() sub procedure.

```
                Application.ScreenUpdating = False
                TwoImageSwap
```

If the selection is valid, a Do-Loop is used to repeatedly call the ScanImages() sub procedure until no more sequences of three identical images are found. The ScanImages() sub procedure must be called repeatedly, in case the images added to the chart from the earlier call to this procedure create a sequence of three or more identical images.

```
                Do
                        scanAgain = False
                        Sheet1.ScanImages
                Loop While scanAgain = True
```

After the chart is updated, variables are reset before the player's next selection.

```
                Range("D28").Value = "Select Two More Aliens"
                ptlSeries = 0
                pt1Point = 0
                pt2Series = 0
                pt2Point = 0
            End If
        End If
    End Sub
```

The ValidatePt2() function procedure serves to validate the player's selection for adjacent cells. That is, the player must select two adjacent images from either the same row or the same column. The procedure is called from the Select() event procedure of the Chart object listed previously, and accepts two arguments that identify the player's second image selection.

```
Private Function ValidatePt2(Arg1 As Long, Arg2 As Long) As Boolean
    Dim c As Range
    Dim testStr(1 To 4) As String
    Dim testRange As Range
```

```
Dim testVal As Integer
Dim seqNums As Integer
Dim tempInt As Integer
Dim I As Integer
Dim col2Index As Integer
ValidatePt2 = True
```

The index of the Point objects selected by the player are stored in the variables pt1Point and Arg2, and the index of the Series objects are stored in pt1Series and Arg1. The difference between these indices for the Point and Series objects should not exceed 1, but the sign can be positive or negative. The Abs() function returns the absolute value and is used in the decision structure listed below to test if the player's selections came from adjacent rows or columns.

```
If Abs(pt1Series - Arg1) > 1 Or Abs(pt1Point - Arg2) > 1 Then
      Worksheets("Alienated").Range("D28").Value = "You must select_
adjacent cells."
      ValidatePt2 = False
```

The next listing in the decision structure tests for diagonal selections by the player; diagonal selections are not allowed.

```
ElseIf (Abs(pt1Series - Arg1) = 1 And (pt1Point <> Arg2)) Then
      Worksheets("Alienated").Range("D28").Value = "You must select_
adjacent cells."
      ValidatePt2 = False
```

The final test is for selecting the same point twice, which can occur after the player selects the first point, selects another series, and then returns to select the first point.

```
ElseIf (pt1Series = Arg1) And (pt1Point = Arg2) Then
      Worksheets("Alienated").Range("D28").Value = "You must select_
adjacent cells."
      ValidatePt2 = False
   End If
```

If any of the conditionals evaluate as true in this If/Then/ElseIf decision structure, then the ValidatePt2() function procedure is assigned the value false. The ValidatePt2() function then returns false to the calling procedure and the player must make another selection.

```
If ValidatePt2 = False Then
   pt1Series = 0
```

```
        Exit Function
    End If
End Function
```

The TwoImageSwap() and ImageIDSwap() sub procedures serve to swap the two selected chart images and their corresponding identification numbers from the Images worksheet, respectively. The call from the Select() event procedure to the TwoImageSwap() sub procedure is made after the player's selection has been validated to prevent automatic screen updating of the chart between procedure calls.

```
Private Sub TwoImageSwap()
  Dim ms As Integer
  On Error GoTo ErrorHandler
  ActiveChart.SeriesCollection(pt1Series).Points(pt1Point).Fill.UserPicture _
              PictureFile:=filePath &
Worksheets("Images").Cells(pt1Series + 1, pt1Point + 1).Value & ".png"
  ActiveChart.SeriesCollection(pt2Series).Points(pt2Point).Fill.UserPicture _
                 PictureFile:=filePath &
Worksheets("Images").Cells(pt2Series + 1, pt2Point + 1).Value & ".png"
    Exit Sub
ErrorHandler:
    ms = MsgBox(Err.Description, vbCritical, "Error")
    End
End Sub
'
Private Sub ImageIDSwap()
    Dim tempInt As Integer
    tempInt = Worksheets("Images").Cells(pt1Series + 1, pt1Point + 1)
    Worksheets("Images").Cells(pt1Series + 1, pt1Point + 1) =
Worksheets("Images").Cells(pt2Series + 1, pt2Point + 1)
    Worksheets("Images").Cells(pt2Series + 1, pt2Point + 1) = tempInt
End Sub
```

The SeriesChange() event procedure of the Chart object is triggered whenever the user selects a single data point on the chart and changes its value by dragging the data point with the mouse. This is an undesirable event, as it can make the chart hard to read depending on how far the point was moved. The solution is to reassign the original values to the affected series using SeriesIndex and PointIndex parameters passed to the procedure. The entire series must be used, because the Point object does not have xValue or Value properties.

```
Private Sub myChartClass_SeriesChange(ByVal SeriesIndex As Long, ByVal_
PointIndex As Long)
    Dim yVal As Integer
    yVal = 10 - SeriesIndex
    Application.ScreenUpdating = False
    ActiveSheet.ChartObjects("Alienated").Activate
    ActiveChart.SeriesCollection(SeriesIndex).XValues = Array(0, 1, 2, 3, 4,_
5, 6, 7, 8, 9)
    ActiveChart.SeriesCollection(SeriesIndex).Values = Array(yVal, yVal,_
yVal, yVal, yVal, yVal, yVal, yVal, yVal, yVal)
End Sub
```

The last sub procedure I'll discuss is not involved in the game, but was used to create the chart and embed it on the worksheet. It is included in a standard module called Create Chart with the Alienated game project, and is listed here.

```
Public Sub AddChart()
```

To create an embedded chart, the Add method of the ChartObject object must be used, specifying parameters for position (Left and Top properties), width, and height. The Chart object is selected before setting the Name property.

The value of the Name property is very important because it can be used to select a specific chart on a worksheet. If the Name property is not assigned a value in code, then VBA automatically assigns values of "Chart 1," "Chart 2," and so on, as charts are added to a worksheet. Furthermore, if all charts are deleted from a worksheet, VBA adds one to the previous index value in the Name property when adding the next chart. For example, if two charts are added to a worksheet (either from a VBA program or by the user) and the charts are subsequently deleted, the next chart added to the worksheet will have a Name property of "Chart 3." This can make the selection of a chart via its Name property unpredictable. Therefore, it is a good idea to assign a value to the Name property of a chart object to remove any ambiguity when selecting the chart from a VBA program.

```
ActiveSheet.ChartObjects.Add(124.5, 33.75, 282, 283.5).Select
Selection.Name = "Alienated"
ActiveSheet.ChartObjects("Alienated").Activate
```

After the newly added chart is activated, values for several properties of the Chart object and its subordinate objects can be assigned. The bubble chart is somewhat different than other charts because data must be included in the chart before assigning a value to the ChartType property. The SetSourceData method is used to set the data range for the chart. At least two cells must be used for a bubble chart, although a third cell can be used to assign a size to the data point. The `PlotBy` parameter specifies whether the data is arranged in worksheet columns or rows.

```
With ActiveChart
    .SetSourceData Source:=Sheets("Images").Range("A15:C15"), PlotBy:=xlColumns
    .ChartType = xlBubble
    .Legend.Delete
    .PlotArea.ClearFormats
    .Axes(xlValue).MajorGridlines.Delete
    .Axes(xlCategory).MinimumScale = 0
    .Axes(xlCategory).MaximumScale = 9.2
    .Axes(xlValue).MinimumScale = 0
    .Axes(xlValue).MaximumScale = 9
End With
```

The axes scales are set (the preceding list) to prevent the chart from automatically determining these values. The data from the game ranges from 0 to 9 for both x and y variables, so comparable values are assigned for the `MaximumScale` property of the Axis objects.

The size of the PlotArea object is set to its maximum by equating it to the size of the ChartArea object. Finally, an image simulating outer space is added to the plot area.

```
With ActiveChart.PlotArea
    .Width = ActiveChart.ChartArea.Width
    .Height = ActiveChart.ChartArea.Height
    .Left = 0
    .Top = 0
    Selection.Fill.UserPicture PictureFile:=ActiveWorkbook.Path &_
"\AlienImages\backgrnd.bmp"
    End With
    ActiveSheet.ChartObjects("Alienated").Chart.ChartGroups(1).BubbleScale = 1
End Sub
```

This concludes the Alienated game project. The program serves as a demonstration of programming Excel's Chart object and several (but certainly not all) of its subordinate objects. Possible enhancements include the addition of sound, multiple levels of difficulty, and animation. To animate charted data points, the data should be assigned to the chart from a worksheet. By changing the values of the cells holding the data in a looping code structure (with a delay), the charted points will move. The problem with animating data is that screen updating has to be turned on and this can make the animation of more than two or three points very slow.

Chapter Summary

In this chapter, you took a close look at Excel's Chart object and many of its related or subordinate objects. You learned how to use specific objects to access charts existing as chart sheets or embedded charts. You also saw several examples of manipulating existing charts through the use of the properties and methods of the chart object and its subordinate objects, and learned how to create charts (chart sheets or embedded charts) using a VBA procedure. Finally, you saw some of the unique event procedures associated with the Chart object and learned how to activate the event procedures of an embedded chart.

CHALLENGES

1. With Excel's macro recorder turned on, create a column chart (chart sheet or embedded) in Excel and format the chart to a desired appearance. Stop the macro recorder and examine the recorded code. Remove any unnecessary code in the macro and change the structure of the procedure to make it more readable. Now run the code from the Excel application.

2. Add an embedded chart to a worksheet along with a ScrollBar control. Attach code to the Change() event procedure of the ScrollBar control that changes the maximum value y-axis scale.

3. Add a scatter chart to a worksheet from x- and y-data points entered in two columns of the worksheet. Create a VBA procedure that animates one of the charted points by changing its x- and y-values in a looping structure. Include a delay in the loop as discussed in previous chapters.

4. Write a VBA procedure that adds a chart to a worksheet and formats it to a desired appearance. The chart should be added after the user selects the data and clicks on a Command Button control.

5. Add a scatter chart to an existing worksheet and write a VBA procedure that enables the charts event procedures (use a class module and the declarations described in this chapter). Using the Select() event procedure of the scatter chart, create a procedure that outputs the values of the ElementID, Arg1, and Arg2 parameters to the worksheet as the user clicks on various elements of the chart.

6. Spice up the Alienated game by adding different levels of difficulty. For example, after the player reaches a certain score, start adding new images to the chart with new identification numbers. This reduces the number of potential moves the player can make.

7. Add sound, such as a small ding or knock that plays once for each image that is scored, to the Alienated game.

VBA Shapes

VBA shapes refer to those objects added to a document
or worksheet from the Drawing toolbar in the application. This includes AutoShapes, freeforms, images,
and text. The Drawing toolbar is common to most Microsoft
Office applications, so programming its components only differs in terms of the document to which its shapes are added (for
example, an Excel worksheet, Word document, or a Power-
Point slide).

The following topics are discussed in this chapter:

- **The Shapes collection and Shape objects**

- **Manipulating a Shape object**

- **The ShapeRange collection object**

- **Activating Shape objects**

- **The OLEObjects collection**

- **Chapter project: Excetris**

Project: Excetris

Excetris is modeled after the classic *Tetris* computer game. The object of the game is to fill a predefined region on an Excel worksheet with five basic shapes so that gaps between the shapes are avoided. The player is continuously given one shape to add to the game board within a limited time period. When an entire row across the game board is filled with shapes, the row is removed and the shapes above moved down. Play continues until the player runs out of room for adding more shapes. You will find Excetris on the accompanying CD-ROM, stored as Excetris.xls. Figure 10.1 shows the Excel version of Excetris.

The Shapes Collection and Shape Objects

The Shapes Collection object represents all Shape objects in the drawing layer of the worksheet. The Shapes property of the Worksheet object is used to return the entire collection of Shape objects in the drawing layer. The following line of code uses the Count property of the Shapes Collection object to return the total number of shapes in the drawing layer of the active worksheet:

```
ActiveSheet.Shapes.Count
```

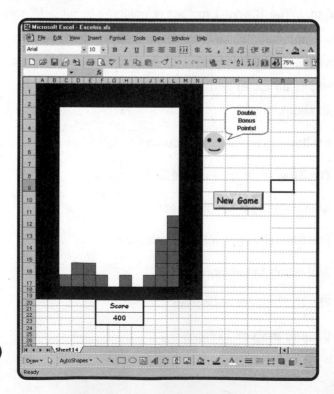

FIGURE 10.1

The Excetris game

You can think of the drawing layer as a sheet of clear plastic cellophane draped over the top of the worksheet. Therefore, shapes added to the drawing layer are positioned on top of the worksheet and mask the cells underneath. The masked cells can still be used to hold data.

Like other collection objects, an index or name can be specified to return a single Shape object from the collection. To return a Shape object by index, specify a number.

```
ActiveSheet.Shapes(1).Select
```

Or, to return a Shape object by name, include the name in quotes.

```
ActiveSheet.Shapes("Oval 1").Select
```

To add a shape to a worksheet, use one of several Add methods of the Shapes Collection object. For example to add a line, use the AddLine method.

```
ActiveSheet.Shapes.AddLine(10, 100, 250, 500).Select
```

The AddLine method accepts four parameters for the starting and ending x- and y-values representing the x,y coordinate pairs of the two points used to define the line. The coordinates are specified in points relative to the upper-left corner of the worksheet. In the preceding example, a line is drawn on the active worksheet from point x=10, y=100 to the point x=250, y=500.

The Add methods of the Shapes Collection object also return a reference to the newly added Shape object, so it is possible to immediately apply a property or method to the shape in the same statement. It is often convenient to select the object then use a With/End With **structure to manipulate several properties of the object. You'll see an example of this in the section "Manipulating a Shape Object."**

Other Add methods of the Shapes Collection object include AddShape, AddPicture, AddOLEObject, and AddPolyline, to name just a few. The AddShape method refers to the AutoShapes found on the Drawing toolbar (see Figure 10.2). The example that follows adds and selects a rectangle to the active worksheet:

```
ActiveSheet.Shapes.AddShape(msoShapeIsoscelesTriangle, 230, 220, 25, 20).Select
```

The AddShape method requires five parameters representing, in order, the shape type (a VBA defined constant, msoShapeIsoscelesTriangle in the example), and the Left, Top, Width, and Height properties of the object.

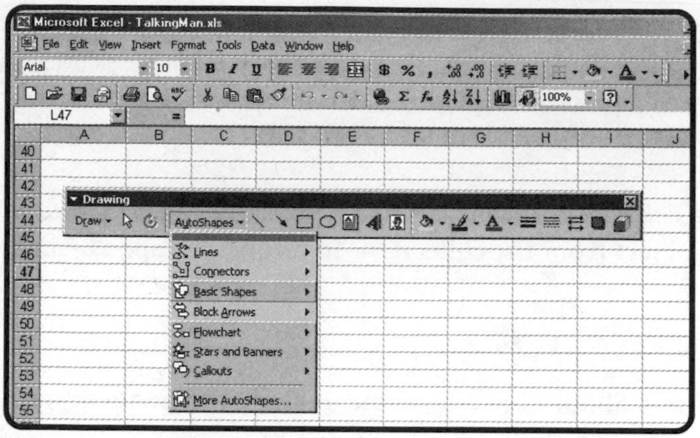

FIGURE 10.2

The Drawing
toolbar

All of the Add methods are implemented in a manner similar to that of the
AddShape method, but the required parameters are specific to the shape type. You
will see more examples of different shape types in the remainder of the chapter.
For details about each method and the parameters it requires, consult the online
help by typing the name of the method in the keyword field.

Manipulating a Shape Object

After a Shape object is selected from the Shapes Collection object, you can edit the
shape through its properties and methods. As always, the properties and methods
available are specific to the type of Shape object. Also, there may be properties and
methods of subordinate objects available for editing. The following example adds
a rectangle to the active worksheet and manipulates a few of its properties; the
result is shown in Figure 10.3.

```
ActiveSheet.Shapes.AddShape(msoShapeRectangle, 100, 100, 50, 50).Select
With Selection
        .Name = "Red Square"
        .Left = 10
        .Top = 10
End With
With ActiveSheet.Shapes("Red Square")
        .Fill.ForeColor.RGB = RGB(255, 0, 0)
        .ZOrder msoBringToFront
End With
```

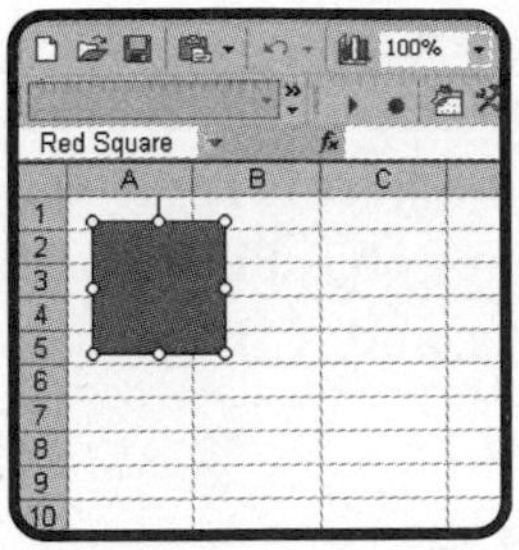

FIGURE 10.3

Adding a Shape object to a worksheet

The AddShape method of the Shapes Collection object is used to add a rectangle to the drawing layer. In the preceding example, the constant msoShapeRectangle sets the Shape type. The Shape type is followed by four parameters that represent the Left, Top, Width, and Height properties of the AutoShape, respectively. After the shape is added to the drawing layer, its Name, Left, and Top properties are edited. The color of the shape is set as red (using the RGB() function) by returning a Fill-Format object via the Fill property. Finally, the ZOrder method of the Shape object is used to bring the shape to the front of the drawing layer.

HINT

Not all properties and subordinate objects are immediately available from an object selected using the Select method. In the previous example, the Fill property and ZOrder method are not available for the Shape object when it has been selected using the Select method. Instead, another With/End With structure is needed to return the Shape object without selecting it before the Fill property and ZOrder method can be applied.

Unfortunately, it is not always clear which properties and methods are available for a selected object. The best way to learn what properties and methods are available is through the online help.

The previous example illustrates some of the properties and methods common to most shapes. As is the case with the Chart object discussed in Chapter 9, some shapes and their subordinate objects have unique properties and methods that cannot be applied to all Shape objects. For example, the TextEffect property of the Shape object cannot be applied to shapes that do not contain text. Therefore, when manipulating a shape through a VBA program, be careful to use the properties and methods that apply to that specific shape to avoid runtime errors.

Looping through a Collection of Shapes

Looping through a collection of Shape objects is essentially the same as looping through any other collection object. The code listed here loops through the Shapes Collection object of the active workbook. This is comparable to the methods discussed in earlier chapters for looping through worksheet cells contained within a range. A variable of type Shape is declared and used as the looping variable in a For/Each loop. The Shape Collection object is returned using the Shapes property of the Worksheet object. As each Shape object is returned in the For/Each loop it is tested for type via the Type property, and if the shape represents a line its name is copied to the worksheet.

```
Public Sub LoopThruShapes()
    Dim sh As Shape
    Dim I As Integer
    I = 1
    For Each sh In ActiveSheet.Shapes
        If sh.Type = msoLine Then
            Cells(I, 1).Value = sh.Name
            I = I + 1
        End If
    Next
End Sub
```

The preceding example represents one possible method for selecting and manipulating specific shapes from a collection. Next you'll see a method for selecting a subset of shapes from a shape collection using the ShapeRange Collection object.

Sample code listed in this chapter and a couple of additional examples illustrating the use of various Shape objects can be found in the ShapeDemos.xls Excel file on the CD-ROM that accompanies this book. Select different worksheets in the workbook to view the different demonstrations. The worksheet labeled Misc Shapes is shown in Figure 10.4.

The ShapeRange Collection Object

The ShapeRange Collection object represents a collection of Shape objects that may contain all, some, or just one of the Shape objects in the drawing layer of a worksheet. A ShapeRange Collection object can be constructed from the current shapes using any of several criteria defined in decision structures (If/Then). For example, a ShapeRange Collection object could be constructed out of just those shapes that are of type AutoShape, or perhaps only those Shape objects that are lines.

If you want to return all Shape objects to a ShapeRange Collection object, use the ShapeRange property of the Selection object when it represents a group of selected Shape objects.

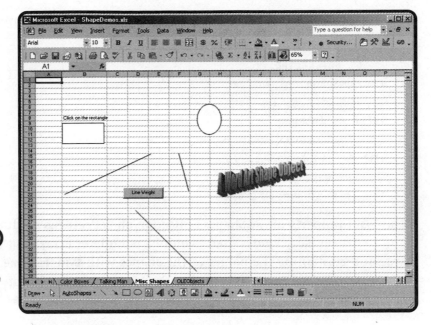

```
ActiveSheet.Shapes.SelectAll
Selection.ShapeRange.Rotation = 30
Selection.ShapeRange(1).Rotation = 60
```

The first line selects all Shape objects in the active workbook. The second line sets the angle of rotation to 30 degrees for all selected Shape objects. The third line sets the angle of rotation to 60 degrees for the first Shape object that was added to the collection (out of those objects currently selected).

To return a subset of the Shape objects as a ShapeRange Collection object, use the Range property of the Shapes Collection object.

```
ActiveSheet.Shapes.Range(1).Select
ActiveSheet.Shapes.Range("Line 1").Select
ActiveSheet.Shapes.Range(Array(1, 2, 3, 4)).Select
ActiveSheet.Shapes.Range(Array("Line 1", "WordArt 2")).Select
```

The Range property of the Shapes Collection object accepts an integer, string, or parameter array as arguments. A parameter array specified with the Array() function is more practical because the Range property is not needed to select a single shape from the Shapes Collection object. The parameter array may contain a list of integers representing the index values of the Shape objects or strings representing their names. Alternatively, you can build a parameter array holding the integers or strings representing specific objects based on various conditions. Consider the following procedure, used to select all the lines in the drawing layer of the active worksheet:

```
Public Sub SelectLines()
    Dim numShapes As Integer
    Dim numLines As Integer
    Dim I As Integer
    Dim lineNames()
    With ActiveSheet.Shapes
        numShapes = .Count
        If numShapes > 0 Then
```

If the Count property of the Shapes Collection object returns a value greater than zero, then a For/Next loop is used to build a parameter array (lineNames declared as variant) containing the names of the shapes with type msoLine. The name of each object of type msoLine is copied to the lineNames array for later use.

```
        For I = 1 To numShapes
            If .Item(I).Type = msoLine Then
                ReDim Preserve lineNames(numLines)
                lineNames(numLines) = .Item(I).Name
                numLines = numLines + 1
            End If
        Next I
    End If
```

Finally, the parameter array built here is passed to the Range property of the Shapes Collection object, and objects of type msoLine are returned and selected. Additional code can now be added to modify the selected shapes. In this example, the ShapeRange property is used to return all the selected shapes and set the thickness of the lines via the Weight property.

```
        .Range(lineNames).Select
        Selection.ShapeRange.Line.Weight = 4.5
    End With
End Sub
```

Figure 10.5 shows the result of applying the preceding procedure to the shapes contained in the worksheet displayed in Figure 10.4.

The preceding procedure is somewhat more involved than is the example using the For/Each loop, but it represents another option for selecting a range of Shape objects of a particular type when you don't know the proper names or index values at design time.

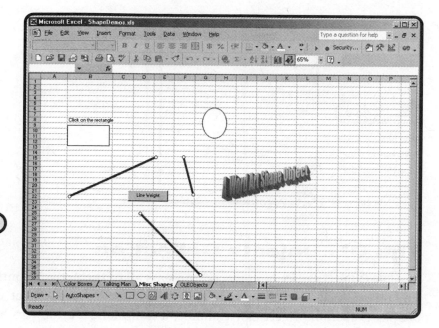

FIGURE 10.5

The Misc Shapes
worksheet after
execution of the
SelectLines()
sub procedure

Activating Shape Objects

Since most Shape objects (with the exception of OLEObjects) do not have any associated event procedures, you can use the OnAction property of the Shape object to simulate a Click() event. After the following code is executed, a Shape object named MyRectangle will activate a VBA procedure called LoopThruShapes() when clicked. Technically, this is not the action of a Click() event procedure but practically it serves the same purpose.

```
ActiveSheet.Shapes.AddShape(msoShapeRectangle, 100, 100, 50, 50).Select
Selection.Name = "MyRectangle"
ActiveSheet.Shapes("MyRectangle").OnAction = "LoopThruShapes"
```

The OnAction property of the Shape object must be executed before a user's click will activate the specified procedure (LoopThruShapes()). This can be done anywhere in the program, but including it in the procedure that adds the shape used to simulate the Click() event is a good idea. The LoopThruShapes() sub procedure is listed earlier in this chapter. The result of the LoopThruShapes() sub procedure after application to the Misc. Shapes worksheet is shown in Figure 10.6

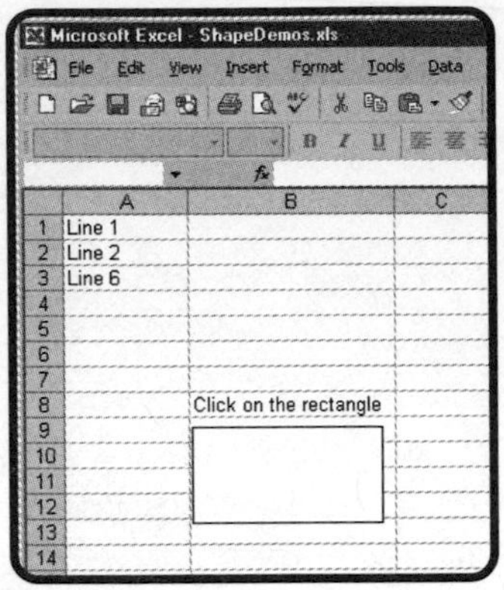

FIGURE 10.6

The Misc Shapes
worksheet after
execution of the
`LoopThruShapes()`
sub procedure

The OLEObjects Collection

The OLEObjects Collection object represents all of the ActiveX controls on a document or worksheet and can be accessed from the Worksheet object or the Shapes Collection object. For example, a Command Button can be added to a worksheet with either the Add method of the OLEObjects Collection object or the AddOLEObject method of the Shapes Collection object.

```
ActiveSheet.OLEObjects.Add(ClassType:="Forms.CommandButton.1").Select
```

Or

```
ActiveSheet.Shapes.AddOLEObject(ClassType:="Forms.CommandButton.1").Select
```

Properties of the newly added OLEObject object are manipulated in one of two ways. First, if the property is listed in the Object Browser under the class OLEObject, then it can be assigned a new value in the usual way by returning the OLEObject from the OLEObjects Collection object. If the property is not listed under the OLEObject class in the Object Browser then you must return the actual Control object by using the Object property before setting the new value of the control's property.

The sub procedure `AddCommandButton()` adds a Command Button control to the active worksheet using the `AddOLEObject` method of the Shapes Collection object. Returning the object from the OLEObjects Collection object sets the Name, Left, and Top properties of the OLEObject. However, to set the Caption property you must first return the control using the Object property of the OLEObject object.

```
Public Sub AddCommandButton()
    ActiveSheet.Shapes.AddOLEObject(ClassType:="Forms.CommandButton.1").
Name = "cmdTest"
    With ActiveSheet.OLEObjects("cmdTest")
        .Left = Range("C1").Left
```

```
        .Top = Range("C4").Top
    End With
    ActiveSheet.OLEObjects("cmdTest").Object.Caption = "Click Me"
End Sub
```

Event procedures for an OLEObject object can be written prior to their addition to a worksheet. You must name the event procedure as VBA would name it when adding the control at design time. For example, if you intend to add a Command Button control at runtime using the `AddCommandButton()` sub procedure listed earlier and you need its `Click()` event procedure, then you must name the procedure `cmdTest_Click()`. Furthermore, the event procedure must be added to the component module of the worksheet to which the Command Button control will be added. The `Click()` event procedure listed here will trigger when the user clicks on the Command Button control `cmdTest` (previously created by running the `AddCommandButton()` sub procedure) provided the `Click()` event procedure is added to the component module of the same worksheet to which the Command Button was added.

```
Private Sub cmdTest_Click()
    MsgBox ("Hello")
End Sub
```

To execute this code, select the worksheet named OLEObjects in the Shape-Demos.xls workbook and click on the button labeled Add Command Button. A Command Button control will immediately appear on the worksheet with the caption "Click Me." With a click on the newly added Command Button control a message box appears with the message "Hello." This sequence of events is shown in Figure 10.7.

It is sometimes desirable to create programs that are completely independent of the active worksheet. The idea is to be able to create programs that run independent of the worksheet, so the user can run the program from any worksheet in the Excel application. This is a relatively simple task when your program does not require ActiveX controls, because all the worksheet formatting can be handled with code.

Considering the sub procedures listed previously, it may seem tempting to try to create programs that add ActiveX controls to a worksheet at runtime in order to avoid the requirements of a specific worksheet. Unfortunately, this task cannot be completed because the event procedures of the control added at runtime must still be added to the component module of a specific worksheet. Therefore, adding ActiveX controls from a VBA program has limited utility and might just as well be added at design time when the event procedures are written.

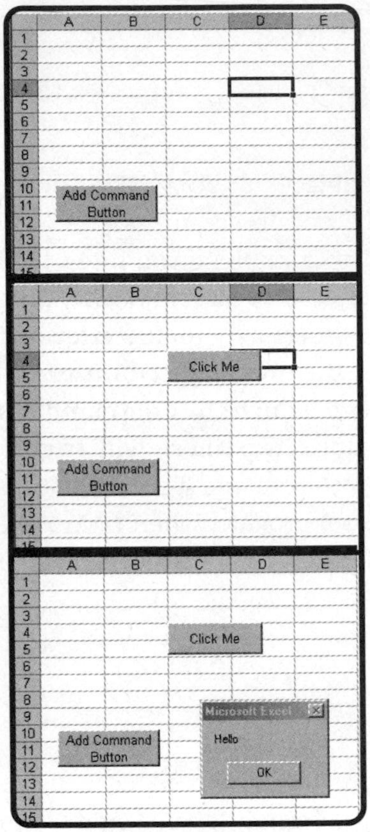

FIGURE 10.7

Adding an
OLEObject object
to a worksheet
with a pre-defined
`Click()` event

Chapter Project: Excetris

The basic objective of the Excetris game was described at the beginning of the chapter. The objective of the program is to demonstrate the use of the Shapes Collection object and some of its component objects while creating a fun program.

Excetris involves a minimal amount of animation involving a small group of Shape objects as they move down the area of the worksheet defined as the game board. The five shapes used for the game are shown in Figure 10.8.

Animation, and some of VBA's limitations when animating objects, were discussed in Chapter 6. The same limitations apply to Excetris with regard to the use of the

FIGURE 10.8

The five shapes
used for the
Excetris game

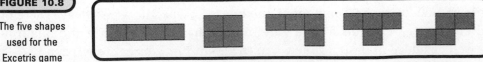

OnTime method of the application object. The minimum one-second interval with the OnTime method limits the level of difficulty at which the game can be played.

Project Statement

I want to create a game modeled after the original *Tetris* with an emphasis on programming Shape objects in Excel. The game should be written such that it can be run from any worksheet in the Excel application. An area of cells on an Excel worksheet provides the game board and the game pieces are constructed out of Shape objects (type rectangle). The program tallies a score based on the number of shapes removed from the game board (worksheet) and assigns bonus points when multiple rows are removed.

Project Tools

Excetris will be constructed using an Excel worksheet with code contained within standard modules to avoid any dependence on specific worksheets. This means that there will not be any ActiveX controls or Form buttons used to start the game.

The game board is simple, and can be constructed entirely from code using many of the properties of the Range object. A rectangular Shape object used to trigger an event procedure that starts a new game can be added to the worksheet from code. The game pieces are constructed out of identical Shape objects and animated using the OnTime method of the Application object. The position of the animated Shape objects can be tracked using a Range object that corresponds to the underlying cells of the worksheet. The OnKey method of the Application object can be used to assign various procedures to simple keystrokes made by the player. This allows the player to direct the movement of the animated shape using the keyboard. The active worksheet can be used to mark shapes that have been "played" in order to determine when a player scores, when shapes should be removed, and when the game is over. Embellishments can be added to the program (preferably involving different Shape objects) once the program is functional.

Project Algorithm

Construct Excetris following the general guidelines listed here.

1. Write the code in standard modules to avoid any dependence on specific worksheets. Format the worksheet selected by the player entirely from the program using a specific sub procedure.

2. The sub procedure used to format the cells on the worksheet should create cells that are identical in size and proportions (height and width). The game board consists of ten columns and 15 rows. Additional formatting is required to define an area on the worksheet below the game board for displaying the player's current score. An area of cells to the right of the game board will display a message signaling when the game is over. Finally, a Shape object will be added to the right of the game board and assigned a procedure with the OnAction property. After the program is functional, images can be added to the Shape object to simulate the look of a button.

3. Another sub procedure functions to randomly create one of five possible shapes and add it to the worksheet at the top of the game board. Each of the five shapes is built out of four AutoShapes of type rectangle. The dimensions of each Shape object match the dimensions of a worksheet cell in the game board. This allows for precise placement of the Shape objects as they move left, right, and down the game board. This procedure also initializes a Range object that is used to track the location of the Shape objects as they move down the game board. This Range object holds the references to the worksheet cells for which the Shape objects are directly above.

4. After a Shape has been added to the top of the game board another sub procedure will be called to initiate its downward movement. This proce-

dure calls itself using the OnTime method of the Application object. With each call to the procedure, the set of four Shape objects move down a distance of one row in the worksheet. The target range must be validated before the shapes are moved.

5. The game is played using the keyboard. The OnKey method of the Application object is used to assign different procedures to specific keystrokes. The left and right arrows call procedures that move the Shape objects one column to the left or right on the worksheet. The up arrow rotates the combination of the four Shape objects 90 degrees counterclockwise and the Tab key drops the shape to the bottom of the game board. Again, the target range for the group of four Shape objects must be validated prior to the move.

6. With each move of the Shape objects down the game board, validation procedures are called that test the target range of the animated Shape objects. The target range (referred to as the active range) must be within the defined area of the game board and cannot overlap with any previously played shapes. The main validation procedure also resets the active range of the animated shape.

7. When the player chooses to rotate the animated shape, the active range corresponding to the cell locations below each shape will be altered based on the type of shape and the number of rotations. The Shape objects then are mapped to the cell references in the altered active range. Figure 10.9 illustrates the allowed rotations for each animated set of Shape objects and the cell references used for deciding how to construct the new active range.

8. When the animated set of Shape objects has moved down the worksheet as far as possible the animation must be turned off by sending false to the OnTime method of the Application object. The four Shape objects are then mapped to their static positions on the worksheet by changing their Name properties to include the column and row indices of the cells they rest above. The corresponding worksheet cells are marked with an x. This is used to determine whether a row has been scored.

9. After each animated set of Shape objects has been placed, the game board will be scanned to see if there are any rows that are completely filled with shapes. If there are, then the row/rows of Shape objects are removed along with the corresponding x's on the worksheet and the score is updated. The player receives ten points for each shape removed. Bonus points are awarded when multiple rows are scored at one time. When bonus points are awarded, Shape objects of type picture and callout will be used to display the message.

10. The game ends when a new shape is added to a group of cells that already contain shapes.

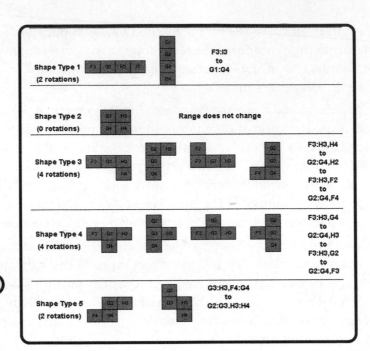

FIGURE 10.9

Mapping shape
rotations to
cell ranges

Adding the Code

The entire program is entered into a single standard module. A main sub procedure is created to initialize variables and call other formatting and initialization procedures. The main sub procedure is called Excetris() and is given public scope so that it can be accessed from the Excel application. Excetris is independent of the worksheet, so the player can run the program from any worksheet in the Excetris.xls workbook.

I begin with a few module-level variable declarations. These will be explained as they appear in the various sub procedures in the program.

```
Option Explicit
Dim sqWidth As Single
Dim sqHeight As Single
Dim shapeType As Integer
Dim activeRange As Range
Dim numRotations As Integer
Const RECTANGLE = 1
```

Because the Excetris game is independent from the worksheet in which it is started, the player must start the program by selecting the Excetris() sub procedure from the Run Macro tool on the Visual Basic toolbar.

```
Public Sub Excetris()
    Dim sh As Shape
```

The block of code in the If/Then conditional is an embellishment added after the program was essentially finished. The purpose of this code block is to change the image in the Shape object used to simulate the action of a button click. This is the Shape object the player can use to start a new game after one game has already been played.

```
    If ActiveSheet.Shapes.Count > 1 Then
        For Each sh In ActiveSheet.Shapes
            If sh.Name = "NewGameButton" Then
                ActiveSheet.Shapes("NewGameButton").Select
                Selection.ShapeRange.Fill.UserPicture ActiveWorkbook.Path_
& "\NewGame2.png"
                Delay (0.5)
            End If
        Next
    End If
```

The rest of the Excetris() sub procedure is making calls to other procedures used to initialize the worksheet and keyboard and begin the game.

```
    NewGame
    FormatSheet
    numRotations = 0
    SetKeys
    AddShape
    Range("A21").Select
```

A small time delay ensures that the added shape can be viewed at the top of the game board (row 3) before it starts to move. The game board refers to worksheet cells C3:L17.

```
    Delay (0.15)
    MoveShape
End Sub
```

The sub procedure NewGame() is called from Excetris() and removes all Shape objects from the worksheet and clears the cells representing the game board, the player's score, and the game over message.

```
Private Sub NewGame()
    Dim sh As Shape
```

```
        For Each sh In ActiveSheet.Shapes
            If sh.Type = msoAutoShape Then
                sh.Delete
            End If
        Next
        Range("C3:L17").ClearContents
        Range("F22").Value = ""
        Range("O12").Value = ""
End Sub
```

The sub procedure FormatSheet() is also called from Excetris(); it sets several properties of the worksheet cells representing the game board, the cells around the game board, and the player's score. Shapes will start on row 3 of the game board and proceed down. The code in the FormatSheet() sub procedure should look quite familiar to you.

```
Private Sub FormatSheet()
    Dim c As Range
    Dim gameBoard As Range
    '
    Set gameBoard = Range("C3:L17")
    gameBoard.ColumnWidth = 4
    gameBoard.RowHeight = 24.75
    gameBoard.Interior.ColorIndex = 2
    '
    Range("A1:B19,M1:N19").ColumnWidth = 4
    Range("A1:L2").RowHeight = 24.75
    Range("A1:B19,M1:N19").Interior.ColorIndex = 1
    Range("A1:N2,A18:N19").Interior.ColorIndex = 1
    '
    Range("O12:Q13").Select
    With Selection
        .HorizontalAlignment = xlCenter
        .VerticalAlignment = xlCenter
        .MergeCells = True
        .Font.Name = "Comic Sans MS"
        .Font.FontStyle = "Bold"
        .Font.Size = 18
    End With
```

The formatting involved for the worksheet range used to display the player's score is a bit lengthy, so I used a separate procedure.

```
FormatScoreCells
```

The Shape object (type msoShapeRectangle) that simulates a button is added to the worksheet with an image loaded into the object. The OnAction property of the Shape object sets the calling procedure to Excetris() when the object is clicked.

```
ActiveSheet.Shapes.AddShape(RECTANGLE, Range("O1").Left + 0.5 *
_Range("O1").Width, _
                                    Range("O10").Top, 104, 35).Select
    Selection.ShapeRange.Fill.UserPicture ActiveWorkbook.Path & "\NewGame.png"
    Selection.Name = "NewGameButton"
    Selection.OnAction = "Excetris"
End Sub
```

The sub procedure FormatScoreCells() is called from FormatSheet() and simply adds a label to the worksheet, merges two ranges, and sets a few of their properties. This procedure is actually a recorded macro that I cleaned up before adding it to the program. The code is straightforward and requires no further explanation.

```
Private Sub FormatScoreCells()
    Range("F20:I21").Select
    With Selection
        .HorizontalAlignment = xlCenter
        .VerticalAlignment = xlCenter
        .MergeCells = True
        .Font.Name = "Comic Sans MS"
        .Font.FontStyle = "Bold"
        .Font.Size = 14
    End With
    With Selection.Borders(xlEdgeLeft)
        .LineStyle = xlContinuous
        .Weight = xlThick
    End With
    With Selection.Borders(xlEdgeTop)
        .LineStyle = xlContinuous
        .Weight = xlThick
    End With
    With Selection.Borders(xlEdgeRight)
        .LineStyle = xlContinuous
        .Weight = xlThick
```

```
        End With
        ActiveCell.Value = "Score"
        Range("F22:I23").Select
        With Selection
            .HorizontalAlignment = xlCenter
            .VerticalAlignment = xlCenter
            .MergeCells = True
            .Font.Name = "Comic Sans MS"
            .Font.FontStyle = "Bold"
            .Font.Size = 14
        End With
        With Selection.Borders(xlEdgeLeft)
            .LineStyle = xlContinuous
            .Weight = xlThick
        End With
        With Selection.Borders(xlEdgeBottom)
            .LineStyle = xlContinuous
            .Weight = xlThick
        End With
        With Selection.Borders(xlEdgeRight)
            .LineStyle = xlContinuous
            .Weight = xlThick
        End With
        With Selection.Borders(xlEdgeTop)
            .LineStyle = xlContinuous
            .Weight = xlThin
        End With
End Sub
```

The sub procedure SetKeys() initializes the keyboard interface required for the game. The OnKey method of the Application object sets the procedures that will be called when either the Tab key, or the left, right, or up arrow keys are pressed by the player. This procedure is called from Excetris() before the game actually begins. If you don't like playing the game with this set of keys, then you can just change the code entered for the OnKey method. For example, to use the down arrow instead of the Tab key to call the sub procedure DropShapes(), change the appropriate statement to Application.OnKey "{DOWN}", "DropShapes". Available keys and their codes can be found in the online help by entering OnKey in the keyword field.

```
Private Sub SetKeys()
    Application.OnKey "{TAB}", "DropShapes"
```

```
    Application.OnKey "{LEFT}", "MoveLeft"
    Application.OnKey "{RIGHT}", "MoveRight"
    Application.OnKey "{UP}", "RotateCC"
End Sub
```

The sub procedure AddShape() randomly adds one of five possible shapes to the game board. The procedure is quite long but the logic is mostly repetitive, so the code is not hard to follow.

```
Private Sub AddShape()
    Dim sqLeft As Single
    Dim sqTop As Single
    Dim I As Integer
    Randomize
```

The shape to be played is constructed out of four Shape objects, each of type AutoShape (msoShapeRectangle). The four shapes are identical in size, and their width and height are set using the module-level variables sqWidth and sqHeight. The width and height of each shape is set to exactly match the width and height of the worksheet cells representing the game board. This is critical for keeping the shapes properly aligned as the game is played. The module-level variable shapeType is assigned a random integer value between 1 and 5 and defines the order in which the four shape objects will be arranged into a single shape (as far as the player is concerned).

```
    sqWidth = 24.75
    sqHeight = sqWidth
    shapeType = Int(5 * Rnd) + 1
```

A Select/Case decision structure operates on the value of the shapeType variable and is used to construct the shape that will be played.

```
    Select Case shapeType
```

The first shape is a sequence of four consecutive squares in a single row (refer to Figure 10.9). With each of four iterations, a For/Next loop adds a new square to the overall shape. The location of each square is set using the Left and Top properties of the worksheet cells to which they are mapped. Each square is added using the AddShape method of the Shapes Collection object, which requires parameters representing the shape type, location (Left and Top properties), and size (Width and Height properties).

The Name property of each Shape object is changed such that the four names are Shape1, Shape2, Shape3, and Shape4. These are the names that will always represent the shapes currently being played (animated). Before the shapes are added to the worksheet the cell location to which they are mapped is tested to see if it holds the value x. If it does, then there is already a shape present in this location and the game must end.

```
Case 1
   For I = 1 To 4
   If Cells(3, I + 5).Value = "x" Then GameOver
   sqLeft = Cells(3, I + 5).Left
   sqTop = Cells(3, I + 5).Top
   ActiveSheet.Shapes.AddShape(RECTANGLE, sqLeft, sqTop, sqWidth,_
sqHeight).Select
      Selection.ShapeRange.Line.Weight = 0.5
      Selection.ShapeRange.Fill.ForeColor.RGB = RGB(125, 125, 125)
      Selection.ShapeRange.Name = "Square" & I
   Next I
```

The module-level variable activeRange is used throughout the program to keep track of the location of the four Shape objects representing the shape being played. At this point in the program the four shapes are added to known locations on the worksheet, so setting the range is easy. With a shape type of 1, the four Shape objects are originally located above cells F3, G3, H3, and I3. Row 3 is the top row of the game board and columns F through I are in the center.

```
Set activeRange = Range("F3:I3")
```

The second shape type is a 2×2 set of four shape objects representing one large square. The logic used in its construction is essentially the same as with the first shape except now two For/Next loops are used to add the four shapes.

```
Case 2
    For I = 1 To 2
        If Cells(3, I + 6).Value = "x" Then GameOver
        sqLeft = Cells(3, I + 6).Left
        sqTop = Cells(3, I + 6).Top
        ActiveSheet.Shapes.AddShape(RECTANGLE, sqLeft, sqTop,_
sqWidth, sqHeight).Select
            Selection.ShapeRange.Line.Weight = 0.5
            Selection.ShapeRange.Fill.ForeColor.RGB = RGB(125, 125, 125)
            Selection.ShapeRange.Name = "Square" & I
    Next I
    For I = 3 To 4
        If Cells(4, I + 4).Value = "x" Then GameOver
        sqLeft = Cells(4, I + 4).Left
```

```
            sqTop = Cells(4, I + 4).Top
            ActiveSheet.Shapes.AddShape(RECTANGLE, sqLeft, sqTop,_
sqWidth, sqHeight).Select
            Selection.ShapeRange.Line.Weight = 0.5
            Selection.ShapeRange.Fill.ForeColor.RGB = RGB(125, 125, 125)
            Selection.ShapeRange.Name = "Square" & I
        Next I
        Set activeRange = Range("G3:H4")
```

The third shape consists of three consecutive shapes in a single row, with a fourth shape added to a second row just below the last square in the first row (see Figure 10.9).

```
        Case 3
            If Cells(4, "H").Value = "x" Then GameOver
            sqLeft = Cells(4, "H").Left
            sqTop = Cells(4, "H").Top
            ActiveSheet.Shapes.AddShape(RECTANGLE, sqLeft, sqTop, sqWidth,_
sqHeight).Select
            Selection.ShapeRange.Line.Weight = 0.5
            Selection.ShapeRange.Fill.ForeColor.RGB = RGB(125, 125, 125)
            Selection.ShapeRange.Name = "Square" & 4
            For I = 2 To 4
                If Cells(3, I + 4).Value = "x" Then GameOver
                sqLeft = Cells(3, I + 4).Left
                sqTop = Cells(3, I + 4).Top
                ActiveSheet.Shapes.AddShape(RECTANGLE, sqLeft, sqTop,_
sqWidth, sqHeight).Select
                Selection.ShapeRange.Line.Weight = 0.5
                Selection.ShapeRange.Fill.ForeColor.RGB = RGB(125, 125, 125)
                Selection.ShapeRange.Name = "Square" & (I - 1)
            Next I
```

With shape type 3, the value of the variable activeRange must be assigned two range areas to include just the cell references representing the location of the four shapes. When setting the range, multiple areas are defined by separating them with a comma.

```
        Set activeRange = Range("F3:H3,H4")
```

If the random selection is shape type 4 or 5, then the four shapes are added in the same manner as the others, albeit at different cell locations.

```
        Case 4
            If Cells(4, "G").Value = "x" Then GameOver
            sqLeft = Cells(4, "G").Left
            sqTop = Cells(4, "G").Top
            ActiveSheet.Shapes.AddShape(RECTANGLE, sqLeft, sqTop, sqWidth,_
sqHeight).Select
            Selection.ShapeRange.Line.Weight = 0.5
            Selection.ShapeRange.Fill.ForeColor.RGB = RGB(125, 125, 125)
            Selection.ShapeRange.Name = "Square" & 4
            For I = 2 To 4
                If Cells(3, I + 4).Value = "x" Then GameOver
                sqLeft = Cells(3, I + 4).Left
                sqTop = Cells(3, I + 4).Top
                ActiveSheet.Shapes.AddShape(RECTANGLE, sqLeft, sqTop,_
sqWidth, sqHeight).Select
                Selection.ShapeRange.Line.Weight = 0.5
                Selection.ShapeRange.Fill.ForeColor.RGB = RGB(125, 125, 125)
                Selection.ShapeRange.Name = "Square" & (I - 1)
            Next I
            Set activeRange = Range("F3:H3,G4")
        Case 5
            For I = 1 To 2
                If Cells(3, I + 6).Value = "x" Then GameOver
                sqLeft = Cells(3, I + 6).Left
                sqTop = Cells(3, I + 6).Top
                ActiveSheet.Shapes.AddShape(RECTANGLE, sqLeft, sqTop,_
sqWidth, sqHeight).Select
                Selection.ShapeRange.Line.Weight = 0.5
                Selection.ShapeRange.Fill.ForeColor.RGB = RGB(125, 125, 125)
                Selection.ShapeRange.Name = "Square" & I
            Next I
            For I = 3 To 4
                If Cells(4, I + 3).Value = "x" Then GameOver
                sqLeft = Cells(4, I + 3).Left
                sqTop = Cells(4, I + 3).Top
                ActiveSheet.Shapes.AddShape(RECTANGLE, sqLeft, sqTop,_
sqWidth, sqHeight).Select
                Selection.ShapeRange.Line.Weight = 0.5
                Selection.ShapeRange.Fill.ForeColor.RGB = RGB(125, 125, 125)
                Selection.ShapeRange.Name = "Square" & I
```

```
            Next I
            Set activeRange = Range("G3:H3, F4:G4")
        Case Else
    End Select
End Sub
```

 TRICK **To randomly change the color of the each shape added to the game board, create three new variables**—colorRed, colorGreen, **and** colorBlue—**and assign them random integer values between 0 and 255 at the beginning of the** AddShape() **sub procedure. Then replace each instance of the statement** Selection.ShapeRange.Fill.ForeColor.RGB = RGB(125, 125, 125) **with** Selection.ShapeRange.Fill.ForeColor.RGB = RGB(colorRed, colorGreen, colorBlue).

The final sub procedure called from Excetris() is MoveShape(). The sub procedure MoveShape() starts the newly added set of four Shape objects on their way down the game board. The shapes are moved down one worksheet row with each call to this procedure. The MoveShape() sub procedure is set to be called every second until the shape being played is stopped.

```
Public Sub MoveShape()
    Dim sh As Shape
    Dim yInc As Integer
    Dim stopShape As Boolean
    Dim I As Integer
```

An error handler is required to keep the program from crashing when the OnTime method of the Application object fails to clear the next procedure call.

```
    On Error GoTo ErrorHandler:
    yInc = sqHeight
    stopShape = False
```

The conditional expression in an If/Then decision structure sends program execution to the validation procedure NewActiveRange() to test the target range for the set of shapes currently being played. If the target range is valid, then the shapes are moved down one row via their Top property. If the target range is invalid, then the Boolean variable stopShape is set to true.

```
    If NewActiveRange("Down") Then
        For Each sh In ActiveSheet.Shapes.Range(Array("Square4", "Square3",_
"Square2", "Square1"))
            sh.Top = sh.Top + yInc
        Next
```

```
    Else
        stopShape = True
    End If
```

Using the OnTime method of the Application object, the MoveShape() procedure is set to be called every second. If the variable stopShape is true, then the OnTime method of the Application object is used to clear the call to the MoveShape() procedure and the sub procedure SetActiveRange() is called to set the four shapes to their current cell locations.

```
    Application.OnTime Now + TimeValue("00:00:01"), "MoveShape", , True
    If stopShape = True Then
        Application.OnTime Now, "MoveShape", , False
        SetActiveRange
    End If
    Exit Sub
```

If the OnTime method fails to clear the next call to MoveShape(), an error is generated and program execution stops. In this case, the solution to the problem is simple but not terribly elegant (keep trying until it works!). Using Resume in the error handler sends program execution back to the line of code that generated the error. This process repeats until the OnTime method succeeds.

```
ErrorHandler:
    Resume
End Sub
```

The sub procedure NewActiveRange() serves two purposes. First, it validates the target range of the group of four Shape objects currently being played. Second, it updates the variable activeRange that is used to keep track of the location of the shapes. The procedure is fairly long, but again the logic is mostly repetitive. The NewActiveRange() sub procedure accepts one string parameter used to specify the direction the program has requested the shapes be moved (left, right, down, or rotated).

```
Private Function NewActiveRange(direction As String) As Boolean
    Dim tempStr As String
    Dim newStr As String
    Dim I As Integer
    Dim c As Range
```

The current location of the four shapes being played is temporarily stored in a string variable. If the target range is determined to be invalid, then this string will be needed at the end of the procedure.

```
    tempStr = activeRange.Address
```

The bulk of this procedure is a `Select/Case` decision structure that operates on the string variable `direction`. The variable `direction` is passed into this procedure and specifies the direction in which the shapes are to be moved.

```
Select Case direction
```

If the program has requested a move down, then the row indices of the range variable `activeRange` must be incremented by one. The string variable `newStr` represents the target range to which the shapes will be moved once the range is validated. Several string functions are used to construct the target range from the current range. The number of characters in the row index changes from row 9 to 10, so this consideration must be included when constructing the value of `newStr`.

```
Case Is = "Down"
        For I = 1 To Len(activeRange.Address)
          If Val(Mid(tempStr, I, 2)) > 1 And Val(Mid(tempStr, I, 2)) < 10_
Then
                newStr = newStr & Trim(Str(Mid(tempStr, I, 1) + 1))
          ElseIf Val(Mid(tempStr, I, 2)) > 1 And Val(Mid(tempStr, I,_
2)) >= 10 Then
                newStr = newStr & Trim(Str(Mid(tempStr, I, 2) + 1))
                I = I + 1
          Else
                newStr = newStr & Mid(tempStr, I, 1)
          End If
        Next I
```

If the program requests a move to the left or right, then the column indices in the variable `activeRange` must be decremented or incremented by one, respectively.

```
        Case Is = "Left"
        For I = 1 To Len(activeRange.Address)
          If Asc(Mid(tempStr, I, 1)) > 64 Then
              newStr = newStr & Chr(Asc(Mid(tempStr, I, 1)) - 1)
          Else
              newStr = newStr & Mid(tempStr, I, 1)
          End If
        Next I
        Case Is = "Right"
        For I = 1 To Len(activeRange.Address)
          If Asc(Mid(tempStr, I, 1)) > 64 Then
              newStr = newStr & Chr(Asc(Mid(tempStr, I, 1)) + 1)
          Else
```

```
            newStr = newStr & Mid(tempStr, I, 1)
        End If
    Next I
```

The request for a rotation is more complicated. The target range is constructed based on the shape type and the number of times the shape has been rotated. Figure 10.9 was used to determine how the column and row indices in the variable `activeRange` are to be altered with a rotation of the shapes.

```
        Case Is = "CC"
```

Shape type 1 contains four shapes in a single row. Only two positions are allowed for this shape—horizontal and vertical. The variable `newStr` is constructed within a `For/Each` loop that iterates through each cell reference in the range variable `activeRange`. In the case of shape type 1, only the first and last cell references must be altered (for example, F3:I3 becomes G1:G4). The variable I tracks the cell reference selected in the `For/Each` loop. When I = 0 or I = 3, the first and last cell reference in the range is selected. The variable `numRotations` is used to determine if the shape is in a horizontal or vertical position.

The cell references used in the previous paragraph represent a static example for determining the magnitude of change required for the row and column indices in the `activeRange` variable. I could have used any range as long as it defined the correct shape type. Consider the first cell reference in the variable `activeRange` as it is rotated by 90 degrees. If the original cell reference is F6, then the target cell reference is G4, a change of +1 in the column index and a change of −2 in the row index. Therefore, when shape type 1 rotates from a horizontal position to a vertical position (I = 0 and `numRotations` = 0 or 2) the column and row indices are incremented by one and decremented by 2, respectively. When rotating from a vertical position back to a horizontal position (I = 0 and `numRotations` = 1 or 3), the opposite change is made where the column index is decremented by one and the row index is incremented by two. I used the same approach to determine the change in the last cell reference of the range.

```
        If shapeType = 1 Then
            For Each c In activeRange
                If I = 0 And (numRotations = 0 Or numRotations = 2)
Then newStr = "$" & Chr(c.Column + 65) & "$" & (c.Row - 2) & ":"
                If I = 3 And (numRotations = 0 Or numRotations = 2)
Then newStr = newStr & "$" & Chr(c.Column + 62) & "$" & (c.Row + 1)
                If I = 0 And (numRotations = 1 Or numRotations = 3)
Then newStr = "$" & Chr(c.Column + 63) & "$" & (c.Row + 2) & ":"
```

```
                    If I = 3 And (numRotations = 1 Or numRotations = 3)
        Then newStr = newStr & "$" & Chr(c.Column + 66) & "$" & (c.Row - 1)
                    I = I + 1
                Next
```

Shape type 2 is the large square. Because of its symmetry, a rotation does not affect this shape. Therefore, the variable newStr is assigned the current range.

```
            ElseIf shapeType = 2 Then newStr = activeRange.Address
```

Shape types 3 and 4 require four rotations to complete one revolution. However, there is still a symmetry element in the first area of their ranges. For both shape types, the first area of the range maps three shapes in a single row. With each rotation, this area changes back and forth between two different ranges (for example, F3:H3 _ G2:G4). In the For/Each loop shown here, when the variable I = 0 or 2, the first area in the range is being altered and when I = 3, the last area (represented by a single cell reference, for example, H4) is altered. The last area in the range changes its cell reference with each rotation until a full revolution is made and it assumes its original value (for example, H4, H2, F2, F4 for shape type 3). The changes in the row and column indices for each cell reference specified in the two range areas are changed accordingly.

```
            ElseIf shapeType = 3 Then
                For Each c In activeRange
                    If I = 0 And (numRotations = 0 Or numRotations = 2)
        Then newStr = "$" & Chr(c.Column + 65) & "$" & (c.Row - 1) & ":"
                    If I = 2 And (numRotations = 0 Or numRotations = 2)
        Then newStr = newStr & "$" & Chr(c.Column + 63) & "$" & (c.Row + 1) & ","
                    If I = 0 And (numRotations = 1 Or numRotations = 3)
        Then newStr = "$" & Chr(c.Column + 63) & "$" & (c.Row + 1) & ":"
                    If I = 2 And (numRotations = 1 Or numRotations = 3)
        Then newStr = newStr & "$" & Chr(c.Column + 65) & "$" & (c.Row - 1) & ","
                    If I = 3 And numRotations = 0 Then newStr = newStr &
        "$" & Chr(c.Column + 64) & "$" & (c.Row - 2)
                    If I = 3 And numRotations = 1 Then newStr = newStr &
        "$" & Chr(c.Column + 62) & "$" & c.Row
                    If I = 3 And numRotations = 2 Then newStr = newStr &
        "$" & Chr(c.Column + 64) & "$" & (c.Row + 2)
                    If I = 3 And numRotations = 3 Then newStr = newStr &
        "$" & Chr(c.Column + 66) & "$" & c.Row
                    I = I + 1
                Next
```

```
        ElseIf shapeType = 4 Then
            For Each c In activeRange
                If I = 0 And (numRotations = 0 Or numRotations = 2)
Then newStr = "$" & Chr(c.Column + 65) & "$" & (c.Row - 1) & ":"
                If I = 2 And (numRotations = 0 Or numRotations = 2)
Then newStr = newStr & "$" & Chr(c.Column + 63) & "$" & (c.Row + 1) & ","
                If I = 0 And (numRotations = 1 Or numRotations = 3)
Then newStr = "$" & Chr(c.Column + 63) & "$" & (c.Row + 1) & ":"
                If I = 2 And (numRotations = 1 Or numRotations = 3)
Then newStr = newStr & "$" & Chr(c.Column + 65) & "$" & (c.Row - 1) & ","
                If I = 3 And numRotations = 0 Then newStr = newStr &
"$" & Chr(c.Column + 65) & "$" & (c.Row - 1)
                If I = 3 And numRotations = 1 Then newStr = newStr &
"$" & Chr(c.Column + 63) & "$" & (c.Row - 1)
                If I = 3 And numRotations = 2 Then newStr = newStr &
"$" & Chr(c.Column + 63) & "$" & (c.Row + 1)
                If I = 3 And numRotations = 3 Then newStr = newStr &
"$" & Chr(c.Column + 65) & "$" & (c.Row + 1)
                I = I + 1
        Next
```

Shape type 5 contains two areas in its range, but is only allowed two rotations before it assumes its original location (see Figure 10.9). In this case, a total of four cell references must be altered (two per area) with each rotation.

```
        ElseIf shapeType = 5 Then
            For Each c In activeRange
                If I = 0 And (numRotations = 0 Or numRotations = 2)
Then newStr = "$" & Chr(c.Column + 63) & "$" & c.Row & ":"
                If I = 1 And (numRotations = 0 Or numRotations = 2)
Then newStr = newStr & "$" & Chr(c.Column + 62) & "$" & (c.Row + 1) & ","
                If I = 2 And (numRotations = 0 Or numRotations = 2)
Then newStr = newStr & "$" & Chr(c.Column + 65) & "$" & c.Row & ":"
                If I = 3 And (numRotations = 0 Or numRotations = 2)
Then newStr = newStr & "$" & Chr(c.Column + 64) & "$" & (c.Row + 1)
                If I = 0 And (numRotations = 1 Or numRotations = 3)
Then newStr = "$" & Chr(c.Column + 65) & "$" & c.Row & ":"
                If I = 1 And (numRotations = 1 Or numRotations = 3)
Then newStr = newStr & "$" & Chr(c.Column + 66) & "$" & (c.Row - 1) & ","
                If I = 2 And (numRotations = 1 Or numRotations = 3)
Then newStr = newStr & "$" & Chr(c.Column + 63) & "$" & c.Row & ":"
```

```
            If I = 3 And (numRotations = 1 Or numRotations = 3)
Then newStr = newStr & "$" & Chr(c.Column + 64) & "$" & (c.Row - 1)
                I = I + 1
            Next
        End If
    End Select
```

The activeRange variable is updated to the target range defined by the variable newStr.

```
    Set activeRange = Range(newStr)
```

A For/Each loop is used to validate the new range. If any of the column or row indices fall outside the allowed values, or if the selected cell already contains an x, then the new range is invalid. The activeRange variable is reset to its original value and the function is exited, returning a value of false to the calling procedure. This is the section of the program that prevents you from rotating a shape when it first appears on the game board (before it has moved down) because the rotation would place a Shape object over worksheet rows 1 or 2.

```
    For Each c In activeRange
        If c.Value = "x" Or c.Column < 3 Or c.Column > 12 Or c.Row < 3 Or_
c.Row > 17 Then
            NewActiveRange = False
            Set activeRange = Range(tempStr)
            Exit Function
        End If
    Next
    NewActiveRange = True
End Function
```

The next four sub procedures listed, DropShapes(), MoveLeft(), MoveRight(), and RotateCC(), are called when the player presses one of the keys assigned to these procedures. The sub procedure DropShapes() is triggered from the Tab key and functions to move the shapes as far down the game board as possible.

```
Private Sub DropShapes()
    Dim I As Integer
    Dim sh As Shape
    Dim moveDown As Boolean
```

An error handler is required to ensure that the OnTime method clears the call to the MoveShape() sub procedure.

```
    On Error GoTo ErrorHandler:
```

A Do-loop repeatedly calls the NewActiveRange() sub procedure listed earlier and passes the string literal "Down". As long as the target range is validated the Boolean variable moveDown will be true and the loop continues. The variable I will hold the number of rows that the shapes are allowed to move down the game board.

```
Do
    I = I + 1
    moveDown = NewActiveRange("Down")
Loop While (moveDown)
```

With the allowed increment stored in the variable I, each Shape object is moved down via its Top property.

```
For Each sh In ActiveSheet.Shapes.Range(Array("Square4", "Square3",
"Square2", "Square1"))
    sh.Top = sh.Top + (I - 1) * sqHeight
Next
```

After the shapes are moved as far down the game board as possible, the next call to the MoveShape() sub procedure is cleared and the range representing the location of the shapes is set with a call to the SetActiveRange() sub procedure.

```
    Application.OnTime Now, "MoveShape", , False
    SetActiveRange
    Exit Sub
ErrorHandler:
    Resume
End Sub
```

The sub procedure MoveLeft() is called when the player presses the left arrow key. A For/Each loop decrements the Left property of each Shape object by one column width after the target range has been validated with a call to the NewActiveRange() sub procedure.

```
Private Sub MoveLeft()
    Dim sh As Shape
    If NewActiveRange("Left") = True Then
        For Each sh In ActiveSheet.Shapes.Range(Array("Square4", "Square3",
_"Square2", "Square1"))
            sh.Left = sh.Left - sqWidth
        Next
    End If
End Sub
```

The MoveRight() sub procedure is triggered with the right arrow key and increments the Left property of each Shape object by one column width after validation.

```
Private Sub MoveRight()
    Dim sh As Shape
    If NewActiveRange("Right") = True Then
        For Each sh In ActiveSheet.Shapes.Range(Array("Square4", "Square3",_
"Square2", "Square1"))
            sh.Left = sh.Left + sqWidth
        Next
    End If
End Sub
```

The sub procedure RotateCC() rotates the shape counterclockwise by 90 degrees. Most of the work is done in the NewActiveRange() sub procedure, which sets the target range for the shapes and stores it in the module-level range variable activeRange. It is then a simple matter of using a For/Each loop to iterate through each cell reference in the activeRange variable and set the Left and Top properties of each shape to the Left and Top properties of the corresponding cell.

```
Private Sub RotateCC()
    Dim c As Range
    Dim I As Integer
    I = 1
    If NewActiveRange("CC") = True Then
        For Each c In activeRange
            ActiveSheet.Shapes("Square" & I).Left = c.Left
            ActiveSheet.Shapes("Square" & I).Top = c.Top
            I = I + 1
        Next
        numRotations = numRotations + 1
        If numRotations = 4 Then numRotations = 0
        ActiveSheet.Range("C20").Select
    End If
End Sub
```

When the set of four shapes currently being played can no longer move down the game board the SetActiveRange() sub procedure is called. The purpose of this procedure is to mark the cell locations on the game board over which the shapes rest and change the Name properties of the Shape objects. This procedure also calls the procedures needed to add the next set of four Shape objects to the game board.

```
Private Sub SetActiveRange()
    Dim c As Range
    Dim I As Integer
    I = 1
```

The activeRange variable holds the cell references representing the location of each of the four Shape objects. It is a simple task to mark these cells by assigning an x to their Value property. The Name property of each Shape object must be altered, because the next set of four shapes added to the game board will be assigned these same names. If you try to assign a name to a Shape object that is already in use, then a runtime error will be generated and program execution stops. The value of the Name property of each Shape object is altered to include the column and row index of the cell it rests above.

```
For Each c In activeRange
    c.Value = "x"
    ActiveSheet.Shapes("Square" & I).Name = "Square" & Chr(c.Column + 64)_
& c.Row
    I = I + 1
Next
```

After the shapes are set, the sub procedure ScanRange() is called to search the game board for a filled row of Shape objects. When program execution returns, the next shape is added with some of the same procedure calls originally used in the Excetris() sub procedure.

```
    ScanRange
    numRotations = 0
    AddShape
    Range("A21").Select
    Delay (0.5)
    MoveShape
End Sub
```

The sub procedure ScanRange() is called every time a played shape is set to the game board. Its purpose is to check each row in the game board to see if it is filled with Shape objects. If such a row is found, the shapes are removed, the shapes above are moved down one row, and the score is updated.

```
Private Sub ScanRange()
    Dim myRow As Range
    Dim c As Range
    Dim scoreRow As Boolean
```

```
Dim numRows As Integer
Dim I As Integer
Dim K As Integer
Dim J As Integer
```

To search the game board for a complete row of shapes, I used a For/Next loop with a looping variable that ranges from the first row to the last row on the game board.

```
For I = 3 To 17
```

I define a range variable (myRow) to represent an individual row in the game board (for example, C3:L3).

```
Set myRow = Range("C" & I & ":" & "L" & I)
scoreRow = True
```

If all Value properties in the range representing the current row hold the value x, then the row must be removed and scored, otherwise the procedure moves on to the next row in the game board.

```
For Each c In myRow
    If c.Value <> "x" Then
        scoreRow = False
        Exit For
    End If
Next
```

If the row is to be scored, then the integer variable numRows is incremented by one. When the value of numRows exceeds 1, the sub procedure BonusCall() is called to display a message to the player indicating he has been awarded bonus points.

```
If scoreRow Then
    numRows = numRows + 1
    If numRows > 1 Then BonusCall (numRows)
```

The contents of the cells in the scored row are cleared and the Shape objects are deleted using the column and row indices referenced in their Name property. The score is calculated by assigning ten points for each shape removed. If multiple rows are removed, bonus points are assigned to each shape according to the number of rows removed (for example, the third row removed scores 30 points for each shape).

```
For Each c In myRow
    c.ClearContents
    ActiveSheet.Shapes("Square" & Chr(c.Column + 64) & c.Row)._
Delete
```

```
            Range("F22").Value = Range("F22").Value + 10 * numRows
        Next
```

After the scored row is removed, any shapes resting above must be moved down one row. This is accomplished by looping up the game board starting from the row that was just removed. Nested `For/Next` loops iterate through each row moving any shapes down one row if an x is found in the corresponding cell. The `Value` properties of the cells are also updated to move any x down one row. The outer loop specifies the row index, and the inner loop specifies the column index as the value of each cell is checked.

```
        For K = myRow.Row To 3 Step -1
            For J = 3 To 12
                If Cells(K - 1, J).Value = "x" Then
                    Cells(K - 1, J).Value = ""
                    Cells(K, J).Value = "x"
                    ActiveSheet.Shapes("Square" & Chr(J + 64) & (K - 1))._
Top = Cells(K, J).Top
                    ActiveSheet.Shapes("Square" & Chr(J + 64) & (K - 1))._
Left = Cells(K, J).Left
                    ActiveSheet.Shapes("Square" & Chr(J + 64) & (K - 1))._
Name = "Square" & Chr(J + 64) & K
                End If
            Next J
        Next K
```

Finally, if a bonus message was displayed, then a call to the sub procedure `DeleteBonus` removes it from the worksheet.

```
            If numRows > 1 Then DeleteBonus
        End If
    Next I
End Sub
```

As another embellishment to the program, I added the `BonusCall()` sub procedure after the game was essentially completed. This procedure adds two new Shape objects to the worksheet, a picture and a callout. The purpose of this procedure is to display an image and message to the player indicating that he has received bonus points for scoring more than one row after a shape is played. The procedure is called from the `ScanRange()` sub procedure, which passes the `numRows` variable.

```
Private Sub BonusCall(factor As Integer)
    Dim bonusStr As String
```

I use a `Select/Case` decision structure to set the image and message displayed. The `AddPicture` method of the Shapes Collection object adds an image to the drawing layer at the specified location. The parameters passed to the `AddPicture` method include the path to the image, and the `Left`, `Top`, `Width`, and `Height` properties of the Shape object to be added.

```
Select Case factor
    Case Is = 2
        bonusStr = "Double Bonus Points!"
        ActiveSheet.Shapes.AddPicture(ActiveWorkbook.Path & "\Smile1.png",_
True, True, Range("O6").Left, Range("P5").Top, 50, 50).Select
    Case Is = 3
        bonusStr = "Triple Bonus Points!"
        ActiveSheet.Shapes.AddPicture(ActiveWorkbook.Path & "\Smile2.png",_
True, True, Range("O6").Left, Range("P5").Top, 50, 50).Select
    Case Is = 4
        bonusStr = "Quadruple Bonus Points!"
        ActiveSheet.Shapes.AddPicture(ActiveWorkbook.Path & "\Smile3.png",_
True, True, Range("O6").Left, Range("P5").Top, 50, 50).Select
End Select
```

The `Name` property is changed to make it easier to delete the shape after it has been displayed.

```
Selection.Name = "BonusPic"
```

Next, I add a Shape object of type `msoShapeRoundedRectangularCallout` to the worksheet and set the `Text` property of the Characters object to the `bonusStr` variable defined earlier in the procedure. The text is also formatted using several properties of the Font object.

```
ActiveSheet.Shapes.AddShape(msoShapeRoundedRectangularCallout,_
Range("P6").Left, Range("P3").Top, 90, 55).Select
Selection.Characters.Text = bonusStr
Selection.Name = "BonusCallout"
With Selection.Characters.Font
    .Name = "Arial"
    .FontStyle = "Bold"
    .Size = 12
End With
Selection.HorizontalAlignment = xlCenter
Range("R9").Select
End Sub
```

The DeleteBonus() sub procedure delays program execution for one second before deleting the image and callout added by the BonusCall() sub procedure.

```
Private Sub DeleteBonus()
    Delay (1)
    ActiveSheet.Shapes("BonusCallout").Delete
    ActiveSheet.Shapes("BonusPic").Delete
End Sub
Private Sub Delay(pauseTime As Single)
    Dim begin As Single
    begin = Timer
    Do While Timer < begin + pauseTime
        DoEvents
    Loop
End Sub
```

When the AddShape() sub procedure attempts to add a new set of shapes to the game board but finds that a shape is already present at the location where the new shapes are to be added, then the GameOver() sub procedure is called to end the game. This procedure calls the ResetKeys() sub procedure to restore the keys used in this game to their default action. In addition, a message is sent to the worksheet indicating that the game is over. The player may then click on the Shape object holding the image to begin a new game.

```
Private Sub GameOver()
    ResetKeys
    Range("O12").Value = "Game Over!"
    End
End Sub
Private Sub ResetKeys()
    Application.OnKey "{TAB}"
    Application.OnKey "{LEFT}"
    Application.OnKey "{RIGHT}"
    Application.OnKey "{UP}"
End Sub
```

This concludes the code listing for the Excel version of Tetris. The next step in the development of Excetris would be to add multiple levels of difficulty to the game. In the original version of *Tetris*, the game is made more challenging by increasing the speed of the shapes as they move down the game board. Unfortunately, the shapes cannot be moved any faster using the OnTime method of the Application object because the program already uses its minimum time interval of one second. The shapes could be incremented down two rows instead of one, which would simulate a faster downward motion of the shapes. Other possibilities include creating additional shape types that make it harder for the player to find a fit, or including an occasional "Hot" shape that automatically drops to the bottom of the game board as soon as it's added (make its color a bright red-orange!). Use your imagination and you'll think of methods for making the game harder and more exciting.

Chapter Summary

In this chapter I discussed the Shape object and the tools available in Excel for adding shapes to a worksheet and manipulating existing shapes. I also discussed the Shapes Collection object and some of its properties and methods used to add and manipulate Shape objects, and demonstrated the use of the ShapeRange Collection object for selecting and manipulating a specific set of Shape objects from a collection. You also saw the OLEObjects Collection object and learned how to add an ActiveX control to a worksheet using a VBA program.

CHALLENGES

1. Create a program in VBA that adds several lines, rectangles, ovals, and triangles to a worksheet. Use a looping code structure.

2. Create a VBA program that creates a ShapeRange Collection object from just the ovals in the drawing layer of a worksheet. Then alter the appearance of the ovals by adding a fill color.

3. Using a For/Each loop in a VBA procedure, select just the rectangles created in the first challenge and align them to column C in the worksheet. Use the Left property of the Range and Shape objects.

4. Add several Shape objects to the drawing layer of an Excel worksheet, then use the Group method of the ShapeRange Collection object to group the range of shapes into a single shape. Rotate the grouped Shape object using its Rotation property.

5. Edit the Excetris program to include an additional shape type, bringing the total number of shape types to six. Build the new shape type out of four rectangular shapes as was done with the other five shape types. Edit all procedures necessary for adding, setting, moving, and keeping track of the location of the new shape type.

A Final Word

Congratulations on finishing this book! You are now ready to tackle your own VBA projects in Excel. You will find that even with the relatively basic programming skills taught in this book you will be able to create robust and helpful projects for the home and business. Don't forget that the accompanying CD-ROM includes two bonus chapters that show you how to use several more VBA objects and methods. The bonus chapters, Chapter 11 and 12, show you how to query external data sources, use some of VBA's Web-related objects, create and use Excel add-ins, and create custom menus and toolbars.

If you want to learn how to do even more with VBA, then I recommend two options. First, learn how to program in Visual Basic. Using Visual Basic 5.0 or 6.0 you can create custom ActiveX controls that can be referenced in VBA and used in your programs. The selection of ActiveX controls that comes with VBA is very limiting, and extending the number of available controls will give you much more flexibility in your projects. I should warn you, though, that Microsoft has effectively killed ActiveX technology with their new release of Visual Basic .NET. Office XP still supports ActiveX technology but it's hard to say if the next version of Office will continue to do so. Second, if you are really gung-ho about programming, then I recommend learning how to use the Windows API. The Windows API will significantly extend your programming capabilities and the power of your programs. Whatever you decide, the most important thing to remember is that you should have fun!

Index

G

s

scientific notation, defined, 28
scope
    defined, 26
    module level variables, 26–27
    procedural level variables, 26
    procedure, 53–54
    sub (subroutine) procedures, 56
    variables, 26–27
Scroll Bar control, animations, 191–194
searches
    Help system, 14
    strings, 34
Select/Case structure, 71–72
SendResult() sub (subroutine) procedure, 58
sequential access files, 272–274
Series object, 324–325
Shape Collection object, 358–362
Shape object
    activating, 365
    adding to worksheet, 360–361
    drawing layer contents, 358
    example code location, 362
    manipulating, 360–362
ShapeRange Collection object, 362–364
shapes
    adding to worksheets, 359
    described, 357
    editing, 360–362
    Excetris project, 368
    looping through collections, 361–362
    selecting size and shape, 377–381
Sheets Collection object, 154, 316, 358–362
Shift parameter, event procedures, 54–55
sounds
    ActiveX controls, 200
    Blackjack project, 251, 257, 266
    Wave Form Audio (wav) file
        playback, 202–203
    Windows API (Application Programming
        Interface), 200–203
spreadsheets
    Fun with Strings, 40–43
    Magic Squares, 30–33
Standard Code window, VBA IDE element, 5–6

standard modules
    Alienated Game project, 353
    described, 24–25
Standard toolbar, VBA IDE element, 4–5
statements
    colorful header project, 16–17
    debugging, 289
    Dim (Dimension), 23–24
    End Sub, 56
    executing, 117
    Exit Do, 92
    Exit For, 92
    GoTo, 285
    On Error, 283–287
    Open, 272
    Option Base 1, 102
    Option Explicit, 24
    Option Private, 54
    Poker Dice project, 73
    ReDim, 106–107
static integer variable, control click counting, 77
Stop Recording button, macros, 114
string concatenation, defined, 43
string data types, 33–34
strings
    ampersand (&) character, 43
    character locations, 42
    constants, 36
    data to numerical conversion, 48
    Internet search, 34
    manipulating with VBA functions, 39–43
    sequential file access, 273
    trimming when validating, 96
    value returns, 58
structures, With/End With 117, 157–159
sub (subroutine) procedures
    addends, 58
    defined, 56
    DisableControls(), 124
    End Sub statement, 56
    GetRandomOperator(), 124
    naming conventions, 58
    outputting answer w/message box, 58
    results determination, 79–81
    scope, 56
    versus event procedures, 57
    worksheet column as array, 100–101

X

Y

Z